Toyota Corolla
Automotive Repair Manual

**by Jeff Killingsworth
and John H Haynes**

Member of the Guild of Motoring Writers

Models covered:

Toyota Corolla models
Series AE101, 102, 112 and ZZE122
1997 – 2006

*Does not include information specific to Sportivo,
turbocharged models*

Haynes Australia Pty Limited
haynes.com   92728-12N1

Acknowledgements

Wiring diagrams provided by Rellim Publications

© Haynes Australia Pty Limited 2007

ABN 59 618 618 992

With permission from J.H. Haynes & Co. Ltd.

A book in the Haynes Automotive Repair Manual Series

ISBN-13: 978-1-56392-668-6

ISBN-10: 1-56392-668-7

While every attempt is made to ensure that the information in this manual is correct, no liability can be accepted by the authors or publishers for loss, damage or injury caused by any errors in, or omissions from, the information given.

Contents

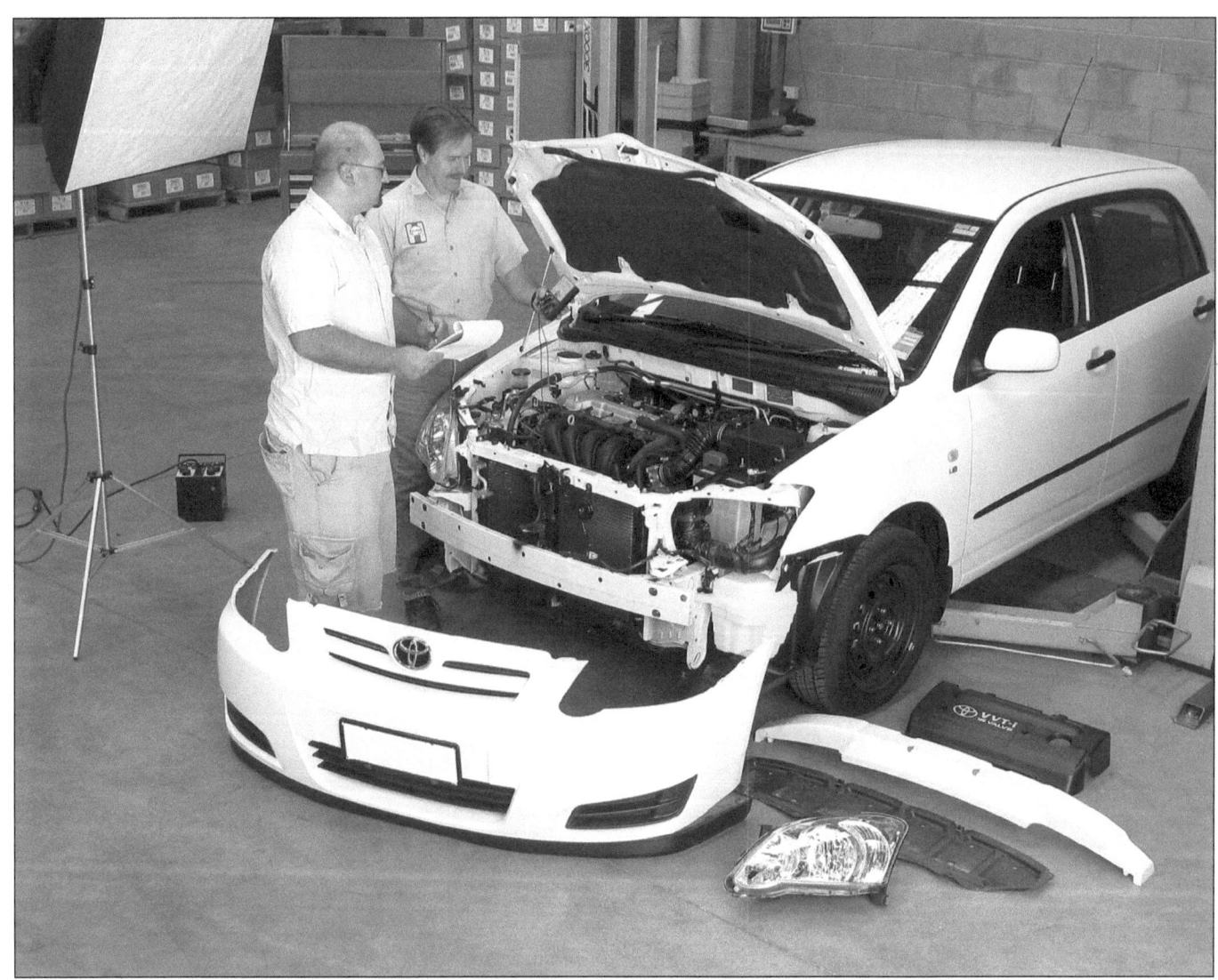

Haynes mechanic and author with 2006 Toyota Corolla

About this manual

Its purpose

The purpose of this manual is to help you get the best value from your vehicle. It can do so in several ways. It can help you decide what work must be done, even if you choose to have it done by a dealer service department or a repair shop; it provides information and procedures for routine maintenance and servicing; and it offers diagnostic and repair procedures to follow when trouble occurs.

We hope you use the manual to tackle the work yourself. For many simpler jobs, doing it yourself may be quicker than arranging an appointment to get the vehicle into a shop and making the trips to leave it and pick it up. More importantly, a lot of money can be saved by avoiding the expense the shop must pass on to you to cover its labor and overhead costs. An added benefit is the sense of satisfaction and accomplishment that you feel after doing the job yourself.

Using the manual

The manual is divided into Chapters. Each Chapter is divided into numbered Sections, which are headed in bold type between horizontal lines. Each Section consists of consecutively numbered paragraphs.

At the beginning of each numbered Section you will be referred to any illustrations which apply to the procedures in that Section. The reference numbers used in illustration captions pinpoint the pertinent Section and the Step within that Section. That is, illustration 3.2 means the illustration refers to Section 3 and Step (or paragraph) 2 within that Section.

Procedures, once described in the text, are not normally repeated. When it's necessary to refer to another Chapter, the reference will be given as Chapter and Section number. Cross references given without use of the word "Chapter" apply to Sections and/or paragraphs in the same Chapter. For example, "see Section 8" means in the same Chapter.

References to the left or right side of the vehicle assume you are sitting in the driver's seat, facing forward.

Even though we have prepared this manual with extreme care, neither the publisher nor the author can accept responsibility for any errors in, or omissions from, the information given.

NOTE

A **Note** provides information necessary to properly complete a procedure or information which will make the procedure easier to understand.

CAUTION

A **Caution** provides a special procedure or special steps which must be taken while completing the procedure where the Caution is found. Not heeding a Caution can result in damage to the assembly being worked on.

WARNING

A **Warning** provides a special procedure or special steps which must be taken while completing the procedure where the Warning is found. Not heeding a Warning can result in personal injury.

Introduction to the Toyota Corolla

The Toyota Corolla models covered by this manual are four-door sedans, wagons and hatchback models.

The transversely-mounted inline four-cylinder engines used in these vehicles are equipped with electronic fuel injection.

The engine drives the front wheels through either a five-speed manual transaxle or a four-speed automatic transaxle via independent driveaxles.

Independent suspension, featuring coil spring/strut damper units, is used on the front of the vehicle. The rack-and-pinion steering unit is mounted behind the engine with power-assist on most models. The rear suspension on 1999 and earlier models uses coil spring/strut damper units, with trailing arms and lateral links. The rear suspension on 2000 and later models uses coil-over shock absorber assemblies, connected to a pressed-steel beam-type axle.

The brakes are disc at the front and either disc or drum at the rear, with power-assist standard. An Anti-lock Brake System (ABS) is available on all models.

Vehicle identification numbers

Modifications are a continuing and unpublVehicle identification numbers

Modifications are a continuing and unpublicized process in vehicle manufacturing. Since spare parts manuals and lists are compiled on a numerical basis, the individual vehicle numbers are essential to correctly identify the component required.

Vehicle Identification Number (VIN)

This very important identification number is stamped on the firewall in the engine compartment (see illustration) and on the manufacturer's compliance plate. The VIN also appears on the Vehicle Certificate of Title and Registration. It contains information such as where and when the vehicle was manufactured, the model year and the body style.

Compliance plate

The manufacturer's Certification Regulation label is attached to the firewall. The plate contains the name of the manufacturer, the month and year of production, the Gross Vehicle Weight Rating (GVWR), the Gross Axle Weight Rating (GAWR) and the certification statement (see illustration).

VIN model year codes

One particularly important piece of information found within the VIN is the model year code. Counting from the left, the model year code designation is the 10th character in the VIN.

Engine and transaxle identification numbers

The engine code number can be found on a pad on the rear side of the block (see illustration). The transaxle identification number is located on a plate attached to the top of the transaxle case (see illustration), or stamped on the transaxle housing.

Location of the Vehicle identification number (VIN)

Location of the Manufacturer compliance plate

Location of the engine identification number

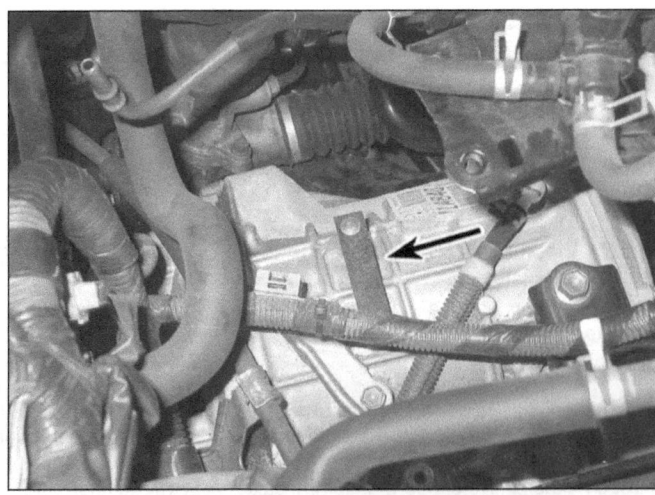

Location of the transaxle identification number

Buying parts

Spare parts are available from many-sources, which generally fall into one of two categories - authorised dealer parts departments and independent retail auto parts stores. Our advice concerning these parts is as follows:

Retail auto parts stores: Good auto parts stores will stock frequently needed components which wear out relatively fast, such as clutch components, exhaust systems, brake parts, tune-up parts, etc. These stores often supply new or reconditioned parts on an exchange basis, which can save a considerable amount of money. Discount auto parts stores are often very good places to buy materials and parts needed for general vehicle maintenance such as oil, grease, filters, spark plugs, belts, touch-up paint, bulbs, etc. They also usually sell tools and general accessories, have convenient hours, charge lower prices and can often be found not far from home.

Authorised dealer parts department: This is the best source for parts which are unique to the vehicle and not generally available elsewhere (such as major engine parts, transmission parts, trim pieces, etc.).

Warranty information: If the vehicle is still covered under warranty, be sure that any renewal parts purchased - regardless of the source - do not invalidate the warranty!

To be sure of obtaining the correct parts, have engine and chassis numbers available and, if possible, take the old parts along for positive identification.

Maintenance techniques, tools and working facilities

Maintenance techniques

There are a number of techniques involved in maintenance and repair that will be referred to throughout this manual. Application of these techniques will enable the home mechanic to be more efficient, better organised and capable of performing the various tasks properly, which will ensure that the repair job is thorough and complete.

Fasteners

Fasteners are nuts, bolts, studs and screws used to hold two or more parts together. There are a few things to keep in mind when working with fasteners. Almost all of them use a locking device of some type, either a lockwasher, locknut, locking tab or thread adhesive. All threaded fasteners should be clean and straight, with undamaged threads and undamaged corners on the hex head where the spanner fits. Develop the habit of all damaged nuts and bolts with new ones. Special locknuts with nylon or fibre inserts can only be used once. If they are removed, they lose their locking ability and must be renewed.

Rusted nuts and bolts should be treated with a penetrating fluid to ease removal and prevent breakage. Some mechanics use turpentine in a spout-type oil can, which works quite well. After applying the rust penetrant, let it work for a few minutes before trying to loosen the nut or bolt. Badly rusted fasteners may have to be chiselled or sawed off or removed with a special nut breaker, available at tool stores.

If a bolt or stud breaks off in an assembly, it can be drilled and removed with a special tool commonly available for this purpose. Most automotive machine shops can perform this task, as well as other repair procedures, such as the repair of threaded holes that have been stripped out.

Flat washers and lockwashers, when removed from an assembly, should always be refitted exactly as removed. Renew any damaged washers. Never use a lockwasher on any soft metal surface (such as aluminium), thin sheet metal or plastic.

Fastener sizes

For a number of reasons, automobile manufacturers are making wider and wider use of metric fasteners. Therefore, it is important to be able to tell the difference between standard (sometimes called US or SAE) and metric hardware, since they cannot be interchanged.

All bolts, whether standard or metric, are sized according to diameter, thread pitch and length. For example, a standard M12 - 1.75 x 25 metric bolt is 12 mm in diameter, has a thread pitch of 1.75 mm (the distance between threads) and is 25 mm long. The two bolts are nearly identical, and easily confused, but they are not interchangeable.

In addition to the differences in diameter, thread pitch and length, metric and standard bolts can also be distinguished by examining the bolt heads. To begin with, the distance across the flats on a standard bolt head is measured in inches, while the same dimen-sion on a metric bolt is sized in millimetres (the same is true for nuts). As a result, a standard spanner should not be used on a metric bolt and a metric spanner should not be used on a standard bolt. Also, most standard bolts have slashes radiating out from the centre of the head to denote the grade or strength of the bolt, which is an indication of the amount of torque that can be applied to it. The greater the number of slashes, the greater the strength of the bolt. Grades 0 through 5 are commonly used on automobiles. Metric bolts have a property class (grade) number, rather than a slash, moulded into their heads to indicate bolt strength. In this case, the higher the number, the stronger the bolt. Property class numbers 8.8, 9.8 and 10.9 are commonly used on automobiles.

Strength markings can also be used to distinguish standard hex nuts from metric hex nuts. Many standard nuts have dots stamped into one side, while metric nuts are marked with a number. The greater the number of dots, or the higher the number, the greater the strength of the nut.

Metric studs are also marked on their ends according to property class (grade). Larger studs are numbered (the same as metric bolts), while smaller studs carry a geometric code to denote grade.

It should be noted that many fasteners, especially Grades 0 through 2, have no distinguishing marks on them. When such is the case, the only way to determine whether it is standard or metric is to measure the thread pitch or compare it to a known fastener of the same size.

Standard fasteners are often referred to as SAE, as opposed to metric. However, it should be noted that SAE technically refers to a non-metric fine thread fastener only. Coarse thread non-metric fasteners are referred to as USS sizes.

Since fasteners of the same size (both

Grade 1 or 2   Grade 5   Grade 8

Bolt strength marking (standard/SAE/USS; bottom - metric)

Grade	Identification	Grade	Identification
Hex Nut Grade 5	3 Dots	Hex Nut Property Class 9	Arabic 9
Hex Nut Grade 8	6 Dots	Hex Nut Property Class 10	Arabic 10

Standard hex nut strength markings   Metric hex nut strength markings

Class 10.9   Class 9.8   Class 8.8

Metric stud strength markings

00-1 HAYNES

standard and metric) may have different strength ratings, be sure to refit any bolts, studs or nuts removed from your vehicle in their original locations. Also, when renewing a fastener, make sure that the new one has a-strength rating equal to or greater than the-original.

Tightening sequences and procedures

Most threaded fasteners should be tightened to a specific torque value (torque is the twisting force applied to a threaded component such as a nut or bolt). Overtightening the fastener can weaken it and cause it to break, while undertightening can cause it to eventually come loose. Bolts, screws and studs, depending on the material they are made of and their thread diameters, have specific torque values, many of which are noted in the Specifications at the beginning of each Chapter. Be sure to follow the torque recommendations closely. For fasteners not assigned a specific torque, a general torque value chart is presented here as a guide. These torque values are for dry (unlubricated) fasteners threaded into steel or cast iron (not aluminium). As was previously mentioned, the size and grade of a fastener determine the amount of torque that can safely be applied to it. The figures listed here are approximate for Grade 2 and Grade 3 fasteners. Higher grades can tolerate higher torque values.

Fasteners laid out in a pattern, such as cylinder head bolts, sump bolts, differential cover bolts, etc., must be loosened or tightened in sequence to avoid warping the component. This sequence will normally be shown in the appropriate Chapter. If a specific pattern is not given, the following procedures can be used to prevent warping.

Initially, the bolts or nuts should be assembled finger-tight only. Next, they should be tightened one full turn each, in a crisscross or diagonal pattern. After each one has

Metric thread sizes	Nm	Ft-lbs
M-6	9 to 12	6 to 9
M-8	19 to 28	14 to 21
M-10	38 to 54	28 to 40
M-12	68 to 96	50 to 71
M-14	109 to 154	80 to 140
Pipe thread sizes		
1/8	7 to 10	5 to 8
1/4	17 to 24	12 to 18
3/8	30 to 44	22 to 33
1/2	34 to 47	25 to 35
U.S. thread sizes		
1/4 - 20	9 to 12	6 to 9
5/16 - 18	17 to 24	12 to 18
5/16 - 24	19 to 27	14 to 20
3/8 - 16	30 to 43	22 to 32
3/8 - 24	37 to 51	27 to 38
7/16 - 14	55 to 74	40 to 55
7/16 - 20	55 to 81	40 to 60
1/2 - 13	75 to 108	55 to 80

00-2 HAYNES

Standard (SAE and USS) bolt dimensions/grade marks

G   *Grade marks (bolt strength)*
L   *Length (in inches)*
T   *Thread pitch (number of threads per inch)*
D   *Nominal diameter (in inches)*

Metric bolt dimensions/grade marks

P   *Property class (bolt strength)*
L   *Length (in millimetres)*
T   *Thread pitch (distance between threads in millimetres)*
D   *Diameter*

been tightened one full turn, return to the first one and tighten them all one-half turn, following the same pattern. Finally, tighten each of them one-quarter turn at a time until each fastener has been tightened to the proper torque. To loosen and remove the fasteners, the procedure would be reversed.

Component disassembly

Component disassembly should be done with care and purpose to help ensure that the parts go back together properly. Always keep track of the sequence in which parts are removed. Make note of special characteristics or marks on parts that can be refit more than one way, such as a grooved-thrust washer on a shaft. It is a good idea to lay the disassembled parts out on a clean surface in the order that they were removed. It may also be helpful to make sketches or take instant photos of components before removal.

When removing fasteners from a component, keep track of their locations. Sometimes threading a bolt back in a part, or putting the washers and nut back on a stud, can prevent mix-ups later. If nuts and bolts cannot be returned to their original locations, they should be kept in a compartmented box or a series of small boxes. A cupcake or muffin tin is ideal for this purpose, since each cavity can hold the bolts and nuts from a particular area (i.e. sump bolts, valve cover bolts,-engine mount bolts, etc.). A pan of this type is especially helpful when working on assemblies with very small parts, such as the carburettor, alternator, valve train or interior dash and trim pieces. The cavities can be marked with paint or tape to identify the contents.

Whenever wiring looms, harnesses or connectors are separated, it is a good idea to identify the two halves with numbered pieces of masking tape so they can be easily reconnected.

Gasket sealing surfaces

Throughout any vehicle, gaskets are used to seal the mating surfaces between two parts and keep lubricants, fluids, vacuum or pressure contained in an assembly.

Many times these gaskets are coated with a liquid or paste-type gasket sealing compound before assembly. Age, heat and pressure can sometimes cause the two parts to stick together so tightly that they are very difficult to separate. Often, the assembly can be loosened by striking it with a soft-face hammer near the mating surfaces. A regular hammer can be used if a block of wood is placed between the hammer and the part. Do not hammer on cast parts or parts that could be easily damaged. With any particularly stubborn part, always recheck to make sure that every fastener has been removed.

Avoid using a screwdriver or bar to prise apart an assembly, as they can easily mar the gasket sealing surfaces of the parts, which must remain smooth. If levering is absolutely necessary, use an old broom handle, but keep in mind that extra clean up will be necessary if the wood splinters.

After the parts are separated, the old gasket must be carefully scraped off and the gasket surfaces cleaned. Stubborn gasket material can be soaked with rust penetrant or treated with a special chemical to soften it so it can be easily scraped off. **Caution:** *Never use gasket removal solutions or caustic chemicals on plastic or other composite components.* A scraper can be fashioned from a piece of copper tubing by flattening and sharpening one end. Copper is recommended because it is usually softer than the surfaces to be scraped, which reduces the chance of gouging the part. Some gaskets can be removed with a wire brush, but regardless of the method used, the mating surfaces must be left clean and smooth. If for some reason the gasket surface is gouged, then a gasket sealer thick enough to fill scratches will have to be used during reassembly of the components. For most applications, a non-drying (or semi-drying) gasket sealer should be used.

Hose removal tips

Warning: *If the vehicle is equipped with air conditioning, do not disconnect any of the A/C hoses without first having the system depressurised by a dealer service department or a service station.*

Hose removal precautions closely parallel gasket removal precautions. Avoid scratching or gouging the surface that the hose mates against or the connection may leak. This is especially true for radiator hoses. Because of various chemical reactions, the rubber in hoses can bond itself to the metal spigot that the hose fits over. To remove a hose, first loosen the hose clamps that secure it to the spigot. Then, with slip-joint pliers, grab the hose at the clamp and rotate it around the spigot. Work it back and forth until it is completely free, then pull it off. Silicone or other lubricants will ease removal if they can be applied between the hose and the outside of the spigot. Apply the same lubricant to the inside of the hose and the outside of the spigot to simplify refitting.

As a last resort (and if the hose is to be renewed anyway), the rubber can be slit with a knife and the hose peeled from the spigot. If this must be done, be careful that the metal connection is not damaged.

If a hose clamp is broken or damaged, do not reuse it. Wire-type clamps usually weaken with age, so it is a good idea to renew them with screw-type clamps whenever a hose is removed.

Tools

A selection of good tools is a basic requirement for anyone who plans to maintain and repair his or her own vehicle. For the owner who has few tools, the initial investment might seem high, but when compared to the spiralling costs of professional auto maintenance and repair, it is a wise one.

To help the owner decide which tools are needed to perform the tasks detailed in this manual, the following tool lists are offered: *Maintenance and minor repair, Repair/overhaul* and *Special.*

The newcomer to practical mechanics should start off with the *maintenance and minor repair* tool kit, which is adequate for the simpler jobs performed on a vehicle. Then, as

Micrometer set

Dial indicator set

Dial caliper

Hand-operated vacuum pump

Timing light

Compression gauge with spark plug hole adapter

Damper/steering wheel puller

General purpose puller

Hydraulic lifter removal tool

Valve spring compressor

Valve spring compressor

Ridge reamer

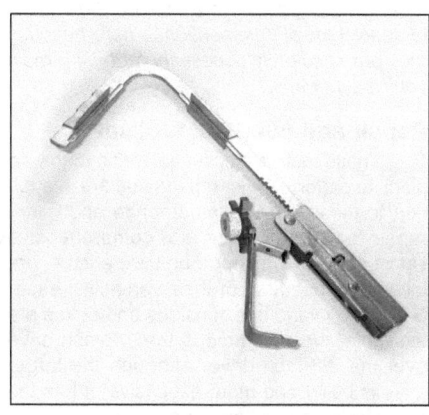

Piston ring groove cleaning tool

Ring removal/refitting tool

Ring compressor

Cylinder hone

Brake hold-down spring tool

Torque angle gauge

Clutch plate alignment tool

Tap and die set

confidence and experience grow, the owner can tackle more difficult tasks, buying additional tools as they are needed. Eventually the basic kit will be expanded into the *repair and overhaul* tool set. Over a period of time, the experienced do-it-yourselfer will assemble a tool set complete enough for most repair and overhaul procedures and will add tools from the special category when it is felt that the expense is justified by the frequency of use.

Maintenance and minor repair tool kit

The tools in this list should be considered the minimum required for performance of routine maintenance, servicing and minor repair work. We recommend the purchase of combination spanners (box-end and open-end combined in one spanner). While more expensive than open end spanners, they offer the advantages of both types of spanner.

> *Combination spanner set (6 mm to 19 mm)*
> *Adjustable spanner*
> *Spark plug spanner with rubber insert*
> *Spark plug gap adjusting tool*
> *Feeler gauge set*
> *Brake bleeder spanner*
> *Standard screwdriver*
> *Phillips screwdriver*
> *Combination pliers*
> *Hacksaw and assortment of blades*

> *Tyre pressure gauge*
> *Grease gun*
> *Oil can*
> *Fine emery cloth*
> *Wire brush*
> *Battery post and cable cleaning tool*
> *Oil filter spanner*
> *Funnel (medium size)*
> *Safety goggles*
> *Jackstands (2)*
> *Drain pan*

Note: *If basic tune-ups are going to be part of routine maintenance, it will be necessary to purchase a good quality stroboscopic timing light and combination tachometer/dwell meter. Although they are included in the list of special tools, it is mentioned here because they are absolutely necessary for tuning most vehicles properly.*

Repair and overhaul tool set

These tools are essential for anyone who plans to perform major repairs and are in addition to those in the maintenance and minor repair tool kit. Included is a comprehensive set of sockets which, though expensive, are invaluable because of their versatility, especially when various extensions and drives are available. We recommend the 1/2-inch drive over the 3/8-inch drive. Although the larger drive is bulky and more expensive, it has the capacity of accepting a very wide range of

large sockets. Ideally, however, the mechanic should have a 3/8-inch drive set and a 1/2-inch drive set.

> *Socket set(s)*
> *Reversible ratchet*
> *Extension*
> *Universal joint*
> *Torque wrench (same size drive as sockets)*
> *Ball peen hammer*
> *Soft-face hammer (plastic/rubber)*
> *Standard screwdriver*
> *Standard screwdriver (stubby)*
> *Phillips screwdriver*
> *Phillips screwdriver (stubby - No. 2)*
> *Pliers - vise grip*
> *Pliers - lineman's*
> *Pliers - needle nose*
> *Pliers - snap-ring (internal and external)*
> *Cold chisel*
> *Scribe*
> *Scraper (made from flattened copper tubing)*
> *Centrepunch*
> *Pin punches*
> *Steel rule/straightedge*
> *Allen wrench set (4 mm to 10 mm)*
> *A selection of files*
> *Wire brush (large)*
> *Jackstands (second set)*
> *Jack (scissor or hydraulic type)*

Note: *Another tool which is often useful is an electric drill with a chuck capacity of 10 mm and a set of good quality drill bits.*

Special tools

The tools in this list include those which are not used regularly, are expensive to buy, or which need to be used in accordance with their manufacturer's instructions. Unless these tools will be used frequently, it is not very economical to purchase many of them. A consideration would be to split the cost and use between yourself and a friend or friends. In addition, most of these tools can be obtained from a tool rental shop on a temporary basis.

This list primarily contains only those tools and instruments widely available to the public, and not those special tools produced by the vehicle manufacturer for distribution to dealer service departments. Occasionally, references to the manufacturer's special tools are included in the text of this manual. Generally, an alternative method of doing the job without the special tool is offered. However, sometimes there is no alternative to their use. Where this is the case, and the tool cannot be purchased or borrowed, the work should be turned over to the dealer service department or an automotive repair shop.

Valve spring compressor
Piston ring groove cleaning tool
Piston ring compressor
Piston ring refitting tool
Cylinder compression gauge
Cylinder ridge reamer
Cylinder surfacing hone
Cylinder bore gauge
Micrometers and/or dial calipers
Hydraulic lifter removal tool
Balljoint separator
Universal-type puller
Impact screwdriver
Dial indicator set
Stroboscopic timing light (inductive pick-up)
Hand operated vacuum/pressure pump
Tachometer/dwell metre
Universal electrical multimeter
Cable hoist
Brake spring removal and refitting tools
Floor jack

Buying tools

For the do-it-yourselfer who is just starting to get involved in vehicle maintenance and repair, there are a number of options available when purchasing tools. If maintenance and minor repair is the extent of the work to be done, the purchase of individual tools is satisfactory. If, on the other hand, extensive work is planned, it would be a good idea to purchase a modest tool set from one of the large retail chain stores. A set can usually be bought at a substantial savings over the individual tool prices, and they often come with a tool box. As additional tools are needed, add-on sets, individual tools and a larger tool box can be purchased to expand the tool selection. Build-ing a tool set gradually allows the cost of the tools to be spread over a longer period of time and gives the mechanic the freedom to choose only those tools that will actually be used.

Tool stores will often be the only source of some of the special tools that are needed, but regardless of where tools are bought, try to avoid cheap ones, especially when buying screwdrivers and sockets, because they won't last very long. The expense involved in renewing cheap tools will eventually be greater than the initial cost of quality tools.

Care and maintenance of tools

Good tools are expensive, so it makes sense to treat them with respect. Keep them clean and in useable condition and store them properly when not in use. Always wipe off any dirt, grease or metal chips before putting them away. Never leave tools lying around in the work area. Upon completion of a job, always check closely under the bonnet for tools that may have been left there so they won't get lost during a test drive.

Some tools, such as screwdrivers, pliers, spanners and sockets, can be hung on a panel mounted on the garage or workshop wall, while others should be kept in a tool box or tray. Measuring instruments, gauges, metres, etc. must be carefully stored where they cannot be damaged by weather or impact from other tools.

When tools are used with care and stored properly, they will last a very long time. Even with the best of care, though, tools will wear out if used frequently. When a tool is damaged or worn out, renew it. Subsequent jobs will be safer and more enjoyable if you do.

How to repair damaged threads

Sometimes, the internal threads of a nut or bolt hole can become stripped, usually from overtightening. Stripping threads is an all-too-common occurrence, especially when working with aluminium parts, because aluminium is so soft that it easily strips out.

Usually, external or internal threads are only partially stripped. After they've been cleaned up with a tap or die, they'll still work. Sometimes, however, threads are badly damaged. When this happens, you've got three choices:

1) *Drill and tap the hole to the next suitable oversize and refit a larger diameter bolt, screw or stud.*

2) *Drill and tap the hole to accept a threaded plug, then drill and tap the plug to the original screw size. You can also buy a plug already threaded to the original size. Then you simply drill a hole to the specified size, then run the threaded plug into the hole with a bolt and jam nut. Once the plug is fully seated, remove the jam nut and bolt.*

3) *The third method uses a patented thread repair kit like Heli-Coil or Slimsert. These easy-to-use kits are designed to repair damaged threads in straight-through holes and blind holes. Both are available as kits which can handle a variety of sizes and thread patterns. Drill the hole, then tap it with the special included tap. Fit the Heli-Coil and the hole is back to its original diameter and thread pitch.*

Regardless of which method you use, be sure to proceed calmly and carefully. A little impatience or carelessness during one of these relatively simple procedures can ruin your whole day's work and cost you a bundle if you wreck an expensive part.

Working facilities

Not to be overlooked when discussing tools is the workshop. If anything more than routine maintenance is to be carried out, some sort of suitable work area is essential.

It is understood, and appreciated, that many home mechanics do not have a good workshop or garage available, and end up removing an engine or doing major repairs outside. It is recommended, however, that the overhaul or repair be completed under the cover of a roof.

A clean, flat workbench or table of comfortable working height is an absolute necessity. The workbench should be equipped with a vise that has a jaw opening of at least 10-cm.

As mentioned previously, some clean, dry storage space is also required for tools, as well as the lubricants, fluids, cleaning solvents, etc. which soon become necessary.

Sometimes waste oil and fluids, drained from the engine or cooling system during normal maintenance or repairs, present a disposal problem. To avoid pouring them on the ground or into a sewage system, pour the used fluids into large containers, seal them with caps and take them to an authorised disposal site or recycling centre. Plastic jugs, such as old antifreeze containers, are ideal for this purpose.

Always keep a supply of old newspapers and clean rags available. Old towels are excellent for mopping up spills. Many mechanics use rolls of paper towels for most work because they are readily available and disposable. To help keep the area under the vehicle clean, a large cardboard box can be cut open and flattened to protect the garage or shop floor.

Whenever working over a painted surface, such as when leaning over a fender to service something under the bonnet, always cover it with an old blanket or bedspread to protect the finish. Vinyl covered pads, made especially for this purpose, are available at auto parts stores.

Anti-theft audio system

General information

1   Some models are equipped with the anti-theft audio system which includes an anti-theft feature that will render the stereo inoperative if stolen. If the power source to the stereo is cut with the anti-theft feature activated, the stereo will be inoperative. Even if the power source is immediately re-connected, the stereo will not function. If your vehicle is equipped with this anti-theft system, do not disconnect the battery, remove the stereo or disconnect related components unless you have either turned off the feature or have the individual ID (code) number for the stereo.

2   Refer to your vehicle's owner's manual for more complete information on this audio system and its anti-theft feature.

Disabling the anti-theft feature

3   Press the stereo's 1 and 4 buttons at the same time for five seconds with the ignition on and the radio power off. The display will show SEC, indicating the unit is in the secure mode (anti-theft feature enabled).

4   Press the SEEK left arrow until the first digit of your code appears.

5   Press the SEEK right arrow until the second digit of your code appears.

6   Press the TUNE left arrow until the third digit of your code appears.

7   Press the TUNE right arrow until the fourth digit of your code appears.

8   Press the AM/FM knob. "0000" will be displayed if you entered the correct code.

9   If Err is displayed, the code you entered was incorrect and the anti-theft feature is still enabled.

Unlocking the stereo after a power loss

10   When power is restored to the stereo, the stereo won't turn on and LOC will appear on the display. Enter your ID code as follows; pause no more than 15 seconds between Steps.

11   Turn the ignition switch to ON, but leave the stereo off.

12   Press the SEEK left arrow until the first digit of your code appears.

13   Press the SEEK right arrow until the second digit of your code appears.

14   Press the TUNE left arrow until the third digit of your code appears.

15   Press the TUNE right arrow until the fourth digit of your code appears.

16   Press the AM/FM knob. If the time of day appears, the numbers you entered were correct and the stereo will work. If Err appears, the numbers you entered were not correct and the stereo is still inoperative.

Booster battery (jump) starting

Observe these precautions when using a booster battery to start a vehicle:

a) Before connecting the booster battery, make sure the ignition switch is in the Off position.

b) Turn off the lights, heater and other electrical loads.

c) Your eyes should be shielded. Safety goggles are a good idea.

d) Make sure the booster battery is the same voltage as the dead one in the vehicle.

e) The two vehicles MUST NOT TOUCH each other!

f) Make sure the transmission is in Neutral (manual) or Park (automatic).

g) If the booster battery is not a maintenance-free type, remove the vent caps and lay a cloth over the vent holes.

Connect the red jumper cable to the positive (+) terminals of each battery (see illustration).

Connect one end of the black jumper cable to the negative (-) terminal of the booster battery. The other end of this cable should be connected to a good ground on the vehicle to be started, such as a bolt or bracket on the body.

Start the engine using the booster battery, then, with the engine running at idle speed, disconnect the jumper cables in the reverse order of connection.

A good earth point on the vehicle with the flat battery

Jumper or booster battery

Dead battery

Make the booster battery cable connections in the numerical order shown (note that the negative cable of the booster battery is NOT attached to the negative terminal of the dead battery)

Jacking and towing

Jacking

Warning: *The jack supplied with the vehicle should only be used for changing a tyre or placing jackstands under the frame. Never work under the vehicle or start the engine while this jack is being used as the only means of support.*

The vehicle should be on level ground. Place the shift lever in Park, if you have an automatic, or Reverse if you have a manual transaxle. Block the wheel diagonally opposite the wheel being changed. Set the parking brake.

Remove the spare tyre and jack from stowage. Remove the wheel cover and trim ring (if so equipped) with the tapered end of the lug nut wrench by inserting and twisting the handle and then prying against the back of the wheel cover. Loosen, but do not remove, the lug nuts (one-half turn is sufficient).

Place the scissors-type jack under the side of the vehicle and adjust the jack height until it fits between the notches in the vertical rocker panel flange nearest the wheel to be changed. There is a front and rear jacking point on each side of the vehicle (**see illustration**).

Turn the jack handle clockwise until the tyre clears the ground. Remove the lug nuts and pull the wheel off. Replace it with the spare.

Install the lug nuts with the beveled edges facing in. Tighten them snugly. Don't attempt to tighten them completely until the vehicle is lowered or it could slip off the jack. Turn the jack handle counterclockwise to lower the vehicle. Remove the jack and tighten the lug nuts in a diagonal pattern.

Install the cover (and trim ring, if used) and be sure it's snapped into place all the way around.

Stow the tyre, jack and spanner. Unblock the wheels.

Towing

The manufacturer does not recommend towing except with a towing dolly under the front wheels. In an emergency the vehicle can be towed a short distance with a cable or chain attached to one of the towing eyelets located under the front or rear bumpers following the precautions above. The driver must remain in the vehicle to operate the steering and brakes (remember that power steering and power brakes will not work with the engine off).

The jack fits over the rocker panel flange, between the two notches (there are two jacking points on each side of the vehicle)

Automotive chemicals and lubricants

A number of automotive chemicals and lubricants are available for use during vehicle maintenance and repair. They include a wide variety of products ranging from cleaning solvents and degreasers to lubricants and protective sprays for rubber, plastic and vinyl.

Cleaners

Carburettor cleaner and choke cleaner is a strong solvent for gum, varnish and carbon. Most carburettor cleaners leave a dry-type lubricant film which will not harden or gum up. Because of this film it is not recommended for use on electrical components.

Brake system cleaner is used to remove brake dust, grease and brake fluid from the brake system, where clean surfaces are absolutely necessary. It leaves no residue and often eliminates brake squeal caused by contaminants.

Electrical cleaner removes oxidation, corrosion and carbon deposits from electrical contacts, restoring full current flow. It can also be used to clean spark plugs, carburettor jets, voltage regulators and other parts where an oil-free surface is desired.

Demoisturants remove water and moisture from electrical components such as alternators, voltage regulators, electrical connectors and fuse blocks. They are non-conductive and non-corrosive.

Degreasers are heavy-duty solvents used to remove grease from the outside of-the engine and from chassis components. They can be sprayed or brushed on and, depending on the type, are rinsed off either with water or solvent.

Lubricants

Motor oil is the lubricant formulated for use in engines. It normally contains a wide variety of additives to prevent corrosion and reduce foaming and wear. Motor oil comes in various weights (viscosity ratings) from 0 to 50. The recommended weight of the oil depends on the season, temperature and the demands on the engine. Light oil is used in cold climates and under light load conditions. Heavy oil is used in hot climates and where high loads are encountered. Multi-viscosity oils are designed to have characteristics of both light and heavy oils and are available in a number of weights from 5W-20 to 20W-50.

Gear oil is designed to be used in differentials, manual transmissions and other areas where high-temperature lubrication is required.

Chassis and wheel bearing grease is a heavy grease used where increased loads and friction are encountered, such as for wheel bearings, balljoints, tie-rod ends and universal joints.

High-temperature wheel bearing grease is designed to withstand the extreme temperatures encountered by wheel bearings in disc brake equipped vehicles. It usually contains molybdenum disulfide (moly), which is a dry-type lubricant.

White grease is a heavy grease for metal-to-metal applications where water is a problem. White grease stays soft under both low and high temperatures (usually from -56 to +106-degrees C), and will not wash off or dilute in the presence of water.

Assembly lube is a special extreme pressure lubricant, usually containing moly, used to lubricate high-load parts (such as main and rod bearings and cam lobes) for initial start-up of a new engine. The assembly lube lubricates the parts without being squeezed out or washed away until the engine oiling system begins to function.

Silicone lubricants are used to protect rubber, plastic, vinyl and nylon parts.

Graphite lubricants are used where oils cannot be used due to contamination problems, such as in locks. The dry graphite will lubricate metal parts while remaining uncontaminated by dirt, water, oil or acids. It is electrically conductive and will not foul electrical contacts in locks such as the ignition switch.

Moly penetrants loosen and lubricate seized, rusted and corroded fasteners and prevent future rusting or freezing.

Heat-sink grease is a special electrically non-conductive grease that is used for mounting electronic ignition modules where it is essential that heat is transferred away from the module.

Sealants

RTV sealant is one of the most widely used gasket compounds. Made from silicone, RTV is air curing, it seals, bonds, waterproofs, fills surface irregularities, remains flexible, doesn't shrink, is relatively easy to remove, and is used as a supplementary sealer with almost all low and medium temperature gaskets.

Anaerobic sealant is much like RTV in that it can be used either to seal gaskets or to form gaskets by itself. It remains flexible, is solvent resistant and fills surface imperfections. The difference between an anaerobic sealant and an RTV-type sealant is in the curing. RTV cures when exposed to air, while an anaerobic sealant cures only in the absence of air. This means that an anaerobic sealant cures only after the assembly of parts, sealing them together.

Thread and pipe sealant is used for sealing hydraulic and pneumatic fittings and vacuum lines. It is usually made from a Teflon compound, and comes in a spray, a paint-on liquid and as a wrap-around tape.

Chemicals

Anti-seize compound prevents seizing, galling, cold welding, rust and corrosion in fasteners. High-temperature anti-seize, usually made with copper and graphite lubricants, is used for exhaust system and exhaust manifold bolts.

Anaerobic locking compounds are used to keep fasteners from vibrating or working loose and cure only after installation, in the absence of air. Medium strength locking compound is used for small nuts, bolts and screws that may be removed later. High-strength locking compound is for large nuts, bolts and studs which aren't removed on a regular basis.

Oil additives range from viscosity index improvers to chemical treatments that claim to reduce internal engine friction. It should be noted that most oil manufacturers caution against using additives with their oils.

Fuel additives perform several functions, depending on their chemical makeup. They usually contain solvents that help dissolve gum and varnish that build up on carburettor, fuel injection and inlet parts. They also serve to break down carbon deposits that form on the inside surfaces of the combustion chambers. Some additives contain upper cylinder lubricants for valves and piston rings, and others contain chemicals to remove condensation from the fuel tank.

Miscellaneous

Brake fluid is specially formulated hydraulic fluid that can withstand the heat and pressure encountered in brake systems. Care must be taken so this fluid does not come in contact with painted surfaces or plastics. An opened container should always be resealed to prevent contamination by water or dirt.

Weatherstrip adhesive is used to bond weatherstripping around doors, windows and luggage compartment lids. It is sometimes used to attach trim pieces.

Undercoating is a petroleum-based, tar-like substance that is designed to protect metal surfaces on the underside of the vehicle from corrosion. It also acts as a sound-deadening agent by insulating the bottom of the vehicle.

Waxes and polishes are used to help protect painted and plated surfaces from the weather. Different types of paint may require the use of different types of wax and polish. Some polishes utilise a chemical or abrasive cleaner to help remove the top layer of oxidised (dull) paint on older vehicles. In recent years many non-wax polishes that contain a wide variety of chemicals such as polymers and silicones have been introduced. These non-wax polishes are usually easier to apply and last longer than conventional waxes and polishes.

Conversion factors

Length (distance)
Inches (in)	X	25.4	= Millimetres (mm)	X 0.0394	= Inches (in)
Feet (ft)	X	0.305	= Metres (m)	X 3.281	= Feet (ft)
Miles	X	1.609	= Kilometres (km)	X 0.621	= Miles

Volume (capacity)
Cubic inches (cu in; in^3)	X	16.387	= Cubic centimetres (cc; cm^3)	X 0.061	= Cubic inches (cu in; in^3)
Imperial pints (Imp pt)	X	0.568	= Litres (l)	X 1.76	= Imperial pints (Imp pt)
Imperial quarts (Imp qt)	X	1.137	= Litres (l)	X 0.88	= Imperial quarts (Imp qt)
Imperial quarts (Imp qt)	X	1.201	= US quarts (US qt)	X 0.833	= Imperial quarts (Imp qt)
US quarts (US qt)	X	0.946	= Litres (l)	X 1.057	= US quarts (US qt)
Imperial gallons (Imp gal)	X	4.546	= Litres (l)	X 0.22	= Imperial gallons (Imp gal)
Imperial gallons (Imp gal)	X	1.201	= US gallons (US gal)	X 0.833	= Imperial gallons (Imp gal)
US gallons (US gal)	X	3.785	= Litres (l)	X 0.264	= US gallons (US gal)

Mass (weight)
Ounces (oz)	X	28.35	= Grams (g)	X 0.035	= Ounces (oz)
Pounds (lb)	X	0.454	= Kilograms (kg)	X 2.205	= Pounds (lb)

Force
Ounces-force (ozf; oz)	X	0.278	= Newtons (N)	X 3.6	= Ounces-force (ozf; oz)
Pounds-force (lbf; lb)	X	4.448	= Newtons (N)	X 0.225	= Pounds-force (lbf; lb)
Newtons (N)	X	0.1	= Kilograms-force (kgf; kg)	X 9.81	= Newtons (N)

Pressure
Pounds-force per square inch (psi; lbf/in^2; lb/in^2)	X	0.070	= Kilograms-force per square centimetre (kgf/cm^2; kg/cm^2)	X 14.223	= Pounds-force per square inch (psi; lbf/in^2; lb/in^2)
Pounds-force per square inch (psi; lbf/in^2; lb/in^2)	X	0.068	= Atmospheres (atm)	X 14.696	= Pounds-force per square inch (psi; lbf/in^2; lb/in^2)
Pounds-force per square inch (psi; lbf/in^2; lb/in^2)	X	0.069	= Bars	X 14.5	= Pounds-force per square inch (psi; lbf/in^2; lb/in^2)
Pounds-force per square inch (psi; lbf/in^2; lb/in^2)	X	6.895	= Kilopascals (kPa)	X 0.145	= Pounds-force per square inch (psi; lbf/in^2; lb/in^2)
Kilopascals (kPa)	X	0.01	= Kilograms-force per square centimetre (kgf/cm^2; kg/cm^2)	X 98.1	= Kilopascals (kPa)

Torque (moment of force)
Pounds-force inches (lbf in; lb in)	X	1.152	= Kilograms-force centimetre (kgf cm; kg cm)	X 0.868	= Pounds-force inches (lbf in; lb in)
Pounds-force inches (lbf in; lb in)	X	0.113	= Newton metres (Nm)	X 8.85	= Pounds-force inches (lbf in; lb in)
Pounds-force inches (lbf in; lb in)	X	0.083	= Pounds-force feet (lbf ft; lb ft)	X 12	= Pounds-force inches (lbf in; lb in)
Pounds-force feet (lbf ft; lb ft)	X	0.138	= Kilograms-force metres (kgf m; kg m)	X 7.233	= Pounds-force feet (lbf ft; lb ft)
Pounds-force feet (lbf ft; lb ft)	X	1.356	= Newton metres (Nm)	X 0.738	= Pounds-force feet (lbf ft; lb ft)
Newton metres (Nm)	X	0.102	= Kilograms-force metres (kgf m; kg m)	X 9.804	= Newton metres (Nm)

Vacuum
Inches mercury (in. Hg)	X	3.377	= Kilopascals (kPa)	X 0.2961	= Inches mercury
Inches mercury (in. Hg)	X	25.4	= Millimetres mercury (mm Hg)	X 0.0394	= Inches mercury

Power
Horsepower (hp)	X	745.7	= Watts (W)	X 0.0013	= Horsepower (hp)

Velocity (speed)
Miles per hour (miles/hr; mph)	X	1.609	= Kilometres per hour (km/hr; kph)	X 0.621	= Miles per hour (miles/hr; mph)

Fuel consumption*
Miles per gallon, Imperial (mpg)	X	0.354	= Kilometres per litre (km/l)	X 2.825	= Miles per gallon, Imperial (mpg)
Miles per gallon, US (mpg)	X	0.425	= Kilometres per litre (km/l)	X 2.352	= Miles per gallon, US (mpg)

Temperature

Degrees Fahrenheit = (°C x 1.8) + 32

Degrees Celsius (Degrees Centigrade; °C) = (°F - 32) x 0.56

*It is common practice to convert from miles per gallon (mpg) to litres/100 kilometres (l/100km), where mpg (Imperial) x l/100 km = 282 and mpg (US) x l/100 km = 235

Safety first!

Regardless of how enthusiastic you may be about getting on with the job at hand, take the time to ensure that your safety is not jeopardised. A moment's lack of attention can result in an accident, as can failure to observe certain simple safety precautions. The possibility of an accident will always exist, and the following points should not be considered a comprehensive list of all dangers. Rather, they are intended to make you aware of the risks and to encourage a safety conscious approach to all work you carry out on your vehicle.

Essential DOs and DON'Ts

DON'T rely on a jack when working under the vehicle. Always use approved jackstands to support the weight of the vehicle and place them under the recommended lift or support points.

DON'T attempt to loosen extremely tight fasteners (i.e. wheel lug nuts) while the vehicle is on a jack - it may fall.

DON'T start the engine without first making sure that the transmission is in Neutral (or Park where applicable) and the parking brake is set.

DON'T remove the radiator cap from a hot cooling system - let it cool or cover it with a cloth and release the pressure gradually.

DON'T attempt to drain the engine oil until you are sure it has cooled to the point that it will not burn you.

DON'T touch any part of the engine or exhaust system until it has cooled sufficiently to avoid burns.

DON'T siphon toxic liquids such as petrol, antifreeze and brake fluid by mouth, or allow them to remain on your skin.

DON'T inhale brake lining dust - it is potentially hazardous (see *Asbestos* below).

DON'T allow spilled oil or grease to remain on the floor - wipe it up before someone slips on it.

DON'T use loose fitting spanners or other tools which may slip and cause injury.

DON'T push on spanners when loosening or tightening nuts or bolts. Always try to pull the spanner toward you. If the situation calls for pushing the spanner away, push with an open hand to avoid scraped knuckles if the spanner should slip.

DON'T attempt to lift a heavy component alone - get someone to help you.

DON'T rush or take unsafe shortcuts to finish a job.

DON'T allow children or animals in or around the vehicle while you are working on it.

DO wear eye protection when using power tools such as a drill, sander, bench grinder, etc. and when working under a vehicle.

DO keep loose clothing and long hair well out of the way of moving parts.

DO make sure that any hoist used has a safe working load rating adequate for the job.

DO get someone to check on you periodically when working alone on a vehicle.

DO carry out work in a logical sequence and make sure that everything is correctly assembled and tightened.

DO keep chemicals and fluids tightly capped and out of the reach of children and pets.

DO remember that your vehicle's safety affects that of yourself and others. If in doubt on any point, get professional advice.

Asbestos

Certain friction, insulating, sealing, and other products - such as brake linings, brake bands, clutch linings, torque converters, gaskets, etc. - may contain asbestos. Extreme care must be taken to avoid inhalation of dust from such products, since it is hazardous to health. If in doubt, assume that they do contain asbestos.

Fire

Remember at all times that petrol is highly flammable. Never smoke or have any kind of open flame around when working on a vehicle. But the risk does not end there. A spark caused by an electrical short circuit, by two metal surfaces contacting each other, or even by static electricity built up in your body under certain conditions, can ignite petrol vapours, which in a confined space are highly explosive. Do not, under any circumstances, use petrol for cleaning parts. Use an approved safety solvent.

Always disconnect the battery earth (-) cable at the battery before working on any part of the fuel system or electrical system. Never risk spilling fuel on a hot engine or exhaust component. It is strongly recommended that a fire extinguisher suitable for use on fuel and electrical fires be kept handy in the garage or workshop at all times. Never try to extinguish a fuel or electrical fire with water.

Fumes

Certain fumes are highly toxic and can quickly cause unconsciousness and even death if inhaled to any extent. Petrol vapour falls into this category, as do the vapours from some cleaning solvents. Any draining or pouring of such volatile fluids should be done in a well ventilated area.

When using cleaning fluids and solvents, read the instructions on the container carefully. Never use materials from unmarked containers.

Never run the engine in an enclosed space, such as a garage. Exhaust fumes contain carbon monoxide, which is extremely poisonous. If you need to run the engine, always do so in the open air, or at least have the rear of the vehicle outside the work area.

If you are fortunate enough to have the use of an inspection pit, never drain or pour petrol and never run the engine while the vehicle is over the pit. The fumes, being heavier than air, will concentrate in the pit with possibly lethal results.

The battery

Never create a spark or allow a bare light bulb near a battery. They normally give off a certain amount of hydrogen gas, which is highly explosive.

Always disconnect the battery earth (-) cable at the battery before working on the fuel or electrical systems.

If possible, loosen the filler caps or cover when charging the battery from an external source (this does not apply to sealed or maintenance-free batteries). Do not charge at an excessive rate or the battery may burst.

Take care when adding water to a non maintenance-free battery and when carrying a battery. The electrolyte, even when diluted, is very corrosive and should not be allowed to contact clothing or skin.

Always wear eye protection when cleaning the battery to prevent the caustic deposits from entering your eyes.

Household current

When using an electric power tool, inspection light, etc., which operates on household current, always make sure that the tool is correctly connected to its plug and that, where necessary, it is properly earthed. Do not use such items in damp conditions and, again, do not create a spark or apply excessive heat in the vicinity of fuel or fuel vapour.

Secondary ignition system voltage

A severe electric shock can result from touching certain parts of the ignition system (such as the spark plug wires) when the engine is running or being cranked, particularly if components are damp or the insulation is defective. In the case of an electronic ignition system, the secondary system voltage is much higher and could prove fatal.

DECIMALS to MILLIMETRES

Decimal	mm	Decimal	mm
0.001	0.0254	0.500	12.7000
0.002	0.0508	0.510	12.9540
0.003	0.0762	0.520	13.2080
0.004	0.1016	0.530	13.4620
0.005	0.1270	0.540	13.7160
0.006	0.1524	0.550	13.9700
0.007	0.1778	0.560	14.2240
0.008	0.2032	0.570	14.4780
0.009	0.2286	0.580	14.7320
		0.590	14.9860
0.010	0.2540		
0.020	0.5080		
0.030	0.7620		
0.040	1.0160	0.600	15.2400
0.050	1.2700	0.610	15.4940
0.060	1.5240	0.620	15.7480
0.070	1.7780	0.630	16.0020
0.080	2.0320	0.640	16.2560
0.090	2.2860	0.650	16.5100
		0.660	16.7640
0.100	2.5400	0.670	17.0180
0.110	2.7940	0.680	17.2720
0.120	3.0480	0.690	17.5260
0.130	3.3020		
0.140	3.5560		
0.150	3.8100		
0.160	4.0640	0.700	17.7800
0.170	4.3180	0.710	18.0340
0.180	4.5720	0.720	18.2880
0.190	4.8260	0.730	18.5420
		0.740	18.7960
0.200	5.0800	0.750	19.0500
0.210	5.3340	0.760	19.3040
0.220	5.5880	0.770	19.5580
0.230	5.8420	0.780	19.8120
0.240	6.0960	0.790	20.0660
0.250	6.3500		
0.260	6.6040		
0.270	6.8580	0.800	20.3200
0.280	7.1120	0.810	20.5740
0.290	7.3660	0.820	21.8280
		0.830	21.0820
0.300	7.6200	0.840	21.3360
0.310	7.8740	0.850	21.5900
0.320	8.1280	0.860	21.8440
0.330	8.3820	0.870	22.0980
0.340	8.6360	0.880	22.3520
0.350	8.8900	0.890	22.6060
0.360	9.1440		
0.370	9.3980		
0.380	9.6520		
0.390	9.9060		
		0.900	22.8600
0.400	10.1600	0.910	23.1140
0.410	10.4140	0.920	23.3680
0.420	10.6680	0.930	23.6220
0.430	10.9220	0.940	23.8760
0.440	11.1760	0.950	24.1300
0.450	11.4300	0.960	24.3840
0.460	11.6840	0.970	24.6380
0.470	11.9380	0.980	24.8920
0.480	12.1920	0.990	25.1460
0.490	12.4460	1.000	25.4000

FRACTIONS to DECIMALS to MILLIMETRES

Fraction	Decimal	mm	Fraction	Decimal	mm
1/64	0.0156	0.3969	33/64	0.5156	13.0969
1/32	0.0312	0.7938	17/32	0.5312	13.4938
3/64	0.0469	1.1906	35/64	0.5469	13.8906
1/16	0.0625	1.5875	9/16	0.5625	14.2875
5/64	0.0781	1.9844	37/64	0.5781	14.6844
3/32	0.0938	2.3812	19/32	0.5938	15.0812
7/64	0.1094	2.7781	39/64	0.6094	15.4781
1/8	0.1250	3.1750	5/8	0.6250	15.8750
9/64	0.1406	3.5719	41/64	0.6406	16.2719
5/32	0.1562	3.9688	21/32	0.6562	16.6688
11/64	0.1719	4.3656	43/64	0.6719	17.0656
3/16	0.1875	4.7625	11/16	0.6875	17.4625
13/64	0.2031	5.1594	45/64	0.7031	17.8594
7/32	0.2188	5.5562	23/32	0.7188	18.2562
15/64	0.2344	5.9531	47/64	0.7344	18.6531
1/4	0.2500	6.3500	3/4	0.7500	19.0500
17/64	0.2656	6.7469	49/64	0.7656	19.4469
9/32	0.2812	7.1438	25/32	0.7812	19.8438
19/64	0.2969	7.5406	51/64	0.7969	20.2406
5/16	0.3125	7.9375	13/16	0.8125	20.6375
21/64	0.3281	8.3344	53/64	0.8281	21.0344
11/32	0.3438	8.7312	27/32	0.8438	21.4312
23/64	0.3594	9.1281	55/64	0.8594	21.8281
3/8	0.3750	9.5250	7/8	0.8750	22.2250
25/64	0.3906	9.9219	57/64	0.8906	22.6219
13/32	0.4062	10.3188	29/32	0.9062	23.0188
27/64	0.4219	10.7156	59/64	0.9219	23.4156
7/16	0.4375	11.1125	15/16	0.9375	23.8125
29/64	0.4531	11.5094	61/64	0.9531	24.2094
15/32	0.4688	11.9062	31/32	0.9688	24.6062
31/64	0.4844	12.3031	63/64	0.9844	25.0031
1/2	0.5000	12.7000	1	1.0000	25.4000

Troubleshooting

Contents

This section provides an easy reference guide to the more common problems which may occur during the operation of your vehicle. These problems and their possible causes are grouped under headings denoting various components or systems, such as Engine, Cooling system, etc. They also refer you to the chapter and/or section which deals with the problem.

Remember that successful trouble-shooting is not a mysterious black art practiced only by professional mechanics. It is simply the result of the right knowledge combined with an intelligent, systematic approach to the problem. Always work by a process of elimination, starting with the simplest solution and working through to the most complex - and never overlook the obvious. Anyone can run the petrol tank dry or leave the lights on overnight, so don't assume that you are exempt from such oversights.

Finally, always establish a clear idea of why a problem has occurred and take steps to ensure that it doesn't happen again. If the electrical system fails because of a poor connection, check the other connections in the system to make sure that they don't fail as well. If a particular fuse continues to blow, find out why - don't just replace one fuse after another. Remember, failure of a small component can often be indicative of potential failure or incorrect functioning of a more important component or system.

Engine

1 Engine will not rotate when attempting to start

1   Battery terminal connections loose or corroded (Chapter 1).
2   Battery discharged or faulty (Chapter 1).
3   Automatic transaxle not completely engaged in Park (Chapter 7) or clutch pedal not completely depressed (Chapter 8).
4   Broken, loose or disconnected wiring in the starting circuit (Chapters 5 and 12).
5   Starter motor pinion jammed in flywheel ring gear (Chapter 5).
6   Starter solenoid faulty (Chapter 5).
7   Starter motor faulty (Chapter 5).
8   Ignition switch faulty (Chapter 12).
9   Starter pinion or flywheel teeth worn or broken (Chapter 5).

2 Engine rotates but will not start

1   Fuel tank empty.
2   Battery discharged (engine rotates slowly) (Chapter 5).
3   Battery terminal connections loose or corroded (Chapter 1).
4   Leaking fuel injector(s), faulty fuel pump, pressure regulator, etc. (Chapter 4).

5   Broken or stripped timing belt (Chapter 2).
6   Ignition components damp or damaged (Chapter 5).
7   Worn, faulty or incorrectly gapped spark plugs (Chapter 1).
8   Broken, loose or disconnected wiring in the starting circuit (Chapter 5).
9   Loose distributor is changing ignition timing (Chapter 5).
10   Broken, loose or disconnected wires at the ignition coil or faulty coil (Chapter 5).

3 Engine hard to start when cold

1   Battery discharged or low (Chapter 1).
2   Malfunctioning fuel system (Chapter 4).
3   Faulty coolant temperature sensor or intake air temperature sensor (Chapter 6).
4   Injector(s) leaking (Chapter 4).
5   Faulty ignition system (Chapter 5).

4 Engine hard to start when hot

1   Air filter clogged (Chapter 1).
2   Fuel not reaching the fuel injection system (Chapter 4).
3   Corroded battery connections, especially ground (Chapter 1).
4   Faulty coolant temperature sensor or intake air temperature sensor (Chapter 6).

5 Starter motor noisy or excessively rough in engagement

1   Pinion or flywheel gear teeth worn or broken (Chapter 5).
2   Starter motor mounting bolts loose or missing (Chapter 5).

6 Engine starts but stops immediately

1   Loose or faulty electrical connections at distributor, coil or alternator (Chapter 5).
2   Insufficient fuel reaching the fuel injector(s) (Chapters 1 and 4).
3   Vacuum leak at the gasket between the intake manifold/plenum and throttle body (Chapter 4).
4   Idle speed incorrect (Chapter 1).

7 Oil puddle under engine

1   Oil pan gasket and/or oil pan drain bolt washer leaking (Chapter 2).
2   Oil pressure sending unit leaking (Chapter 2).
3   Cylinder head covers leaking (Chapter 2).

4   Engine oil seals leaking (Chapter 2).
5   Oil pump housing leaking (Chapter 2).

8 Engine lopes while idling or idles erratically

1   Vacuum leakage (Chapters 2 and 4).
2   Leaking EGR valve (Chapter 6).
3   Air filter clogged (Chapter 1).
4   Malfunction in the fuel injection or engine control system (Chapters 4 and 6).
5   Leaking head gasket (Chapter 2).
6   Timing belt and/or pulleys worn (Chapter 2).
7   Camshaft lobes worn (Chapter 2).

9 Engine misses at idle speed

1   Spark plugs worn or not gapped properly (Chapter 1).
2   Faulty spark plug wires (Chapter 1).
3   Vacuum leaks (Chapter 1).
4   Incorrect ignition timing (Chapter 1).
5   Uneven or low compression (Chapter 2).
6   Problem with the fuel injection system (Chapter 4).

10 Engine misses throughout driving speed range

1   Fuel filter clogged and/or impurities in the fuel system (Chapter 1).
2   Low fuel output at the injector(s) (Chapter 4).
3   Faulty or incorrectly gapped spark plugs (Chapter 1).
4   Incorrect ignition timing (Chapter 5).
5   Cracked distributor cap, disconnected distributor wires or damaged distributor components (Chapters 1 and 5).
6   Leaking spark plug wires (Chapters 1 or 5).
7   Faulty emission system components (Chapter 6).
8   Low or uneven cylinder compression pressures (Chapter 2).
9   Weak or faulty ignition system (Chapter 5).
10   Vacuum leak in fuel injection system, intake manifold, air control valve or vacuum hoses (Chapter 4).

11 Engine stumbles on acceleration

1   Spark plugs fouled (Chapter 1).
2   Problem with fuel injection or engine control system (Chapters 4 and 6).
3   Fuel filter clogged (Chapters 1 and 4).
4   Incorrect ignition timing (Chapter 5).
5   Intake manifold air leak (Chapters 2 and 4).
6   Problem with the emissions control system (Chapter 6).

12 Engine surges while holding accelerator steady

1   Intake air leak (Chapter 4).
2   Fuel pump or fuel pressure regulator faulty (Chapter 4).
3   Problem with fuel injection system (Chapter 4).
4   Problem with the emissions control system (Chapter 6).

13 Engine stalls

1   Idle speed incorrect (Chapter 1).
2   Fuel filter clogged and/or water and impurities in the fuel system (Chapters 1 and 4).
3   Distributor components damp or damaged (Chapter 5).
4   Faulty emissions system components (Chapter 6).
5   Faulty or incorrectly gapped spark plugs (Chapter 1).
6   Faulty spark plug wires (Chapter 1).
7   Vacuum leak in the fuel injection system, intake manifold or vacuum hoses (Chapters 2 and 4).
8   Valve clearances incorrectly set (Chapter 1).

14 Engine lacks power

1   Incorrect ignition timing (Chapter 5).
2   Excessive play in distributor shaft (Chapter 5).
3   Worn rotor, distributor cap, spark plug wires or faulty coil (Chapters 1 and 5).
4   Faulty or incorrectly gapped spark plugs (Chapter 1).
5   Problem with the fuel injection system (Chapter 4).
6   Plugged air filter (Chapter 1).
7   Brakes binding (Chapter 9).
8   Automatic transaxle fluid level incorrect (Chapter 1).
9   Clutch slipping (Chapter 8).
10   Fuel filter clogged and/or impurities in the fuel system (Chapters 1 and 4).
11   Emission control system not functioning properly (Chapter 6).
12   Low or uneven cylinder compression pressures (Chapter 2).
13   Obstructed exhaust system (Chapter 4).

15 Engine backfires

1   Emission control system not functioning properly (Chapter 6).
2   Ignition timing incorrect (Chapter 5).
3   Faulty secondary ignition system (cracked spark plug insulator, faulty plug wires, distributor cap and/or rotor) (Chapters 1 and 5).
4   Problem with the fuel injection system (Chapter 4).

5   Vacuum leak at fuel injector(s), intake manifold, air control valve or vacuum hoses (Chapters 2 and 4).
6   Valve clearances incorrectly set and/or valves sticking (Chapter 1).

16 Pinging or knocking engine sounds during acceleration or uphill

1   Incorrect grade of fuel.
2   Ignition timing incorrect (Chapter 5).
3   Fuel injection system faulty (Chapter 4).
4   Improper or damaged spark plugs or wires (Chapter 1).
5   Worn or damaged distributor components (Chapter 5).
6   EGR valve not functioning (Chapter 6).
7   Vacuum leak (Chapters 2 and 4).

17 Engine runs with oil pressure light on

1   Low oil level (Chapter 1).
2   Idle rpm below specification (Chapter 1).
3   Short in wiring circuit (Chapter 12).
4   Faulty oil pressure sender (Chapter 2).
5   Worn engine bearings and/or oil pump (Chapter 2).

18 Engine diesels (continues to run) after switching off

1   Idle speed too high (Chapter 1).
2   Excessive engine operating temperature (Chapter 3).
3   Ignition timing in need of adjustment (Chapter 5).

Engine electrical system

19 Battery will not hold a charge

1   Alternator drivebelt defective or not adjusted properly (Chapter 1).
2   Battery electrolyte level low (Chapter 1).
3   Battery terminals loose or corroded (Chapter 1).
4   Alternator not charging properly (Chapter 5).
5   Loose, broken or faulty wiring in the charging circuit (Chapter 5).
6   Short in vehicle wiring (Chapter 12).
7   Internally defective battery (Chapters 1 and 5).

20 Alternator light fails to go out

1   Faulty alternator or charging circuit (Chapter 5).
2   Alternator drivebelt defective or out of

adjustment (Chapter 1).
3   Alternator voltage regulator inoperative (Chapter 5).

21 Alternator light fails to come on when key is turned on

1   Warning light bulb defective (Chapter 12).
2   Fault in the printed circuit, dash wiring or bulb holder (Chapter 12).

Fuel system

22 Excessive fuel consumption

1   Dirty or clogged air filter element (Chapter 1).
2   Incorrectly set ignition timing (Chapter 5).
3   Emissions system not functioning properly (Chapter 6).
4   Fuel injection system not functioning properly (Chapter 4).
5   Low tyre pressure or incorrect tyre size (Chapter 1).

23 Fuel leakage and/or fuel odor

1   Leaking fuel feed or return line (Chapters 1 and 4).
2   Tank overfilled.
3   Evaporative canister filter clogged (Chapters 1 and 6).
4   Problem with fuel injection system (Chapter 4).

Cooling system

24 Overheating

1   Insufficient coolant in system (Chapter 1).
2   Water pump drivebelt defective or out of adjustment (Chapter 1).
3   Radiator core blocked or grille restricted (Chapter 3).
4   Thermostat faulty (Chapter 3).
5   Electric coolant fan inoperative or blades broken (Chapter 3).
6   Radiator cap not maintaining proper pressure (Chapter 3).
7   Ignition timing incorrect (Chapter 5).

25 Overcooling

1   Faulty thermostat (Chapter 3).
2   Inaccurate temperature gauge sending unit (Chapter 3).

26 External coolant leakage

1 Deteriorated/damaged hoses; loose clamps (Chapters 1 and 3).
2 Water pump defective (Chapter 3).
3 Leakage from radiator core or coolant reservoir bottle (Chapter 3).
4 Engine drain or water jacket core plugs leaking (Chapter 2).

27 Internal coolant leakage

1 Leaking cylinder head gasket (Chapter 2).
2 Cracked cylinder bore or cylinder head (Chapter 2).

28 Coolant loss

1 Too much coolant in reservoir (Chapter 1).
2 Coolant boiling away because of overheating (Chapter 3).
3 Internal or external leakage (Chapter 3).
4 Faulty radiator cap (Chapter 3).

29 Poor coolant circulation

1 Inoperative water pump (Chapter 3).
2 Restriction in cooling system (Chapters 1 and 3).
3 Water pump drivebelt defective/out of adjustment (Chapter 1).
4 Thermostat sticking (Chapter 3).

Clutch

30 Pedal travels to floor - no pressure or very little resistance

1 Master or release cylinder faulty (Chapter 8).
2 Hose/pipe burst or leaking (Chapter 8).
3 Connections leaking (Chapter 8).
4 No fluid in reservoir (Chapter 8).
5 If fluid level in reservoir rises as pedal is depressed, master cylinder centre valve seal is faulty (Chapter 8).
6 If there is fluid on dust seal at master cylinder, piston primary seal is leaking (Chapter 8).
7 Broken release bearing or fork (Chapter 8).

31 Fluid in area of master cylinder dust cover and on pedal

Rear seal failure in master cylinder (Chapter 8).

32 Fluid on release cylinder

Release cylinder plunger seal faulty (Chapter 8).

33 Pedal feels spongy when depressed

Air in system (Chapter 8).

34 Unable to select gears

1 Faulty transaxle (Chapter 7).
2 Faulty clutch disc or pressure plate (Chapter 8).
3 Faulty release lever or release bearing (Chapter 8).
4 Faulty shift lever assembly or control cables (Chapter 8).

35 Clutch slips (engine speed increases with no increase in vehicle speed)

1 Clutch plate worn (Chapter 8).
2 Clutch plate is oil soaked by leaking rear main seal (Chapter 8).
3 Clutch plate not seated (Chapter 8).
4 Warped pressure plate or flywheel (Chapter 8).
5 Weak diaphragm springs (Chapter 8).
6 Clutch plate overheated. Allow to cool.

36 Grabbing (chattering) as clutch is engaged

1 Oil on clutch plate lining, burned or glazed facings (Chapter 8).
2 Worn or loose engine or transaxle mounts (Chapters 2 and 7).
3 Worn splines on clutch plate hub (Chapter 8).
4 Warped pressure plate or flywheel (Chapter 8).
5 Burned or smeared resin on flywheel or pressure plate (Chapter 8).

37 Transaxle rattling (clicking)

1 Release lever loose (Chapter 8).
2 Clutch plate damper spring failure (Chapter 8).
3 Low engine idle speed (Chapter 1).

38 Noise in clutch area

1 Fork shaft improperly installed (Chapter 8).
2 Faulty bearing (Chapter 8).

39 Clutch pedal stays on floor

1 Clutch master cylinder piston binding in bore (Chapter 8).
2 Broken release bearing or fork (Chapter 8).

40 High pedal effort

1 Piston binding in bore (Chapter 8).
2 Pressure plate faulty (Chapter 8).
3 Incorrect size master or release cylinder (Chapter 8).

Manual transaxle

41 Knocking noise at low speeds

1 Worn driveaxle constant velocity (CV) joints (Chapter 8).
2 Worn side gear shaft counterbore in differential case (Chapter 7A).*

42 Noise most pronounced when turning

Differential gear noise (Chapter 7A).*

43 Clunk on acceleration or deceleration

1 Loose engine or transaxle mounts (Chapters 2 and 7A).
2 Worn differential pinion shaft in case.*
3 Worn side gear shaft counterbore in differential case (Chapter 7A).*
4 Worn or damaged driveaxle inboard CV joints (Chapter 8).

44 Clicking noise in turns

Worn or damaged outboard CV joint (Chapter 8).

45 Vibration

1 Rough wheel bearing (Chapters 1 and 10).
2 Damaged driveaxle (Chapter 8).
3 Out of round tyres (Chapter 1).
4 Tire out of balance (Chapters 1 and 10).
5 Worn CV joint (Chapter 8).

46 Noisy in neutral with engine running

1   Damaged input gear bearing (Chapter 7A).*
2   Damaged clutch release bearing (Chapter 8).

47 Noisy in one particular gear

1   Damaged or worn constant mesh gears (Chapter 7A).*
2   Damaged or worn synchronizers (Chapter 7A).*
3   Bent reverse fork (Chapter 7A).*
4   Damaged fourth speed gear or output gear (Chapter 7A).*
5   Worn or damaged reverse idler gear or idler bushing (Chapter 7A).*

48 Noisy in all gears

1   Insufficient lubricant (Chapter 7A).
2   Damaged or worn bearings (Chapter 7A).*
3   Worn or damaged input gear shaft and/or output gear shaft (Chapter 7A).*

49 Slips out of gear

1   Worn or improperly adjusted linkage (Chapter 7A).
2   Transaxle loose on engine (Chapter 7A).
3   Shift linkage does not work freely, binds (Chapter 7A).
4   Input gear bearing retainer broken or loose (Chapter 7A).*
5   Dirt between clutch cover and engine housing (Chapter 7A).
6   Worn shift fork (Chapter 7A).*

50 Leaks lubricant

1   Side gear shaft seals worn (Chapter 7).
2   Excessive amount of lubricant in transaxle (Chapters 1 and 7A).
3   Loose or broken input gear shaft bearing retainer (Chapter 7A).*
4   Input gear bearing retainer O-ring and/or lip seal damaged (Chapter 7A).*

51 Locked in gear

Lock pin or interlock pin missing (Chapter 7A).*

* Although the corrective action necessary to remedy the symptoms described is beyond the scope of this manual, the above information should be helpful in isolating the cause of the condition so that the owner can communicate clearly with a professional mechanic.

Automatic transaxle

Note: *Due to the complexity of the automatic transaxle, it is difficult for the home mechanic to properly diagnose and service this component. For problems other than the following, the vehicle should be taken to a dealer or transaxle shop.*

52 Fluid leakage

1   Automatic transaxle fluid is a deep red colour. Fluid leaks should not be confused with engine oil, which can easily be blown onto the transaxle by air flow.
2   To pinpoint a leak, first remove all built-up dirt and grime from the transaxle housing with degreasing agents and/or steam cleaning. Then drive the vehicle at low speeds so air flow will not blow the leak far from its source. Raise the vehicle and determine where the leak is coming from. Common areas of leakage are:
a) *Pan (Chapters 1 and 7)*
b) *Dipstick tube (Chapters 1 and 7)*
c) *Transaxle oil lines (Chapter 7)*
d) *Speed sensor (Chapter 7)*
e) *Driveaxle oil seals (Chapter 7).*

53 Transaxle fluid brown or has a burned smell

Transaxle fluid overheated (Chapter 1).

54 General shift mechanism problems

1   Chapter 7, Part B, deals with checking and adjusting the shift linkage on automatic transaxles. Common problems which may be attributed to poorly adjusted linkage are:
a) *Engine starting in gears other than Park or Neutral.*
b) *Indicator on shifter pointing to a gear other than the one actually being used.*
c) *Vehicle moves when in Park.*
2   Refer to Chapter 7B for the shift linkage adjustment procedure.

55 Transaxle will not downshift with accelerator pedal pressed to the floor

Throttle valve cable out of adjustment (Chapter 7B).

56 Engine will start in gears other than Park or Neutral

Neutral start switch malfunctioning (Chapter 7B).

57 Transaxle slips, shifts roughly, is noisy or has no drive in forward or reverse gears

There are many probable causes for the above problems, but the home mechanic should be concerned with only one possibility - fluid level. Before taking the vehicle to a repair shop, check the level and condition of the fluid as described in Chapter 1. Correct the fluid level as necessary or change the fluid and filter if needed. If the problem persists, have a professional diagnose the cause.

Driveaxles

58 Clicking noise in turns

Worn or damaged outboard CV joint (Chapter 8).

59 Shudder or vibration during acceleration

1   Excessive toe-in (Chapter 10).
2   Incorrect spring heights (Chapter 10).
3   Worn or damaged inboard or outboard CV joints (Chapter 8).
4   Sticking inboard CV joint assembly (Chapter 8).

60 Vibration at highway speeds

1   Out of balance front wheels and/or tyres (Chapters 1 and 10).
2   Out of round front tyres (Chapters 1 and 10).
3   Worn CV joint(s) (Chapter 8).

Brakes

Note: *Before assuming that a brake problem exists, make sure that:*
a) *The tyres are in good condition and properly inflated (Chapter 1).*
b) *The front end alignment is correct (Chapter 10).*
c) *The vehicle is not loaded with weight in an unequal manner.*

61 Vehicle pulls to one side during braking

1   Incorrect tyre pressures (Chapter 1).
2   Front end out of alignment (have the front end aligned).
3   Front, or rear, tyre sizes not matched to one another.
4   Restricted brake lines or hoses (Chap-

ter 9).

5 Malfunctioning drum brake or caliper assembly (Chapter 9).
6 Loose suspension parts (Chapter 10).
7 Loose calipers (Chapter 9).
8 Excessive wear of brake shoe or pad material or disc/drum on one side.

62 Noise (high-pitched squeal when the brakes are applied)

Front and/or rear disc brake pads worn out. The noise comes from the wear sensor rubbing against the disc (does not apply to all vehicles). Replace pads with new ones immediately (Chapter 9).

63 Brake roughness or chatter (pedal pulsates)

1 Excessive lateral runout (Chapter 9).
2 Uneven pad wear (Chapter 9).
3 Defective disc (Chapter 9).

64 Excessive brake pedal effort required to stop vehicle

1 Malfunctioning power brake booster (Chapter 9).
2 Partial system failure (Chapter 9).
3 Excessively worn pads or shoes (Chapter 9).
4 Piston in caliper or wheel cylinder stuck or sluggish (Chapter 9).
5 Brake pads or shoes contaminated with oil or grease (Chapter 9).
6 Brake disc grooved and/or glazed (Chapter 1).
7 New pads or shoes installed and not yet seated. It will take a while for the new material to seat against the disc or drum.

65 Excessive brake pedal travel

1 Partial brake system failure (Chapter 9).
2 Insufficient fluid in master cylinder (Chapters 1 and 9).
3 Air trapped in system (Chapters 1 and 9).

66 Dragging brakes

1 Incorrect adjustment of brake light switch (Chapter 9).
2 Master cylinder pistons not returning correctly (Chapter 9).
3 Restricted brakes lines or hoses (Chapters 1 and 9).
4 Incorrect parking brake adjustment (Chapter 9).

67 Grabbing or uneven braking action

1 Malfunction of proportioning valve (Chapter 9).
2 Malfunction of power brake booster unit (Chapter 9).
3 Binding brake pedal mechanism (Chapter 9).

68 Brake pedal feels spongy when depressed

1 Air in hydraulic lines (Chapter 9).
2 Master cylinder mounting bolts loose (Chapter 9).
3 Master cylinder defective (Chapter 9).

69 Brake pedal travels to the floor with little resistance

1 Little or no fluid in the master cylinder reservoir caused by leaking caliper piston(s) (Chapter 9).
2 Loose, damaged or disconnected brake lines (Chapter 9).

70 Parking brake does not hold

Parking brake linkage improperly adjusted (Chapters 1 and 9).

Suspension and steering systems

Note: *Before attempting to diagnose the suspension and steering systems, perform the following preliminary checks:*
a) *Tires for wrong pressure and uneven wear.*
b) *Steering universal joints from the column to the rack and pinion for loose connectors or wear.*
c) *Front and rear suspension and the rack and pinion assembly for loose or damaged parts.*
d) *Out-of-round or out-of-balance tyres, bent rims and loose and/or rough wheel bearings.*

71 Vehicle pulls to one side

1 Mismatched or uneven tyres (Chapter 10).
2 Broken or sagging springs (Chapter 10).
3 Wheel alignment out-of-specifications (Chapter 10).
4 Front brake dragging (Chapter 9).

72 Abnormal or excessive tyre wear

1 Wheel alignment out-of-specifications (Chapter 10).

2 Sagging or broken springs (Chapter 10).
3 Tire out-of-balance (Chapter 10).
4 Worn strut damper (Chapter 10).
5 Overloaded vehicle.
6 Tires not rotated regularly.

73 Wheel makes a thumping noise

1 Blister or bump on tyre (Chapter 10).
2 Improper strut damper action (Chapter 10).

74 Shimmy, shake or vibration

1 Tire or wheel out-of-balance or out-of-round (Chapter 10).
2 Loose or worn wheel bearings (Chapters 1, 8 and 10).
3 Worn tie-rod ends (Chapter 10).
4 Worn balljoints (Chapters 1 and 10).
5 Excessive wheel runout (Chapter 10).
6 Blister or bump on tyre (Chapter 10).

75 Hard steering

1 Lack of lubrication at balljoints, tie-rod ends and rack and pinion assembly (Chapter 10).
2 Front wheel alignment out-of-specifications (Chapter 10).
3 Low tyre pressure(s) (Chapters 1 and 10).

76 Poor returnability of steering to centre

1 Lack of lubrication at balljoints and tie-rod ends (Chapter 10).
2 Binding in balljoints (Chapter 10).
3 Binding in steering column (Chapter 10).
4 Lack of lubricant in steering gear assembly (Chapter 10).
5 Front wheel alignment out-of-specifications (Chapter 10).

77 Abnormal noise at the front end

1 Lack of lubrication at balljoints and tie-rod ends (Chapters 1 and 10).
2 Damaged strut mounting (Chapter 10).
3 Worn control arm bushings or tie-rod ends (Chapter 10).
4 Loose stabilizer bar (Chapter 10).
5 Loose wheel nuts (Chapters 1 and 10).
6 Loose suspension bolts (Chapter 10).

78 Wander or poor steering stability

1 Mismatched or uneven tyres (Chapter 10).

2　Lack of lubrication at balljoints and tie-rod ends (Chapters 1 and 10).
3　Worn strut assemblies (Chapter 10).
4　Loose stabilizer bar (Chapter 10).
5　Broken or sagging springs (Chapter 10).
6　Wheels out of alignment (Chapter 10).

79　Erratic steering when braking

1　Wheel bearings worn (Chapter 10).
2　Broken or sagging springs (Chapter 10).
3　Leaking wheel cylinder or caliper (Chapter 10).
4　Warped rotors or drums (Chapter 10).

80　Excessive pitching and/or rolling around corners or during braking

1　Loose stabilizer bar (Chapter 10).
2　Worn strut dampers or mountings (Chapter 10).
3　Broken or sagging springs (Chapter 10).
4　Overloaded vehicle.

81　Suspension bottoms

1　Overloaded vehicle.

2　Worn strut dampers (Chapter 10).
3　Incorrect, broken or sagging springs (Chapter 10).

82　Cupped tyres

1　Front wheel or rear wheel alignment out-of-specifications (Chapter 10).
2　Worn strut dampers (Chapter 10).
3　Wheel bearings worn (Chapter 10).
4　Excessive tyre or wheel runout (Chapter 10).
5　Worn balljoints (Chapter 10).

83　Excessive tyre wear on outside edge

1　Inflation pressures incorrect (Chapter 1).
2　Excessive speed in turns.
3　Front end alignment incorrect (excessive toe-in). Have professionally aligned.
4　Suspension arm bent or twisted (Chapter 10).

84　Excessive tyre wear on inside edge

1　Inflation pressures incorrect (Chapter 1).

2　Front end alignment incorrect (toe-out). Have professionally aligned.
3　Loose or damaged steering components (Chapter 10).

85　Tire tread worn in one place

1　Tires out-of-balance.
2　Damaged or buckled wheel. Inspect and replace if necessary.
3　Defective tyre (Chapter 1).

86　Excessive play or looseness in steering system

1　Wheel bearing(s) worn (Chapter 10).
2　Tie-rod end loose (Chapter 10).
3　Steering gear loose (Chapter 10).
4　Worn or loose steering intermediate shaft (Chapter 10).

87　Rattling or clicking noise in rack and pinion

1　Steering gear loose (Chapter 10).
2　Steering gear defective.

Chapter 1
Tune-up and routine maintenance

Contents

Specifications

Recommended lubricants and fluids

Note: *Listed here are manufacturer recommendations at the time this manual was written. Manufacturers occasionally upgrade their fluid and lubricant specifications, so check with your local auto parts store for current recommendations.*

Engine oil
    Type .... API "Certified for petrol engines"
    Viscosity .... See accompanying chart

Recommended engine oil viscosity

Recommended lubricants and fluids

Fuel .... Unleaded petrol, 87 octane or higher
Engine coolant .... Toyota Genuine Long Life Coolant or equivalent
Automatic transaxle fluid .... Toyota ATF Type T-IV automatic transmission fluid
Manual transaxle lubricant .... API GL-5 75W-90 gear oil
Brake fluid .... DOT 4 brake fluid
Clutch fluid .... DOT 4 brake fluid
Power steering system .... DEXRON III automatic transmission fluid

Capacities*

Engine oil (with filter change)	3.7 litres
Coolant	6.8 litres
Transaxle (drain and refill)	
Automatic	3 litres
Manual	2 litres

*All capacities approximate. Add as necessary to bring up to appropriate level.

Ignition system

Spark plug type and gap	
Type	
1997 models	NGK BKR5EYA or equivalent
1998 and 1999 models	NGK BKR5EKB11 or equivalent
2000 and later	NGK IFR5A11 or equivalent
Gap	
1997 and earlier	0.8 mm
1998 and later	1.09 mm
Firing order	1-3-4-2
Spark plug wire resistance	10,000 to 25,000 ohms

92036 1-specs HAYNES

**Cylinder location and distributor rotation
(1997 models)**

*The blackened terminal shown on the
distributor cap indicates the Number One
spark plug wire position*

FRONT
OF
VEHICLE

1998 AND 1999

2000 AND LATER

92036-2B SPECS HAYNES

**Cylinder numbering
diagram (1998 and
later models)**

Valve clearances (engine cold)

Intake valve	0.152 to 0.254 mm
Exhaust valve	0.254 to 0.457 mm

Cooling system

Thermostat rating fully open	95-degrees C

Clutch pedal

Freeplay	4.76 to 15.8 mm
Height	134.6 to 144.7 mm

Brakes

Disc brake pad thickness (minimum)	2.38 mm
Drum brake shoe lining thickness (minimum)	1.58 mm
Parking brake adjustment	6 to 9 clicks

Suspension and steering

Steering wheel freeplay limit	30.4 mm
Balljoint allowable movement	0 mm

Torque specifications

	Nm (unless otherwise noted)
Wheel lug nuts	103
Spark plugs	25
Seat bolts/nuts	37
Drivebelt tensioner	
To cylinder head	29
To block	69
Engine oil sump drain plug	37
Automatic transaxle pan bolts	4.5
Automatic transaxle fluid pan drain plug	17.5

Typical engine compartment components - 1997 models

1	Brake fluid reservoir	7	Air cleaner assembly	13	Radiator cap
2	Engine oil dipstick	8	Coolant reservoir	14	Spark plug
3	Power steering fluid reservoir	9	Automatic transaxle dipstick	15	Oil filler cap
4	Fuse/relay block	10	Distributor	16	Drivebelt
5	Relay block	11	Radiator hose	17	Windscreen washer fluid reservoir
6	Battery	12	PCV valve		

Typical engine compartment components - 1998 through 2002 models

1	Engine oil dipstick	10	Air cleaner assembly
2	Drivebelt	11	Fuse/relay block
3	Fuse/relay block	12	Fuse/relay block
4	Windscreen washer fluid reservoir	13	Battery
5	Power steering fluid reservoir	14	Automatic transaxle dipstick
6	Ignition coils (2000 and later models only)	15	Coolant reservoir
7	PCV valve	16	Radiator cap
8	Oil filler cap	17	Radiator hoses
9	Brake fluid reservoir		

Typical engine compartment components (engine cover removed) - 2003 and later models

1	Engine oil dipstick	6	Ignition coils	11	Battery
2	Drivebelt	7	PCV valve	12	Automatic transaxle dipstick
3	Fuse/relay block	8	Oil filler cap	13	Coolant reservoir
4	Windscreen washer fluid reservoir	9	Brake fluid reservoir	14	Radiator cap
5	Power steering fluid reservoir	10	Air filter housing	15	Upper radiator hose

Typical engine compartment underside components - 1997 through 2002 models

1	Driveaxle boot	6	Front suspension strut unit
2	Automatic transaxle drain plug	7	Radiator drain fitting
3	Exhaust system catalytic converter	8	Engine oil filter
4	Steering gear boot	9	Front disc brake caliper
5	Engine oil drain plug		

Typical engine compartment underside components - 2003 and later models

1	Driveaxle boot	4	Steering gear boot	7	Radiator drain fitting
2	Automatic transaxle drain plug	5	Engine oil drain plug	8	Engine oil filter
3	Catalytic converter	6	Front suspension strut unit	9	Front disc brake caliper

Typical rear underside components - 1997 through 2002 models

1	Fuel tank filler pipe	3	Suspension strut	5	Fuel tank
2	Muffler	4	Exhaust system rear exhaust pipe	6	Rear brake assembly

Typical rear underside components - 2003 and later models

1	Fuel tank filler pipe	4	Exhaust system	6	Rear brake assembly
2	Muffler	5	Fuel tank	7	Rear axle beam
3	Shock absorber/coil spring assembly				

1 Toyota Corolla Maintenance schedule

The maintenance intervals in this manual are provided with the assumption that you, not the dealer, will be doing the work. These are the minimum maintenance intervals recommended by the factory for vehicles that are driven daily. If you wish to keep your vehicle in peak condition at all times, you may wish to perform some of these procedures even more often. Because frequent maintenance enhances the efficiency, performance and resale value of your car, we encourage you to do so. If you drive in dusty areas, tow a trailer, idle or drive at low speeds for extended periods or drive for short distances (less than 6 kilometres) in below freezing temperatures, shorter intervals are also recommended.

When your vehicle is new, it should be serviced by a factory authorised dealer service department to protect the factory warranty. In many cases, the initial maintenance check is done at no cost to the owner.

Every 500 kilometres or weekly, whichever comes first

Check the engine oil level (Section 4)
Check the engine coolant level (Section 4)
Check the windscreen washer fluid level (Section 4)
Check the brake fluid level (Section 4)
Check the power steering fluid level (Section 4)
Check the tyres and tyre pressures (Section 5)

Every 5000 kilometres or 3 months, whichever comes first

All items listed above plus:
Change the engine oil and oil filter (Section 6)

Every 10,000 kilometres or 6 months, whichever comes first

Inspect (and replace, if necessary) the windscreen wiper blades (Section 7)
Check the clutch pedal for proper freeplay (Section 8)
Check and service the battery (Section 9)
Check the engine drivebelt (Section 10)
Inspect (and replace if, necessary) all under bonnet hoses (Section 11)
Check the cooling system (Section 12)
Rotate the tyres (Section 13)
Check the seat belts (Section 14)

Every 20,000 kilometres or 12 months, whichever comes first

All items listed above plus:
Inspect the brake system (Section 15)*
Replace the air filter (Section 16)

Inspect the fuel system (Section 17)
Check the manual transaxle lubricant level (Section 18)
Inspect the suspension and steering components (Section 19)*
Check the driveaxle boots (Section 19)
Replace the cabin air filter (Section 20)

Every 40,000 kilometres or 24 months, whichever comes first

All items listed above plus:
Change the brake fluid (Section 21)
Check (and replace, if necessary) the spark plugs (Section 22)
Service the cooling system (drain, flush and refill) (Section 23) **Note:** *On models with factory filled Toyota Super Long Life coolant the initial replacement is 160,000 km*
Inspect the evaporative emissions control system (Section 24)
Inspect the exhaust system (Section 25)
Change the automatic transaxle fluid and filter and differential lubricant (Section 26)**
Change the manual transaxle lubricant (Section 27)**
Check and replace if necessary the PCV valve (Section 28)
Spark plug wire, distributor cap and rotor check and replacement (every 40,000 kilometres or 24 months) Section 30)

Every 80,000 kilometres or 48 months, whichever comes first

Check and adjust the valve clearances (Section 31)
Replace the fuel filter (Section 29)
Replace the timing belt (Chapter 2)

*This item is affected by "severe" operating conditions as described below. If your vehicle is operated under "severe" conditions, perform all maintenance indicated with an asterisk (*) at 5000 km/3 month intervals. Severe conditions are indicated if you mainly operate your vehicle under one or more of the following conditions:

Operating in dusty areas
Towing a trailer
Idling for extended periods and/or low speed operation
Operating when outside temperatures remain below freezing and when most trips are less than 6 kilometres

** If operated under one or more of the following conditions, change the manual or automatic transaxle fluid and differential lubricant every 25,000 kilometres:

In heavy city traffic where the outside temperature regularly reaches 32-degrees C or higher
In hilly or mountainous terrain
Frequent trailer pulling

2 Introduction

This Chapter is designed to help the home mechanic maintain the Toyota Corolla for peak performance, economy, safety and long life.

Included is a master maintenance schedule, followed by sections dealing specifically with each item on the schedule. Visual checks, adjustments, component replacement and other helpful items are included. Refer to the **accompanying illustrations** of the engine compartment and the underside of the vehicle for the location of various components.

Servicing your Corolla in accordance with the mileage/time maintenance schedule and the following Sections will provide it with a planned maintenance program that should result in a long and reliable service life. This is a comprehensive plan, so maintaining some items but not others at the specified service intervals will not produce the same results.

As you service your Corolla, you will discover that many of the procedures can - and should - be grouped together because of the nature of the particular procedure you're performing or because of the close proximity of two otherwise unrelated components to one another.

For example, if the vehicle is raised for any reason, you should inspect the exhaust, suspension, steering and fuel systems while you're under the vehicle. When you're rotating the tyres, it makes good sense to check the brakes and wheel bearings since the wheels are already removed.

Finally, let's suppose you have to borrow or rent a torque wrench. Even if you only need to tighten the spark plugs, you might as well check the torque of as many critical fasteners as time allows.

The first step of this maintenance program is to prepare yourself before the actual work begins. Read through all sections pertinent to the procedures you're planning to do, then make a list of and gather together all the parts and tools you will need to do the job. If it looks as if you might run into problems during a particular segment of some procedure, seek advice from your local parts counterperson or dealer service department.

3 Tune-up general information

The term tune-up is used in this manual to represent a combination of individual operations rather than one specific procedure.

If, from the time the vehicle is new, the routine maintenance schedule is followed closely and frequent checks are made of fluid levels and high wear items, as suggested throughout this manual, the engine will be kept in relatively good running condition and the need for additional work will be minimised.

More likely than not, however, there will be times when the engine is running poorly due to lack of regular maintenance. This is even more likely if a used vehicle, which has not received regular and frequent maintenance checks, is purchased. In such cases, an engine tune-up will be needed outside of the regular routine maintenance intervals.

The first step in any tune-up or engine diagnosis to help correct a poor running engine would be a cylinder compression check. A check of the engine compression (Chapter 2 Part C) will give valuable information regarding the overall performance of many internal components and should be used as a basis for tune-up and repair procedures. If, for instance, a compression check indicates serious internal engine wear, a conventional tune-up will not help the running condition of the engine and would be a waste of time and money.

The following series of operations are those most often needed to bring a generally poor running engine back into a proper state of tune.

Minor tune-up

Check all engine related fluids (Section 4)
Clean, inspect and test the battery
  (Section 9)
Check the drivebelt (Section 10)
Check all underbonnet hoses (Section 11)
Check the cooling system (Section 12)

Check the air filter (Section 16)
Replace the spark plugs (Section 24)

Major tune-up

All items listed under Minor tune-up, plus . . .

Replace the air filter (Section 16)
Check the fuel system (Section 17)
Check the charging system (Chapter 5)
Check plug wire, distributor cap and rotor
  (1997 models) (Section 29)

4 Fluid level checks (every 500 kilometres or weekly)

1 Fluids are an essential part of the lubrication, cooling, brake, clutch and other systems. Because these fluids gradually become depleted and/or contaminated during normal operation of the vehicle, they must be periodically replenished. See *Recommended lubricants and fluids* and *Capacities* at the beginning of this Chapter before adding fluid to any of the following components. **Note:** *The vehicle must be on level ground before fluid levels can be checked.*

Engine oil

Refer to illustrations 4.2, 4.4 and 4.6

2 The engine oil level is checked with a dipstick located at the front of the engine **(see illustration)**. The dipstick extends through a metal tube from which it protrudes down into the engine oil sump.

3 The oil level should be checked before the vehicle has been driven, or about 5 minutes after the engine has been shut off. If the oil is checked immediately after driving the vehicle, some of the oil will remain in the upper engine components, producing an inaccurate reading on the dipstick.

4 Pull the dipstick from the tube and wipe all the oil from the end with a clean rag or paper towel. Insert the clean dipstick all the way back into its metal tube and pull it out again. Observe the oil at the end of the dipstick. At its highest point, the level should be between the two dimples **(see illustration)**.

4.2 The engine oil dipstick (A) is located at the front of the engine - the oil filler cap (B) is in the valve cover

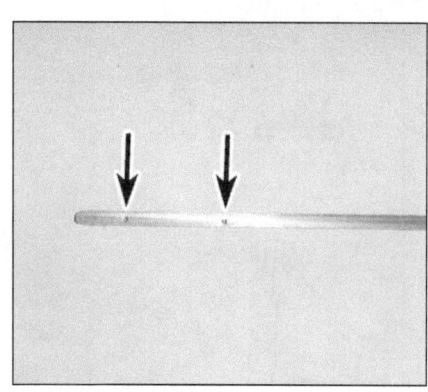

4.4 On 1998 and later models, the engine oil dipstick has two dimples - keep the oil level at or near the upper dimple

4.6 The threaded oil filler cap is located on the valve cover - always make sure the area around the opening is clean before unscrewing the cap to prevent dirt from contaminating the engine

4.8a On 1997 models, the coolant reservoir is located next to the battery - make sure the level is between the Low and Full marks on the reservoir

5   It takes one quart of oil to raise the level from the lower dimple to the upper dimple on the dipstick. Do not allow the level to drop below the lower dimple or oil starvation may cause engine damage. Conversely, overfilling the engine (adding oil above the upper dimple) may cause oil fouled spark plugs, oil leaks or oil seal failures.

6   Remove the threaded cap from the valve cover to add oil **(see illustration)**. Use a funnel to prevent spills. After adding the oil, install the filler cap hand tight. Start the engine and look carefully for any small leaks around the oil filter or drain plug. Stop the engine and check the oil level again after it has had sufficient time to drain from the upper block and cylinder head galleys.

7   Checking the oil level is an important preventive maintenance step. A continually dropping oil level indicates oil leakage through damaged seals, from loose connections, or past worn rings or valve guides. If the oil looks milky in colour or has water droplets in it, a cylinder head gasket may be blown. The

engine should be checked immediately. The condition of the oil should also be checked. Each time you check the oil level, slide your thumb and index finger up the dipstick before wiping off the oil. If you see small dirt or metal particles clinging to the dipstick, the oil should be changed (see Section 6).

Engine coolant

Refer to illustrations 4.8a, 4.8b and 4.8c

Warning: *Do not allow antifreeze to come in contact with your skin or painted surfaces of the vehicle. Flush contaminated areas immediately with plenty of water. Don't store new coolant or leave old coolant lying around where it's accessible to children or pets - they're attracted by its sweet smell and may drink it. Ingestion of even a small amount of coolant can be fatal! Wipe up garage floor and drip pan spills immediately. Keep antifreeze containers covered and repair cooling system leaks as soon as they're noticed.*

8   All vehicles covered by this manual are equipped with a pressurised coolant recovery system. A white coolant reservoir located at the left side of the engine compartment on 2002 and earlier models and the right side of

the radiator in the engine compartment on 2003 and later models is connected by a hose to the base of the radiator filler neck **(see illustrations)**. If the coolant heats up during engine operation, coolant can escape through a pressurised filler cap, then through a connecting hose into the reservoir. As the engine cools, the coolant is automatically drawn back into the cooling system to maintain the correct level.

9   The coolant level should be checked regularly. It must be between the Full and Low lines on the tank. The level will vary with the temperature of the engine. When the engine is cold, the coolant level should be at or slightly above the Low mark on the tank. Once the engine has warmed up, the level should be at or near the Full mark. If it isn't, allow the fluid in the tank to cool, then remove the cap from the reservoir and add coolant to bring the level up to the Full line. Use only the coolant listed in this Chapter's Specifications, or its equivalent. Do not use supplemental inhibitor additives. If only a small amount of coolant is required to bring the system up to the proper level, water can be used. However, repeated additions of water will dilute the rec-

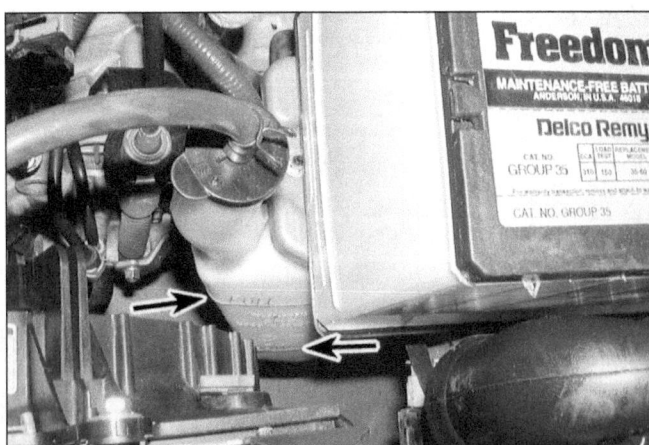

4.8b On 1998 to 2002 models, the coolant reservoir is mounted below the battery, but the Low and Full marks are still visible from above

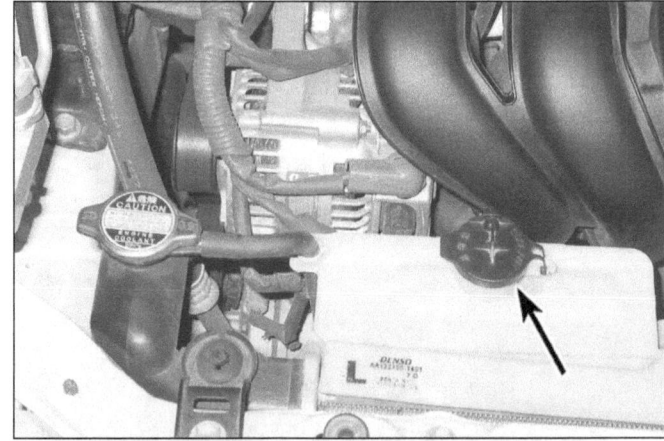

4.8c On 2003 and later models, the coolant reservoir is at the right side of the radiator - make sure the coolant level is between the Low and Full marks on the reservoir

4.14 The windscreen washer fluid reservoir is located in the right front corner of the engine compartment

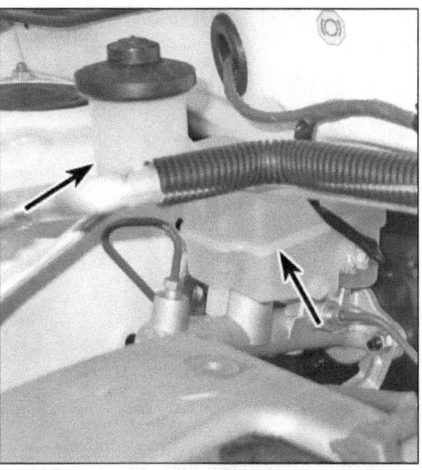

4.17 The brake fluid level should be kept between the MIN and MAX marks on the translucent plastic reservoir

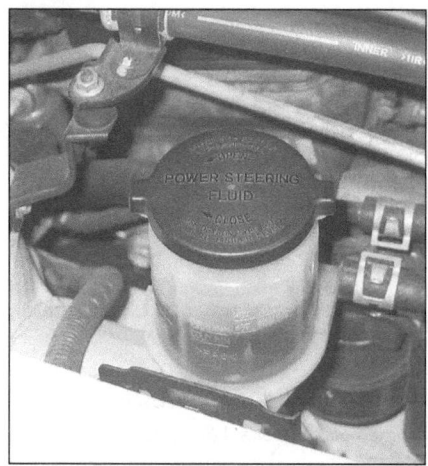

4.25 The power steering fluid reservoir is located near the right shock tower in the engine compartment

ommended antifreeze and water solution. In order to maintain the proper ratio of antifreeze and water, it is advisable to top up the coolant level with the correct mixture.

10   If the coolant level drops within a short time after replenishment, there may be a leak in the system. Inspect the radiator, hoses, engine coolant filler cap, drain plugs, air bleeder plugs and water pump. If no leak is evident, have the radiator cap pressure tested by your dealer. **Warning:** *Never remove the radiator cap or the coolant recovery reservoir cap when the engine is running or has just been shut down, because the cooling system is hot. Escaping steam and scalding liquid could cause serious injury.*

11   If it is necessary to open the radiator cap, wait until the system has cooled completely, then wrap a thick cloth around the cap and turn it to the first stop. If any steam escapes, wait until the system has cooled further, then remove the cap.

12   When checking the coolant level, always note its condition. It should be relatively clear. If it is brown or rust coloured, the system should be drained, flushed and refilled. Even if the coolant appears to be normal, the corrosion inhibitors wear out with use, so it must be replaced at the specified intervals.

13   Do not allow antifreeze to come in contact with your skin or painted surfaces of the vehicle. Flush contacted areas immediately with plenty of water.

Windscreen washer fluid

Refer to illustration 4.14

14   Fluid for the windscreen washer system is stored in a plastic reservoir which is located on the right side of the engine compartment **(see illustration)**. In milder climates, plain water can be used to top up the reservoir, but the reservoir should be kept no more than two-thirds full to allow for expansion should the water freeze. In colder climates, the use of a specially designed windscreen washer fluid, available at your dealer and any auto parts

store, will help lower the freezing point of the fluid. Mix the solution with water in accordance with the manufacturer's directions on the container. Do not use regular antifreeze. It will damage the vehicle's paint.

Battery electrolyte

15   On models not equipped with a sealed battery, remove the filler/vent cap and check the electrolyte level. It must be between the upper and lower levels. If the level is low, add distilled water. Install and securely retighten the cap. **Caution:** *Overfilling the cells may cause electrolyte to spill over during periods of heavy charging, causing corrosion or damage.*

Brake and clutch fluid

Refer to illustration 4.17

16   The brake master cylinder is mounted on the front of the power booster unit in the engine compartment. The clutch master cylinder on vehicles with manual transaxles is connected by a hose to the brake master cylinder.

17   To check the fluid level, simply look at the MAX and MIN marks on the reservoir **(see illustration)**. The level should be at or near the maximum fill line.

18   If the level is low, wipe the top of the reservoir cover with a clean rag to prevent contamination of the brake or clutch system before lifting the cover.

19   Add only the specified brake fluid to the reservoir (refer to *Recommended lubricants and fluids* at the front of this chapter or to your owner's manual). Mixing different types of brake fluid can damage the system. **Warning:** *Use caution when filling the reservoir - brake fluid can harm your eyes and damage painted surfaces. Do not use brake fluid that has been opened for more than one year (even if the cap has been on) or has been left open. Brake fluid absorbs moisture from the air. Excess moisture can cause a dangerous loss of braking.*

20   While the reservoir cap is removed,

inspect the master cylinder reservoir for contamination. If deposits, dirt particles or water droplets are present, the fluid in the brake system should be changed (see Section 21 for the brake fluid replacement procedure or Chapter 8 for the clutch hydraulic system bleeding procedure).

21   After filling the reservoir to the proper level, make sure the lid is properly seated to prevent fluid leakage and/or system pressure loss.

22   The brake fluid in the master cylinder will drop slightly as the brake pads at each wheel wear down during normal operation. If the master cylinder requires repeated replenishing to keep it at the proper level, this is an indication of leakage in the brake system, which should be corrected immediately. Check all brake lines and connections, along with the calipers, wheel cylinders and booster (see Section 15 for more information).

23   If, upon checking the master cylinder fluid level, you discover the reservoir empty or nearly empty, the brake and clutch systems must be diagnosed immediately (see Chapters 8 and 9).

Power steering fluid

Refer to illustrations 4.25 and 4.29

24   Unlike manual steering, the power steering system relies on fluid which may, over a period of time, require replenishing.

25   The fluid reservoir for the power steering pump is located on the driver's side inner fender panel, just behind the windscreen washer fluid reservoir **(see illustration)**.

26   For the check, the front wheels should be pointed straight ahead and the engine should be off.

27   Use a clean rag to wipe off the reservoir cap and the area around the cap. This will help prevent any foreign matter from entering the reservoir during the check.

28   Remove the cap and check the temperature of the fluid with your finger.

29   On 1997 models, check the fluid level on

the dipstick. On 1998 and later models, view the level of power steering fluid through the translucent reservoir **(see illustration)**. At no time should the fluid level drop below the upper mark for each heat range.

30   If additional fluid is required, pour the specified type directly into the reservoir, using a funnel to prevent spills.

31   If the reservoir requires frequent fluid additions, all power steering hoses, hose connections, the power steering pump and the rack and pinion assembly should be carefully checked for leaks.

Automatic transaxle fluid

Refer to illustrations 4.35a and 4.35b

32   The level of the automatic transaxle fluid should be carefully maintained. Low fluid level can lead to slipping or loss of drive, while overfilling can cause foaming, loss of fluid and transaxle damage.

33   The transaxle fluid level should only be checked when the transaxle is hot (at its normal operating temperature). If the vehicle has just been driven over 15 kilometres (20 kilometres in a frigid climate), and the fluid temperature is 71 to 79-degrees C, the transaxle is hot. **Caution:** *If the vehicle has just been driven for a long time at high speed or in city traffic in hot weather, or if it has been pulling a trailer, an accurate fluid level reading cannot be obtained. Allow the fluid to cool down for about 30 minutes.*

34   If the vehicle has not just been driven, park the vehicle on level ground, set the parking brake and start the engine. While the engine is idling, depress the brake pedal and move the selector lever through all the gear ranges, beginning and ending in Park.

35   With the engine still idling, remove the dipstick from its tube **(see illustration)**. Check the level of the fluid on the dipstick **(see illustration)** and note its condition.

36   Wipe the fluid from the dipstick with a clean rag and reinsert it back into the filler tube until the cap seats.

37   Pull the dipstick out again and note the fluid level. If the transaxle is cold, the level should be in the COLD or COOL range on the dipstick. If it is hot, the fluid level should be in the HOT range. If the level is at the low side of either range, add the specified automatic transmission fluid through the dipstick tube with a funnel.

38   Add just enough of the recommended fluid to fill the transaxle to the proper level. It takes about one pint to raise the level from the low mark to the high mark when the fluid is hot, so add the fluid a little at a time and keep checking the level until it is correct.

39   The condition of the fluid should also be checked along with the level. If the fluid at the end of the dipstick is black or a dark reddish brown colour, or if it emits a burned smell, the fluid should be changed (see Section 26). If you are in doubt about the condition of the fluid, purchase some new fluid and compare the two for colour and smell.

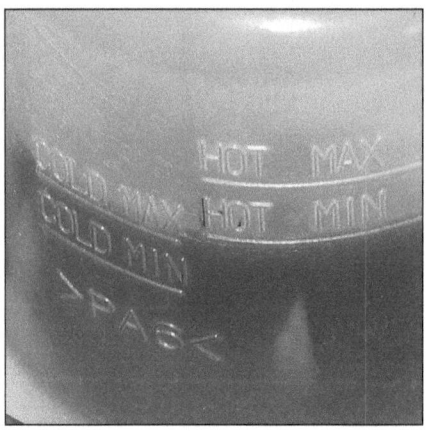

4.29 The power steering fluid level is checked by looking through the plastic reservoir (1998 and later models)

4.35a The automatic transaxle dipstick is located in a tube which extends forward from the transaxle

4.35b If the automatic transaxle fluid is cold, the level should be between the two lower notches; if it's at operating temperature, the level should be between the two upper notches

5   Tyre and tyre pressure checks (every 500 kilometres or weekly)

Refer to illustrations 5.2, 5.3, 5.4a, 5.4b and 5.8

1   Periodic inspection of the tyres may spare you from the inconvenience of being stranded with a flat tyre. It can also provide you with vital information regarding possible problems in the steering and suspension systems before major damage occurs.

2   Normal tread wear can be monitored with a simple, inexpensive device known as a tread depth indicator **(see illustration)**. When the tread depth reaches the specified minimum, replace the tyre(s).

3   Note any abnormal tread wear **(see illustration)**. Tread pattern irregularities such as cupping, flat spots and more wear on one side than the other are indications of front end alignment and/or balance problems. If any of these conditions are noted, take the vehicle to a tyre shop or service station to correct the problem.

4   Look closely for cuts, punctures and embedded nails or tacks. Sometimes a tyre will hold its air pressure for a short time or leak down very slowly even after a nail has embedded itself into the tread. If a slow leak persists, check the valve stem core to make sure it is

tight **(see illustration)**. Examine the tread for an object that may have embedded itself into the tyre or for a "plug" that may have begun to leak (radial tyre punctures are repaired with a plug that is installed in a puncture). If a puncture is suspected, it can be easily verified by spraying a solution of soapy water onto the puncture area **(see illustration)**. The soapy

5.2 A tyre tread depth indicator should be used to monitor tyre wear - they are available at auto parts stores and service stations and cost very little

UNDERINFLATION

CUPPING

OVERINFLATION

Cupping may be caused by:
- Underinflation and/or mechanical irregularities such as out-of-balance condition of wheel and/or tire, and bent or damaged wheel.
- Loose or worn steering tie-rod or steering idler arm.
- Loose, damaged or worn front suspension parts.

INCORRECT TOE-IN OR EXTREME CAMBER

FEATHERING DUE TO MISALIGNMENT

5.3 This chart will help you determine the condition of your tyres, the probable cause(s) of abnormal wear and the corrective action necessary

solution will bubble if there is a leak. Unless the puncture is inordinately large, a tyre shop or service station can usually repair the punctured tyre.

5   Carefully inspect the inner sidewall of each tyre for evidence of brake fluid leakage. If you see any, inspect the brakes immediately.

6   Correct tyre air pressure adds kilometres to the lifespan of the tyres, improves mileage and enhances overall ride quality. Tyre pressure cannot be accurately estimated by looking at a tyre, particularly if it is a radial. A tyre pressure gauge is therefore essential. Keep an accurate gauge in the glovebox. The pressure gauges fitted to the nozzles of air hoses at service stations are often inaccurate.

7   Always check tyre pressure when the tyres are cold. "Cold," in this case, means the vehicle has not been driven over a mile in the three hours preceding a tyre pressure check. A pressure rise of four to eight pounds is not uncommon once the tyres are warm.

8   Unscrew the valve cap protruding from the wheel or hubcap and push the gauge firmly onto the valve **(see illustration)**. Note the reading on the gauge and compare this

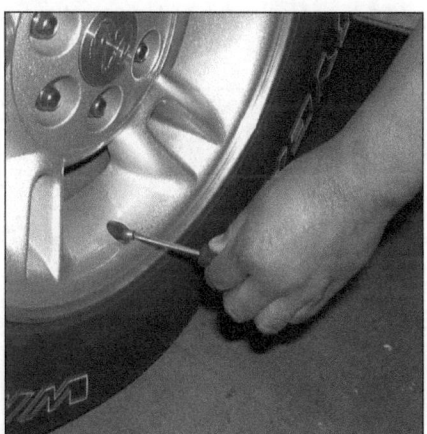

5.4a If a tyre loses air on a steady basis, check the valve core first to make sure it's snug (special inexpensive spanners are commonly available at auto parts stores)

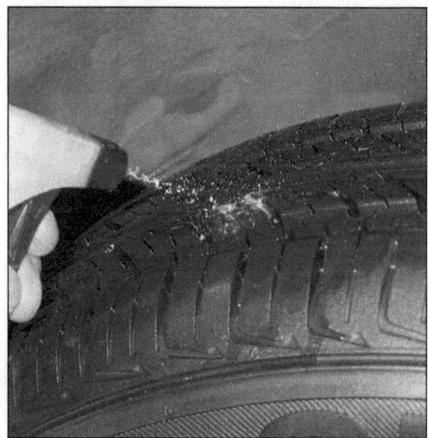

5.4b If the valve core is tight, raise the corner of the vehicle with the low tyre and spray a soapy water solution onto the tread as the tyre is turned slowly - slow leaks will cause small bubbles to appear

5.8 To extend the life of your tyres, check the air pressure at least once a week with an accurate gauge (don't forget the spare!)

6.2 These tools are required when changing the engine oil and filter

1   ***Drain pan*** *- It should be fairly shallow in depth, but wide in order to prevent spills*
2   ***Rubber gloves*** *- When removing the drain plug and filter, it is inevitable that you will get oil on your hands (the gloves will prevent burns)*
3   ***Breaker bar*** *- Sometimes the oil drain plug is pretty tight and a long breaker bar is needed to loosen it*
4   ***Socket*** *- To be used with the breaker bar or a ratchet (must be the correct size to fit the drain plug)*
5   ***Filter wrench*** *- This is a metal band-type wrench, which requires clearance around the filter to be effective*
6   ***Filter wrench*** *- This type fits on the bottom of the filter and can be turned with a ratchet or beaker bar (different size wrenches are available for different types of filters)*

figure to the recommended tyre pressure shown on the tyre placard on the left door. Be sure to reinstall the valve cap to keep dirt and moisture out of the valve stem mechanism. Check all four tyres and, if necessary, add enough air to bring them up to the recommended pressure levels.

9   Don't forget to keep the spare tyre inflated to the specified pressure (consult your owner's manual). Note that the air pressure specified for the compact spare is significantly higher than the pressure of the regular tyres.

---

6   Engine oil and oil filter change (every 5000 kilometres or 3 months)

Refer to illustrations 6.2, 6.7, 6.13 and 6.15

1   Frequent oil changes are the best preventive maintenance the home mechanic can give the engine, because aging oil becomes diluted and contaminated, which leads to premature engine wear.

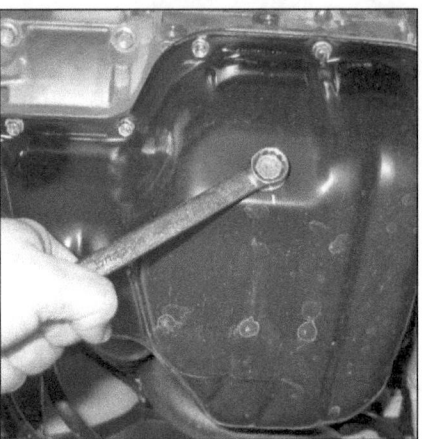

6.7 Use a proper size box-end wrench or socket to remove the oil drain plug and avoid rounding it off

2   Make sure that you have all the necessary tools before you begin this procedure **(see illustration)**. You should also have plenty of rags or newspapers handy for mopping up any spills.
3   Access to the underside of the vehicle is greatly improved if the vehicle can be lifted on a hoist, driven onto ramps or supported by jackstands. **Warning:** *Do not work under a vehicle which is supported only by a bumper, hydraulic or scissors-type jack.*
4   If this is your first oil change, get under the vehicle and familiarise yourself with the location of the oil drain plug. The engine and exhaust components will be warm during the actual work, so try to anticipate any potential problems before the engine and accessories are hot.
5   Park the vehicle on a level spot. Start the engine and allow it to reach its normal operating temperature (the needle on the temperature gauge should be at least above the bottom mark). Warm oil and sludge will flow out more easily. Turn off the engine when it's warmed up. Remove the filler cap in the rear cam cover.
6   Raise the vehicle and support it on jackstands. **Warning:** *To avoid personal injury, never get beneath the vehicle when it is supported by only by a jack. The jack provided with your vehicle is designed solely for raising the vehicle to remove and replace the wheels. Always use jackstands to support the vehicle when it becomes necessary to place your body underneath the vehicle.*
7   Being careful not to touch the hot exhaust components, place the drain pan under the drain plug in the bottom of the pan and remove the plug **(see illustration)**. You may want to wear gloves while unscrewing the plug the final few turns if the engine is really hot.
8   Allow the old oil to drain into the pan. It may be necessary to move the pan farther under the engine as the oil flow slows to a trickle. Inspect the old oil for the presence of metal shavings and chips.
9   After all the oil has drained, wipe off the

6.13 The oil filter points straight down from the engine block (arrow)

drain plug with a clean rag. Even minute metal particles clinging to the plug would immediately contaminate the new oil.
10   Clean the area around the drain plug opening, reinstall the plug and tighten it securely, but do not strip the threads.
11   Move the drain pan into position under the oil filter.
12   Remove all tools, rags, etc. from under the vehicle, being careful not to spill the oil in the drain pan, then lower the vehicle.
13   Loosen the oil filter **(see illustration)** by turning it anticlockwise with the filter wrench. Any standard filter wrench should work. Once the filter is loose, use your hands to unscrew it from the block.
14   With a clean rag, wipe off the mounting surface on the block. If a residue of old oil is allowed to remain, it will smoke when the block is heated up. It will also prevent the new filter from seating properly. Also make sure that the none of the old gasket remains stuck to the mounting surface. It can be removed with a scraper if necessary.
15   Compare the old filter with the new one to make sure they are the same type. Smear some engine oil on the rubber gasket of the new filter and screw it into place **(see illus-**

6.15 Lubricate the oil filter gasket with clean engine oil before installing the filter on the engine

7.5 Push on the release lever and slide the wiper assembly down out of the hook in the end of the wiper arm

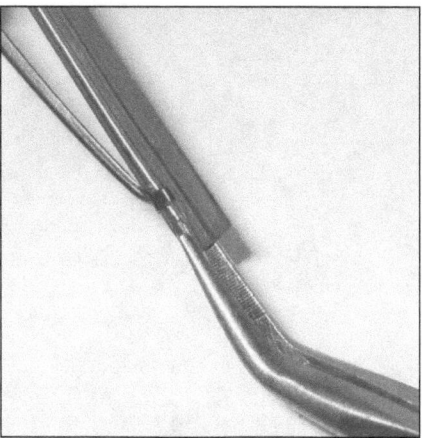

7.6 After detaching the end of the element, slide it out of the end of the frame

7.7 Slide the element into place until the cutouts seat into the locking claw

tration). Because overtightening the filter will damage the gasket, do not use a filter wrench to tighten the filter. Tighten it by hand following the directions on the canister or packing box.

16   Add new oil to the engine through the oil filler cap in the valve cover. Use a funnel to prevent oil from spilling onto the top of the engine. Pour three quarts of fresh oil into the engine. Wait a few minutes to allow the oil to drain into the pan, then check the level on the oil dipstick (see Section 4 if necessary). If the oil level is at or near the F mark, install the filler cap hand tight, start the engine and allow the new oil to circulate.

17   Allow the engine to run for about a minute. While the engine is running, look under the vehicle and check for leaks at the oil sump drain plug and around the oil filter. If either is leaking, stop the engine and tighten the plug or filter slightly.

18   Wait a few minutes to allow the oil to trickle down into the pan, then recheck the level on the dipstick and, if necessary, add enough oil to bring the level to the F mark.

19   During the first few trips after an oil change, make it a point to check frequently for leaks and proper oil level.

20   The old oil drained from the engine cannot be reused in its present state and should be discarded. Check with your local refuse disposal company, disposal facility or environmental agency to see if they will accept the oil for recycling. Don't pour used oil into drains or onto the ground. After the oil has cooled, it can be drained into a suitable container (capped plastic jugs, topped bottles, milk cartons, etc.) for transport to one of these disposal sites.

---

7   Windscreen wiper blade inspection and replacement (every 12,000 kilometres or 6 months)

Refer to illustrations 7.5, 7.6 and 7.7

1   The windscreen wiper and blade assem-

bly should be inspected periodically for damage, loose components and cracked or worn blade elements.

2   Road film can build up on the wiper blades and affect their efficiency, so they should be washed regularly with a mild detergent solution.

3   The action of the wiping mechanism can loosen bolts, nuts and fasteners, so they should be checked and tightened, as necessary, at the same time the wiper blades are checked.

4   If the wiper blade elements are cracked, worn or warped, or no longer clean adequately, they should be replaced with new ones.

5   Remove the wiper blade assembly from the arm by pushing on the release lever, then sliding the assembly down and out of the hook in the end of the arm **(see illustration)**.

6   Squeeze the end of the wiper element and pull it out of the wiper frame **(see illustration)**.

7   Insert the new element end without the cutouts into the wiper frame. Slide the element fully into place, then seat the protrusions in the end of the frames to secure it **(see illustration)**.

---

8   Clutch pedal freeplay check and adjustment (every 12,000 kilometres or 6 months)

Refer to illustration 8.1

1   Peel back the carpet and check the clutch pedal height **(see illustration)**. If pedal height is incorrect, loosen the locknut and turn the stopper bolt until the height is correct. Tighten the locknut.

2   Press down lightly on the clutch pedal and measure the distance that it moves freely before the clutch resistance is felt. The freeplay should be within the specified limits. If it isn't, it must be adjusted.

3   Loosen the locknut on the pedal end of the clutch pushrod **(see illustration 8.1)**.

4   Turn the pushrod until pedal freeplay is correct.

5   Tighten the locknut.

6   After adjusting the pedal freeplay, check the pedal height again, adjusting it if necessary.

---

9   Battery check, maintenance and charging (every 12,000 kilometres or 6 months)

Refer to illustrations 9.1, 9.6a, 9.6b, 9.7a, 9.7b and 9.8

Warning: *Certain precautions must be followed when checking and servicing the battery. Hydrogen gas, which is highly flammable, is always present in the battery cells, so keep lighted tobacco and all other open flames and sparks away from the battery. The elec-*

92037-1-8.2 HAYNES

8.1 Clutch pedal height and freeplay measuring points and adjustments

A   Pedal freeplay adjustment point
B   Pedal height adjustment point
C   Pedal height measurement point
D   Freeplay measurement point

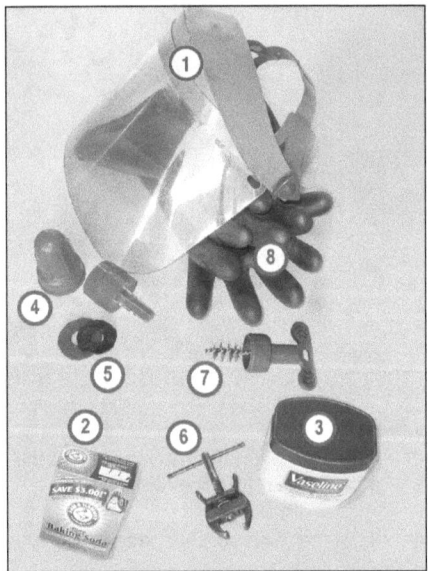

9.1 Tools and materials required for battery maintenance

1 **Face shield/safety goggles** - *When removing corrosion with a brush, the acidic particles can easily fly up into your eyes*
2 **Baking soda** - *A solution of baking soda and water can be used to neutralise corrosion*
3 **Petroleum jelly** - *A layer of this on the battery posts will help prevent corrosion*
4 **Battery post/cable cleaner** - *This wire brush cleaning tool will remove all traces of corrosion from the battery posts and cable clamps*
5 **Treated felt washers** - *Placing one of these on each post, directly under the cable clamps, will help prevent corrosion*
6 **Puller** - *Sometimes the cable clamps are very difficult to pull off the posts, even after the nut/bolt has been completely loosened. This tool pulls the clamp straight up and off the post without damage*
7 **Battery post/cable cleaner** - *Here is another cleaning tool which is a slightly different version of number 4 above, but it does the same thing*
8 **Rubber gloves** - *Another safety item to consider when servicing the battery; remember that's acid inside the battery*

trolyte inside the battery is actually dilute sulfuric acid, which will cause injury if splashed on your skin or in your eyes. It will also ruin clothes and painted surfaces. When removing the battery cables, always detach the negative cable first and hook it up last!

1   A routine preventive maintenance program for the battery in your vehicle is the only way to ensure quick and reliable starts. But before performing any battery maintenance, make sure that you have the proper equipment necessary to work safely around the battery **(see illustration)**.
2   There are also several precautions that

9.6a Battery terminal corrosion usually appears as light, fluffy powder

9.7a When cleaning the cable clamps, all corrosion must be removed (the inside of the clamp is tapered to match the taper on the post, so don't remove too much material)

should be taken whenever battery maintenance is performed. Before servicing the battery, always turn the engine and all accessories off and disconnect the cable from the negative terminal of the battery.
3   The battery produces hydrogen gas, which is both flammable and explosive. Never create a spark, smoke or light a match around the battery. Always charge the battery in a ventilated area.
4   Electrolyte contains poisonous and corrosive sulfuric acid. Do not allow it to get in your eyes, on your skin on your clothes. Never ingest it. Wear protective safety glasses when working near the battery. Keep children away from the battery.
5   Note the external condition of the battery. If the positive terminal and cable clamp on your vehicle's battery is equipped with a rubber protector, make sure that it's not torn or damaged. It should completely cover the terminal. Look for any corroded or loose connections, cracks in the case or cover or loose hold-down clamps. Also check the entire length of each cable for cracks and frayed conductors.
6   If corrosion, which looks like white, fluffy

9.6b Removing a cable from the battery post with a spanner - sometimes a pair of special battery pliers are required for this procedure if corrosion has caused deterioration of the nut hex (always remove the ground (-) cable first and hook it up last!)

9.7b Regardless of the type of tool used to clean the battery posts, a clean, shiny surface should be the result

deposits **(see illustration)** is evident, particularly around the terminals, the battery should be removed for cleaning. Loosen the cable clamp bolts with a spanner, being careful to remove the ground cable first, and slide them off the terminals **(see illustration)**. Then disconnect the hold-down clamp bolt and nut, remove the clamp and lift the battery from the engine compartment.
7   Clean the cable clamps thoroughly with a battery brush or a terminal cleaner and a solution of warm water and baking soda **(see illustration)**. Wash the terminals and the top of the battery case with the same solution but make sure that the solution doesn't get into the battery. When cleaning the cables, terminals and battery top, wear safety goggles and rubber gloves to prevent any solution from coming in contact with your eyes or hands. Wear old clothes too - even diluted, sulfuric acid splashed onto clothes will burn holes in them. If the terminals have been extensively corroded, clean them up with a terminal cleaner **(see illustration)**. Thoroughly wash

9.8 Make sure the battery clamp nut and bolt are tight

ACCEPTABLE

Cracks Running Across "V" Portions of Belt

5 mm

Missing Two or More Adjacent Ribs 5 mm or longer

UNACCEPTABLE

Cracks Running Parallel to "V" Portions of Belt

10.3 Check the multi-ribbed belt for signs of wear like these - if the belt looks worn, replace it

all cleaned areas with plain water.

8   Make sure that the battery tray is in good condition and the hold-down nut and bolt are tight **(see illustration)**. If the battery is removed from the tray, make sure no parts remain in the bottom of the tray when the battery is reinstalled. When reinstalling the hold-down clamp bolt or nut, do not overtighten it.

9   Information on removing and installing the battery can be found in Chapter 5. Information on jump starting can be found at the front of this manual. For more detailed battery checking procedures, refer to the *Haynes Automotive Electrical Manual*.

Cleaning

10   Corrosion on the hold-down components, battery case and surrounding areas can be removed with a solution of water and baking soda. Thoroughly rinse all cleaned areas with plain water.

11   Any metal parts of the vehicle damaged by corrosion should be covered with a zinc-based primer, then painted.

Charging

Warning: *When batteries are being charged, hydrogen gas, which is very explosive and flammable, is produced. Do not smoke or allow open flames near a charging or a recently charged battery. Wear eye protection when near the battery during charging. Also, make sure the charger is unplugged before connecting or disconnecting the battery from the charger.*

12   Slow-rate charging is the best way to restore a battery that's discharged to the point where it will not start the engine. It's also a good way to maintain the battery charge in a vehicle that's only driven a few kilometres between starts. Maintaining the battery charge is particularly important in the winter when the battery must work harder to start the engine and electrical accessories that drain the battery are in greater use.

13   It's best to use a one or two-amp battery charger (sometimes called a "trickle" charger). They are the safest and put the least strain on the battery. They are also the least expensive. For a faster charge, you can use a higher amperage charger, but don't use one

rated more than 1/10th the amp/hour rating of the battery. Rapid boost charges that claim to restore the power of the battery in one to two hours are hardest on the battery and can damage batteries not in good condition. This type of charging should only be used in emergency situations.

14   The average time necessary to charge a battery should be listed in the instructions that come with the charger. As a general rule, a trickle charger will charge a battery in 12 to 16 hours.

10   Drivebelt check and replacement (every 12,000 kilometres or 6 months)

Check

Refer to illustrations 10.3, 10.4 and 10.5

1   The alternator, power steering pump and air conditioning compressor drivebelts, also referred to as simply "fan" belts, are located at the right end of the engine. The good condition and proper adjustment of the alternator belt is critical to the operation of the engine. Because of their composition and the high stresses to which they are subjected, drivebelts stretch and deteriorate as they get older. They must

therefore be periodically inspected.

2   On 1997 models, multiple belts are used; one belt transmits power from the crankshaft to the alternator, and one drives the air conditioning compressor, if equipped. If the vehicle is equipped with power steering, the pump is driven by it's own belt, powered by the water pump pulley. On 1998 and later models, a single "serpentine" drivebelt is used.

3   With the engine off, open the bonnet and locate the drivebelt(s). With a flashlight, check each belt for separation of the adhesive rubber on both sides of the core, core separation from the belt side, a severed core, separation of the ribs from the adhesive rubber, cracking or separation of the ribs, and torn or worn ribs or cracks in the inner ridges of the ribs (see illustration). Also check for fraying and glazing, which gives the belt a shiny appearance. Both sides of the belt should be inspected, which means you will have to twist the belt to check the underside. Use your fingers to feel the belt where you can't see it. If any of the above conditions are evident, replace the belt (go to Step 8).

4   Belt tension on 1997 models must be manually adjusted, while on 1998 and later models the tension is adjusted automatically. To check the tension of each belt in accordance with factory specifications, install either a Nippondenso or Burroughs belt tension

Nippondenso   Burroughs

10.4 If you are able to borrow either a Nippondenso or Burroughs belt tension gauge, this is how it's installed on the belt - compare the reading on the scale with the specified drivebelt tension

10.5 Measuring drivebelt deflection with a straightedge and ruler

10.7 After loosening the idler pulley lock nut, turn the adjusting bolt to tension the air conditioning compressor drivebelt

gauge on the belt **(see illustration)**. Measure the tension in accordance with the manufacturer's instructions and compare your measurement to the specified drivebelt tension for either a used or new belt. **Note:** *A "used" belt is defined as any belt which has been operated more than five minutes on the engine; a "new" belt is one that has been used for less than five minutes.*

5   If you don't have either of the above tools, and cannot borrow one, the following rule of thumb method is recommended: Push firmly on the belt with your thumb at a distance halfway between the pulleys and note how far the belt can be pushed (deflected). Measure this deflection with a ruler **(see illustration)**. The belt should deflect 6 mm if the distance from pulley centre to pulley centre is between 177 and 279 mm; the belt should deflect 12.7 mm if the distance from pulley centre to pulley centre is between 304 and 406 mm.

Adjustment
1997 models
Refer to illustration 10.7

6   To adjust the alternator belt, loosen the alternator pivot bolt and the lock bolt at the alternator bracket. Now turn the adjusting bolt and measure the belt tension in accordance with one of the above methods. When the proper tension is achieved, tighten the lock

bolt and pivot bolt securely.

7   To adjust the air conditioning compressor drivebelt, loosen the idler pulley lock nut and turn the adjusting bolt **(see illustration)** until the belt is properly tensioned. When the proper tension is achieved, tighten the lock bolt and pivot bolt securely.

8   Adjust the power steering pump belt by loosening the pivot bolt and the lock bolt that secures the pump to the slotted bracket, then pivot the pump (away from the engine to tighten the belt, toward it to loosen it) until the proper tension is reached. When the proper tension is achieved, tighten the lock bolt and pivot bolt securely.

1998 and later models
9   Drivebelt tension on 1998 and later models is adjusted automatically by a spring-loaded tensioner.

Replacement
1997 models
Refer to illustration 10.12

10   To replace a belt, follow the above procedures for drivebelt adjustment but slip the belt off the crankshaft pulley and remove it. If you are replacing the power steering pump belt, you will have to remove the air condi-

tioning compressor belt first because of the way they are arranged on the crankshaft pulley. Because of this and because belts tend to wear out more or less together, it is a good idea to replace both belts at the same time. Mark each belt and its appropriate pulley groove so the replacement belts can be installed in their proper positions.

11   Take the old belts to the parts store in order to make a direct comparison for length, width and design.

12   After replacing the drivebelt, make sure that it fits properly in the ribbed grooves in the pulleys **(see illustration)**. It is essential that the belt be properly centred.

13   Adjust the belt(s) in accordance with the procedure outlined above.

1998 and later models
Refer to illustrations 10.14 and 10.15

14   Rotate the belt tensioner clockwise to release the tension, then slip the belt off the pulleys **(see illustration)**. Slowly release the tensioner.

15   Route the new belt over the pulleys (see illustration), again rotating the tensioner to allow the belt to be installed, then release the belt tensioner.

16   Make sure the belt is properly centred in the pulleys **(see illustration 10.12)**.

CORRECT

WRONG

10.12 When installing a multi-ribbed belt, make sure that it is centred - it must not overlap either edge of the pulley

10.14 To release the tension on the drivebelt, place a long spanner or socket and ratchet on the hex-shaped boss, then turn the tensioner clockwise (1998 and later models)

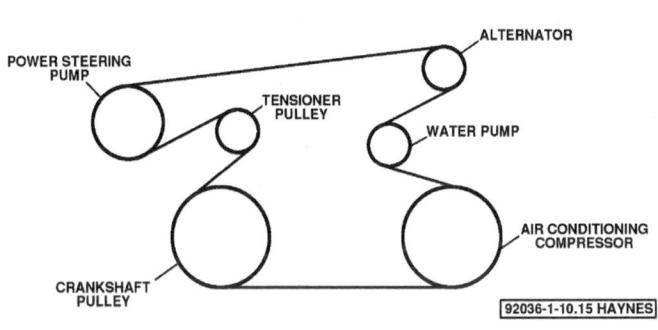

10.15 Drivebelt routing diagram (1998 and later models)

10.17 The drivebelt tensioner on 1998 and later models is retained by a nut and a bolt

Drivebelt tensioner replacement (1998 and later models)

Refer to illustration 10.17

17   To replace a tensioner that can't properly tension the belt, or one that exhibits binding or a worn-out bearing/pulley, remove the drivebelt (see Step 14) then unscrew the mounting bolt and nut **(see illustration)**.
18   Installation is the reverse of the removal procedure. Tighten the fasteners to the torque values listed in this Chapter's Specifications.
19   Install the drivebelt (see Steps 15 and 16).

11   Underbonnet hose check and replacement (every 12,000 kilometres or 6 months)

Caution: *Replacement of air conditioning hoses must be left to a dealer service department or air conditioning shop that has the equipment to depressurise the system safely. Never remove air conditioning components or hoses until the system has been depressurised.*

General

1   High temperatures in the engine compartment can cause the deterioration of the rubber and plastic hoses used for engine, accessory and emission systems operation. Periodic inspection should be made for cracks, loose clamps, material hardening and leaks.
2   Information specific to the cooling system hoses can be found in Section 12.
3   Some, but not all, hoses are secured to the fittings with clamps. Where clamps are used, check to be sure they haven't lost their tension, allowing the hose to leak. If clamps aren't used, make sure the hose has not expanded and/or hardened where it slips over the fitting, allowing it to leak.

Vacuum hoses

4   It's quite common for vacuum hoses, especially those in the emissions system, to be colour coded or identified by coloured stripes molded into them. Various systems require hoses with different wall thickness, collapse resistance and temperature resistance. When replacing hoses, be sure the new ones are made of the same material.
5   Often the only effective way to check a hose is to remove it completely from the vehicle. If more than one hose is removed, be sure to label the hoses and fittings to ensure correct installation.
6   When checking vacuum hoses, be sure to include any plastic T-fittings in the check. Inspect the fittings for cracks and the hose where it fits over the fitting for distortion, which could cause leakage.
7   A small piece of vacuum hose (6 to 8 mm inside diameter) can be used as a stethoscope to detect vacuum leaks. Hold one end of the hose to your ear and probe around vacuum hoses and fittings, listening for the "hissing" sound characteristic of a vacuum leak. **Warning:** *When probing with the vacuum hose stethoscope, be very careful not to come into contact with moving engine components such as the drivebelt, cooling fan, etc.*

Fuel hose

Warning: *Petrol is extremely flammable, so take extra precautions when you work on any part of the fuel system. Don't smoke or allow open flames or bare light bulbs near the work area, and don't work in a garage where a gas-type appliance (such as a water heater or a clothes dryer) is present. Since petrol is carcinogenic, wear latex gloves when there's a possibility of being exposed to fuel, and, if you spill any fuel on your skin, rinse it off immediately with soap and water. Mop up any spills immediately and do not store fuel-soaked rags where they could ignite. The fuel system is under constant pressure, so, if any fuel lines are to be disconnected, the fuel pressure in the system must be relieved first. When you perform any kind of work on the fuel system,*

wear safety glasses and have a Class B type fire extinguisher on hand.
8   Check all rubber fuel lines for deterioration and chafing. Check especially for cracks in areas where the hose bends and just before fittings, such as where a hose attaches to the fuel filter.
9   High quality fuel line, specifically designed for fuel injection systems, must be used for fuel line replacement. **Warning:** *Never use anything other than the proper fuel line for fuel line replacement.*
10   Spring-type clamps are commonly used on fuel lines. These clamps often lose their tension over a period of time, and can be "sprung" during removal. Replace all spring-type clamps with screw clamps whenever a hose is replaced.

Metal lines

11   Sections of metal line are often used for fuel line between the fuel pump and fuel injection unit. Check carefully to be sure the line has not been bent or crimped and that cracks have not started in the line.
12   If a section of metal fuel line must be replaced, only seamless steel tubing should be used, since copper and aluminum tubing don't have the strength necessary to withstand normal engine vibration.
13   Check the metal brake lines where they enter the master cylinder and brake proportioning unit (if used) for cracks in the lines or loose fittings. Any sign of brake fluid leakage calls for an immediate thorough inspection of the brake system.

12   Cooling system check (every 12,000 kilometres or 6 months)

Refer to illustration 12.4

1   Many major engine failures can be attributed to a faulty cooling system. If the vehicle is equipped with an automatic transaxle, the cooling system also cools the transaxle fluid and thus plays an important role in prolonging

Check for a chafed area that could fail prematurely.

Check for a soft area indicating the hose has deteriorated inside.

Overtightening the clamp on a hardened hose will damage the hose and cause a leak.

Check each hose for swelling and oil-soaked ends. Cracks and breaks can be located by squeezing the hose.

12.4 Hoses, like drivebelts, have a habit of failing at the worst possible time - to prevent the inconvenience of a blown radiator or heater hose, inspect them carefully as shown here

transaxle life.

2   The cooling system should be checked with the engine cold. Do this before the vehicle is driven for the day or after the engine has been shut off for at least three hours.

3   Remove the radiator cap by turning it to the left until it reaches a stop. If you hear a hissing sound (indicating there is still pressure in the system), wait until it stops. Now press down on the cap with the palm of your hand and continue turning to the left until the cap can be removed. Thoroughly clean the cap, inside and out, with clean water. Also clean the filler neck on the radiator. All traces of corrosion should be removed. The coolant inside the radiator should be relatively transparent. If it's rust coloured, the system should be drained and refilled (see Section 23). If the coolant level isn't up to the top, add additional antifreeze/coolant mixture (see Section 4).

4   Carefully check the large upper and

lower radiator hoses along with the smaller diameter heater hoses which run from the engine to the firewall. Inspect each hose along its entire length, replacing any hose which is cracked, swollen or shows signs of deterioration. Cracks may become more apparent if the hose is squeezed **(see illustration)**. Regardless of condition, it's a good idea to replace hoses with new ones every two years.

5   Make sure that all hose connections are tight. A leak in the cooling system will usually show up as white or rust coloured deposits on the areas adjoining the leak. If wire-type clamps are used at the ends of the hoses, it may be a good idea to replace them with more secure screw-type clamps.

6   Use compressed air or a soft brush to remove bugs, leaves, etc. from the front of the radiator or air conditioning condenser. Be careful not to damage the delicate cooling fins or cut yourself on them.

7   Every other inspection, or at the first indication of cooling system problems, have the cap and system pressure tested. If you don't have a pressure tester, most service stations and repair shops will do this for a minimal charge.

13   Tyre rotation (every 12,000 kilometres or 6 months)

Refer to illustration 13.2

1   The tyres should be rotated at the specified intervals and whenever uneven wear is noticed. Since the vehicle will be raised and the tyres removed anyway, check the brakes (see Section 15) at this time.

2   Radial tyres must be rotated in a specific pattern **(see illustration)**.

3   Refer to the information in *Jacking and towing* at the front of this manual for the proper procedures to follow when raising the vehicle and changing a tyre. If the brakes are to be checked, do not apply the parking brake as stated. Make sure the tyres are blocked to prevent the vehicle from rolling.

4   Preferably, the entire vehicle should be raised at the same time. This can be done on a hoist or by jacking up each corner and then lowering the vehicle onto jackstands placed under the frame rails. Always use four jackstands and make sure the vehicle is firmly supported.

5   After rotation, check and adjust the tyre pressures as necessary and be sure to check the lug nut tightness.

6   For further information on the wheels and tyres, refer to Chapter 10.

14   Seat belt check (every 12,000 kilometres or 6 months)

1   Check the seat belts, buckles, latch plates and guide loops for obvious damage and signs of wear. Seat belts that exhibit fraying along the edges should be replaced.

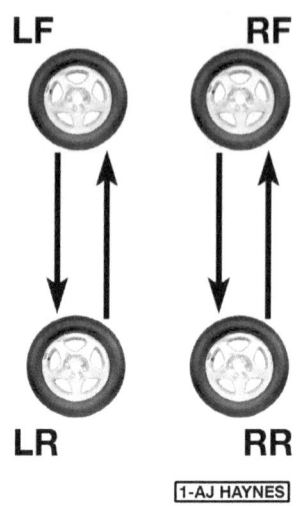

1-AJ HAYNES

13.2 The recommended tyre rotation pattern for these vehicles

2   Where the seat belt receptacle bolts to the floor of the vehicle, check that the bolts are secure.

3   See if the seat belt reminder light comes on when the key is turned to the Run or Start position. A chime should also sound.

15   Brake check (every 20,000 kilometres or 12 months)

Warning: *Dust created by the brake system is harmful to your health. Never blow it out with compressed air and don't inhale any of it. An approved filtering mask should be worn when working on the brakes. Do not, under any circumstances, use petroleum-based solvents to clean brake parts. Use brake system cleaner only!*
Note: *For detailed photographs of the brake system, refer to Chapter 9.*

1   In addition to the specified intervals, the brakes should be inspected every time the wheels are removed or whenever a defect is suspected. Any of the following symptoms could indicate a potential brake system defect: The vehicle pulls to one side when the brake pedal is depressed; the brakes make squealing or dragging noises when applied; brake travel is excessive; the pedal pulsates; brake fluid leaks, usually onto the inside of the tyre or wheel.

2   The disc brake pads have built-in wear indicators which should make a high-pitched squealing or scraping noise when they are worn to the replacement point. When you hear this noise, replace the pads immediately or expensive damage to the discs can result.

3   Loosen the wheel lug nuts.

4   Raise the vehicle and place it securely on jackstands.

5   Remove the wheels (see *Jacking and towing* at the front of this book, or your owner's manual, if necessary).

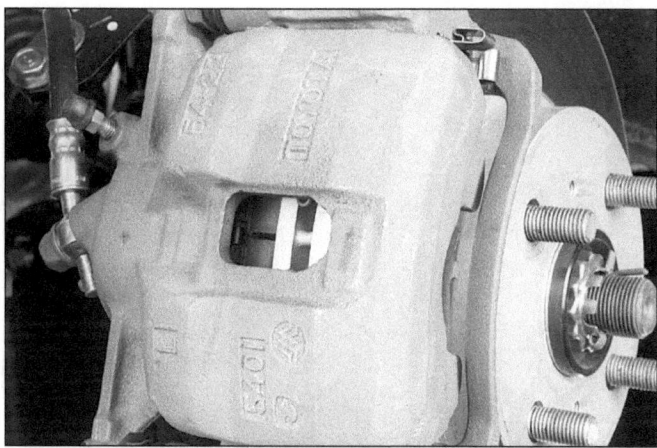

15.6 You will find an inspection hole like this in each caliper - placing a ruler across the hole should enable you to determine the thickness of remaining pad material for both inner and outer pads

15.15 If the lining is bonded to the brake shoe, measure the lining thickness from the outer surface to the metal shoe, as shown here; if the lining is riveted to the shoe, measure from the lining outer surface to the rivet head

Disc brakes

Refer to illustration 15.6

6   There are two pads - an outer and an inner - in each caliper. The pads are visible through small inspection holes in each caliper **(see illustration)**.

7   Check the pad thickness by looking at each end of the caliper and through the inspection hole in the caliper body. If the lining material is less than the thickness listed in this Chapter's Specifications, replace the pads. **Note:** *Keep in mind that the lining material is riveted or bonded to a metal backing plate and the metal portion is not included in this measurement.*

8   If it is difficult to determine the exact thickness of the remaining pad material by the above method, or if you are at all concerned about the condition of the pads, remove the caliper(s), then remove the pads for further inspection (refer to Chapter 9).

9   Once the pads are removed from the calipers, clean them with brake cleaner and re-measure them.

10   Measure the disc thickness with a micrometer to make sure that it still has service life remaining. If any disc is thinner than the specified minimum thickness, replace it (refer to Chapter 9). Even if the disc has service life remaining, check its condition. Look for scoring, gouging and burned spots. If these conditions exist, remove the disc and have it resurfaced (see Chapter 9).

11   Before installing the wheels, check all brake lines and hoses for damage, wear, deformation, cracks, corrosion, leakage, bends and twists, particularly in the vicinity of the rubber hoses at the calipers.

12   Check the clamps for tightness and the connections for leakage. Make sure that all hoses and lines are clear of sharp edges, moving parts and the exhaust system. If any of the above conditions are noted, repair, reroute or replace the lines and/or fittings as necessary (see Chapter 9).

Rear drum brakes

Refer to illustrations 15.15 and 15.17

13   To check the brake shoe lining thickness without removing the brake drums, remove the rubber plug from the backing plate and use a flashlight to inspect the linings. For a more thorough brake inspection, follow the procedure below.

14   Refer to Chapter 9 and remove the rear brake drums.

15   Note the thickness of the lining material on the rear brake shoes **(see illustration)** and look for signs of contamination by brake fluid and grease. If the lining material is within 1.5 mm of the recessed rivets or metal shoes, replace the brake shoes with new ones. The shoes should also be replaced if they are cracked, glazed (shiny lining surfaces) or contaminated with brake fluid or grease. See Chapter 9 for the replacement procedure.

16   Check the shoe return and hold-down springs and the adjusting mechanism to make sure they're installed correctly and in good

condition. Deteriorated or distorted springs, if not replaced, could allow the linings to drag and wear prematurely.

17   Check the wheel cylinders for leakage by carefully peeling back the rubber boots **(see illustration)**. If brake fluid is noted behind the boots, the wheel cylinders must be replaced (see Chapter 9).

18   Check the drums for cracks, score marks, deep scratches and hard spots, which will appear as small discoloured areas. If imperfections cannot be removed with emery cloth, the drums must be resurfaced by an automotive machine shop (see Chapter 9 for more detailed information).

19   Install the brake drums.

20   Install the wheels and lug nuts.

21   Remove the jackstands and lower the vehicle.

22   Tighten the wheel lug nuts to the torque listed in this Chapter's Specifications.

Brake booster check

23   Sit in the driver's seat and perform the following sequence of tests.

24   With the brake fully depressed, start the engine - the pedal should move down a little when the engine starts.

25   With the engine running, depress the brake pedal several times - the travel distance should not change.

26   Depress the brake, stop the engine and hold the pedal in for about 30 seconds - the pedal should neither sink nor rise.

27   Restart the engine, run it for about a minute and turn it off. Then firmly depress the brake several times - the pedal travel should decrease with each application.

28   If your brakes do not operate as described above when the preceding tests are performed, the brake booster has failed. Refer to Chapter 9 for the replacement procedure.

Parking brake

29   Slowly pull up on the parking brake and

15.17 Carefully peel back the wheel cylinder boot and check for leaking fluid indicating that the cylinder must be replaced

16.2a Detach the clips and separate the cover from the air cleaner housing

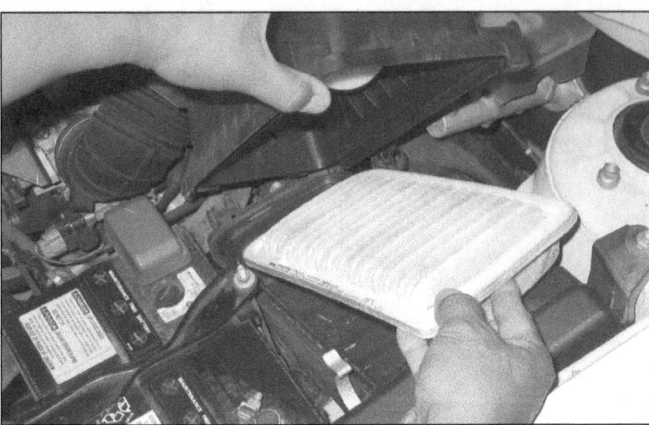

16.2b Hold the cover up out of the way and lift the element out

count the number of clicks you hear until the handle is up as far as it will go. The adjustment is correct if you hear the specified number of clicks. If you hear more or fewer clicks, it's time to adjust the parking brake (refer to Chapter 9).

30   An alternative method of checking the parking brake is to park the vehicle on a steep hill with the parking brake set and the transaxle in Neutral (be sure to stay in the vehicle for this procedure). If the parking brake cannot prevent the vehicle from rolling, it is in need of adjustment (see Chapter 9).

16   Air filter replacement (every 20,000 kilometres or 12 months)

Refer to illustrations 16.2a and 16.2b

1   The air filter is located inside a housing at the left (driver's) side of the engine compartment.

2   To remove the air filter, release the spring clips that keep the two halves of the air cleaner housing together, then lift the cover up and remove the air filter element **(see illustrations)**.

3   Inspect the outer surface of the filter element. If it is dirty, replace it. If it is only moderately dusty, it can be reused by blowing it clean from the back to the front surface with

compressed air. Because it is a pleated paper type filter, it cannot be washed or oiled. If it cannot be cleaned satisfactorily with compressed air, discard and replace it. While the cover is off, be careful not to drop anything down into the housing. **Caution:** *Never drive the vehicle with the air cleaner removed. Excessive engine wear could result and backfiring could even cause a fire under the bonnet.*

4   Wipe out the inside of the air cleaner housing.

5   Place the new filter into the air cleaner housing, making sure it seats properly.

6   Installation of the cover is the reverse of removal.

17   Fuel system check (every 20,000 kilometres or 12 months)

Refer to illustrations 17.2 and 17.5

Warning: *Petrol is extremely flammable, so take extra precautions when you work on any part of the fuel system. Don't smoke or allow open flames or bare light bulbs near the work area, and don't work in a garage where a gas-type appliance (such as a water heater or a clothes dryer) is present. Since petrol is carcinogenic, wear latex gloves when there's a possibility of being exposed to fuel, and, if you*

spill any fuel on your skin, rinse it off immediately with soap and water. Mop up any spills immediately and do not store fuel-soaked rags where they could ignite. The fuel system is under constant pressure, so, if any fuel lines are to be disconnected, the fuel pressure in the system must be relieved first. When you perform any kind of work on the fuel system, wear safety glasses and have a Class B type fire extinguisher on hand.

1   If you smell petrol while driving or after the vehicle has been sitting in the sun, inspect the fuel system immediately.

2   Remove the petrol filler cap and inspect it for damage and corrosion. The gasket should have an unbroken sealing imprint. If the gasket is damaged or corroded, remove it and install a new one **(see illustration)**.

3   Inspect the fuel feed and return lines for cracks. Make sure that the threaded flare-nut type connectors which secure the metal fuel lines to the fuel injection system are tight.

4   Since some components of the fuel system - the fuel tank and part of the fuel feed and return lines, for example - are underneath the vehicle, they can be inspected more easily with the vehicle raised on a hoist. If that's not possible, raise the vehicle and support it securely on jackstands.

5   With the vehicle raised and safely supported, inspect the petrol tank and filler neck for punctures, cracks and other damage. The

17.2 Use a small screwdriver to carefully pry out the old gasket - take care not to damage the cap

17.5 Inspect the filler hose for cracks and make sure the clamps are tight

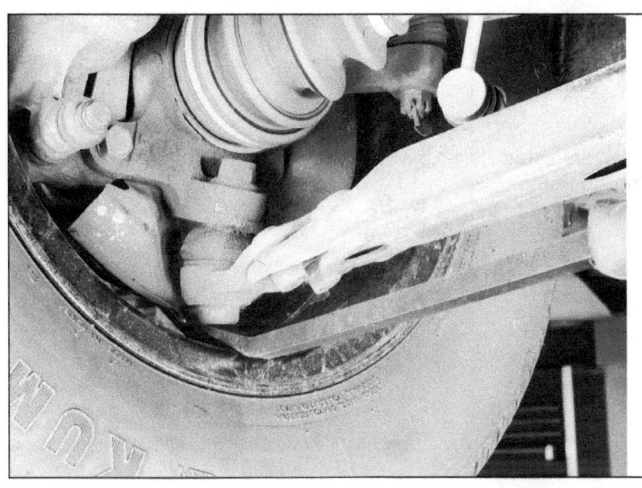

19.7 To check a balljoint for wear, try to move the control arm up and down with a prybar to make sure there is no play in the balljoint (if there is, replace it)

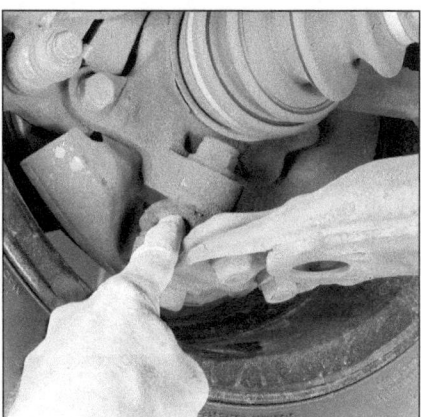

19.8 Push on the balljoint boot to check for damage

connection between the filler neck and the tank is particularly critical. Sometimes a rubber filler neck will leak because of loose clamps or deteriorated rubber **(see illustration)**. These are problems a home mechanic can usually rectify. **Warning:** *Do not, under any circumstances, try to repair a fuel tank (except rubber components). A welding torch or any open flame can easily cause fuel vapors inside the tank to explode.*

6   Carefully check all rubber hoses and metal lines leading away from the fuel tank. Check for loose connections, deteriorated hoses, crimped lines and other damage. Carefully inspect the lines from the tank to the fuel injection system. Repair or replace damaged sections as necessary (see Chapter 4).

---

18   Manual transaxle lubricant level check (every 20,000 kilometres or 12 months)

1   The manual transaxle does not have a dipstick. To check the fluid level, raise the vehicle and support it securely on jackstands. On the lower front side of the transaxle housing, you will see a plug. Remove it. If the lubricant level is correct, it should be up to the lower edge of the hole.
2   If the transaxle needs more lubricant (if the level is not up to the hole), use a syringe or a gear oil pump to add more. Stop filling the transaxle when the lubricant begins to run out the hole.
3   Install the plug and tighten it securely. Drive the vehicle a short distance, then check for leaks.

---

19   Steering, suspension and driveaxle boot check (every 20,000 kilometres or 12 months)

Refer to illustrations 19.7 and 19.8

Note: *For detailed illustrations of the steering and suspension components, refer to Chapter 10.*

Steering and suspension check

With the wheels on the ground

1   With the vehicle stopped and the front wheels pointed straight ahead, rock the steering wheel gently back and forth. If freeplay **(see illustration)** is excessive, a front wheel bearing, main shaft yoke, intermediate shaft yoke, lower arm balljoint or steering system joint is worn or the steering gear is out of adjustment or broken. Refer to Chapter 10 for the appropriate repair procedure.
2   Other symptoms, such as excessive vehicle body movement over rough roads, swaying (leaning) around corners and binding as the steering wheel is turned, may indicate faulty steering and/or suspension components.
3   Check the shock absorbers by pushing down and releasing the vehicle several times at each corner. If the vehicle does not come back to a level position within one or two bounces, the shocks/struts are worn and must be replaced. When bouncing the vehicle up and down, listen for squeaks and noises from the suspension components. Additional information on suspension components can be found in Chapter 10.

Under the vehicle

4   Raise the vehicle with a floor jack and support it securely on jackstands. See *Jacking and towing* at the front of this book for the proper jacking points.
5   Check the tyres for irregular wear patterns and proper inflation. See Section 5 in this Chapter for information regarding tyre wear and Chapter 10 for the wheel bearing replacement procedures.
6   Inspect the universal joint between the steering shaft and the steering gear housing. Check the steering gear housing for grease leakage or oozing. Make sure that the dust seals and boots are not damaged and that the boot clamps are not loose. Check the steering linkage for looseness or damage. Check the tie-rod ends for excessive play. Look for loose bolts, broken or disconnected parts and deteriorated rubber bushings on all suspension and steering components. While an

assistant turns the steering wheel from side to side, check the steering components for free movement, chafing and binding. If the steering components do not seem to be reacting with the movement of the steering wheel, try to determine where the slack is located.
7   Move each control arm up and down with a lever **(see illustration)** to ensure that its balljoint has no play. If any balljoint does have play, replace it. See Chapter 10 for the balljoint replacement procedure.
8   Inspect the balljoint boots for damage and leaking grease **(see illustration)**. Replace the balljoints with new ones if they are damaged (see Chapter 10).

Driveaxle boot check

Refer to illustration 19.10

9   The driveaxle boots are very important because they prevent dirt, water and foreign material from entering and damaging the constant velocity (CV) joints. Oil and grease can cause the boot material to deteriorate prematurely, so it's a good idea to wash the boots with soap and water. Because it constantly pivots back and forth following the steering action of the front hub, the outer CV boot wears out sooner and should be inspected regularly.
10   Inspect the boots for tears and cracks as well as loose clamps **(see illustration)**.

19.10 Flex the driveaxle boots by hand to check for cracks and/or leaking grease

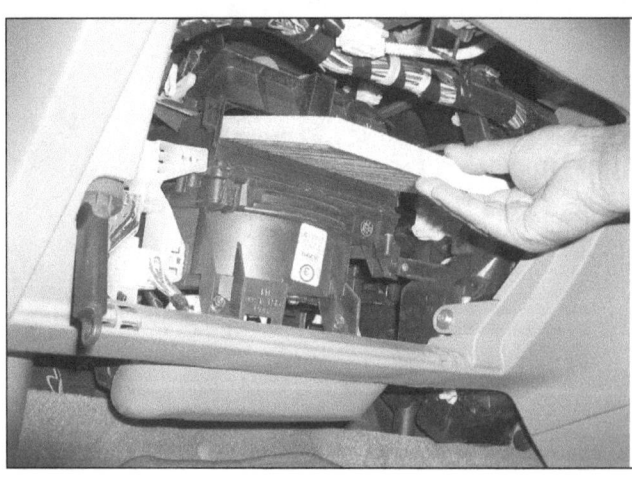

20.3 Open the cabin air filter door and slide the filter out

22.1 Tools required for changing spark plugs

1   *Spark plug socket - This will have special padding inside to protect the spark plug porcelain insulator*
2   *Torque wrench - Although not mandatory, use of this tool is the best way to ensure that the plugs are tightened properly*
3   *Ratchet - Standard hand tool to fit the plug socket*
4   *Extension - Depending on model and accessories, you may need special extensions and universal joints to reach one or more of the plugs*
5   *Spark plug gap gauge - This gauge for checking the gap comes in a variety of styles. Make sure the gap for your engine is included*

If there is any evidence of cracks or leaking lubricant, they must be replaced as described in Chapter 8.

20   Cabin air filter - replacement (every 20,000 kilometres or 12 months)

Refer to illustration 20.3

1   The covered models are equipped with a cabin air filter in the blower housing. The filter traps dust and pollen before the air enters the passenger compartment.
2   For access to the cabin air filter, remove the glove box (see Chapter 11).
3   Release the two clips on the filter door, open the door and remove the filter **(see illustration)**.
4   Installation is the reverse of the removal procedure.

21   Brake fluid change (every 40,000 kilometres or 24 months)

Warning: *Brake fluid can harm your eyes and damage painted surfaces, so use extreme caution when handling or pouring it. Do not use brake fluid that has been standing open or is more than one year old. Brake fluid absorbs moisture from the air. Excess moisture can cause a dangerous loss of braking effectiveness.*

1   At the specified intervals, the brake fluid should be drained and replaced. Since the brake fluid may drip or splash when pouring it, place plenty of rags around the master cylinder to protect any surrounding painted surfaces.
2   Before beginning work, purchase the specified brake fluid (see *Recommended lubricants and fluids* at the beginning of this Chapter).
3   Remove the cap from the master cylinder reservoir.
4   Using a hand suction pump or similar device, withdraw the fluid from the master cylinder reservoir.

5   Add new fluid to the master cylinder until it rises to the line indicated on the reservoir.
6   Bleed the brake system as described in Chapter 9 at all four brakes until new and uncontaminated fluid is expelled from the bleeder screw. Be sure to maintain the fluid level in the master cylinder as you perform the bleeding process. If you allow the master cylinder to run dry, air will enter the system.
7   Refill the master cylinder with fluid and check the operation of the brakes. The pedal should feel solid when depressed, with no sponginess. **Warning:** *Do not operate the vehicle if you are in doubt about the effectiveness of the brake system.*

22   Spark plug check and replacement (every 40,000 kilometres or 24 months)

Refer to illustrations 22.1, 22.4a, 22.4b, 22.6, 22.10a and 22.10b

1   Spark plug replacement requires a spark plug socket which fits onto a ratchet wrench. This socket is lined with a rubber grommet to protect the porcelain insulator of the spark plug and to hold the plug while you insert it into the spark plug hole. You will also need a wire-type feeler gauge to check and adjust the spark plug gap and a torque wrench to tighten the new plugs to the specified torque **(see illustration)**.
2   If you are replacing the plugs, purchase the new plugs, adjust them to the proper gap and then replace each plug one at a time. **Note:** *When buying new spark plugs, it's essential that you obtain the correct plugs for your specific vehicle.*
3   Inspect each of the new plugs for defects. If there are any signs of cracks in the porcelain insulator of a plug, don't use it.
4   Check the electrode gaps of the new plugs. Check the gap by inserting the wire gauge of the proper thickness between the electrodes at the tip of the plug **(see illustrations)**. **Caution:** *Don't attempt to adjust the gap on a used iridium-coated plug.*
5   If the side electrode is not exactly over

the centre electrode, use the notched adjuster to align them. **Caution:** *If the gap of a new plug must be adjusted, bend only the base of the ground electrode - do not touch the tip.*

Removal

6   Remove the engine cover **(see illustration)** if equipped, then remove the ignition coils (see Chapter 5) if equipped.
7   If compressed air is available, blow any

22.4a Spark plug manufacturers recommend using a wire-type gauge when checking the gap - if the wire does not slide between the electrodes with a slight drag, adjustment is required

22.4b To change the gap, bend the side electrode only, as indicated by the arrows, and be very careful not to crack or chip the porcelain insulator surrounding the centre electrode

22.6 Engine cover fastener locations

A Nut
B Plastic fastener

dirt or foreign material away from the spark plug area before proceeding.

8 Remove the spark plug.

9 Whether you are replacing the plugs at this time or intend to reuse the old plugs, compare each old spark plug with the chart on the inside back cover of this manual to determine the overall running condition of the engine.

Installation

10 Prior to installation, it's a good idea to coat the spark plug threads with anti-seize compound **(see illustration)**. Also, it's often difficult to insert spark plugs into their holes without cross-threading them. To avoid this possibility, fit a length of snug-fitting rubber hose over the end of the spark plug **(see illustration)**. The flexible hose acts as a universal joint to help align the plug with the plug hole. Should the plug begin to cross-thread, the hose will slip on the spark plug, preventing thread damage. Tighten the plug to the torque listed in this Chapter's Specifications.

11 Install the ignition coil.

12 Follow the above procedure for the remaining spark plugs.

---

23 Cooling system servicing (draining, flushing and refilling) (every 40,000 kilometres or 24 months)

Warning: *Do not allow engine coolant (antifreeze) to come in contact with your skin or painted surfaces of the vehicle. Rinse off spills immediately with plenty of water. Antifreeze is highly toxic if ingested. Never leave antifreeze lying around in an open container or in puddles on the floor; children and pets are attracted by it's sweet smell and may drink it. Check with local authorities on disposing of used antifreeze. Many communities have collection centres which will see that antifreeze*

22.10a Apply a thin coat of anti-seize compound to the spark plug threads

is disposed of safely. Antifreeze is flammable under certain conditions - be sure to read the precautions on the container.

Note: *Non-toxic antifreeze is available at most auto parts stores. Although the antifreeze is non-toxic when fresh, proper disposal is still required.*

1 Periodically, the cooling system should be drained, flushed and refilled to replenish the antifreeze mixture and prevent formation of rust and corrosion, which can impair the performance of the cooling system and cause engine damage. When the cooling system is serviced, all hoses and the radiator cap should be checked and replaced if necessary.

22.10b A length of snug-fitting rubber hose will save time and prevent damaged threads when installing the spark plugs

Draining

Refer to illustrations 23.4 and 23.5

2 Apply the parking brake and block the wheels. If the vehicle has just been driven, wait several hours to allow the engine to cool down before beginning this procedure.

3 Once the engine is completely cool, remove the radiator cap.

4 Move a large container under the radiator drain to catch the coolant. Attach a 9 mm inner diameter hose to the drain fitting to direct the coolant into the container (some models are already equipped with a hose), then open the drain fitting (a pair of pliers may be required to turn it) **(see illustration)**.

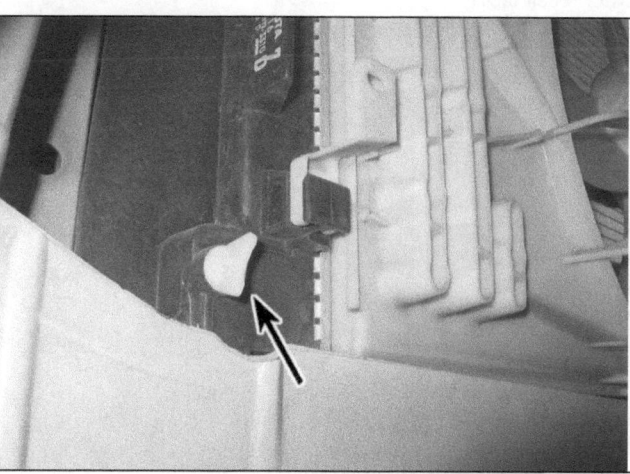

23.4 On most models you will have to remove a cover for access to the radiator drain fitting located at the bottom of the radiator - before opening the valve, push a short section of 9 mm ID hose onto the plastic fitting to prevent the coolant from splashing

23.5 Attach a length of tubing to the spigot on the engine block drain, then loosen the drain bolt and allow the block to drain

Garden Hose

Upper Hose →
Expels Water

23.9 With the thermostat removed, disconnect the upper radiator hose and flush the radiator and engine block with a garden hose

36022-1-22.10 HAYNES

Radiator

5   After the coolant stops flowing out of the radiator, move the container under the engine block drain plug **(see illustration)**. Loosen the plug and allow the coolant in the block to drain.

6   While the coolant is draining, check the condition of the radiator hoses, heater hoses and clamps (refer to Section 12 if necessary). Replace any damaged clamps or hoses.

Flushing

Refer to illustration 23.9

7   Once the system is completely drained, remove the thermostat from the engine (see Chapter 3). Then reinstall the thermostat housing without the thermostat. This will allow the system to be thoroughly flushed.

8   Tighten the radiator drain plug. Turn your heating system controls to Hot, so that the heater core will be flushed at the same time as the rest of the cooling system.

9   Disconnect the upper radiator hose from the radiator, then place a garden hose in the upper radiator inlet and flush the system until the water runs clear at the upper radiator hose **(see illustration)**.

10   In severe cases of contamination or clogging of the radiator, remove the radiator (see Chapter 3) and have a radiator repair facility clean and repair it if necessary.

11   Many deposits can be removed by the chemical action of a cleaner available at auto parts stores. Follow the procedure outlined in the manufacturer's instructions. **Note:** *When the coolant is regularly drained and the system refilled with the correct antifreeze/water mixture, there should be no need to use chemical cleaners or descalers.*

12   Remove the overflow hose from the coolant recovery reservoir. Drain the reservoir and flush it with clean water, then reconnect the hose.

Refilling

13   Close and tighten the radiator drain. Install and/or tighten the block drain plug.

Reinstall the thermostat (see Chapter 3).

14   Place the heater temperature control in the maximum heat position.

15   Slowly add new coolant (a 50/50 mixture of water and antifreeze) to the radiator until it's full. Squeeze the radiator hoses, then add more coolant, if possible. Add coolant to the reservoir up to the lower mark.

16   Install the radiator cap and run the engine in a well-ventilated area until the thermostat opens (coolant will begin flowing through the radiator and the upper radiator hose will become hot).

17   Turn the engine off and let it cool. Add more coolant mixture to bring the level back up to the lip on the radiator filler neck.

18   Squeeze the upper radiator hose to expel air, then add more coolant mixture if necessary. Reinstall the radiator cap.

19   Start the engine, allow it to reach normal operating temperature and check for leaks.

24 Evaporative emissions control system check (every 40,000 kilometres or 24 months)

Refer to illustration 24.2

1   The function of the evaporative emissions control system is to draw fuel vapors from the petrol tank and fuel system, store them in a charcoal canister and then burn them during normal engine operation.

2   The most common symptom of a fault in the evaporative emissions control system is a strong fuel odor from the rear of the vehicle. If a fuel odor is detected, inspect the charcoal canister duct **(see illustration)** located under the rear of the vehicle, above the rear suspension crossmember. Check the canister and all hoses for damage and deterioration.

3   The evaporative emissions control system is explained in more detail in Chapter 6.

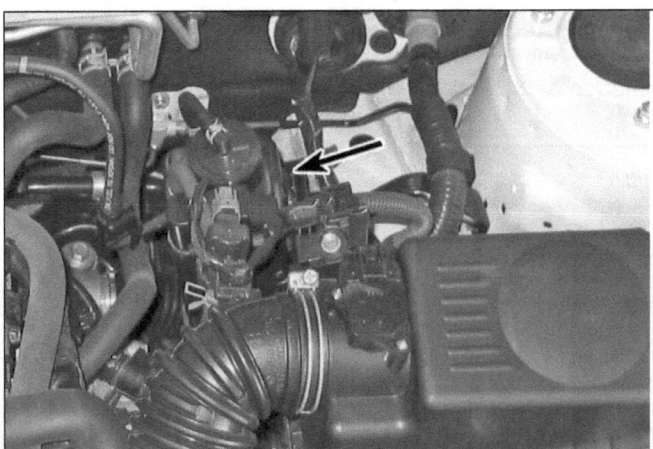

24.2 The charcoal canister in the engine compartment on later models (arrow)

25.4 Be sure to check each exhaust system rubber hanger for damage

26.8a After loosening the front bolts, remove the rear transaxle pan bolts . . .

25 Exhaust system check (every 40,000 kilometres or 24 months)

Refer to illustration 25.4

1   With the engine cold (at least three hours after the vehicle has been driven), check the complete exhaust system from its starting point at the engine to the end of the tailpipe. This should be done on a hoist where unrestricted access is available.

2   Check the pipes and connections for evidence of leaks, severe corrosion or damage. Make sure that all brackets and hangers are in good condition and tight.

3   At the same time, inspect the underside of the body for holes, corrosion, open seams, etc. which may allow exhaust gases to enter the passenger compartment. Seal all body openings with silicone or body putty.

4   Rattles and other noises can often be traced to the exhaust system, especially the mounts and hangers. Try to move the pipes, muffler and catalytic converter. If the components can come in contact with the body or suspension parts, secure the exhaust system with new mounts **(see illustration)**.

5   Check the running condition of the engine by inspecting inside the end of the tailpipe. The exhaust deposits here are an indication of engine state-of-tune. If the pipe is black and sooty or coated with white deposits, the engine is in need of a tune-up, including a thorough engine control system inspection.

26 Automatic transaxle fluid and filter change (every 40,000 kilometres or 24 months)

Refer to illustrations 26.8a, 26.8b, 26.9 and 26.11

Note: *Toyota does not recommend changing the ATF fluid under normal driving conditions for later models, see Owners manual for details.*

1   At the specified time intervals, the automatic transaxle fluid should be drained and replaced.

2   Before beginning work, purchase the specified transmission fluid (see *Recommended fluids and lubricants* at the front of this Chapter).

3   Other tools necessary for this job include jackstands to support the vehicle in a raised position, spanners, drain pan capable of holding at least four quarts, newspapers and clean rags.

4   The fluid should be drained immediately after the vehicle has been driven. Hot fluid is more effective than cold fluid at removing built up sediment. **Warning:** *Fluid temperature can exceed 176-degrees C in a hot transaxle. Wear protective gloves.*

5   After the vehicle has been driven to warm up the fluid, raise it and support it on jackstands for access to the transaxle and differential drain plugs.

6   Move the necessary equipment under the vehicle, being careful not to touch any of the hot exhaust components.

7   Place the drain pan under the drain plug in the transaxle pan and remove the drain plug. Be sure the drain pan is in position, as fluid will come out with some force. Once the fluid is drained, reinstall the drain plug securely.

8   Remove the front transaxle pan bolts, then loosen the rear bolts and carefully prise the pan loose with a screwdriver and allow the remaining fluid to drain **(see illustrations)**. Once the fluid has drained, remove the bolts and lower the pan.

9   Remove the filter retaining bolts, disconnect the clip (some models) and lower the filter from the transaxle **(see illustration)**. Be careful when lowering the filter as it contains residual fluid.

10   Place the new filter in position, connect

26.8b . . . and allow the remaining fluid to drain out

26.9 Remove the filter bolts and lower the filter (be careful, there will be some residual fluid) - note that here one of the pan magnets is stuck to the filter (arrow); be sure to clean any magnets and return them to the pan

26.11 Noting their locations, remove any magnets and wash them and the pan in solvent before reinstalling them

28.1 The PCV valve is threaded into the valve cover

the clip (if equipped) and install the bolts. Tighten the bolts securely.

11   Carefully clean the gasket surfaces of the fluid pan, removing all traces of old gasket material. Noting their location, remove the magnets, wash the pan in clean solvent and dry it. Be sure to clean and reinstall any magnets **(see illustration)**.

12   Install a new gasket, place the fluid pan in position and install the bolts in their original positions. Tighten the bolts to the torque listed in this Chapter's Specifications.

13   Lower the vehicle.

14   With the engine off, add new fluid to the transaxle through the dipstick tube (see *Recommended fluids and lubricants* for the recommended fluid type and capacity). Use a funnel to prevent spills. It is best to add a little fluid at a time, continually checking the level with the dipstick (see Section 4). Allow the fluid time to drain into the pan.

15   Start the engine and shift the selector into all positions from P through L, then shift into P and apply the parking brake.

16   With the engine idling, check the fluid level. Add fluid up to the Cool level on the dipstick.

27   Manual transaxle lubricant change (every 40,000 kilometres or 24 months)

1   Raise the vehicle and support it securely on jackstands.

2   Remove the filler plug and drain plug(s) and drain the fluid.

3   Reinstall the drain plug(s) and tighten securely.

4   Add new fluid until it is even with the lower edge of the filler hole. See *Recommended lubricants and fluids* for the specified lubricant type.

29.4a Using a backup wrench to prevent the filter from turning, remove the banjo bolt at the top and . . .

28   Positive Crankcase Ventilation (PCV) valve and hose check and replacement (every 40,000 kilometres or 24 months)

Refer to illustration 28.1

1   The PCV valve and hose is located in the valve cover. It's threaded into the left (passenger's) end of the valve cover **(see illustration)**.

2   Detach the hose, unscrew the valve from the cover, then reattach the hose to the valve.

3   With the engine idling at normal operating temperature, place your finger over the end of the valve. If there's no vacuum at the valve, check for a plugged hose or valve. Replace any plugged or deteriorated hoses.

4   Turn off the engine. Remove the PCV valve from the hose. Connect a clean piece of hose and blow through the valve from the valve cover (cylinder head) end. If air will not pass through the valve in this direction, replace it with a new one.

**29.4b . . . loosen the fitting at the bottom of the filter
1997 mdoels**

5   When purchasing a replacement PCV valve, make sure it's for your particular vehicle and engine size. Compare the old valve with the new one to make sure they're the same.

29   Fuel filter replacement (every 80,000 kilometres or 48 months)

Refer to illustrations 29.4a and 29.4b

Note: *The fuel filter on 1998 and later models is located in the fuel tank. It is necessary to remove the fuel pump to access the fuel filter. Refer to Chapter 4 for the fuel pump and fuel filter removal procedure. For 1997 models, use the following procedure.*

1   Relieve the fuel system pressure (see Chapter 4). Disconnect the negative battery cable.

2   The canister filter is mounted in a bracket on the firewall near the brake master cylinder.

3   Remove any components that would interfere with access to the top of the filter.

4   Using a backup wrench to steady the

30.8 Use a small screwdriver to lift the lock claw up when detaching the spark plug wire boot from the distributor

30.11a Remove the screws (arrows) and detach the distributor cap (third screw not visible in this photo)

filter, remove the banjo bolt at the top and, using a flare-nut wrench, if available, loosen the fitting at the bottom of the fuel filter **(see illustrations)**.

5   Remove both bracket bolts from the firewall and remove the old filter and the filter support bracket assembly.

6   Note that the inlet and outlet pipes are clearly labeled on their respective ends of the filter and that the flanged end of the filter faces down. Make sure the new filter is installed so that it's facing the proper direction as noted above. When correctly installed, the filter should be installed so that the outlet pipe faces up and the inlet pipe faces down.

7   Connect the threaded fitting to the bottom of the filter and tighten it securely. Using new sealing washers, connect the banjo fitting to the top of the filter and tighten the banjo bolt to the torque listed in this Chapter's Specifications.

8   The remainder of installation is the reverse of the removal procedure.

30   Spark plug wire, distributor cap and rotor check and replacement (every 40,000 kilometres or 24 months)

Refer to illustrations 30.8, 30.11a, 30.11b, 30.12 and 30.13

Note: *Only 1997 models are equipped with distributors. All 1999 and earlier models have spark plug wires, but 2000 and later models have "coil over plug" ignition systems, where the ignition coils fit directly over the spark plugs. Therefore, this procedure does not apply to 2000 and later models.*

1   The spark plug wires should be checked whenever new spark plugs are installed.

2   Begin this procedure by making a visual check of the spark plug wires while the engine is running. In a darkened garage (make sure there is ventilation) start the engine and observe each plug wire. Be careful not to come into contact with any moving engine parts. If there is a break in the wire, you

will see arcing or a small spark at the damaged area. If arcing is noticed, make a note to obtain new wires, then allow the engine to cool and check the distributor cap and rotor.

3   The spark plug wires should be inspected one at a time to prevent mixing up the order, which is essential for proper engine operation. Each original plug wire should be numbered to help identify its location. If the number is illegible, a piece of tape can be marked with the correct number and wrapped around the plug wire.

4   Disconnect the plug wire from the spark plug. A removal tool can be used for this purpose or you can grasp the rubber boot, twist the boot half a turn and pull the boot free. Do not pull on the wire itself.

5   Check inside the boot for corrosion, which will look like a white crusty powder.

6   Push the wire and boot back onto the end of the spark plug. It should fit tightly onto the end of the plug. If it doesn't, remove the wire and use pliers to carefully crimp the metal connector inside the wire boot until the fit is snug.

7   Using a clean rag, wipe the entire length of the wire to remove built-up dirt and grease.

Once the wire is clean, check for burns, cracks and other damage. Do not bend the wire sharply, because the conductor might break.

8   Disconnect the wire from the distributor cap (1997 models) or coil pack (1998 and 1999 models), using a small screwdriver to lift up on the lock claw, if equipped **(see illustration)**. Check for corrosion and a tight fit. Reconnect the wire.

9   Inspect the remaining spark plug wires, making sure that each one is securely fastened at the distributor or coil pack and spark plug when the check is complete.

10   If new spark plug wires are required, purchase a set for your specific engine model. Pre-cut wire sets with the boots already installed are available. Remove and replace the wires one at a time to avoid mix-ups in the firing order.

11   On 1997 models, detach the distributor cap by removing the retaining screws **(see illustration)**. Look inside it for cracks, carbon tracks and worn, burned or loose contacts **(see illustration)**.

12   Pull the rotor off the distributor shaft and examine it for cracks and carbon tracks **(see illustration)**. Replace the cap and rotor if any damage or defects are noted.

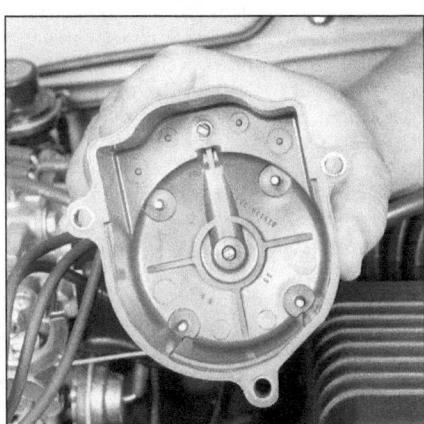

30.11b Inspect the distributor cap for carbon tracks, charred or eroded terminals and other damage (if in doubt about its condition, install a new one)

30.12 Check the rotor for damage, wear and corrosion (if in doubt about its condition, buy a new one)

30.13 Measure the resistance value of the distributor cap and the spark plug wires - if it exceeds the specified maximum value, replace either the cap, or the wires, or both

31.6a When the No. 1 piston is at TDC on the compression stroke, the valve clearance for the No. 1 and No. 3 cylinder exhaust valves and the No. 1 and No. 2 intake valves can be measured

31.6b Check the clearance for each valve with a feeler gauge of the specified thickness - if the clearance is correct, you should feel a slight drag on the gauge as you pull it out

31.7 When the No. 4 piston is at TDC on the compression stroke, the valve clearance for the No. 2 and No. 4 exhaust valves and the No. 3 and No. 4 intake valves can be measured

13   It is common practice to install a new cap and rotor whenever new spark plug wires are installed, but if you wish to continue using the old cap, check the resistance between the spark plug wires and the cap first **(see illustration)**. If the indicated resistance is more than the maximum value listed in this Chapter's Specifications, replace the cap and/or wires.

14   When installing a new cap, remove the wires from the old cap one at a time and attach them to the new cap in the exact same location - do not simultaneously remove all the wires from the old cap or firing order mix-ups may occur.

31   Valve clearance check and adjustment (every 80,000 kilometres or 48 months)

Warning: *These models are equipped with airbags. Always disable the airbag system before working in the vicinity of any airbag system component to avoid the possibility of accidental deployment of the airbag(s), which could cause personal injury (see Chapter 12).*

Check

Refer to illustrations 31.6a, 31.6b and 31.7

1   Disconnect the negative cable from the battery.

2   Remove the ignition coils (see Chapter 5) and remove any other components that will interfere with valve cover removal.

3   Blow out the recessed area around the spark plug openings with compressed air, if available, to remove any debris that might fall into the cylinders, then remove the spark plugs (see Section 22).

4   Remove the valve cover (refer to Chapter 2).

5   Refer to Chapter 2A and position the number 1 piston at TDC on the compression stroke.

6   Measure the clearances of the indicated valves with feeler gauges **(see illustrations)**. Record the measurements which are out of specification. They will be used later to determine the required replacement lifters.

7   Turn the crankshaft one complete revolution and realign the timing marks. Measure the remaining valves **(see illustration)**.

Adjustment

Refer to illustrations 31.9, 31.10a and 31.10b

8   If any of the valve clearances were out of adjustment, remove the camshaft(s) from over the lifter(s) that was/were out of the specified clearance range (see Chapter 2, Part C).

9   Measure the thickness of the lifter with a micrometer **(see illustration)**. To calculate the correct thickness of a replacement shim or

31.9 Measure the thickness of each lifter head with a micrometer

lifter that will place the valve clearance within the specified value, use the following formula:

$N = T + (A - V)$

T = thickness of the old shim or lifter
A = valve clearance measured
N = thickness of the new shim or lifter
V = desired valve clearance (see this Chapter's Specifications)

10 Select a lifter with a thickness as close as possible to the valve clearance calculated. The lifters are available in 35 sizes in increments of 0.020 mm, range in size from 5.060 mm to 5.740 mm **(see illustrations)**. **Note:** *Through careful analysis of the lifter sizes needed to bring the out-of-specification valve clearance within specification, it is often possible to simply move a lifter that has to come out anyway to another location requiring a lifter of that particular size, thereby reducing the number of new lifters that must be purchased.*

11 Install the proper thickness lifter(s) in position, making sure to lubricate them with camshaft installation lube first. **Note:** *Apply*

New shim thickness   mm (in.)

Shim No.	Thickness	Shim No.	Thickness
1	2.55 (0.1004)	9	2.95 (0.1161)
2	2.60 (0.1024)	10	3.00 (0.1181)
3	2.65 (0.1043)	11	3.05 (0.1201)
4	2.70 (0.1063)	12	3.10 (0.1220)
5	2.75 (0.1083)	13	3.15 (0.1240)
6	2.80 (0.1102)	14	3.20 (0.1260)
7	2.85 (0.1122)	15	3.25 (0.1280)
8	2.90 (0.1142)	16	3.30 (0.1299)

31.10a Valve lifter thickness chart - 1997 models

the lubricant to the underside of the lifter where it contacts the valve stem, the walls of the lifter and the face of the lifter.

12 Install the camshaft(s) (see Chapter 2).

13 Recheck the valve clearances.

14 Installation of the spark plugs, valve cover, spark plug wires and boots (or ignition coils), etc. is the reverse of removal.

LIFTER NO.	THICKNESS	LIFTER NO.	THICKNESS	LIFTER NO.	THICKNESS
06	5.059 mm	30	5.300 mm	54	5.539 mm
08	5.080 mm	32	5.318 mm	56	5.560 mm
10	5.100 mm	34	5.339 mm	58	5.580 mm
12	5.120 mm	36	5.359 mm	60	5.600 mm
14	5.140 mm	38	5.379 mm	62	5.621 mm
16	5.158 mm	40	5.400 mm	64	5.638 mm
18	5.179 mm	42	5.420 mm	66	5.659 mm
20	5.199 mm	44	5.440 mm	68	5.679 mm
22	5.219 mm	46	5.461 mm	70	5.699 mm
24	5.240 mm	48	5.478 mm	72	5.720 mm
26	5.260 mm	50	5.499 mm	74	5.740 mm
28	5.280 mm	52	5.519 mm		

31.10b Valve lifter thickness chart - 1998 and later models

Notes

Chapter 2 Part A
4A-FE and 7A-FE engines

Contents

Specifications

General

Engine type	DOHC, inline four-cylinder, four valves per cylinder
Cylinder numbers (drivebelt end-to-transaxle end)	1-2-3-4
Firing order	1-3-4-2
Displacement	
4A-FE	1.6L
7A-FE	1.8L

Timing belt

Tensioner spring free length	
1.6L	35.3 mm
1.8L	31.8 mm
Timing belt deflection	5 to 6 mm

920036 1-specs HAYNES

**Cylinder location and
distributor rotation**

Camshaft

Journal diameter	
Exhaust camshaft, no. 1 journal	24.949 to 24.965 mm
All others	22.949 to 22.965 mm
Bearing oil clearance	
Standard	0.035 to 0.072 mm
Service limit	0.10 mm
Runout limit	0.04 mm

Camshaft (continued)

Lobe height
    Intake (standard)... 42.610 to 42.710 mm
    Intake service limit, minimum... 42.20 mm
    Exhaust (standard)... 41.960 to 42.060 mm
    Exhaust service limit, minimum.. 41.55mm
Camshaft thrust clearance (endplay)
    Intake camshaft
        Standard .... 0.030 to 0.085 mm
        Service limit, maximum.. 0.11 mm
    Exhaust camshaft
        Standard .... 0.35 to 0.90 mm
        Service limit, maximum.. 0.11 mm
Camshaft gear spring free length .... 17.0 to 17.6 mm
Camshaft gear backlash
    Standard.. 0.020 to 0.200 mm
    Service limit.. 0.30 mm
Valve lifter
    Diameter.. 30.966 to 30.976 mm
    Bore diameter.. 31.000 to 31.025 mm
Lifter oil clearance
    Standard.. 0.024 to 0.059 mm
    Service limit.. 0.07 mm

Oil pump

Rotor-to-body clearance
    Standard.. 0.080 to 0.180 mm
    Service limit.. 0.20 mm
Rotor tip clearance
    Standard.. 0.025 to 0.085 mm
    Service limit.. 0.35 mm
Rotor-to-cover clearance
    Standard.. 0.025 to 0.085 mm
    Service limit.. 0.10 mm

Torque specifications

Nm (unless otherwise indicated)

Intake manifold bolts.. 19
Intake manifold brace bolts
    At manifold 19
    At block 39
Intake air chamber cover 19
Exhaust manifold nuts/bolts.. 34
Exhaust manifold brace bolts 63
Crankshaft pulley-to-crankshaft bolt 118
Flywheel/driveplate bolts
    Flywheel (manual transaxle) 78
    Driveplate (automatic transaxle) 64
Idler pulley bolts... 37
Cylinder head bolts
    Step 1 29
    Step 2 .... Tighten an additional 90-degrees
    Step 3 .... Tighten an additional 90-degrees
Camshaft bearing cap bolts.. 13
Camshaft sprocket bolt... 59
Oil pump bolts... 21
Oil pick-up/strainer nuts/bolts 9.3
Oil sump bolts
    1.6L 4.9
    1.8L
        Reinforcement section-to-block 14
        Pan-to-reinforcement section................................... 4.9
Centre chassis brace bolts 60
Engine/transaxle stiffener bolts (1.6L)..................................... 22
Rear crankshaft oil seal retainer bolts 9.3

1 General information

This Part of Chapter 2 is devoted to in-vehicle repair procedures for the four-cylinder engines. Information concerning engine removal and installation and engine overhaul can be found in Part C of this Chapter.

The following repair procedures are based on the assumption that the engine is installed in the vehicle. If the engine has been removed from the vehicle and mounted on a stand, many of the steps outlined in this Part of Chapter 2 will not apply.

The four-cylinder engines covered by this chapter are designated the 4A-FE (1.6L) and the 7A-FE (1.8L). The two engines are almost identical, and incorporate dual overhead camshafts (DOHC) and four valves per cylinder.

2 Repair operations possible with the engine in the vehicle

Many major repair operations can be accomplished without removing the engine from the vehicle.

Clean the engine compartment and the exterior of the engine with some type of degreaser before any work is done. It will make the job easier and help keep dirt out of the internal areas of the engine.

Depending on the components involved, it may be helpful to remove the bonnet to improve access to the engine as repairs are performed (refer to Chapter 11 if necessary). Cover the fenders to prevent damage to the paint. Special pads are available, but an old bedspread or blanket will also work.

If vacuum, exhaust, oil or coolant leaks develop, indicating a need for gasket or seal replacement, the repairs can generally be made with the engine in the vehicle. The intake and exhaust manifold gaskets, oil sump gasket, crankshaft oil seals and cylinder head gasket are all accessible with the engine in place.

Exterior engine components, such as the intake and exhaust manifolds, the oil sump, the oil pump, the water pump, the starter motor, the alternator, the distributor and the fuel system components can be removed for repair with the engine in place, although when replacing the oil pump an engine hoist is required to support the engine from above, while the right engine mount is removed.

Since the cylinder head can be removed without pulling the engine, camshaft and valve component servicing can also be accomplished with the engine in the vehicle. Replacement of the timing belt and pulleys is also possible with the engine in the vehicle.

In extreme cases caused by a lack of necessary equipment, repair or replacement of piston rings, pistons, connecting rods and rod bearings is possible with the engine in the vehicle. However, this practice is not recommended because of the cleaning and preparation work that must be done to the components involved.

3 Top Dead Centre (TDC) for number one piston - locating

Refer to illustration 3.8

Note: *The following procedure is based on the assumption that the distributor is correctly installed. If you are trying to locate TDC to install the distributor correctly, piston position must be determined by feeling for compression at the number one spark plug hole, then aligning the ignition timing marks as described in Step 8.*

1   Top Dead Centre (TDC) is the highest point in the cylinder that each piston reaches as it travels up the cylinder bore. Each piston reaches TDC on the compression stroke and again on the exhaust stroke, but TDC generally refers to piston position on the compression stroke.

2   Positioning the piston(s) at TDC is an essential part of many procedures such as camshaft and timing belt/pulley removal and distributor removal.

3   Before beginning this procedure, be sure to place the transmission in Neutral and apply the parking brake or block the rear wheels. Also, disable the ignition system by detaching the coil wire from the centre terminal of the distributor cap and grounding it on the block with a jumper wire. Remove the spark plugs (see Chapter 1).

4   In order to bring any piston to TDC, the crankshaft must be turned using one of the methods outlined below. When looking at the timing belt end of the engine, normal crankshaft rotation is clockwise.

a)   *The preferred method is to turn the crankshaft with a socket and ratchet attached to the bolt threaded into the front of the crankshaft. Apply pressure on the bolt in a clockwise direction only. Never turn the bolt anti-clockwise.*

b)   *A remote starter switch, which may save some time, can also be used. Follow the instructions included with the switch. Once the piston is close to TDC, use a socket and ratchet as described in the previous paragraph.*

c)   *If an assistant is available to turn the ignition switch to the Start position in short bursts, you can get the piston close to TDC without a remote starter switch. Make sure your assistant is out of the vehicle, away from the ignition switch, then use a socket and ratchet as described in Paragraph a) to complete the procedure.*

5   Note the position of the terminal for the number one spark plug wire on the distributor cap. If the terminal isn't marked, follow the

3.8 Align the crankshaft drivebelt pulley notch (arrow) with the 0 (zero) on the timing plate

plug wire from the number one cylinder spark plug to the cap.

6   Use a felt-tip pen or chalk to make a mark on the distributor body directly under the number one terminal.

7   Detach the cap from the distributor and set it aside (see Chapter 1 if necessary).

8   Turn the crankshaft until the notch in the crankshaft pulley is aligned with the 0 on the timing plate located at the front of the engine **(see illustration)**.

9   Look at the distributor rotor - it should be pointing directly at the mark you made on the distributor body. If so, you are at TDC for number 1.

10   If the rotor is 180-degrees off, the number one piston is at TDC on the exhaust stroke.

11   To get the piston to TDC on the compression stroke, turn the crankshaft one complete turn (360-degrees) clockwise. The rotor should now be pointing at the mark on the distributor. When the rotor is pointing at the number one spark plug wire terminal in the distributor cap and the ignition timing marks are aligned, the number one piston is at TDC on the compression stroke. **Note:** *If it's impossible to align the ignition timing marks when the rotor is pointing at the mark on the distributor body, the timing belt may have jumped the teeth on the pulleys or may have been installed incorrectly.*

12   After the number one piston has been positioned at TDC on the compression stroke, TDC for any of the remaining pistons can be located by turning the crankshaft and following the firing order. Mark the remaining spark plug wire terminal locations on the distributor body just like you did for the number one terminal, then number the marks to correspond with the cylinder numbers. As you turn the crankshaft, the rotor will also turn. When it's pointing directly at one of the marks on the distributor, the piston for that particular cylinder is at TDC on the compression stroke.

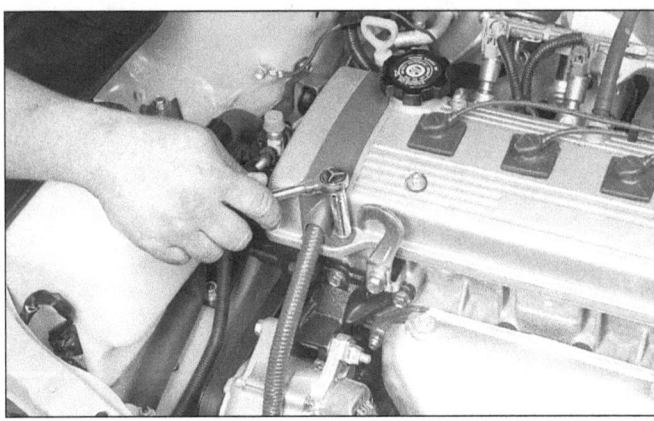

4.4 Remove the two harness-cover mounting bolts at the right end of the valve cover, allowing the wiring harness to be pulled up and clear of the valve cover

4.5 The valve cover is held in place by four nuts (arrows)

4.6 The valve cover gasket (left arrow) is a rubber O-ring-like seal - it can be reused if it hasn't hardened - make sure the spark plug tube seals (arrow) are in place before replacing the valve cover

RTV SEALANT

4.7 Apply sealant to the five points indicated by the shaded areas before installing the valve cover

4   Valve cover - removal and installation

Removal

Refer to illustrations 4.4 and 4.5

1   Disconnect the negative cable from the battery. **Caution:** *If the stereo in your vehicle is equipped with an anti-theft system, make sure you have the correct activation code before disconnecting the battery.*
2   Detach the PCV hoses from the valve cover.
3   Remove the spark plug wires from the spark plugs, handling them by the boots, not pulling on the wires.
4   Remove two bolts at the timing-belt end of the valve cover, then pull up the wiring harness cover and wiring **(see illustration)**.
5   Remove the valve cover mounting nuts, then detach the valve cover and gasket from the cylinder head **(see illustration)**. If the valve cover is stuck to the cylinder head, bump the end with a wood block and a hammer to jar it loose. If that doesn't work, try to slip a flexible putty knife between the cylinder head and valve cover to break the seal. **Cau-**

tion: *Don't prise at the valve cover-to-cylinder head joint or damage to the sealing surfaces may occur, leading to oil leaks after the valve cover is reinstalled.*

Installation

Refer to illustrations 4.6 and 4.7

6   The mating surfaces of the housing or cylinder head and valve cover must be clean when the valve cover is installed. The rubber sealing gasket can be reused unless it has high mileage and the rubber has hardened or cracked, then pull out the rubber seal and clean the mating surfaces with lacquer thinner or acetone. Install a new rubber gasket, pressing it evenly into the groove around the underside of the valve cover. If there's residue or oil on the mating surfaces when the valve cover is installed, oil leaks may develop. **Note:** *Make sure that the spark plug tube gaskets are in place on the underside of the valve cover before reinstalling it* **(see illustration)**.
7   Apply RTV sealant near the rubber plug, cam seal cap and distributor **(see illustration)**.
8   Position a new gasket on the cylinder head, then install the valve cover and nuts.

9   Tighten the nuts to the torque listed in this Chapter's Specifications in three or four equal steps.
10   Reinstall the remaining parts, run the engine and check for oil leaks.

5   Intake manifold - removal and installation

Removal

Refer to illustrations 5.3, 5.6, 5.7a and 5.7b

Note: *If the intake manifold is to be unbolted only for removal of the cylinder head, then the intake manifold can be unbolted from the cylinder head and pushed toward the firewall, without disconnecting any hoses, wires or linkage. The following procedure is for complete removal of the manifold from the vehicle.*

1   Disconnect the negative cable from the battery. **Caution:** *If the stereo in your vehicle is equipped with an anti-theft system, make sure you have the correct activation code before disconnecting the battery.*
2   Refer to Chapter 4 to remove the throttle

5.3 The various hoses should be marked to insure correct reinstallation

5.6 From underneath the vehicle, remove the bolt retaining this brace (arrow) to the intake manifold (intake manifold removed for clarity)

body and linkages, and safely relieve the fuel system pressure.

3 Label and detach the PCV and vacuum hoses connected to the intake manifold, including those from the MAP sensor, brake booster and the air conditioning idle-up actuator **(see illustration)**.

4 The intake manifold can be removed with the injectors and fuel rail in place. If the injectors are to be removed from the intake manifold, refer to Chapter 4.

5 Disconnect the electrical connector from the EGR valve, label and disconnect the vacuum hose, and unbolt the EGR pipe from the intake manifold (see Chapter 4). Set the EGR assembly aside.

6 Unbolt the upper end of the intake manifold-to-block brace **(see illustration)**.

7 Remove the ground strap and mounting nuts/bolts, then detach the manifold from the engine **(see illustrations)**. Note: *From under the vehicle, it will be necessary to unbolt the wiring harness, the lower intake manifold bolts, and the two nuts securing the pair of steel lines to the underside of the intake manifold.*

Installation

8 Clean the mating surfaces of the intake

manifold and the cylinder head mounting surface with lacquer thinner or acetone. If the gasket shows signs of leaking, have the manifold checked for warpage at an automotive machine shop and resurfaced if necessary.

9 The manifold is a two piece design, and a new gasket set may include the gasket for the air chamber cover. Unless the engine has high mileage or you suspect a vacuum leak at the mating surfaces, don't unbolt the air chamber cover. If it's necessary to replace the gasket, unbolt the cover, clean the surfaces, position the new gasket and reinstall the cover, tightening it to Specifications (see Chapter 4).

10 Install a new gasket, then position the manifold on the cylinder head and install the nuts/bolts.

11 Tighten the nuts/bolts in three or four equal steps to the torque listed in this Chapter's Specifications. Work from the centre out towards the ends to avoid warping the manifold.

12 Install the remaining parts in the reverse order of removal.

13 Before starting the engine, check the throttle linkage for smooth operation.

14 Run the engine and check for coolant and vacuum leaks.

15 Road test the vehicle and check for proper operation of all accessories, including the cruise control system, if equipped.

6 Exhaust manifold - removal and installation

Warning: *The engine must be completely cool before beginning this procedure.*

Removal

Refer to illustrations 6.2, 6.4 and 6.5

1 Disconnect the negative cable from the battery. **Caution:** *If the stereo in your vehicle is equipped with an anti theft system, make sure you have the correct activation code before disconnecting the battery.*

2 Remove the upper heat insulator from the manifold **(see illustration)**. Note: *There is also a lower heat insulator, but is attached*

5.7a From underneath the vehicle, unbolt the wiring harness (right arrow) from the water neck and cylinder head, then remove the lower manifold bolts (left arrow indicates one of the four bolts)

5.7b Remove the intake manifold bolts/nuts and remove the intake manifold

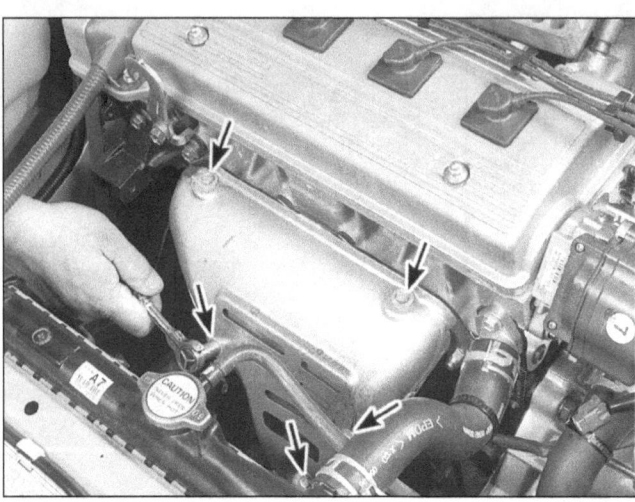

6.2 Remove the five upper heat insulator bolts (arrows)

to the manifold from underneath and does not need to be removed.

3   Apply penetrating oil to the exhaust manifold mounting nuts/bolts, and the nuts retaining the exhaust pipe to the manifold. After the nuts have soaked, remove the nuts retaining the exhaust pipe to the manifold (see Chapter 4).

4   Unbolt the exhaust manifold brace **(see illustration)**.

5   Remove the nuts/bolts and detach the manifold and gasket **(see illustration)**.

Installation

6   Use a scraper to remove all traces of old gasket material and carbon deposits from the manifold and cylinder head mating surfaces. If the gasket was leaking, have the manifold checked for warpage at an automotive machine shop and resurfaced if necessary.

7   Position a new gasket over the cylinder head studs. **Note:** The marks on the gasket should face out (away from the cylinder head) and the arrow should point toward the rear (transaxle end) of the engine.

8   Install the manifold and thread the mounting nuts/bolts into place.

9   Working from the centre out, tighten the nuts/bolts to the torque listed in this Chapter's

Specifications in three or four equal steps.

10   Reinstall the remaining parts in the reverse order of removal.

11   Run the engine and check for exhaust leaks.

7   Timing belt and sprockets - removal, inspection and installation

Removal

Refer to illustrations 7.7, 7.12, 7.13, 7.14, 7.17a, 7.17b, 7.17c and 7.19

1   Disconnect the negative cable from the battery. **Caution:** If the stereo in your vehicle is equipped with an anti-theft system, make sure you have the correct activation code before disconnecting the battery.

2   Block the rear wheels and set the parking brake.

3   Loosen the lug nuts on the right front wheel and raise the vehicle. Support the front of the vehicle securely on jackstands.

4   Remove the right front wheel and fender apron seal.

5   Remove the coolant overflow tank (see Chapter 3).

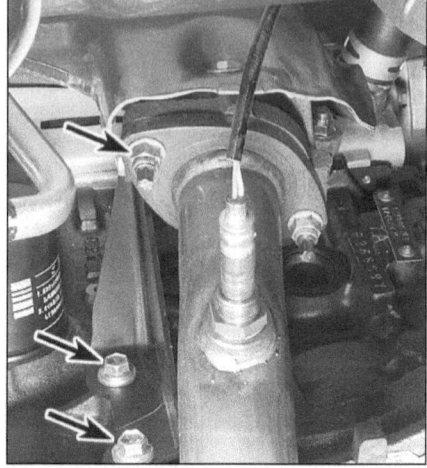

6.4 Remove the upper bolt retaining the exhaust brace to the manifold (top arrow), and loosen the two bolts retaining the brace to the block (lower arrows)

6   Remove the spark plugs and drivebelts (see Chapter 1).

7   Remove the air conditioning compressor belt idler pulley **(see illustration)**.

8   Unbolt the cruise control actuator (if equipped) and set it aside.

9   Refer to Section 4 and remove the valve cover.

10   Support the engine from underneath with a jack (use a wood block on the jack but don't place the block under the oil sump drain plug. **Note:** If you're planning on removing the oil sump in addition to the timing belt, support the engine with a hoist from above (see Chapter 2, Part C).

11   Position the number one piston at TDC on the compression stroke (see Section 3).

12   Prise the flywheel inspection cover out (see Chapter 7A) and wedge a large screwdriver into the flywheel teeth to hold the engine while an assistant loosens the crankshaft pulley bolt **(see illustration)**.

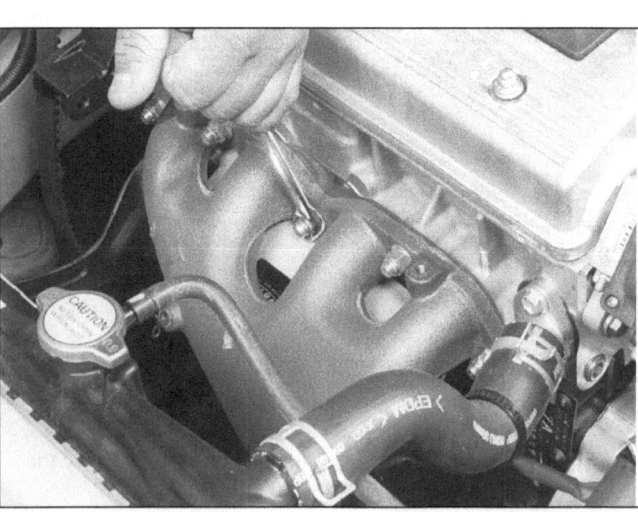

6.5 Remove the bolts and nuts and remove the exhaust manifold

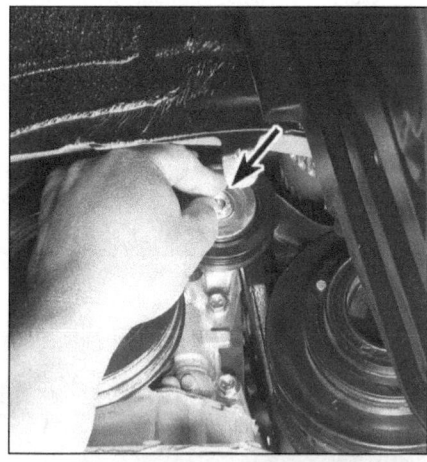

7.7 With the belts removed, unbolt and remove the air conditioning idler pulley (arrow, shown from below through the right fenderwell)

7.12 Use a lever wedged into the flywheel (arrow) to keep the engine from rotating while loosening the crankshaft pulley bolt

7.13 After removing the centre bolt, remove the crankshaft pulley

13 The crankshaft pulley should slide off the crankshaft without a puller **(see illustration)**.

14 Remove the three timing belt covers **(see illustration)**.

15 Remove the timing belt guide, noting that the cupped side faces out and the smooth side is next to the belt.

16 If you plan to re-use the timing belt, apply match marks on the sprocket and belt and an arrow indicating direction of rotation on the belt.

17 Loosen the belt tensioner adjustment bolt, prise the tensioner to the left and retighten the bolt in this position **(see illustration)**. Slip the timing belt off the sprocket. If you're removing the belt for camshaft seal replacement or cylinder head removal, it isn't necessary to detach the belt from the crankshaft sprocket, or unbolt the right engine mount. If you are removing the belt completely, remove the two nuts from the right engine mount (from underneath) and the bolt from above **(see illustrations)**.

18 If the camshaft sprocket is worn or dam-

No.3 Timing Belt Cover

No.2 Timing Belt Cover

Grommet

Crankshaft Pulley

Timing Belt

7.14 Timing belt cover details

Timing Belt Guide

No.1 Timing Belt Cover

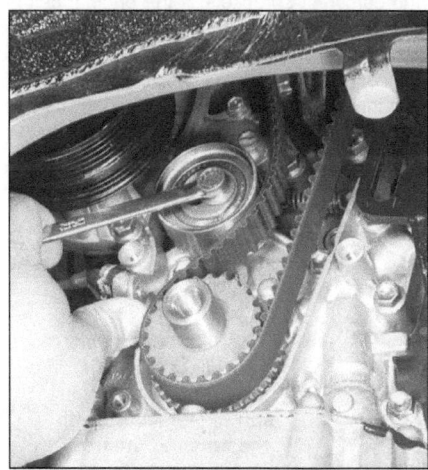

7.17a Loosen the centre bolt on the belt tensioner, prise it to the rear of the car, then retighten to keep tension off the belt for removal/installation

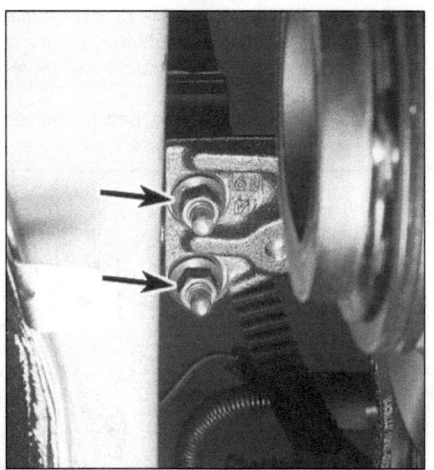

7.17b With the engine supported by a jack, remove these two nuts (arrows) from the right engine mount

7.17c Remove the upper engine mount bolt (arrow) and lower the engine, then pull the upper part of the mount up (the rubber will allow movement) until the belt can be slipped out between the upper and lower sections of the mount - this saves removing the mount completely

7.19 The crankshaft sprocket should slide off the crankshaft easily - If its stuck, protect the oil pump case with rags and prise the sprocket off with two screwdrivers. While the engine is at TDC, paint marks (arrows) on the crankshaft sprocket and oil pump case, so you can find TDC without the crankshaft pulley in place

aged, hold the front (exhaust) camshaft with a large wrench and remove the bolt, then detach the sprocket (see Section 9).

19   Slip the timing belt off the crankshaft sprocket and remove it. If the sprocket is worn or damaged, or if you need to replace the crankshaft front oil seal, remove the sprocket from the crankshaft. Before removing it, paint matching marks on the crankshaft sprocket and the oil pump case, so that you can find the TDC position without the crankshaft pulley in place **(see illustration)**.

Inspection

Refer to illustrations 7.21, 7.22, 7.23 and 7.25
Caution: *Do not bend, twist or turn the timing belt inside out. Do not allow it to come in contact with oil, coolant or fuel. Do not utilize timing belt tension to keep the camshaft or crankshaft from turning when installing the sprocket bolts. Do not turn the crankshaft or*

7.21 Check the timing belt for cracked and missing teeth

camshaft more than a few degrees (if necessary for tooth alignment) while the timing belt is removed.
20   If the timing belt broke during engine operation, the belt may have been contaminated or over-tightened. **Caution:** If the timing belt broke during engine operation, the valves may have come in contact with the pistons, causing damage. Check the valve clearance (see Chapter 1) - bent valves usually will have excessive clearance, indicating damage that will require cylinder head removal to repair.
21   If the belt teeth are cracked or missing **(see illustration)**, the distributor, oil pump or camshafts may have seized.
22   If there is noticeable wear or cracks on the face of the belt, check to see if there are nicks or burrs on the idler pulleys **(see illustration)**.
23   If there is wear or damage on only one side of the belt, check the belt guide and the alignment of the sprockets **(see illustration)**.
24   Replace the timing belt with a new one if obvious wear or damage is noted or if it is the least bit questionable. Correct any problems which contributed to belt failure prior to belt installation. **Note:** *Professionals recommend replacing the belt whenever it is removed, since belt failure can lead to expensive engine damage. The manufacturer recommends replacing the belt at 80,000-kilometer intervals.*
25   Release the bolt on the belt tensioner,

7.22 If the face of the belt is cracked or worn, check the idler pulleys for nicks or burrs

7.23 Wear on one side of the belt indicates sprocket misalignment problems

then remove the tensioner and its spring. Check the idler for free rotation and measure the spring's free length **(see illustration)**. Replace the spring if it doesn't meet Specifications. reinstall the tensioner and spring.

Installation

Refer to illustration 7.27
26   Remove all dirt, oil and grease from the timing belt area at the front of the engine.
27   Recheck the camshaft and crankshaft timing marks to be sure they are properly aligned **(see illustration)**. If the camshaft sprocket had been removed, reinstall it with the timing mark hole in the sprocket aligned with the notch in the front bearing cap of the exhaust camshaft. Make sure the crankshaft sprocket is still aligned at the TDC marks you made in Step 19.
28   Install the timing belt on the crankshaft and camshaft sprockets. If the original belt is being reinstalled, align the marks made during removal.
29   Slip the belt guide onto the crankshaft with the cupped side facing out.
30   Reinstall the lower timing belt cover

7.25 Check the idler pulley bearing for smooth operation and measure the free length of the tension spring for comparison to this Chapter's Specifications

Free length

7.27 The camshaft sprocket is at TDC when the hole in the sprocket lines up with the notch in the front bearing cap

8.2a Wrap tape around the screwdriver tip and carefully work the crankshaft front oil seal out of the bore - DO NOT nick or scratch the crankshaft in the process!

8.2b The seal may be removed more easily by carefully cutting the lip as indicated

and crankshaft pulley and recheck the TDC marks.

31 Keeping tension on the side of the belt nearest the front of the vehicle, loosen the idler pulley bolt 1/2-turn, allowing the spring to apply pressure to the idler pulley.

32 Slowly turn the crankshaft clockwise two complete revolutions (720-degrees), then tighten the idler pulley mounting bolt to the torque listed in this Chapter's Specifications. Measure the deflection of the belt on the radiator side, halfway between the camshaft and crankshaft sprockets, and compare it to this Chapter's Specifications.

33 Recheck the timing marks. With the crankshaft at TDC for number one cylinder, the hole in the camshaft sprocket must align with the timing mark **(see illustration 7.27)**. If the marks are not aligned exactly, repeat the belt installation procedure. **Caution:** *DO NOT start the engine until you're absolutely certain that the timing belt is installed correctly. Serious and costly engine damage could occur if the belt is installed out-of-time.*

34 Reinstall the remaining parts in the reverse order of removal.

35 Run the engine and check for proper operation.

8 Crankshaft front oil seal - replacement

Refer to illustrations 8.2a, 8.2b and 8.4

1 Remove the timing belt and crankshaft sprocket (see Section 7).

2 Note how far the seal is recessed in the bore, then carefully prise it out of the oil pump housing with a screwdriver or seal removal tool **(see illustration)**. Don't scratch the housing bore or damage the crankshaft in the process (if the crankshaft is damaged, the new seal will end up leaking). **Note:** *The seal may be easier to remove if the old seal lip is cut with a sharp utility knife first* **(see illustration)**.

3 Clean the bore in the housing and coat the outer edge of the new seal with engine oil or multi-purpose grease. Apply moly-base grease to the seal lip.

4 Using a socket with an outside diam-

eter slightly smaller than the outside diameter of the seal, carefully drive the new seal into place with a seal driver or large socket **(see illustration)**. Make sure it's installed squarely and driven in to the same depth as the original. If a socket isn't available, a short section of large diameter pipe will also work. Check the seal after installation to make sure the spring didn't pop out of place.

5 Reinstall the crankshaft sprocket and timing belt (see Section 7).

6 Run the engine and check for oil leaks at the front seal.

9 Camshaft oil seal - replacement

Refer to illustrations 9.2, 9.3 and 9.5

1 Refer to Section 4 and remove the valve cover, then remove the timing belt.

2 Use a large wrench to hold the exhaust camshaft at its hex portion, while removing the bolt from the camshaft sprocket **(see illustration)**, then pull off the sprocket.

3 Note how far the seal is seated in the

8.4 Gently drive the new seal into place with the spring side installed toward the engine

9.2 Use an end wrench to hold the camshaft while removing the camshaft sprocket bolt

9.3 Carefully prise the camshaft seal out of the bore - DO NOT nick or scratch the camshaft journal

9.5 The new camshaft seal can be pressed into place squarely with an appropriate-size socket and a lever working against the engine mount

10.4 Mount a dial indicator as shown to measure camshaft endplay - with the dial zeroed, prise the camshaft forward and back and read the endplay on the dial

10.5 Place the EXHAUST camshaft knock pin between the 9 o'clock and 10 o'clock position

bore, then carefully prise it out with a small screwdriver **(see illustration)**. Don't scratch the bore or damage the camshaft in the process (if the camshaft is damaged, the new seal will end up leaking).

4   Clean the bore and coat the outer edge of the new seal with engine oil or multi-purpose grease. Apply multi-purpose grease to the seal lip.

5   Using a socket with an outside diameter slightly smaller than the outside diameter of the seal, carefully drive the new seal into place with a seal installer or large socket. Make sure it's installed squarely and driven into the same depth as the original. If a socket isn't available, a short section of pipe will also work. **Note:** *There isn't much room for a hammer, so you can also prise between the engine mount and the socket to press the seal in* **(see illustration)**.

6   Reinstall the camshaft sprocket and timing belt (see Section 7). Refer to Section 4 and reinstall the valve cover.

7   Run the engine and check for oil leaks at the camshaft seal.

10 Camshafts and valve lifters - removal, inspection and installation

Note: *Before beginning this procedure, obtain two 6 x 1.0 mm bolts 16 to 20 mm long. They will be referred to as service bolts in the text.*

Removal

Refer to illustrations 10.4, 10.5, 10.6, 10.7, 10.10, 10.14a, 10.14b, 10.15, 10.16a and 10.16b

1   Remove the valve cover as described in Section 4.

2   Refer to Section 3 and place the engine on TDC for number 1 cylinder. Apply a dab of paint to the camshaft gear TDC alignment marks (the marks where the gears mesh just at the valve cover/head interface line). **Note:** *There are two sets of marks on the camshaft gears. The marks that align at TDC are for TDC reference only, the other two marks are used to align the camshafts during installation.*

3   Remove the distributor (see Chapter 5). Remove the timing belt and camshaft sprocket (see Sections 7 and 9).

4   Measure the camshaft thrust clearance (endplay) with a dial indicator **(see illustration)**. If the clearance is greater than the service limit, replace the camshaft and/or the cylinder head.

Intake camshaft

5   Position the knock pin in the EXHAUST camshaft just above the top of the cylinder head **(see illustration)**. This will position the intake camshaft lobes so the camshaft will be pushed up evenly by valve spring pressure. **Caution:** *This positioning is important to avoid damaging the cylinder head or camshaft as the camshaft is removed.*

6   Remove the two bolts and the front bearing cap from the intake camshaft **(see illustration)**.

7   Secure the intake camshaft sub-gear to the main gear by installing one of the service bolts into the threaded hole **(see illustration)**.

10.6 Remove the two bolts and the front camshaft bearing cap from the intake camshaft

10.7 Install a service bolt through the sub-gear and thread it into the main gear (arrow)

8   Following the reverse of the tightening sequence (**see Illustration 10.40**), loosen the remaining intake camshaft bearing cap bolts in 1/4-turn increments until the bolts can be removed by hand. Lift the bearing caps straight up and off.

9   Lift the camshaft straight up and out of the cylinder head.

Exhaust camshaft

10   Position the knock pin in the exhaust camshaft at approximately the 5 o'clock position (**see illustration**).

11   Remove the front (timing belt end) exhaust camshaft bearing cap bolts and detach the bearing cap and oil seal. **Caution:** *Do not prise the cap off. If it doesn't come loose easily, leave it in place without bolts.*

12   Following the reverse of the tightening sequence (**see illustration 10.30**), loosen the remaining exhaust camshaft bearing cap bolts in 1/4-turn increments until the bolts can be removed by hand. Lift off the bearing caps. **Caution:** *As the centre bearing cap bolts are being loosened, make sure the camshaft is moving up evenly. If one end or the other stops moving and the cam gets cocked, start over by reinstalling the bearing caps and resetting the knock pin. DO NOT try to prise or force the camshaft out.*

10.10 Turn the exhaust camshaft until the knock pin is pointed at about the 5 o'clock position

13   Lift the camshaft straight up and out of the cylinder head.

14   Clean the oil off the valve lifter shims, mark them with a felt-tip marker and remove the lifters, keeping the shims with their lifters (**see illustration**). Store the camshaft bearing caps, lifters and shims so they can be reinstalled without mixing them up (**see illustration**).

15   Position the intake camshaft in a vise, clamping it on the hex portion. Using a two-

10.14a Mark the lifters/shims (I for inlet, E for exhaust, and number their location) and remove them with a magnetic retrieval tool

pin spanner, rotate the sub-gear clockwise and remove the service bolt from the threaded hole, then allow the subgear to rotate back until all tension is relieved (**see illustration**).

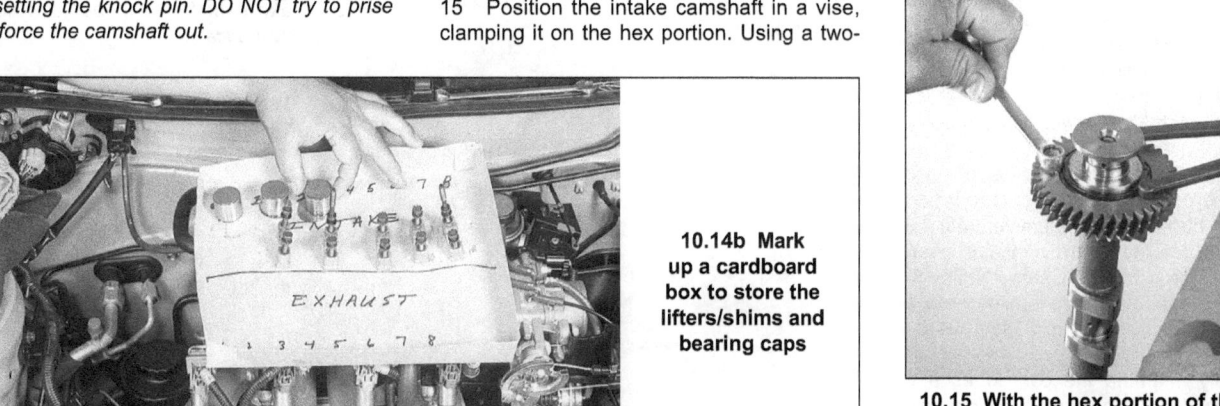

10.14b Mark up a cardboard box to store the lifters/shims and bearing caps

10.15 With the hex portion of the intake camshaft clamped in a vise, use a spanner to relieve the tension on the service bolt, remove the bolt, then release the tension on the subgear

10.16a Remove the snap-ring with a pair of snap-ring pliers

10.16b Remove the wave washer (1), the camshaft subgear (2) and the gear spring (3)

10.17 Measure the distance between the ends of the camshaft gear spring

10.18 Wipe off the oil and inspect each lifter for wear and scuffing

10.21 Measure the lobe heights on each camshaft - if any lobe height is less than the specified allowable minimum, replace that camshaft

16   Remove the sub-gear snap-ring **(see illustration)**. The wave washer, sub-gear and camshaft gear spring can now be removed from the camshaft **(see illustration)**.

Inspection

Refer to illustrations 10.17, 10.18, 10.21, 10.22, 10.23a, 10.23b and 10.24

17   Measure the free length (distance between the ends) of the camshaft gear spring **(see illustration)** and compare it to this Chapter's Specifications. If not as specified, replace the spring.
18   Inspect each lifter for scuffing and score marks **(see illustration)**.
19   Measure the outside diameter of each lifter and the corresponding lifter bore inside diameter. Subtract the lifter diameter from the lifter bore diameter to determine the oil clearance. Compare it to this Chapter's Specifications. If the oil clearance is excessive, a new cylinder head and/or new lifters will be required.
20   Visually examine the cam lobes and bearing journals for score marks, pitting, galling and evidence of overheating (blue, discoloured areas). Look for flaking away of the hardened surface layer of each lobe.
21   Using a micrometer, measure the

height of each camshaft lobe **(see illustration)**. Compare your measurements with this Chapter's Specifications. If the height for any one lobe is less than the specified minimum, replace the camshaft.
22   Using a micrometer, measure the diameter of each journal at several points **(see illustration)**. Compare your measurements with this Chapter's Specifications. If the diameter of any one journal is less than specified, replace the camshaft.

23   Check the oil clearance for each camshaft journal as follows:
a) *Clean the bearing caps and the camshaft journals with lacquer thinner or acetone.*
b) *Carefully lay the camshaft(s) in place in the cylinder head. Don't install the lifters or intake camshaft subgear and don't use any lubrication.*

10.22 Measure each journal diameter with a micrometer (if any journal measures less than the specified limit, replace the camshaft)

10.23a The camshaft bearing caps are numbered and have an arrow that should face the timing belt end of the engine

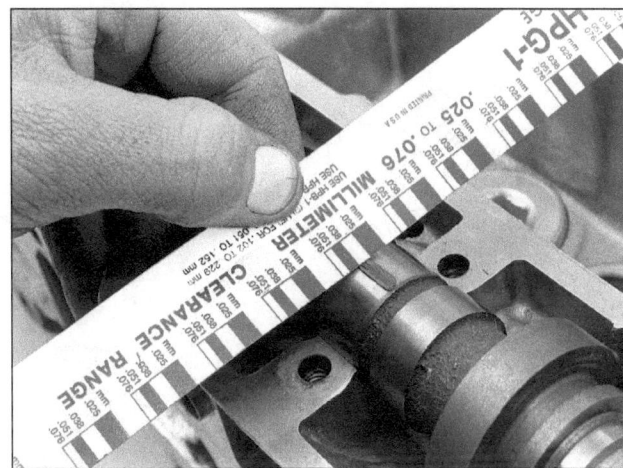

10.23b Compare the width of the crushed Plastigage to the scale on the envelope to determine the oil clearance

10.24 Position a dial indicator as shown here to measure gear backlash - hold one camshaft steady with a wrench while moving the other camshaft with another wrench

10.28 Apply sealer to the shaded areas of the front exhaust camshaft bearing cap

c) Lay a strip of Plastigage on each journal.

d) Install the bearing caps with the arrows pointing toward the front (timing belt end) of the engine (see illustration).

e) Tighten the bolts to the torque listed in this Chapter's Specifications in 1/4-turn increments. Note: Don't turn the camshaft while the Plastigage is in place.

f) Remove the bolts and detach the caps.

g) Compare the width of the crushed Plastigage (at its widest point) to the scale on the Plastigage envelope (see illustration).

h) If the clearance is greater than specified, replace the camshaft and/or cylinder head.

i) Scrape off the Plastigage with your fingernail or the edge of a credit card - don't scratch or nick the journals or bearing caps.

24 With the caps reinstalled temporarily, use a dial indicator to measure the backlash between the two camshaft gears. Hold one camshaft from turning (using a wrench on the hex portion) while measuring the movement in the other camshaft gear, and compare the results to Specifications (see illustration). If the backlash is beyond Specifications, replace both camshafts.

Installation

Refer to illustrations 10.28, 10.30, 10.37 and 10.40

Exhaust camshaft

25 Apply moly-base grease or engine assembly lube to the lifters, then install them in their original locations. Make sure the valve adjustment shims are on place on the lifters.

26 Apply moly-base grease or engine assembly lube to the camshaft lobes and bearing journals.

27 Position the exhaust camshaft in the cylinder head with the knock pin at approximately the 5 o'clock position (see illustration 10.10).

28 Apply a thin coat of RTV sealant to the outer edge of the front bearing-cap-to-cylinder-head mating surface (see illustration). Note: The cap must be installed immediately or the sealer will dry prematurely.

29 Install the bearing caps in numerical order with the arrows pointing toward the timing belt end of the engine.

30 Following the recommended tightening sequence (see illustration), tighten the bearing cap bolts in 1/4-turn increments to the torque listed in this Chapter's Specifications.

10.30 Exhaust camshaft bearing cap bolt TIGHTENING sequence

Installation Mark

Timing Mark

Installation Mark

10.37 Align the camshaft gears as shown here - use the installation marks, NOT the TDC marks

10.40 INLET camshaft bearing cap bolt tightening sequence

31   Refer to Section 9 and install a new camshaft oil seal.

Intake camshaft

32   Reassemble the intake camshaft subgear. Install the camshaft gear spring, subgear and wave washer. Secure them with the snap-ring **(see illustrations 10.16a and 10.16b)**.

33   Refer to Step 15 and install a service bolt.

34   Apply moly-base grease or engine assembly lube to the lifters, then install them in their original locations. Make sure the valve adjustment shims are in place on the lifters.

35   Apply moly-base grease or engine assembly lube to the camshaft lobes and bearing journals.

36   Rotate the EXHAUST camshaft until the knock pin is positioned between the 9 o'clock and 10 o'clock position **(see illustration 10.5)**.

37   Align the intake camshaft gear with the exhaust camshaft gear by matching up the "installation" marks on the gears **(see illustration)**. **Caution:** *There are two sets of marks. Do not use the TDC marks you applied paint to in Step 2. The camshaft installation marks are the only marks that are duplicated on both front and rear sides of the two camshaft gears.*

38   Roll the intake camshaft down into position. Turn the exhaust camshaft back and forth a little until the intake camshaft sits in the bearings evenly.

39   Install the intake camshaft bearing caps in numerical order with the arrows pointing toward the timing belt end of the engine.

40   Following the recommended sequence **(see illustration)**, tighten the bearing cap bolts in 1/4-turn increments to the torque listed in this Chapter's Specifications.

41   Remove the service bolt from the intake camshaft gear.

42   Install the timing belt pulley on the exhaust camshaft and tighten the bolt to the torque listed in this Chapter's Specifications. Prevent the camshaft from turning by holding

it with a wrench on the large hex.

43   Install the timing belt (see Section 7).

44   The remainder of installation is the reverse of the removal procedure.

11   Cylinder head - removal and installation

Note: *The engine must be completely cool before beginning this procedure.*

Removal

Refer to illustration 11.14

1   Disconnect the negative cable from the battery. **Caution:** *If the stereo in your vehicle is equipped with an anti-theft system, make sure you have the correct activation code before disconnecting the battery.*

2   Drain the coolant from the engine block and radiator (see Chapter 1).

3   Drain the engine oil and remove the oil filter (see Chapter 1).

4   Remove the throttle body, fuel injectors and fuel rail (see Chapter 4).

5   Remove the intake manifold (see Section 5).

6   Remove the exhaust manifold (see Sec-

tion 6). **Note:** *It is possible to leave the intake and exhaust manifolds attached to the cylinder head, to be removed along with the cylinder head for disassembly on the bench.*

7   Remove the timing belt and camshaft sprocket (see Sections 7 and 9).

8   Remove the camshafts and lifters (see Section 10).

9   Remove the alternator and distributor (see Chapter 5).

10   Unbolt the upper bracket of the power steering pump and set the pump aside without disconnecting the hoses.

11   Label and remove any remaining items, such as coolant fittings, tubes, cables, hoses or wires.

12   Refer to Chapter 3 and detach the water necks from each end of the cylinder head. At this point the cylinder head should be ready for removal.

13   Using an 8 mm hex-head socket bit and a breaker bar, loosen the cylinder head bolts in 1/4-turn increments until they can be removed by hand. Loosen the cylinder head bolts opposite of the recommended tightening sequence **(see illustration 11.25)** to avoid warping or cracking the cylinder head.

14   Lift the cylinder head off the engine block. If it's stuck, very carefully prise up at

11.14 If the cylinder head is stuck, prise only at the overhang, not between the mating surfaces

11.17 Remove all traces of old gasket material - the cylinder head and block mating surfaces must be perfectly clean to ensure a good gasket seal

11.22 Place the new cylinder head gasket over the dowels in the block, noting the markings for UP on the gasket

the transaxle end, beyond the gasket surface **(see illustration)**.

15   Remove all external components from the cylinder head to allow for thorough cleaning and inspection. See Chapter 2, Part C, for cylinder head servicing procedures.

Installation

Refer to illustrations 11.17, 11.22 and 11.25

16   The mating surfaces of the cylinder head and block must be perfectly clean when the cylinder head is installed.

17   Use a gasket scraper to remove all traces of carbon and old gasket material **(see illustration)**, then clean the mating surfaces with lacquer thinner or acetone. If there's oil on the mating surfaces when the cylinder head is installed, the gasket may not seal correctly and leaks could develop. When working on the block, stuff the cylinders with clean shop rags to keep out debris. Use a vacuum cleaner to remove material that falls into the cylinders.

18   Check the block and cylinder head mating surfaces for nicks, deep scratches and other damage. If damage is slight, it can be removed with a file; if it's excessive, machining may be the only alternative.

19   Use a tap of the correct size to chase the threads in the cylinder head bolt holes, then clean the holes with compressed air - make sure that nothing remains in the holes. **Warning:** *Wear eye protection when using compressed air!*

20   Mount each bolt in a vise and run a die down the threads to remove corrosion and restore the threads. Dirt, corrosion, sealant and damaged threads will affect torque readings.

21   Install the components that were removed from the cylinder head.

22   Position the new gasket over the dowel pins in the block **(see illustration)**.

23   Carefully set the cylinder head on the block without disturbing the gasket.

24   Before installing the cylinder head bolts, apply a small amount of clean engine oil to the threads and under the bolt heads.

25   Install the bolts in their original locations and tighten them finger tight. Install the shorter bolts along the intake side of the cylinder head and the longer bolts along the exhaust side. Following the recommended sequence, tighten the bolts in three steps to the torque listed in this Chapter's Specifications **(see illustration)**. Steps 2 and 3 of the tightening sequence each require the bolts to be tightened an additional 90 degrees. If you don't have an angle-torque attachment for your torque wrench, simply apply a paint mark at one edge of each cylinder head bolt and tighten the bolt until that mark is 90 degrees from where you started (Step 2). After Step 3, the marks will be 180 degrees from where they started.

26   The remaining installation steps are the reverse of removal. **Note:** *If the semi-circular rubber plug had been removed from the cylinder head (ahead of the intake camshaft), reinstall it with some RTV sealant.*

27   Check and adjust the valves as necessary (see Chapter 1).

28   Refill the cooling system, install a new oil filter and add oil to the engine (see Chapter 1).

29   Run the engine and check for leaks. Set the ignition timing (see Chapter 5) and road test the vehicle.

12   Oil sump - removal and installation

Removal

Refer to illustration 12.8

1   Disconnect the negative cable from the battery. **Caution:** *If the stereo in your vehicle is equipped with an anti-theft system, make sure you have the correct activation code before disconnecting the battery.*

2   Set the parking brake and block the rear wheels.

3   Raise the front of the vehicle and support it securely on jackstands.

4   Remove the two plastic splash shields under the engine.

5   Drain the engine oil and remove the oil filter (see Chapter 1). Remove the oil dipstick.

6   Disconnect the electrical connector to the oxygen sensor (see Chapter 6).

7   Remove the two nuts retaining the front exhaust pipe to the exhaust manifold, then the two bolts/nuts connecting the pipe to the rear of the exhaust system (see Chapter 4).

8   Remove the two front bolts of the longitu-

INTAKE SIDE

EXHAUST SIDE

11.25 Cylinder head bolt TIGHTENING sequence

12.8 Remove the front bolts of the chassis brace (arrows) - for better access for oil sump removal, you'll have to insert a large lever between the brace and the chassis to prise the brace down

12.9 Unbolt the block-to-transaxle brace on 1.6L models

dinal chassis brace and the two nuts securing the radiator-side engine mount (see illustration).

1.6L engine

Refer to illustrations 12.9 and 12.10

9   Unbolt and remove the block-to-transaxle brace (see illustration).
10   Remove the bolts and detach the oil sump. If it's stuck, prise it loose very carefully with a small screwdriver or putty knife (see illustration). Don't damage the mating surfaces of the pan and block or oil leaks could develop.

1.8L engine

Refer to illustrations 12.12, 12.13, 12.15a and 12.15b

11   The 1.8L engine uses a steel oil sump mounted to a large cast aluminum reinforcement section that stiffens the block/transaxle mounting. There is no separate engine/transaxle brace as on the 1.6L engine. **Note:** *The manufacturer uses a very tough sealant on the oil sump flange which make the steel and aluminum components difficult to separate. Take your time and use a putty knife rather than a screwdriver to break the seal.*

12   Remove the bolts and stud nuts around the perimeter of the oil sump, then carefully prise between the steel and aluminum sections to loosen the oil sump (see illustration). Be careful not to gouge the softer aluminum or distort the flange of the steel pan.
13   Remove the two bolts and two nuts retaining the oil baffle and remove the baffle (see illustration).
14   Unbolt the pick-up tube/oil strainer assembly and remove it for cleaning.
15   If necessary, remove the bolts and nuts retaining the aluminum reinforcement section to the block and transaxle (see illustrations). Carefully prise the aluminum section down

12.10 Carefully prise the oil sump away from the block - if the mating surfaces are damaged, oil leaks could develop

12.12 Remove the bolts and nuts securing the oil sump to the reinforcement section, then break its seal with a putty knife

12.13 Remove the oil baffle plate and the pick-up tube/strainer

12.15a Unbolt the six fasteners inside the area concealed by the oil sump - one is an Allen-head bolt (arrow)

12.15b To access the bolts between the reinforcement section and the transaxle (arrows), you'll need to bend the exhaust pipe down at its flex joint and prise the longitudinal chassis brace down

12.20a RTV sealant application details - 1.6L engine oil sump

without gouging the sealing surface. Six of the fasteners are inside the area originally covered by the oil sump. **Caution:** *Do not prise on the reinforcement section until you are certain all fasteners are removed. There are two Allen bolts near the right front which will require using a ball-hex wrench to remove. If you don't have this type wrench (which allows you to turn an Allen bolt from a slight angle), you will have to remove the air conditioning compressor and bracket to allow using a L-shaped Allen wrench.*

Installation

Refer to illustrations 12.20a, 12.20b and 12.20c

16   Use a scraper to remove all traces of old gasket material and sealant from the block and oil sump. Clean the mating surfaces with lacquer thinner or acetone.
17   Make sure the threaded bolt holes in the block are clean.
18   Check the oil sump flange for distortion, particularly around the bolt holes. If necessary, place the oil sump on a wood block and use a hammer to flatten and restore the gasket surface.

19   Inspect the oil pump pick-up tube assembly for cracks and a blocked strainer. On 1.6L models, if the pick-up was removed, clean it thoroughly and install it now, using a new O-ring or gasket. Tighten the nuts/bolts to the torque listed in this Chapter's Specifications.
20   Apply a 5 mm wide bead of RTV sealant to the oil sump flange (1.6L engine) or reinforcement section (1.8L engine) **(see illustrations)**. **Note:** *Installation must be completed within 5 minutes once the sealer has been applied.*
21   Carefully position the oil sump or reinforcement section on the engine block and install the bolts. Working from the centre out. Tighten the bolts to the torque listed in this Chapter's Specifications in three or four steps. On 1.8L engines, reinstall the oil baffle plate and the pick-up tube/strainer. Be sure to use a new gasket on the pick-up tube. On 1.8L engines, apply RTV to the oil sump flange and install it after the aluminum reinforcement section has been sealed and tightened to specifications.

22   The remainder of installation is the reverse of removal. Be sure to add oil and install a new oil filter. Use new gasket/seals on the front exhaust pipe.
23   Run the engine and check for oil pressure and leaks.

13   Oil pump - removal, inspection and installation

Removal

Refer to illustrations 13.3, 13.4 and 13.6

1   Remove the oil dipstick, oil sump, baffle plate (1.8L only) and the oil pick-up/strainer assembly (see Section 12).
2   Support the engine securely from above and remove the timing belt, crankshaft pulley and sprocket (see Section 7).
3   On 1996 and some 1995 models, remove the crankshaft position sensor **(see illustration)**. Unbolt and remove the oil dipstick pipe (see Chapter 3).

12.20b RTV sealant application details - 1.8L engine oil sump

12.20c RTV sealant application details - 1.8L engine aluminum reinforcement section

13.3 Remove the bolt (arrow) and withdraw the crankshaft position sensor from the oil pump body

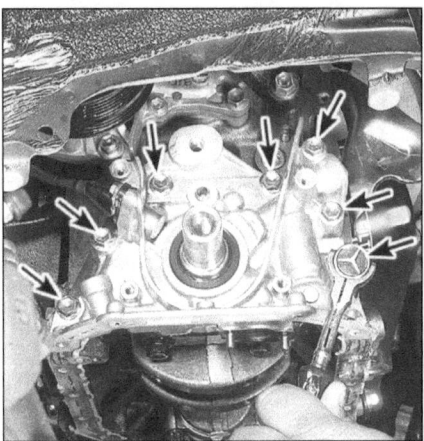

13.4 Remove the oil pump body-to-block bolts (arrows)

13.6 Oil pump components

13.10a Measure the driven rotor-to-body clearance with a feeler gauge

4   Remove the seven bolts and detach the oil pump body from the engine **(see illustration)**. You may have to prise carefully between the front main bearing cap and the pump body with a screwdriver, or tap behind the oil pump with a soft-faced hammer.

5   Use a scraper to remove all traces of sealant and old gasket material from the pump body and engine block, then clean the mating

surfaces with lacquer thinner or acetone.

6   Remove the five Torx screws and separate the pump cover from the body. Lift out the drive and driven rotors **(see illustration)**.

7   Remove the oil pressure relief valve snap-ring retainer, spring and piston. **Warning:** *The spring is tightly compressed - be careful and wear eye protection.*

Inspection

Refer to illustrations 13.10a, 13.10b and 13.10c

8   Clean all components with solvent, inspect them for wear and damage.

9   Check the oil pressure relief valve piston sliding surface and valve spring. If either the spring or the valve is damaged, they must be replaced as a set.

10   Check the driven rotor-to-body clearance, rotor-to-cover clearance and drive

rotor tip clearance with a feeler gauge **(see illustrations)** and compare the results to this Chapter's Specifications. If any clearance is excessive, replace the rotors as a set. If necessary, replace the oil pump body.

Installation

Refer to illustration 13.15

11   Lubricate the drive and driven rotors with clean engine oil and place them in the pump body with the marks facing out **(see illustration 13.10c)**.

12   Pack the pump cavity with petroleum jelly and attach the pump cover, tighten the screws to the torque listed in this Chapter's Specifications.

13   Lubricate the oil pressure relief valve piston with clean engine oil and reinstall the valve components in the pump body.

14   Place a new gasket on the engine block

13.10b Using a straightedge and feeler gauge, measure the rotor-to-cover clearance

13.10c Measure the rotor tip clearance with a feeler gauge - install the rotors with the marks facing out, against the cover (arrows)

13.15 When installing the oil pump, align the flats in the pump rotor with the flats on the crankshaft (arrows)

14.3 Mark the flywheel/driveplate and the crankshaft so they can be reassembled in the same relative positions

(the dowel pins should hold it in place).

15   Position the pump assembly against the block and install the mounting bolts. Make sure that the flats on the oil pump drive rotor aligns with the flats on the crankshaft **(see illustration)**.

16   Tighten the bolts to the torque listed in this Chapter's Specifications in three or four steps. Follow a criss-cross pattern to avoid warping the body.

17   Reinstall the remaining parts in the reverse order of removal.

18   Using a new gasket, install the oil pick-up tube/strainer assembly and baffle plate (see Section 12). Tighten the fasteners to the torque listed in this Chapter's Specifications. When reinstalling the dipstick tube, use a new O-ring on the oil-pump end.

19   Add oil, start the engine and check for oil pressure and leaks.

20   Recheck the engine oil level.

14   Flywheel/driveplate - removal and installation

Removal

Refer to illustrations 14.3 and 14.5

1   Raise the vehicle and support it securely on jackstands, then refer to Chapter 7 and remove the transaxle.

2   Remove the pressure plate and clutch disc (Chapter 8) (manual transaxle equipped vehicles).

3   Use a centre punch or paint to make alignment marks on the flywheel/driveplate and crankshaft to ensure correct alignment during reinstallation **(see illustration)**.

4   Remove the bolts that secure the flywheel/driveplate to the crankshaft. If the crankshaft turns, wedge a screwdriver in the ring gear teeth to jam the flywheel **(see illustration 7.12)**.

5   Remove the flywheel/driveplate from the crankshaft. Since the flywheel is fairly heavy, be sure to support it while removing the last bolt. Automatic transaxle equipped vehicles have spacers on both sides of the driveplate

(see illustration). Keep them with the drive-plate. **Warning:** *The ring-gear teeth may be sharp, wear gloves to protect your hands.*

Installation

6   Clean the flywheel to remove grease and oil. Inspect the surface for cracks, rivet grooves, burned areas and score marks. Light scoring can be removed with emery cloth. Check for cracked and broken ring gear teeth. Lay the flywheel on a flat surface and use a straightedge to check for warpage.

7   Clean and inspect the mating surfaces of the flywheel/driveplate and the crankshaft. If the crankshaft rear seal is leaking, replace it before reinstalling the flywheel/driveplate (see Section 15).

8   Position the flywheel/driveplate against the crankshaft. Be sure to align the marks made during removal. Note that some engines have an alignment dowel or staggered bolt holes to ensure correct installation. Before installing the bolts, apply thread-locking compound to the threads.

9   Wedge a screwdriver in the ring gear teeth to keep the flywheel/driveplate from turning and tighten the bolts to the torque listed in this Chapter's Specifications. Follow a criss-cross pattern and work up to the final torque in three or four steps.

10   The remainder of installation is the reverse of the removal procedure.

15   Rear main oil seal - replacement

Refer to illustrations 15.2, 15.5 and 15.6

1   Remove the transaxle (see Chapter 7). Remove the rear end plate.

2   The seal can be replaced without removing the oil sump or seal retainer. However, this method is not recommended because the lip of the seal is quite stiff and it's possible to cock the seal in the retainer bore or damage it during installation. If you want to take the chance, prise out the old seal with a screwdriver **(see illustration)**. Apply multi-purpose grease to the crankshaft seal journal and the lip of the new seal and carefully push the new

14.5 On vehicles equipped with a spacer plate, note the position of the locating pin (arrow)

15.2 The quick way to replace the rear crankshaft oil seal is to simply prise the old one out with a screwdriver, lubricate the crankshaft journal and the lip of the new seal with moly-base grease and push the new seal into place - the seal lip is very stiff and can be easily damaged during installation if you're not careful

seal into place. The lip is stiff so carefully work it onto the seal journal of the crankshaft with a smooth object like the end of an extension as you tap the seal into place. Don't rush it or you may damage the seal.

3   The following method is recommended

15.5 After removing the retainer assembly from the block, support it between two wooden blocks and drive out the old seal with a screwdriver and hammer

15.6 Drive the new seal into the retainer with a wood block or a section of pipe - make sure hat you don't cock the seal in the retainer bore

but requires resealing the rear of the oil sump (see Section 12) and removing the seal retainer.

4   After removing the two rearmost oil sump bolts that go into the seal retainer, break the seal between the rear of the oil sump and the bottom of the seal retainer with a putty knife. Remove the bolts, detach the seal retainer and remove all the old gasket material. remove the sealant from the top of the oil sump flange. **Note:** *Cover the open area of the oil sump with clean rags to keep debris out while bracing the pan flange.*

5   Position the seal and retainer assembly between two wood blocks on a workbench and drive the old seal out from the back side with a screwdriver **(see illustration)**.

6   Drive the new seal into the retainer with a wood block **(see illustration)** or a section of pipe slightly smaller in diameter than the outside diameter of the seal.

7   Lubricate the crankshaft seal journal and the lip of the new seal with multi-purpose grease. Position a new gasket on the engine block. Apply a bead of RTV sealant to the exposed portion of oil sump flange and particularly at the pan-to-block mating surface.

8   Slowly and carefully push the seal and retainer onto the crankshaft. The seal lip is stiff, so work it onto the crankshaft with a smooth object such as the end of an extension as you push the retainer against the block.

9   Install and tighten the retainer bolts to the torque listed in this Chapter's Specifications.

10   The remainder of installation is the reverse of removal.

16   Engine mounts - check and replacement

1   Engine mounts seldom require attention, but broken or deteriorated mounts should be replaced immediately or the added strain placed on the driveline components may cause damage or wear.

Check

Refer to illustration 16.4

2   During the check, the engine must be raised slightly to remove the weight from the mounts.

3   Raise the vehicle and support it securely on jackstands, then position a jack under the engine oil sump. Place a large wood block between the jack head and the oil sump, then carefully raise the engine just enough to take the weight off the mounts. Do not position the wood block under the drain plug. **Warning:** *DO NOT place any part of your body under the engine when it's supported only by a jack!*

4   Check the mounts **(see illustration)** to see if the rubber is cracked, hardened or separated from the metal plates. Sometimes the

rubber will split right down the centre.

5   Check for relative movement between the mount plates and the engine or frame (use a large screwdriver or lever to attempt to move the mounts). If movement is noted, lower the engine and tighten the mount fasteners.

6   Rubber preservative should be applied to the mounts to slow deterioration.

Replacement

7   Disconnect the negative battery cable from the battery, then raise the vehicle and support it securely on jackstands (if not already done). Support the engine as described in Step 3. **Caution:** *If the stereo in your vehicle is equipped with an anti-theft system, make sure you have the correct activation code before disconnecting the battery.*

8   To remove the right engine mount, remove the two nuts from underneath, one bolt from above, and the upper section will separate from the engine bracket **(see illustrations 7.17b and 7.17c)**.

9   Remove the mount-to-chassis nuts and detach the mount.

10   To remove the rear engine mount, pull the rubber plugs from the longitudinal chassis brace to access the two nuts.

11   To remove the front engine mount, remove the two nuts retaining the insulator to the longitudinal chassis brace **(see illustration 12.8)**, then the three nuts retaining the insulator to the chassis.

12   Installation is the reverse of removal. Use thread locking compound on the mount bolts/nuts and be sure to tighten them securely.

13   See Chapter 7 for transaxle mount replacement.

16.4 Typical engine mount components

Chapter 2 Part B
1ZZ-FE engines

Contents

Specifications

General

Engine type	DOHC, inline four-cylinder, four valves per cylinder
Cylinder numbers (drivebelt end-to-transaxle end)	1-2-3-4
Firing order	1-3-4-2
Displacement	
1ZZ-FE	1.8 litres (1769 cc)

Timing chain

Timing chain sprocket wear limit (minimum diameter)	
Camshaft sprocket(s) (w/chain)	
2004 and earlier	97.3 mm
2005 and later	96.8 mm
Crankshaft sprocket (w/chain)	
2004 and earlier	51.6 mm
2005 and later	51.0 mm
Timing chain stretch limit	
8 links (16 pins)	
2004 and earlier	112.6 mm
2005 and later	115.2 mm
Timing chain guide wear limit	1.0 mm
Crankshaft sprocket (w/chain)	51.6 mm

FRONT OF VEHICLE

1999 AND EARLIER

2000 AND LATER

92036-2B SPECS HAYNES

Cylinder location and distributor rotation

Camshaft and lifters

Journal diameter	
No. 1 journal..	34.449 to 34.465 mm
All others	22.949 to 22.965 mm
Bearing oil clearance	
Standard..	0.035 to 0.072 mm
Service limit (maximum).................................	1.0 mm
Runout limit..	0.03 mm
Thrust clearance (endplay)	
Standard..	0.040 to 0.095 mm
Service limit (maximum).................................	0.11 mm
Lobe height	
Inlet camshaft	
Standard	44.333 to 44.433 mm
Service limit (minimum)	44.18 mm
Exhaust camshaft	
Standard	43.761 to 43.861 mm
Service limit (minimum)	43.61 mm
Valve lifter	
Diameter...	30.966 to 30.976 mm
Bore diameter...	31.000 to 31.025 mm
Lifter oil clearance	
Standard..	0.024 to 0.059 mm
Service limit..	0.1 mm

Oil pump

Rotor-to-body clearance	
2002 and earlier	
Standard	0.260 to 0.325 mm
Service limit	0.300 mm
2003 and later	96.8 mm
Standard	0.259 to 0.325 mm
Service limit	0.325 mm
Rotor tip clearance	
2002 and earlier	
Standard	0.040 to 0.160 mm
Service limit	0.35 mm
2003 and later	96.8 mm
Standard	0.040 to 0.160 mm
Service limit	0.350 mm
Rotor side clearance	
2002 and earlier	
Standard	0.025 to 0.071 mm
Service limit	0.15 mm
2003 and later	96.8 mm
Standard	0.254 to 0.0711 mm
Service limit	0.0711 mm

Torque specifications

	Nm (unless otherwise indicated)
Camshaft bearing cap bolts	
Journal No.1	23
All others	13
Camshaft sprocket bolts	
1998 and earlier	44
1999 and later	54
Crankshaft pulley/vibration damper bolt	138
Cylinder head bolts	
Step 1	25
Step 2	49
Step 3	Tighten an additional 90-degrees
Drivebelt tensioner	
Bolt...	69
Nut...	29
Engine mounts	
Passenger's side mount	
Mount-to-frame bolts......................................	54
Mount bracket-to engine mount bracket nuts/bolts....................	54

Torque specifications

Nm (unless otherwise indicated)

Engine mounts	
Driver's side mount	
Mount-to-frame bolts...	60
Mount through-bolt...	60
Mount bracket (manual transaxle)...	20
Front and rear mounts	
Mount-to-frame bolts...	60
Mount through-bolt	
2002 and earlier models	60
2003 and 2004 models	89
2005 and later models	66
Engine mount bracket-to timing chain cover bolts............................	48
Exhaust manifold nuts/bolts...	37
Exhaust manifold brace bolts..	50
Exhaust manifold heat shield bolts..	12
Exhaust pipe-to-exhaust manifold bolts.......................................	63
Flywheel/driveplate bolts	
Manual transaxle	
Step 1	49
Step 2	Tighten an additional 90-degrees
Automatic transaxle..	86
Inlet manifold nuts/bracket bolts..	18
Oil pump bolts	
Pump cover-to-body screws..	9.9
Relief valve plug..	37
Oil pump-to-engine block	9
Oil pick-up/strainer nuts/bolts...	9
Oil sump bolts...	9
Timing chain guide bolts (stationary)..	9
Timing chain tensioner pivot arm bolt.......................................	18
Timing chain cover bolts **(see illustrations 7.14a and 7.14b)**	
10 mm head	9.5
12 mm head	18
Timing chain tensioner nuts/bolts	9
Valve cover..	9.5
Water pump mounting bolts	
10 mm head	9.5
12 mm head	18

1 General information

This Part of Chapter 2 is devoted to in-vehicle repair procedures for the 1.8L four-cylinder engine with variable valve timing. Information concerning engine removal and overhaul or replacement can be found in Chapter 2, Part C.

The following repair procedures are based on the assumption that the engine is installed in the vehicle. If the engine has been removed from the vehicle and mounted on a stand, many of the steps outlined in this Part of Chapter 2 will not apply.

The four-cylinder engine covered by this Chapter is designated 1ZZ-FE (1.8L). It incorporates an aluminum cylinder block with a bedplate to strengthen the lower half of the block. The camshafts are driven from a single timing chain off the crankshaft, and all 2000 and later models are equipped with Variable Valve Timing (VVT) on the inlet camshaft to increase horsepower and decrease emissions.

2 Repair operations possible with the engine in the vehicle

Many major repair operations can be accomplished without removing the engine from the vehicle.

Clean the engine compartment and the exterior of the engine with some type of degreaser before any work is done. It will make the job easier and help keep dirt out of the internal areas of the engine.

Depending on the components involved, it may be helpful to remove the bonnet to improve access to the engine as repairs are performed (refer to Chapter 11 if necessary). Cover the fenders to prevent damage to the paint. Special pads are available, but an old bedspread or blanket will also work.

If vacuum, exhaust, oil or coolant leaks develop, indicating a need for gasket or seal replacement, the repairs can generally be made with the engine in the vehicle. The inlet and exhaust manifold gaskets, oil sump gasket, crankshaft oil seals and cylinder head gasket are all accessible with the engine in place.

Exterior engine components, such as the inlet and exhaust manifolds, the oil sump, the oil pump, the water pump, the starter motor, the alternator and the fuel system components can be removed for repair with the engine in place.

Since the cylinder head can be removed without pulling the engine, camshaft and valve component servicing can also be accomplished with the engine in the vehicle. Replacement of the timing chain and sprockets is also possible with the engine in the vehicle.

In extreme cases caused by a lack of necessary equipment, repair or replacement of piston rings, pistons, connecting rods and rod bearings is possible with the engine in the vehicle. However, this practice is not recommended because of the cleaning and preparation work that must be done to the components involved.

3 Top Dead Centre (TDC) for number one piston - locating

Refer to illustrations 3.5 and 3.8

1 Top Dead Centre (TDC) is the highest point in the cylinder that each piston reaches

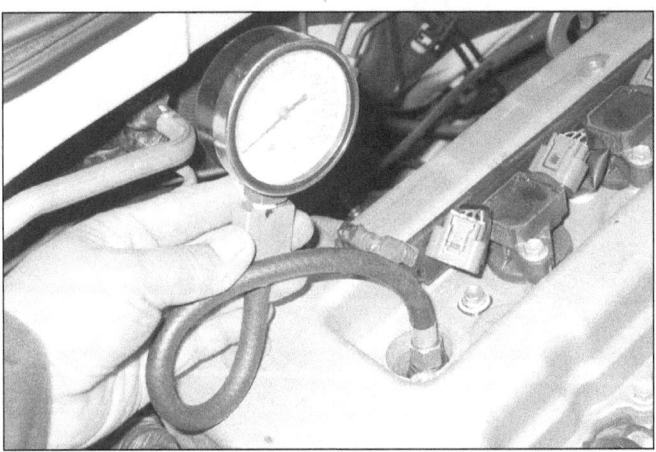

3.5 A compression gauge can be used in the number one plug hole to assist in finding TDC

3.8 Align the groove in the damper with the "0" mark on the front timing chain cover

as it travels up the cylinder bore. Each piston reaches TDC on the compression stroke and again on the exhaust stroke, but TDC generally refers to piston position on the compression stroke.

2   Positioning the piston(s) at TDC is an essential part of many procedures such as valve timing, camshaft and timing chain/sprocket removal.

3   Before beginning this procedure, be sure to place the transmission in Neutral and apply the parking brake or block the rear wheels. Also, disable the ignition system by disconnecting the primary electrical connectors at the ignition coils and remove the spark plugs (see Chapter 1).

4   In order to bring any piston to TDC, the crankshaft must be turned using one of the methods outlined below. When looking at the front of the engine, normal crankshaft rotation is clockwise.

a) *The preferred method is to turn the crankshaft with a socket and ratchet attached to the bolt threaded into the front of the crankshaft. Turn the bolt in a clockwise direction only.*

b) *A remote starter switch, which may save some time, can also be used. Follow the instructions included with the switch.*

Once the piston is close to TDC, use a socket and ratchet as described in the previous paragraph.

c) *If an assistant is available to turn the ignition switch to the Start position in short bursts, you can get the piston close to TDC without a remote starter switch. Make sure your assistant is out of the vehicle, away from the ignition switch, then use a socket and ratchet as described in Paragraph (a) to complete the procedure.*

5   Install a compression gauge in the number one spark plug hole **(see illustration)**. It should be a gauge with a screw-in fitting and a hose at least 15 cm long.

6   Rotate the crankshaft using one of the methods described above while observing for pressure on the compression gauge. The moment the gauge shows pressure indicates that the number one cylinder has begun the compression stroke.

7   Once the compression stroke has begun, TDC for the compression stroke is reached by bringing the piston to the top of the cylinder.

8   Continue turning the crankshaft until the notch in the crankshaft damper is aligned with the "TDC" or the "0" mark on the timing chain cover **(see illustration)**. At this point, the

number one cylinder is at TDC on the compression stroke. If the marks are aligned but there was no compression, the piston was on the exhaust stroke; continue rotating the crankshaft 360-degrees (1-turn). **Note:** *If a compression gauge is not available, you can simply place a blunt object over the spark plug hole and listen for compression as the engine is rotated. Once compression at the No.1 spark plug hole is noted the remainder of the Step is the same.*

9   After the number one piston has been positioned at TDC on the compression stroke, TDC for any of the remaining cylinders can be located by turning the crankshaft 180 degrees and following the firing order (refer to the Specifications). Rotating the engine 180 degrees past TDC #1 will put the engine at TDC compression for cylinder #3.

---

4   Valve cover - removal and installation

Removal

Refer to illustrations 4.2a, 4.2b and 4.6

1   Disconnect the cable from the negative terminal of the battery. **Caution:** *If the stereo*

4.2a On 1999 and earlier models, remove the fuel injector wiring harness cover - arrows indicate the fasteners which secure the cover to the valve cover and the inlet manifold

4.2b On 2000 and later models, remove the engine cover - upper arrows indicate plastic retaining clips, lower arrows indicate two retaining nuts

4.6 Valve cover fastener locations

4.7 The valve cover gasket and the spark plug tube seals are incorporated into a single rubber O-ring-like seal (arrow) - press the gasket evenly into the grooves around the underside of the valve cover and the spark plug openings

in your vehicle is equipped with an anti-theft system, make sure you have the correct activation code before disconnecting the battery.

2   Remove the engine cover or the fuel injector wire harness cover (see illustrations).

3   On 1999 and earlier models, remove the spark plug wires from the spark plugs and position them aside. Handle the spark plug wires by the boots only - do not pull on the wires.

4   On 2000 and later models, disconnect the electrical connectors from the ignition coils, remove the nuts securing the wiring harness to the valve cover and position the ignition coil wiring harness aside. Then remove the ignition coil pack from each of the spark plugs (see Chapter 5).

5   Detach the PCV hoses from the valve cover.

6   Remove the valve cover mounting nuts, then detach the valve cover and gasket from the cylinder head (see illustration). If the valve cover is stuck to the cylinder head, bump the end with a wood block and a hammer to jar it loose. If that doesn't work, try to slip a flexible putty knife between the cylinder head and valve cover to break the seal. **Caution:** *Don't prise at the valve cover-to-cylinder head joint or damage to the sealing surfaces may occur, leading to oil leaks after the valve cover is reinstalled.*

Installation

Refer to illustrations 4.7 and 4.8

7   Remove the valve cover gasket from the valve cover and clean the mating surfaces with lacquer thinner or acetone. Install a new rubber gasket, pressing it evenly into the grooves around the underside of the valve cover. **Note:** *Make sure the spark plug tube seals are in place on the underside of the valve cover before reinstalling it (see illustration). The mating surfaces of the timing chain cover, the cylinder head and valve cover must be perfectly clean when the valve cover is installed. If there's residue or oil on the mating*

ADD SEALANT

4.8 Apply sealant at the timing chain cover-to-cylinder head joint before installing the valve cover

surfaces when the valve cover is installed, oil leaks may develop.

8   Apply RTV sealant at the timing chain cover-to-cylinder head joint, then install the valve cover and fasteners (see illustration).

9   Tighten the nuts/bolts to the torque listed in this Chapter's Specifications in three or four equal steps.

10   Reinstall the remaining parts, run the engine and check for oil leaks.

5   Variable Valve Timing (VVT) system - description and component check

1   The VVT system was introduced on all 2000 and later models. The differences between the 1999 and earlier 1.8L engines and the 2000 and later models is strictly in the VVT system components and operation of the valve train. The engine short block, oiling and cooling systems are identical, as are all attached components.

2   The VVT system varies inlet camshaft timing by directing oil pressure to advance or retard the inlet camshaft sprocket/actuator assembly. Changing the inlet camshaft timing

during certain engine conditions increases engine power output, fuel economy and reduces emissions.

3   System components include the Powertrain Control Module (PCM), the VVT oil control valve (OCV), the VVT oil control valve filter and the inlet camshaft sprocket/actuator assembly.

4   The PCM uses inputs from the following sensors to turn the oil control valve ON or OFF:

a) *Vehicle Speed Sensor (VSS)*
b) *Throttle Position Sensor (TPS)*
c) *Mass Air Flow (MAF) sensor*
d) *Engine Coolant Temperature (ECT) sensor*

5   Once the VVT oil control valve is actuated by the PCM it directs the specified amount of oil pressure from the engine to advance or retard the inlet camshaft sprocket/actuator assembly.

6   The inlet camshaft sprocket/actuator assembly is equipped with an inner hub that is attached to the camshaft. The inner hub consists of a series of fixed vanes that use oil pressure as a wedge against the vanes to rotate the camshaft. The higher the oil pressure (or flow) the more the actuator assembly

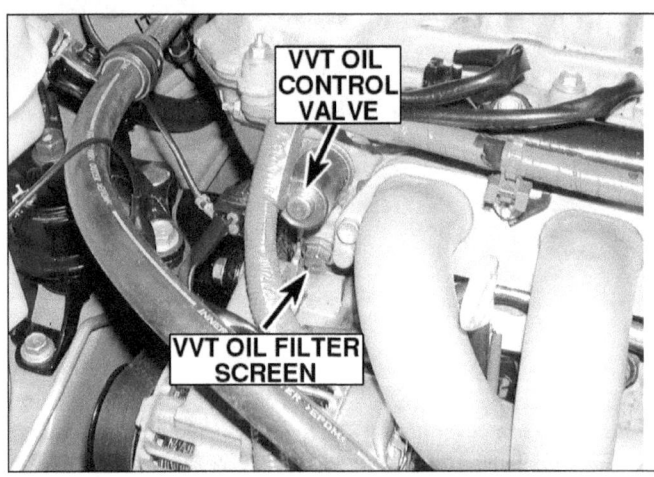

5.9a The Variable Valve Timing (VVT) oil control valve and filter are located at the front of the cylinder head

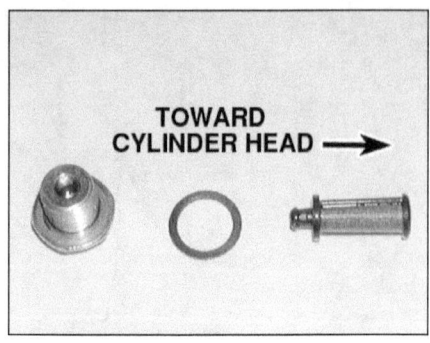

5.9b Whenever problems are suspected in the VVT system, check the oil control valve filter for clogging - note that the big end of the filter must be installed in the direction shown

will rotate, thereby advancing or retarding the camshaft.

7   When oil is applied to the advance side of the vanes, the actuator can advance the camshaft up to 21 degrees in a clockwise direction. When oil is applied to the retard side of the vanes, the actuator will start to rotate the camshaft counterclockwise back to 0 degrees which is the normal position of the actuator during engine operation under no load or at idle. The PCM can also send a signal to the oil control valve to stop oil flow to both (advance and retard) passages to hold camshaft advance in its current position.

8   Under light engine loads, the VVT system will retard the camshaft timing to decrease valve overlap and stabilize engine output. Under medium engine loads, the VVT system will advance the camshaft timing to increase valve overlap, thereby increasing fuel economy and decreasing exhaust emissions. Under heavy engine loads at low RPM, the VVT system will advance the camshaft timing to help close the inlet valve faster, which improves low to midrange torque. Under heavy engine loads at high RPM, the VVT system will retard the camshaft timing to slow the closing of the inlet valve to improve engine horsepower.

5.10 Measure the resistance between the terminals of the VVT oil control valve

Component checks

VVT oil control valve and filter

Refer to illustrations 5.9a, 5.9b, 5.10 and 5.11

Note 1: *A problem in the VVT oil control valve circuit will set a diagnostic trouble code and turn on the Check Engine light on the dash. Refer to Chapter 6 for accessing trouble codes.*

Note 2: *Most problems in the VVT system are with the oil control valve and its filter. Regular engine oil and filter changes are necessary for trouble-free operation of the valve.*

Note 3: *Some checks and inspections of the VVT system require removal of the valve cover, the inlet camshaft sprocket/actuator assembly and the inlet camshaft.*

9   The first check of the VVT system components begins with removing the oil control valve filter from the cylinder head and check the filter/O-ring for clogging **(see illustrations)**. Clean and reinstall with a new O-ring. A clogged filter screen is often the cause of system problems.

10   The second and third check of the VVT system involve checking the operation of the oil control valve. Disconnect the electrical connector from the oil control valve and measure the resistance between the terminals of the control valve **(see illustration)**. There should be 6.9 to 7.9 ohms; if not, replace the VVT oil control valve.

11   If the resistance figures check out OK,

remove the oil control valve from the cylinder head and check the operation of the control valve plunger. Using a pair of fused jumper wires, apply battery voltage to terminal No. 1 on the control valve, then apply earth to terminal No. 2 on the oil control valve. With battery voltage applied to the oil control valve, check for free movement of the plunger **(see illustration)**. The plunger should move out when voltage is applied and move back inward when voltage is not applied. If the oil control valve does not operate as described, replace the VVT oil control valve. Always use a new O-ring when reinstalling the control valve.

VVT camshaft sprocket/actuator assembly

Refer to illustrations 5.13 and 5.15

12   The fourth and final check of the VVT system requires removing the valve cover, the inlet camshaft and the camshaft sprocket/actuator assembly from the engine. Refer to Section 8 and perform Steps 1 through 10, removing the inlet camshaft and sprocket from the engine only. Do not remove the exhaust camshaft or sprocket from the engine.

13   Clean the snout of the inlet camshaft with lacquer thinner or acetone to remove all traces of oil from the front journals and the VVT oil control orifices. Apply vinyl tape over all the oil control orifices at the front of the camshaft, except the advance side oil port

5.11 The oil control valve plunger (A) can be seen through the slots in the housing - the plunger should move outward when voltage is applied and inward when voltage is released

5.13 To test the actuator assembly, it will be necessary to block off all of the oil control orifices except the advance side port

5.15 With air pressure applied to the advance side oil port, try to rotate the actuator in the direction shown

6.4 You'll need an air hose adapter this long to reach down into the spark plug tubes - they're commonly available from auto parts stores

(see illustration). Do not apply tape over the front of the camshaft were the sprocket fits.

14   Install the inlet camshaft sprocket/actuator assembly onto the inlet camshaft and tighten the bolt to 54 Nm. Check that the actuator assembly will not rotate from the locked position. The locked position is a "neutral position" in which the actuator is placed during idle and no load conditions or when the VVT system is not activated by the PCM.

15   Apply 96 kPa of air pressure to the advance side oil port and try to rotate the actuator assembly by hand (see illustration). The actuator should rotate approximately 30 degrees in a counterclockwise direction from the locked position. Also check that it rotates freely with no obvious binding. **Note:** *It is critical to have an airtight seal between the air gun nozzle and the advance oil port hole to accomplish this task, as the lock pin in the actuator may not be forced out of its locating hole. If leakage at the air gun nozzle occurs, it may be necessary to apply a greater amount of air pressure to the advance side oil port in order to force the lock pin from the locating hole.*

16   If the actuator does not rotate freely as described, replace the inlet camshaft sprocket/actuator assembly.

17   Reassembly is the reverse of removal.

6   Valve springs, retainers and seals - replacement

Refer to illustrations 6.4, 6.8a, 6.8b, 6.10, 6.15a, 6.15b and 6.17

Note: *Broken valve springs and defective valve stem seals can be replaced without removing the cylinder head. Two special tools and a compressed air source are normally required to perform this operation, so read through this Section carefully. The universal shaft-type valve spring compressor required for the tight valve spring pockets of this vehicle may not be available at all tool rental yards, so check on the availability before beginning the job.*

1   Remove the valve cover (see Section 4). Refer to Section 7 and remove the timing chain, then refer to Section 8 and remove the camshafts and lifters from the cylinder head.

2   Remove the spark plug from the cylinder that has the defective component. If all of the valve stem seals are being replaced, all of the spark plugs should be removed.

3   Turn the crankshaft until the piston in the affected cylinder is at top dead centre (TDC) on the compression stroke (see Section 3 for instructions). If you're replacing all of the valve stem seals, begin with cylinder number one

and work on the valves for one cylinder at a time. Move from cylinder-to-cylinder following the firing order sequence (see the Specifications listed at the beginning of this Chapter).

4   Thread an adapter into the spark plug hole (see illustration) and connect an air hose from a compressed air source to it. Most auto parts stores can supply the air hose adapter. **Note:** *Many cylinder compression gauges utilize a screw-in fitting that may work with your air hose quick-disconnect fitting.*

5   Apply compressed air to the cylinder. The valves should be held in place by the air pressure. **Warning:** *If the cylinder isn't exactly at TDC, air pressure may force the piston down, causing the engine to quickly rotate. DO NOT leave a wrench on the crankshaft drive sprocket bolt or you may be injured by the tool.*

6   Stuff shop rags into the cylinder head holes around the valves to prevent parts and tools from falling into the engine.

7   Using a socket and a hammer, gently tap on the top of each valve spring retainer several times. This will break the bond between the valve keepers and the spring retainer and allow the keepers to separate from the valve spring retainer as the valve spring is compressed.

8   Use a valve spring compressor to compress the spring, then remove the keepers with small needle-nose pliers or a magnet (see illustrations). **Note:** *Several different types of tools are available for compressing*

6.8a Compress the valve spring enough to release the keepers . . .

6.8b . . . and lift them out with a magnet or needle-nose pliers

6.10 A pair of pliers will be required to remove the valve seal from the valve guide

6.15a Valve seal installation details

the valve springs with the head in place. Be sure to purchase or rent the "import type" that bolts to the top of the cylinder head. This type uses a support bar across the cylinder head for leverage as the valve spring is compressed. The lack of clearance surrounding the valve springs on these engines prohibits typical types of valve spring compressors from being used.

9   Remove the valve spring and retainer.
Note: *If air pressure fails to retain the valve in the closed position during this operation, the valve face or seat may be damaged. If so, the cylinder head will have to be removed for repair.*

10   Remove the old valve stem seals, noting differences between the inlet and exhaust seals **(see illustration)**.

11   Wrap a rubber band or tape around the top of the valve stem so the valve won't fall into the combustion chamber, then release the air pressure.

12   Inspect the valve stem for damage. Rotate the valve in the guide and check the end for eccentric movement, which would indicate that the valve is bent.

13   Move the valve up-and-down in the guide and make sure it doesn't bind. If the valve stem binds, either the valve is bent or

the guide is damaged. In either case, the head will have to be removed for repair.

14   Reapply air pressure to the cylinder to retain the valve in the closed position, then remove the tape or rubber band from the valve stem.

15   Lubricate the valve stem with engine oil and install a new seal on the valve guide **(see illustrations)**.

16   Install the valve spring and the spring retainer in position over the valve.

17   Compress the valve spring and carefully position the keepers in the groove. Apply a small dab of grease to the inside of each keeper to hold it in place **(see illustration)**.

18   Remove the pressure from the spring tool and make sure the keepers are seated.

19   Disconnect the air hose and remove the adapter from the spark plug hole.

20   Install the camshaft, lifters, timing chain and the valve cover by referring to the appropriate Sections.

21   Install the spark plug(s) and the spark plug wires (on 1999 and earlier models) or the ignition coils (on 2000 and later models).

22   Start and run the engine, then check for oil leaks and unusual sounds coming from the valve cover area.

7   Timing chain and sprockets - removal, inspection and installation

Note: *Special tools are required for this procedure. Read through the entire procedure and acquire the necessary tools and equipment before beginning work.*

Removal

Refer to illustrations 7.7, 7.9, 7.11, 7.13, 7.14a, 7.14b, 7.14c, 7.15, 7.16 and 7.19

1   Detach the cable from the negative terminal of the battery. **Caution:** *On models equipped with the Theftlock audio system, be sure the lockout feature is turned off before performing any procedure which requires disconnecting the battery (see the front of this manual).*

2   Remove the drivebelt (see Chapter 1) and the alternator (see Chapter 5).

3   Remove the windscreen washer reservoir and the valve cover (see Section 4).

4   With the parking brake applied and the shifter in Park (automatic) or in gear (manual), loosen the lug nuts from the right front wheel,

6.15b Using a deep socket and hammer, gently tap the new seals onto the valve guide only until seated

6.17 Apply a small dab of grease to each keeper as shown here before installation - it will hold them in place on the valve stem as the spring is released

7.7 Verify the engine is at TDC by observing the position of the camshaft sprocket marks (upper arrows) - they must be in a straight line and parallel with the top of the timing chain cover (lower arrow)

7.9 If an engine support fixture is not available, the engine can be supported from below using a floor jack and a block of wood

then raise the front of the vehicle and support it securely on jackstands. Remove the right front wheel and the right splash shield from the wheelwell.

5   Drain the cooling system (see Chapter 1).

6   While the coolant is draining, refer to Chapter 10 and remove the power steering pump from the engine without disconnecting the fluid lines. Tie the power steering pump to the body with a piece of wire and position it out of the way.

7   Position the number one piston at TDC on the compression stroke (see Section 3). Visually confirm the engine is at TDC on the compression stroke by verifying that the timing mark on the crankshaft pulley/vibration damper is aligned with the "0" mark on the timing chain cover and the camshaft sprocket marks are aligned and parallel with the top of the timing chain cover **(see illustration 3.8 and the accompanying illustration)**. **Note:** *There are two sets of marks on the camshaft sprockets. The marks that align at TDC are for TDC reference only; the other two marks are used to align the sprockets with the timing chain during installation.*

8   Remove the crankshaft pulley/vibration damper, being careful not to rotate the engine from TDC (see Section 12). If the engine rotates off TDC during this step, reposition the engine back to TDC before proceeding. The engine should be left at TDC for the No. 1 piston during this entire procedure.

9   Support the engine from above, using an engine support fixture (available at rental yards), or from below using a floor jack. Use a wood block between the floor jack and the engine to prevent damage **(see illustration)**.

10   Remove the passenger side engine mount (see Section 18).

11   Remove the drivebelt tensioner, the engine mount bracket and the crankshaft position sensor from the timing chain cover **(see illustration)**. Also remove the bolt securing the crankshaft position sensor wiring harness to the timing chain cover.

12   Remove the water pump (see Chapter 3).

13   Remove the timing chain tensioner from the rear side of the timing chain cover **(see illustration)**.

7.11 Remove the drivebelt tensioner, the engine mount bracket and the crankshaft position sensor from the timing chain cover - mounting bolt locations are indicated by arrows

14   Remove the timing chain cover fasteners and prise the cover off the engine **(see illustrations)**.

7.13 Timing chain tensioner mounting nuts (arrows)

7.14a Timing chain cover upper fasteners - this stud (A) will have to be removed with a torx bit and tightened to 9.0 Nm during installation

7.14b Timing chain cover lower fasteners - make a note of the
fastener sizes, locations and lengths as your removing them as
they must be installed back in the original position

7.14c Prise the timing chain cover off by the casting protrusion

7.15 Slide the crankshaft position sensor
reluctor ring off the crankshaft - note the
"F" mark (arrow) on the front (it must be
facing outward upon installation)

**7.16 Timing chain
guide mounting
details**

A   *Pivot bolt*
B   *Tensioner pivot
arm/chain guide*
C   *Stationary chain
guide mounting
bolts*
D   *Stationary chain
guide*

15   Slide the crankshaft position sensor
reluctor ring off the crankshaft (see illustration).
16   Remove the timing chain tensioner pivot
arm/chain guide (see illustration).
17   Lift the timing chain off the camshaft
sprockets and remove the timing chain and

the crankshaft sprocket as an assembly from
the engine. The crankshaft sprocket should
slip off the crankshaft by hand. If not, use several flat bladed screwdrivers to evenly prise
the sprocket off the crankshaft. **Note:** *If you
intend to reuse the timing chain, use white
paint or chalk to make a mark indicating the
front of the chain. If a used timing chain is
reinstalled with the wear pattern in the opposite direction noise and increased wear may
occur.*

18   Remove the stationary timing chain
guide (see illustration 7.16).
19   To remove the camshaft sprockets,
loosen the bolts while holding the lug on the
camshaft with a wrench (see illustration).
Note the identification marks on the camshaft
sprockets before removal, then remove the
bolts. Pull on the sprockets by hand until they
slip off the dowels. If necessary, use a small
puller, with the legs inserted in the relief holes,
to pull the sprockets off. **Note 1:** *All 2000 and*

7.19 Hold the lug on the camshaft with a wrench to keep it from
rotating as the sprocket bolts are loosened - 2000 and later
models are equipped with a variable valve timing actuator on the
inlet camshaft sprocket - loosen the centre bolt (arrow) securing
the sprocket to the camshaft only

7.20a Timing chain stretch is measured by checking the length of
the chain between 8 links (16 pins) at 3 or more places (selected
randomly) around the chain - if chain stretch exceeds the
specifications between any 8 links, the chain must be replaced

7.20b Wrap the chain around each of the timing sprockets and measure the diameter of the sprockets across the chain rollers - if the measurement exceeds the minimum sprocket diameter, the chain and the timing sprockets must be replaced

7.21 Timing chain guide wear is measured from the top of the chain contact surface to the bottom of the wear grooves

later models are equipped with variable valve timing, which consists of an actuator assembly attached to the inlet camshaft sprocket. When removing the inlet camshaft sprocket on these models only loosen and remove the centre bolt, which fastens the sprocket to the camshaft. Do not loosen the outer four bolts that secure the actuator to the sprocket.

Note 2: *On 1999 and earlier models are not equipped with variable valve timing and have two very similar looking camshaft sprockets. On these models, the camshaft sprockets are marked "EX" for exhaust and "IN" for inlet. When looking at the engine from the front of the vehicle, the forward facing cam is the inlet camshaft and the cam nearest the firewall is the exhaust camshaft. It is very important that the sprockets are returned to their original location during installation.*

Inspection

Refer to illustrations 7.20a, 7.20b and 7.21

20   Visually inspect all parts for wear and damage. Check the timing chain for loose pins, cracks, worn rollers and side plates. Check the sprockets for hook-shaped, chipped and broken teeth. Also check the timing chain for stretching and the diameter of the timing sprockets for wear with the chain assembled on the sprockets **(see illustrations)**. Be sure to measure across the chain rollers when checking the sprocket diameter and to measure chain stretch at three or more places around the chain. Maximum chain elongation and minimum sprocket diameter (with chain) should not exceed the amount listed in this Chapter's Specifications. Replace the timing chain and sprockets as a set if the engine has high mileage or fails inspection.

21   Check the chain guides for excessive wear **(see illustration)**. Replace the chain guides if scoring or wear exceeds the amount listed in this Chapter's Specifications. Note that some scoring of the timing chain guide shoes is normal. If excessive wear is indicated, it will also be necessary to inspect the chain guide oil hole on the front of the oil pump for clogging (see Section 15).

Installation

Refer to illustrations 7.27, 7.28, 7.29, 7.32a, 7.32b, 7.34, 7.35 and 7.37

22   Remove all traces of old sealant from the timing chain cover and the mating surfaces of

the engine block and cylinder head.

23   Make sure the camshafts are positioned with the dowel pins at the top in the 12 o'clock position, then install both camshaft sprockets in their original locations by aligning the dowel pin hole on the rear of the sprockets with dowel pin on the camshaft. Apply medium strength thread locking compound to the camshaft sprocket bolt threads and make sure the washers are in place. Hold the camshaft from turning as described in Step 19 and tighten the bolts to the torque listed in this Chapter's Specifications.

24   Rotate the camshafts as necessary to align the TDC marks on the camshaft sprockets **(see illustration 7.7)**.

25   If the crankshaft has been rotated off TDC during this procedure, it will be necessary to rotate the crankshaft until the keyway is pointing straight up in the 12 o'clock position with the centreline of the cylinder bores.

26   Install the stationary timing chain guide **(see illustration 7.16)**.

27   Loop the timing chain around the crankshaft sprocket and align the No.1 coloured link with the mark on the crankshaft sprocket. Install the chain and crankshaft sprocket as an assembly on the engine **(see illustration)**. **Note:** *There are three coloured links on the timing chain. The No.1 coloured link is the link farthest away from the two coloured links that are closest together.*

28   Slip the timing chain into the lip of the

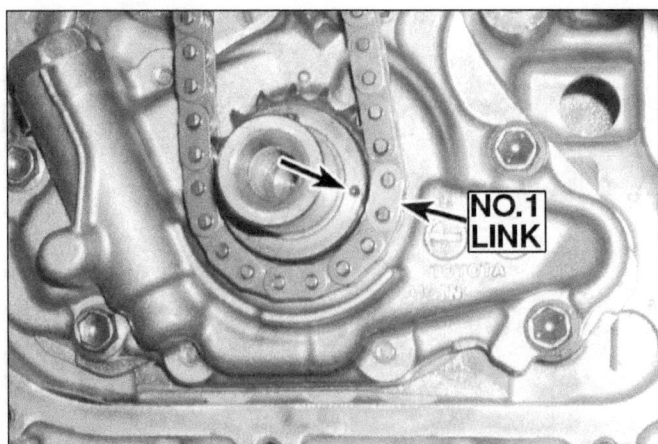

7.27 Loop the timing chain around the crankshaft sprocket and align the No.1 coloured link with the mark on the crankshaft sprocket, then install the chain and crankshaft sprocket as an assembly on the engine

7.28 Loop the timing chain up over the inlet camshaft and around the exhaust camshaft, while aligning the remaining two coloured links with the marks on the camshaft sprockets

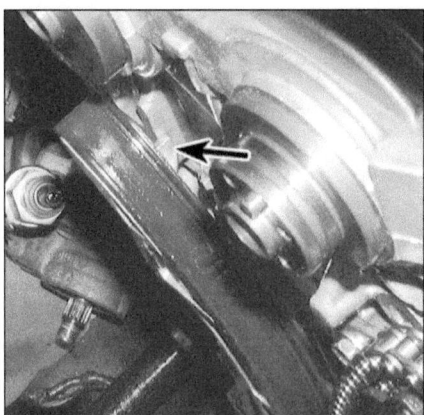

7.29 After the tensioner pivot arm is installed, make sure the tab (arrow) on the pivot arm can't move past the stopper on the cylinder head

7.34 Raise the ratchet pawl and push the plunger inward until the hook on the tensioner body can be engaged with the pin on the plunger to lock the plunger in place

stationary timing chain guide and over the inlet camshaft sprocket, then around the exhaust camshaft sprocket making sure to align the remaining two coloured links with the marks on the camshaft sprockets **(see illustration)**. Make sure to remove all slack from the right side of the chain when doing so.

29   Use one hand to remove the slack from the left side of the chain and install the timing chain tensioner pivot arm/chain guide. Tighten the pivot bolt to torque listed in this Chapter's Specifications. After installation, make sure the tab on the pivot arm can't move past the stopper on the cylinder head **(see illustration)**.

30   Reconfirm that the number one piston is still at TDC on the compression stroke and that the timing marks on the crankshaft and camshaft sprockets are aligned with the coloured links on the chain.

31   Install the crankshaft position sensor reluctor ring with the "F" mark facing outward.

32   Apply a bead of RTV sealant to the timing chain cover sealing surfaces **(see illustrations)**. Place the timing chain cover in position on the engine and install the bolts in their original locations. Tighten the bolts evenly in several steps to the torque listed in this Chap-

Seal Width 4 – 5 mm
Chain Cover Groove
Cylinder Head Groove

7 mm | 4mm | 12 mm | 6 mm | 3 mm

A   B   C

7.32a Timing chain cover sealant installation details

ter's Specifications **(see illustration)**. Be sure to follow the sealant manufacturer's recommendations for assembly and sealant curing times.

33   Install the water pump O-ring, the water pump and the engine mount bracket all within the sealant manufacturer's specified drying times. Before installing the engine mount bracket, apply a small amount of RTV sealant to the threads of the engine mount bracket bolts.

34   Reload and lock the timing chain

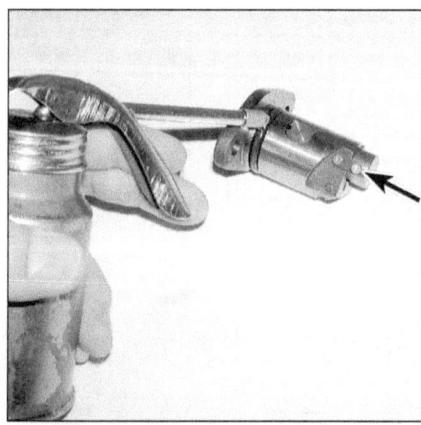

7.35 Apply a small amount of oil to the tensioner O-ring and insert the tensioner into the timing chain cover with the hook facing upward

7.32b Also apply a bead of sealant on each side of the parting line between the cylinder head and the engine block

tensioner to its "zero" position as follows:

a) *Raise the ratchet pawl and push the plunger inward until it bottoms out* **(see illustration)**.

b) *Engage the hook on the tensioner body with the pin on the tensioner plunger to lock the plunger in place.*

35   Lubricate the tensioner O-ring with a small amount of oil and install the tensioner into the timing chain cover with the hook facing up **(see illustration)**.

36   Install the crankshaft pulley/vibration damper (see Section 12).

37   Rotate the engine clockwise slightly to set the chain tension. As the engine is rotated, the hook on the tensioner body should release itself from the pin on the plunger and allow the plunger to spring out and apply tension to the timing chain. If the plunger does not spring outward and apply tension to the timing chain, press downward on the pivot arm and release the hook with a screwdriver **(see illustration)**.

38   Rotate the engine clockwise several turns and reposition the number one piston at TDC on the compression stroke (see Section 3). Visually confirm that the timing mark

7.37 Depress the tensioner pivot arm and disengage the hook from the plunger pin to set tension on the timing chain

8.4 With the TDC marks aligned, apply a dab of paint to the timing chain links where they meet the upper timing marks on the camshaft sprockets

8.7 With the camshaft sprockets removed, hang the timing chain out of the way with a piece of wire and place a shop rag in the timing chain cover opening to prevent foreign objects from falling into the engine

on the crankshaft pulley/vibration damper is aligned with the "0" mark on the timing chain cover and the camshaft sprocket marks are aligned and parallel with the top of the timing chain cover as shown in **illustration 7.7**.

39   The remainder of the installation is the reverse of removal.

8   Camshafts and lifters - removal, inspection and installation

Note: *The camshafts should always be thoroughly inspected before installation and camshaft endplay should always be checked prior to camshaft removal (see Step 13).*

Removal

Refer to illustrations 8.4, 8.7, 8.8, 8.11a and 8.11b

1   Disconnect the cable from the negative terminal of the battery.

2   Remove the valve cover (see Section 4).

3   Refer to Section 3 and place the engine on TDC for number 1 cylinder. Visually confirm the engine is at TDC on the compression stroke by verifying that the timing mark on the crankshaft pulley/vibration damper is aligned with the "0" mark on the timing chain cover and the camshaft sprocket TDC marks are aligned and parallel with the top of the timing

chain cover (**see illustrations 3.8 and 7.7**).

4   With the TDC marks aligned, apply a dab of paint to the timing chain links where they meet the upper timing marks on the camshaft sprockets (**see illustration**). **Note:** *There are two sets of marks on the camshaft sprockets. The marks that align at TDC are for TDC reference only, the other two marks are used to align the sprockets with the timing chain during installation.*

5   Using a wrench to hold the camshaft sprockets from turning, loosen the camshaft sprocket bolts several turns (**see illustration 7.19**). If the camshaft sprockets have rotated during the bolt loosening process, rotate the engine clockwise until the "TDC" marks on the cam sprockets are realigned.

6   Remove the timing chain tensioner from the timing cover (**see illustration 7.13**) and the camshaft position sensor from the cylinder head (see Chapter 6).

7   Remove the camshaft sprocket retaining bolts. Disengage the timing chain from the sprockets and remove the camshaft sprockets from the engine. Make sure to note that the sprockets are marked "IN" for inlet or "EX" for exhaust and cannot be interchanged. After removing the sprockets, hang the timing chain up with a piece of wire and attach it to an object on the firewall (**see illustration**). This will prevent the timing chain from falling into the engine as the remaining steps in this pro-

cedure are performed. Also place a rag into the opening of the timing chain cover to prevent any foreign objects from falling into the engine.

8   Verify the markings on the camshaft bearing caps. The caps should be marked from 1 to 5 with an "I" or an "E" mark on the cap indicating whether they're for the inlet or exhaust camshaft (**see illustration**).

9   Loosen the camshaft bearing caps in two or three steps, in the reverse order of the tightening sequence (**see illustration 8.22**). **Caution:** *Keep the caps in order. They must go back in the same location they were removed from.*

10   Detach the bearing caps, then remove the camshaft(s) from the cylinder head. Mark the camshaft(s) "Inlet" or "Exhaust" to avoid mixing them up. **Note:** *When looking at the engine from the front of the vehicle, the forward facing cam is the inlet camshaft and the cam nearest the firewall is the exhaust camshaft. It is very important that the camshafts are returned to their original locations during installation.*

11   Remove the lifters from the cylinder head, keeping them in order with their respec-

8.8 The camshaft bearing caps are numbered and have an arrow that should face the timing chain end of the engine

8.11a Mark the lifters (I for inlet, E for exhaust, and number their location) and remove them with a magnetic retrieval tool

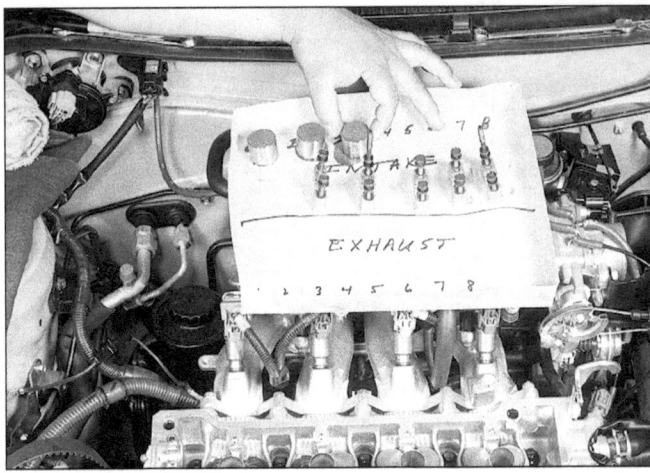

8.11b Mark up a cardboard box to store the lifters and bearing caps in order

8.13 Mount a dial indicator as shown to measure camshaft endplay - with the dial zeroed, prise the camshaft forward and back and read the endplay on the dial

tive valve and cylinder (**see illustrations**). **Caution:** *Keep the lifters in order. They must go back in the position from which they were removed.*

12   Inspect the camshafts and lifters as described below. Also inspect the camshaft sprockets for wear on the teeth. Inspect the chains for cracks or excessive wear of the rollers, and for stretching (see Section 7). If any of the components show signs of excessive wear they must be replaced.

Inspection

Refer to illustrations 8.13, 8.14, 8.15, 8.16, 8.18 and 8.19

13   Before the camshafts are removed from the engine, check the camshaft endplay by placing a dial indicator with the stem in line with the camshaft and touching the snout (**see illustration**). Push the camshaft all the way to the rear and zero the dial indicator. Next, prise the camshaft to the front as far as possible and check the reading on the dial indica-

tor. The distance it moves is the endplay. If it's greater than the Specifications listed in this Chapter, check the bearing caps for wear. If the bearing caps are worn, the cylinder head must be replaced.

14   With the camshafts removed, visually check the camshaft bearing surfaces in the cylinder head for pitting, score marks, galling and abnormal wear. If the bearing surfaces are damaged, the cylinder head may have to be replaced (**see illustration**).

15   Measure the outside diameter of each camshaft bearing journal and record your measurements (**see illustration**). Compare them to the journal outside diameter specified in this Chapter, then measure the inside diameter of each corresponding camshaft bearing and record the measurements. Subtract each cam journal outside diameter from its respective cam bearing bore inside diameter to determine the oil clearance for each bearing. Compare the results to the specified journal-to-bearing clearance. If any of the measurements fall outside the standard specified wear limits

in this Chapter, either the camshaft or the cylinder head, or both, must be replaced. **Note:** *If precision measuring tools are not available, Plastigage may be used to determine the bearing journal oil clearance (see Chapter 2A, Section 10, Step 23).*

16   Using a micrometer, measure the height of each camshaft lobe (**see illustration**). Compare your measurements with this Chapter's Specifications. If the height for any one lobe is less than the specified minimum, replace the camshaft.

17   Check the camshaft runout by placing the camshaft back into the cylinder head and set up a dial indicator on the centre journal. Zero the dial indicator. Turn the camshaft slowly and note the dial indicator readings. Runout should not exceed 0.030 mm. If the measured runout exceeds the specified runout, replace the camshaft.

18   Inspect each lifter for scuffing and score marks (**see illustration**).

19   Measure the outside diameter of each lifter (**see illustration**) and the correspond-

8.14 Inspect the cam bearing surfaces in the cylinder head for pits, score marks and abnormal wear - if wear or damage is noted, the cylinder head must be replaced

8.15 Measure each journal diameter with a micrometer - if any journal measures less than the specified limit, replace the camshaft

8.16 Measure the lobe heights on each camshaft - if any lobe height is less than the specified allowable minimum, replace that camshaft

8.18 Wipe off the oil and inspect each lifter for wear and scuffing

8.19 Measure the outside diameter of each lifter and the inside diameter of each lifter bore to determine the oil clearance measurement

ing lifter bore inside diameter. Subtract the lifter diameter from the lifter bore diameter to determine the oil clearance. Compare it to this Chapter's Specifications. If the oil clearance is excessive, a new cylinder head and/or new lifters will be required.

Installation

Refer to illustrations 8.20 and 8.22

20   Apply moly-based engine assembly lubricant to the camshaft lobes and journals and install the camshaft into the cylinder head with the No.1 cylinder camshaft lobes pointing inward toward each other and the dowel pins facing upward **(see illustration)**. If the old camshafts are being used, make sure they're installed in the exact location from which they came.

21   Install the bearing caps and bolts and tighten them hand tight.

22   Tighten the bearing cap bolts in several equal steps, to the torque listed in this Chapter's Specifications, using the proper tighten-

ing sequence **(see illustration)**.

23   Engage the camshaft sprocket teeth with the timing chain links so that the match marks made during removal align with the upper timing marks on the sprockets, then position the sprockets over the dowels on the camshaft hubs and install the camshaft sprocket bolts finger tight. At this point the mark on the crankshaft pulley should be aligned with the "0" mark on the timing chain cover, the camshaft sprocket TDC marks should be aligned and parallel with the top of the timing chain cover and the timing chain match marks should be aligned with the upper timing sprocket marks with all of the slack in the chain positioned towards the tensioner side of the engine **(see illustration 8.4)**.

24   Double check that the timing sprockets are returned to the proper camshaft and tighten the camshaft sprocket bolts to the torque listed in this Chapter's Specifications.

25   Install the timing chain tensioner as described in Section 7, Steps 34 and 35.

26   The remainder of installation is the reverse of removal.

9   Inlet manifold - removal and installation

Warning: *The engine must be completely cool before beginning this procedure.*

Removal

Refer to illustrations 9.4 and 9.6

1   Relieve the fuel system pressure (see Chapter 4), then disconnect the negative cable from the battery. **Caution:** *If the stereo in your vehicle is equipped with an anti-theft system, make sure you have the correct activation code before disconnecting the battery.*

2   On 1999 and earlier models, remove the fuel injector wiring harness cover **(see illustration 4.2a)**. On 2000 and later models, remove the engine cover **(see illustration)**.

3   Drain the cooling system (see Chapter 1) and remove the upper radiator hose (see Chapter 3).

8.20 Place the camshafts in the cylinder head with the No.1 cylinder lobes pointing inward at approximately a 30 degree angle

8.22 Camshaft bearing cap bolt TIGHTENING sequence

9.4 Label and disconnect the following components required for inlet manifold removal

1   Air inlet duct and upper air cleaner cover
2   PCV hose
3   Throttle body
4   Fuel rail and injectors

4   Remove the fuel rail and injectors as an assembly (see Chapter 4). Also remove the throttle linkage and the throttle body from the inlet manifold **(see illustration)**.

5   Label and detach the PCV and vacuum hoses connected to the rear of the inlet manifold.

6   Remove the inlet manifold mounting nuts, bolts and support bracket bolts and remove the manifold and the gasket from the engine **(see illustration)**.

Installation

7   Clean the mating surfaces of the inlet manifold and the cylinder head mounting surface with lacquer thinner or acetone. If the gasket shows signs of leaking, have the manifold checked for warpage at an automotive machine shop and resurfaced if necessary.

8   Install a new gasket over the manifold studs, then position the manifold on the cylinder head and install the nuts/bolts and brackets.

9   Tighten the manifold-to-cylinder head nuts/bolts in three or four equal steps to the torque listed in this Chapter's Specifications. Work from the centre out towards the ends to avoid warping the manifold. After the manifold-to-cylinder head bolts have been tightened to the proper torque, tighten the lower bracket bolts **(see illustration 9.6)**.

10   Install the remaining parts in the reverse order of removal. Refill the cooling system (see Chapter 1).

9.6 Inlet manifold fastener locations

11   Before starting the engine, check the throttle linkage for smooth operation.

12   Run the engine and check for coolant and vacuum leaks.

13   Road test the vehicle and check for proper operation of all accessories, including the cruise control system, if equipped.

10   Exhaust manifold - removal and installation

Warning: *The engine must be completely cool before beginning this procedure.*

Removal

Refer to illustrations 10.3, 10.5 and 10.6

1   Disconnect the negative cable from the battery. **Caution:** *If the stereo in your vehicle is equipped with an anti-theft system, make sure you have the correct activation code before disconnecting the battery.*

2   Raise the front of the vehicle and support it securely on jackstands.

3   Working below the vehicle, apply penetrating oil to the bolts and springs retaining the exhaust pipe to the manifold. After the bolts have soaked, remove the bolts retaining the exhaust pipe to the manifold. Separate the front exhaust pipe from the manifold, being

10.3 Working below the vehicle, remove the exhaust pipe-to manifold mounting bolts (A) and lower the front exhaust pipe - being careful not to damage the oxygen sensor (C) - (B) indicates the mounting bolts for the lower exhaust manifold brace (early model shown later models similar)

10.5 Working from the engine compartment, remove the upper heat shield mounting bolts (arrows) . . .

10.6 . . . and the exhaust manifold retaining nuts, then pull the manifold off the studs on the cylinder head and remove from above (early model shown later models similar)

11.11 Detach the earth straps (A), the ECT sensor connector (B), the coolant hoses (C) and the bracket retaining bolts (D)

careful not to damage the oxygen sensor **(see illustration)**. **Note:** *It may be necessary to remove the inner heat shield from above the right driveaxle to access one of the exhaust pipe-to-manifold bolts.*

4   Unbolt the lower exhaust manifold brace and remove it from the engine.

5   Working in the engine compartment, remove the upper heat shield from the manifold **(see illustration)**. **Note:** *There is also a lower heat shield, but it is attached to the manifold from underneath and does not need to be removed.*

6   Remove the nuts/bolts and detach the manifold and gasket **(see illustration)**.

Installation

7   Use a scraper to remove all traces of old gasket material and carbon deposits from the manifold and cylinder head mating surfaces. If the gasket was leaking, have the manifold checked for warpage at an automotive machine shop and resurfaced if necessary. **Note:** *If the manifold is being replaced*

with a new one it will be necessary to remove the lower heat shield and fasten it to the new manifold.

8   Position a new gasket over the cylinder head studs noting any directional marks or arrows on the gasket if equipped.

9   Install the manifold and thread the mounting nuts into place.

10   Working from the centre out, tighten the nuts/bolts to the torque listed in this Chapter's Specifications in three or four equal steps.

11   Reinstall the remaining parts in the reverse order of removal.

12   Run the engine and check for exhaust leaks.

11   Cylinder head - removal and installation

Warning: *The engine must be completely cool before beginning this procedure.*

Removal

Refer to illustration 11.11

1   Relieve the fuel system pressure (see

Chapter 4), then disconnect the cable from the negative terminal of the battery. **Caution:** *If the stereo in your vehicle is equipped with an anti-theft system, make sure you have the correct activation code before disconnecting the battery.*

2   Drain the coolant from the engine block and radiator (see Chapter 1).

3   Remove the drivebelt and the alternator (see Chapter 5).

4   Remove the valve cover (see Section 4).

5   Remove the throttle body, fuel injectors and fuel rail (see Chapter 4).

6   Remove the inlet manifold (see Section 9).

7   Remove the exhaust manifold (see Section 10).

8   Remove the timing chain and camshaft sprockets (see Section 7).

9   Remove the camshafts and lifters (see Section 8).

10   On 2000 and later models, refer to Section 5 and remove the variable valve timing control valve and filter.

11   Label and remove the coolant hoses, tubes and electrical connections from the cylinder head **(see illustration)**.

11.24 Cylinder head bolt TIGHTENING sequence

12.4 A puller base and several spacers can be mounted to the centre hub of the pulley to keep the crankshaft from turning as the pulley retaining bolt is loosened - install the socket over the crankshaft bolt head before installing the puller, then insert the extension through the centre hole of the puller

12   Using a 10 mm hex-head socket bit and a breaker bar, loosen the cylinder head bolts in 1/4-turn increments until they can be removed by hand. Loosen the cylinder head bolts in the reverse order of the recommended tightening sequence **(see illustration 11.24)** to avoid warping or cracking the cylinder head.

13   Lift the cylinder head off the engine block. If it's stuck, very carefully prise up at the transaxle end, beyond the gasket surface.

14   Remove any remaining external components from the cylinder head to allow for thorough cleaning and inspection. See Chapter 2C for cylinder head servicing procedures.

Installation

Refer to illustration 11.24

15   The mating surfaces of the cylinder head and block must be perfectly clean when the cylinder head is installed.

16   Use a gasket scraper to remove all traces of carbon and old gasket material, then clean the mating surfaces with lacquer thinner or acetone. If there's oil on the mating surfaces when the cylinder head is installed, the gasket may not seal correctly and leaks could develop. When working on the block, stuff the cylinders with clean shop rags to keep out debris. Use a vacuum cleaner to remove material that falls into the cylinders.

17   Check the block and cylinder head mating surfaces for nicks, deep scratches and other damage. If damage is slight, it can be removed with a file; if it's excessive, machining may be the only alternative.

18   Use a tap of the correct size to chase the threads in the cylinder head bolt holes, then clean the holes with compressed air - make sure that nothing remains in the holes. **Warning:** *Wear eye protection when using compressed air!*

19   Using a wire brush, clean the threads on each bolt to remove corrosion and restore the threads. Dirt, corrosion, sealant and damaged threads will affect torque readings. Also check the cylinder head bolts for stretching.

Measure the entire length of each bolt from the top of head to the tip of the threads. If the length of any bolt exceeds 16 cm, it must be replaced.

20   Install the components that were removed from the cylinder head.

21   Position the new gasket over the dowel pins in the block. Position the gasket with the "Lot #" mark facing up and near the timing chain end of the engine.

22   Carefully set the cylinder head on the block without disturbing the gasket.

23   Before installing the cylinder head bolts, apply a small amount of clean engine oil to the threads and under the bolt heads.

24   Install the bolts in their original locations and tighten them finger tight. Following the recommended sequence, tighten the bolts in three steps to the torque listed in this Chapter's Specifications **(see illustration)**. Step 3 of the tightening sequence requires each bolt to be tightened an additional 90 degrees. If you don't have an angle-torque attachment for your torque wrench, simply apply a paint mark at one edge of each cylinder head bolt and tighten the bolt until that mark is 90 degrees (1/4-turn) from where you started at the beginning of Step 3.

25   The remaining installation steps are the reverse of removal.

26   Check and adjust the valves as necessary (see Chapter 1).

27   Change the engine oil and filter (see Chapter 1.

28   Refill the cooling system (see Chapter 1), run the engine and check for leaks.

12   Crankshaft pulley/vibration damper - removal and installation

Refer to illustrations 12.4, 12.5 and 12.6

1   Detach the cable from the negative terminal of the battery. **Caution:** *If the stereo in your vehicle is equipped with an anti-theft system, make sure you have the correct acti-*

vation code before disconnecting the battery.

2   Remove the drivebelt (see Chapter 1).

3   With the parking brake applied and the shifter in Park (automatic) or in gear (manual), loosen the lug nuts from the right front wheel, then raise the front of the vehicle and support it securely on jackstands. Remove the right front wheel and the right splash shield from the wheelwell.

4   Remove the bolt from the front of the crankshaft. A breaker bar will probably be necessary, since the bolt is very tight **(see illustration)**.

5   Using a puller that bolts to the crankshaft hub, remove the crankshaft pulley from the crankshaft **(see illustration)**. **Note:** *Depending on the type of puller you have it may be necessary to support the engine from above, remove the right side engine mount and lower to engine to gain sufficient clearance to use the puller.*

6   To install the crankshaft pulley, slide the pulley onto the crankshaft as far as it will slide on, then use a vibration damper installation tool to press the pulley onto the crankshaft. Note that the slot (keyway) in the hub must be aligned with the Woodruff key in the end of

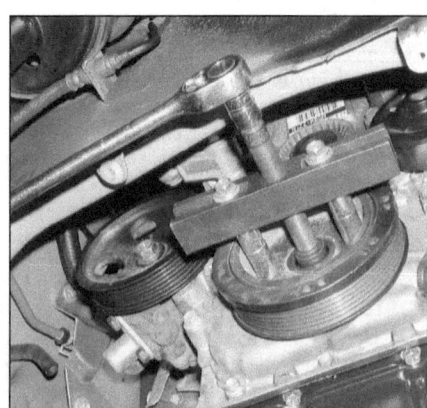

12.5 Reinstall the puller back onto the crankshaft pulley with the centre bolt attached and remove the crankshaft pulley

12.6 Align the keyway in the crankshaft pulley hub with the Woodruff key in the crankshaft (arrow)

13.2 Carefully prise the old seal out of the timing chain cover - don't damage the crankshaft in the process

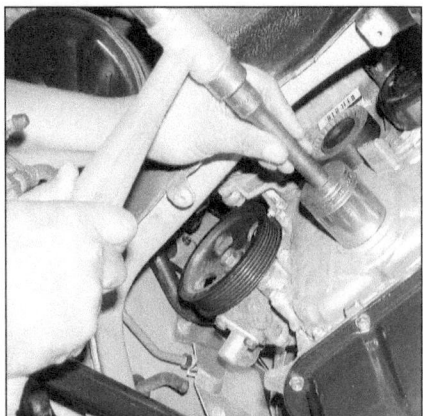

13.3 Drive the new seal into place with a large socket and hammer

the crankshaft **(see illustration)** and that the crankshaft bolt can also be used to press the crankshaft pulley into position.

7   Tighten the crankshaft bolt to the torque and angle of rotation listed in this Chapter's Specifications.

8   The remaining installation steps are the reverse of removal.

13 Crankshaft front oil seal - replacement

Refer to illustrations 13.2 and 13.3

1   Remove the crankshaft pulley (see Sec-

14.4 With the engine supported from above, remove the front crossmember support

tion 12).

2   Note how the seal is installed - the new one must be installed to the same depth and facing the same way. Carefully prise the oil seal out of the cover with a seal puller or a large screwdriver **(see illustration)**. Be very careful not to distort the cover or scratch the crankshaft! Wrap electrician's tape around the tip of the screwdriver to avoid damage to the crankshaft.

3   Apply clean engine oil or multi-purpose grease to the outer edge of the new seal, then install it in the cover with the lip (spring side) facing IN. Drive the seal into place with a seal driver or a large socket and a hammer **(see illustration)**. Make sure the seal enters the bore squarely and stop when the front face is at the proper depth.

4   Check the surface on the pulley hub that the oil seal rides on. if the surface has been grooved from long-time contact with the seal, a press-on sleeve may be available to renew the sealing surface. This sleeve is pressed into place with a hammer and a block of wood and is commonly available at auto parts stores for various applications.

5   Lubricate the pulley hub with clean engine oil and reinstall the crankshaft pulley (see Section 12).

6   Install the crankshaft pulley retaining bolt and tighten it to the torque listed in this Chap-

ter's Specifications.

7   The remainder of installation is the reverse of the removal.

14 Oil sump - removal and installation

Removal

Refer to illustrations 14.4, 14.6a and 14.6b

1   Disconnect the cable from the negative terminal of the battery. **Caution:** *If the stereo in your vehicle is equipped with an anti-theft system, make sure you have the correct activation code before disconnecting the battery.*

2   Set the parking brake and block the rear wheels.

3   Raise the front of the vehicle and support it securely on jackstands.

4   Remove the two plastic splash shields under the engine, if equipped. Support the engine from above with a hoist or engine support fixture and remove the front crossmember support **(see illustration)**.

5   Drain the engine oil and remove the oil filter (see Chapter 1). Remove the oil dipstick.

6   Remove the bolts and detach the oil sump. If it's stuck, prise it loose very carefully with a small screwdriver or putty knife **(see illustrations)**. Don't damage the mating sur-

14.6a Oil sump mounting bolts

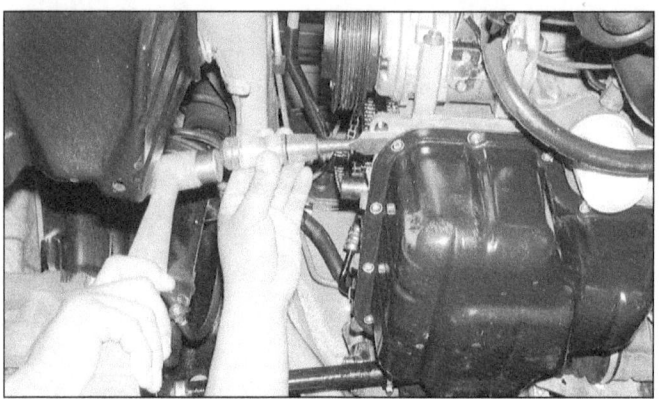

14.6b Prise the oil sump loose with a screwdriver or putty knife - be careful not to damage the mating surfaces of the pan and block or oil leaks may develop

15.2 Oil pump mounting bolts (arrows)

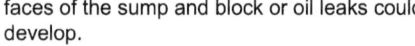

15.4 Oil pump relief valve components

A	Relief valve	C	Plug
B	Spring		

15.8a Measure the driven rotor-to-body clearance with a feeler gauge

faces of the sump and block or oil leaks could develop.

Installation

7   Use a scraper to remove all traces of old sealant from the block and oil sump. Clean the mating surfaces with lacquer thinner or acetone.

8   Make sure the threaded bolt holes in the block are clean.

9   Check the oil sump flange for distortion, particularly around the bolt holes. Remove any nicks or burrs as necessary.

10   Inspect the oil pump pick-up tube assembly for cracks and a blocked strainer. If the pick-up was removed, clean it thoroughly and install it now, using a new gasket. Tighten the nuts/bolts to the torque listed in this Chapter's Specifications.

11   Apply a 4 to 5 mm wide bead of RTV sealant to the mating surface of the oil sump. **Note:** *Be sure follow the sealant manufacturers recommendations for assembly and sealant curing times.*

12   Carefully position the oil sump on the engine block and install the oil sump-to-engine block bolts loosely.

13   Working from the centre out, tighten the oil sump-to-engine block bolts to the torque listed in this Chapter's Specifications in three or four steps.

14   The remainder of installation is the

reverse of removal. Be sure to wait at least one hour before adding oil to allow the sealant to properly cure.

15   Run the engine and check for oil pressure and leaks.

15   Oil pump - removal, inspection and installation

Removal

Refer to illustrations 15.2 and 15.4

1   Refer to Section 7, Steps 1 through 17

15.8b Using a straightedge and feeler gauge, measure the rotor-to-cover clearance

and remove the timing chain and the crankshaft sprocket.

2   Remove the five bolts and detach the oil pump body from the engine **(see illustration)**. You may have to prise carefully between the front of the block and the pump body with a screwdriver to remove it.

3   Use a scraper to remove all traces of sealant and old gasket material from the pump body and engine block, then clean the mating surfaces with lacquer thinner or acetone.

4   Remove the oil pressure relief valve from the pump body **(see illustration)**.

5   Remove the three screws and separate the pump cover from the body. Lift out the drive and driven rotors.

Inspection

Refer to illustrations 15.8a, 15.8b, 15.8c and 15.9

6   Clean all components with solvent, then inspect them for wear and damage.

7   Check the oil pressure relief valve piston sliding surface and valve spring. If either the spring or the valve is damaged, they must be replaced as a set.

8   Check the driven rotor-to-body clearance, rotor-to-cover clearance and drive rotor tip clearance with a feeler gauge **(see illustrations)** and compare the results to this Chapter's Specifications. If any clearance is excessive, replace the rotors as a set. If necessary, replace the oil pump body.

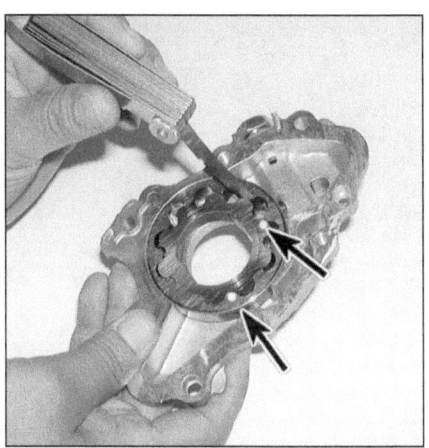

15.8c Measure the rotor tip clearance with a feeler gauge - install the rotors with the marks facing out, against the cover (arrows)

15.9 Check that the oil jet is free of debris - a blockage here will lead to an excessively worn timing chain and guides

15.14 Place the gasket over the dowels (lower arrows) on the engine block - when installing the oil pump, align the flats in the pump rotor with the flats on the crankshaft (upper arrow)

9   Check the timing chain guide oil jet for blockage (see illustration).

Installation

Refer to illustration 15.14

10   Lubricate the drive and driven rotors with clean engine oil and place them in the pump body with the marks facing out (see illustration 15.8c).
11   Pack the pump cavity with petroleum jelly and attach the pump cover, tighten the screws to the torque listed in this Chapter's Specifications.
12   Lubricate the oil pressure relief valve piston with clean engine oil and reinstall the valve components in the pump body.
13   Place a new oil pump gasket on the engine block.
14   Position the pump assembly against the block and install the mounting bolts. Make sure that the flats on the oil pump drive rotor align with the flats on the crankshaft (see illustration).
15   Tighten the bolts to the torque listed in this Chapter's Specifications in three or four

steps. Follow a criss-cross pattern to avoid warping the body.
16   Reinstall the remaining parts in the reverse order of removal.
17   Add oil if necessary, start the engine and check for oil pressure and leaks.

16   Flywheel/driveplate - removal and installation

Removal

Refer to illustrations 16.3 and 16.5

1   Raise the vehicle and support it securely on jackstands, then refer to Chapter 7 and remove the transaxle.
2   Remove the pressure plate and clutch disc (see Chapter 8) (manual transaxle equipped vehicles).
3   Use a centre punch or paint to make alignment marks on the flywheel/driveplate and crankshaft to ensure correct alignment during reinstallation (see illustration).
4   Remove the bolts that secure the flywheel/driveplate to the crankshaft. If the crankshaft turns, have an assistant wedge a

screwdriver in the ring gear teeth to jam the flywheel.
5   Remove the flywheel/driveplate from the crankshaft. Since the flywheel is fairly heavy, be sure to support it while removing the last bolt. Automatic transaxle equipped vehicles have spacers on both sides of the driveplate (see illustration). Keep them with the driveplate. **Warning:** *The ring-gear teeth may be sharp; wear gloves to protect your hands.*

Installation

6   Clean the flywheel to remove grease and oil. Inspect the surface for cracks, rivet grooves, burned areas and score marks. Light scoring can be removed with emery cloth. Check for cracked and broken ring gear teeth. Lay the flywheel on a flat surface and use a straightedge to check for warpage.
7   Clean and inspect the mating surfaces of the flywheel/driveplate and the crankshaft. If the crankshaft rear seal is leaking, replace it before reinstalling the flywheel/driveplate (see Section 17).
8   Position the flywheel/driveplate against the crankshaft. Be sure to align the marks

16.3 Mark the flywheel/driveplate and the crankshaft so they can be reassembled in the same relative positions

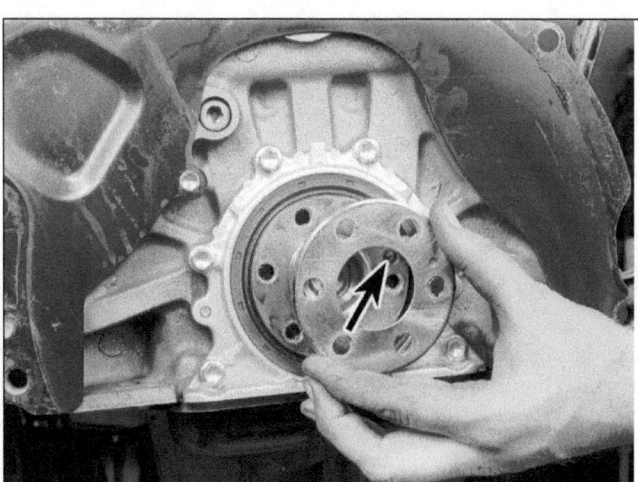

16.5 On vehicles equipped with a spacer plate, note the position of the locating pin

17.3 Carefully prise out the old seal with a screwdriver - it may be helpful to cut the seal lip with a razor blade first to make removal of the seal easier

18.7 The preferred method to support the engine is with a support fixture like this that allows maximum working room around the engine top and bottom

made during removal. Note that some engines have an alignment dowel or staggered bolt holes to ensure correct installation. Before installing the bolts, apply thread-locking compound to the threads.

9   Wedge a screwdriver in the ring gear teeth to keep the flywheel/driveplate from turning and tighten the bolts to the torque listed in this Chapter's Specifications. Follow a criss-cross pattern and work up to the final torque in three or four steps.

10   The remainder of installation is the reverse of the removal procedure.

---

17   Rear main oil seal - replacement

Refer to illustration 17.3

1   Remove the transaxle (see Chapter 7A or 7B).

2   Remove the flywheel/driveplate (see Section 16).

3   Prise the oil seal from the rear of the engine with a screwdriver **(see illustration)**. Be careful not to nick or scratch the crankshaft or the seal bore. Be sure to note how far it's recessed into the bore before removal so the new seal can be installed to the same depth. Thoroughly clean the seal bore in the block with a shop towel. Remove all traces of oil and dirt.

4   Lubricate the outside diameter of the seal and, using a seal installation tool, install the seal over the end of the crankshaft. Drive the new seal squarely into the seal bore and flush with the edge of the seal retainer.

5   Install the flywheel/driveplate (see Section 16).

6   Install the transaxle (see Chapter 7A or 7B).

---

18   Powertrain mounts - check and replacement

1   Engine mounts seldom require attention,

18.8a To remove the driver's side mount, detach the three mount-to-body bolts, the bolt at the engine . . .

but broken or deteriorated mounts should be replaced immediately or the added strain placed on the driveline components may cause damage or wear.

Check

Note: *During the check, the engine must be raised slightly to remove the weight from the mounts.*

2   Raise the vehicle and support it securely on jackstands, then position a jack under the engine oil sump. Place a large wood block between the jack head and the oil sump, then carefully raise the engine just enough to take the weight off the mounts. Do not position the wood block under the drain plug. **Warning:** *DO NOT place any part of your body under the engine* **when** *it's supported only by a jack!*

3   Check the mounts to see if the rubber is cracked, hardened or separated from the metal casing, which would indicate the need for replacement.

4   Check for relative movement between the inner and outer portions of the mount (use a large screwdriver or lever to attempt to move the mounts). If movement is noted,

replace the mount.

5   Check the mount fasteners to make sure they are tight.

6   Rubber preservative should be applied to the mounts to slow deterioration.

Replacement

Refer to illustrations 18.7, 18.8a, 18.8b, 18.9, 18.10a and 18.10b

7   Disconnect the cable from the negative terminal of the battery, then raise the vehicle and support it securely on jackstands (if not already done). The engine should be supported from above, preferably with an engine support fixture available from tool rental yards **(see illustration)**.

8   To remove the right (driver's side) engine mount, remove the three bolts securing the mount to the body, then remove the three bolts and two nuts securing the mount bracket to the engine bracket **(see illustrations)**. If the vehicle is equipped with air conditioning, detach the refrigerant line bracket retaining nut and remove the mount from the engine compartment. Be sure to remove the mount bracket from the old mount and reinstall it on the new mount.

18.8b . . . and the mount bracket-to-engine mount bracket nuts (seen from below)

18.9 Passenger's side engine mount details

A   Mount-to-body bolts
B   Through-bolt

9   To remove the left (passenger's side) engine mount, remove the four bolts securing the mount to the body, then remove the through-bolt securing the mount to the transaxle bracket **(see illustration)**. On manual transaxle equipped vehicles, it will be necessary to remove two bolts and an additional mount support bracket before removing the mount-to-body bolts and the mount through-bolt.

10   To remove the front and rear engine mounts, remove the bolts securing the mount to the lower frame crossmember, then remove the through-bolt securing the mount to the engine bracket **(see illustrations)**.

11   Installation is the reverse of removal. Use thread locking compound on the mount bolts/nuts and be sure to tighten them securely.

18.10a Front engine mount details

A   Mount-to-lower frame (access from below, one shown)
B   Through-bolt (nut indicated)

18.10b Rear engine mount details

A   Mount-to-frame crossmember
B   Through-bolt

Notes

Chapter 2 Part C
General engine overhaul procedures

Contents

Specifications

General

Displacement

4A-FE .... 1.6 litres
7A-FE .... 1.8 litres
1ZZ-FE .... 1.8 litres

Cylinder compression pressure

4A-FE and 7A-FE engines

Standard .... 1,320 kPa
Minimum .... 981 kPa

1ZZ-FE engines

Standard .... 1,303 kPa
Minimum .... 999 kPa

Maximum variation between cylinders .... 96 kPa

Oil pressure (engine warm)

4A-FE and 7A-FE engines

At idle .... 29 kPa minimum
At 3000 rpm .... 248 to 489 kPa

1ZZ-FE engines

At idle .... 39 kPa minimum
At 3000 rpm .... 296 to 537 kPa

Torque specifications

Nm (unless otherwise indicated)

Connecting rod bearing cap nuts/bolts

Step 1

4A-FE engines 29
7A-FE engines 25

Step 2 .... Tighten an additional 90-degrees (1/4 turn)

Connecting rod bearing cap bolts

1ZZ-FE engines

Step 1 20
Step 2 .... Tighten an additional 90-degrees (1/4 turn)

Main bearing cap bolts

4A-FE and 7A-FE engines 60

1ZZ-FE engines

Inner - bolts 1 through 10

Step 1 44
Step 2 .... Tighten an additional 90-degrees (1/4 turn)

Outer - bolts 11 through 20 19

1   General information - engine overhaul

Overhauling an engine is a difficult and time-consuming task. Special tools and knowledge are required. For these reasons, we recommend that engine overhaul is best left to a professional engine rebuilder. A competent engine rebuilder will handle the inspection of your old parts and offer advice concerning the reconditioning or replacement of the original engine.

Be aware that some engine builders can only rebuild the engine you bring them, which can take several weeks, while other rebuilders have rebuilt exchange engines in stock. If time is an issue, an exchange engine may be the best solution. If an exchange engine is fitted, check with your state registry authority as some insist the engine number on the new engine is included on your registration and insurance details.

An engine overhaul involves restoring the internal parts to the specifications of a new engine. During an overhaul, the piston rings are replaced and the cylinder walls are reconditioned (rebored and/or honed). If a rebore is done by an automotive machine shop, new oversize pistons will also be installed. The main bearings and connecting rod bearings are generally replaced with new ones and, if necessary, the crankshaft may be reground to restore the journals. Generally, the valves are serviced as well, since they're usually in less-than-perfect condition at this point. The end result should be a like-new engine that will give many trouble-free kilometres.

For those with engine overhaul experience and access to the necessary tools who wish to undertake the overhaul themselves, engine specifications have been included at the start of this chapter. Also included in this chapter are general information and diagnostic testing procedures for determining the overall mechanical condition of your engine.

It is important to establish the condition of the cylinder block. Never purchase parts or have machine work done on other components until the block has been thoroughly inspected by a professional machine shop.

The following Sections have been written to help you determine whether your engine needs to be overhauled and how to remove and install it once you've determined it needs to be rebuilt. For information concerning in-vehicle engine repair, see Chapter 2A.

The Specifications included relate to engine overhaul. Refer to the previous Engine chapters for additional engine Specifications.

It's not always easy to determine when, or if, an engine should be completely overhauled, because a number of factors must be considered.

High mileage is not necessarily an indication that an overhaul is needed, while low mileage doesn't preclude the need for an overhaul. Frequency of servicing is probably the most important consideration. An engine

2.2a On 1997 models the oil-pressure sending unit (arrow) is located at the front of the engine block, just above the oil filter

that has had regular and frequent oil and filter changes, as well as other required maintenance, will most likely give many thousands of kilometres of reliable service. Conversely, a neglected engine may require an overhaul very early in its service life.

Excessive oil consumption is an indication that piston rings, valve seals and/or valve guides are in need of attention. Make sure that oil leaks aren't responsible before deciding that the rings and/or valve guides are bad. Perform a cylinder compression check to determine the extent of the work required (see Section 3).

Check the oil pressure with a gauge installed in place of the oil pressure sending unit and compare it to this chapter's Specifications (see Section 2). If it's extremely low, the bearings and/or oil pump are probably worn out.

Loss of power, rough running, knocking or metallic engine noises, excessive valve train noise and high fuel consumption rates may also point to the need for an overhaul, especially if they're all present at the same time. If a complete tune-up doesn't remedy the situation, major mechanical work is the only solution.

Note: *Critical cooling system components such as the hoses, drivebelts, thermostat and water pump should be replaced with new parts when an engine is overhauled. The radiator should be checked carefully to ensure*

that it isn't clogged or leaking (see Chapter 3). If you purchase a rebuilt engine or short block, some rebuilders will not warranty their engines unless the radiator has been professionally flushed.

2   Oil pressure check

Refer to illustrations 2.2a and 2.2b

1   Low engine oil pressure can be a sign of an engine in need of rebuilding. A 'low oil pressure' indicator (often called an 'idiot light') is not a test of the oiling system. Such indicators only come on when the oil pressure is dangerously low. Even a factory oil pressure gauge in the instrument panel is only a relative indication, although much better for driver information than a warning light. A better test is with a mechanical (not electrical) oil pressure gauge.

2   Locate the oil pressure indicator sending unit on the engine block **(see illustrations)**.

3   Unscrew and remove the oil pressure sending unit and then screw in the hose for your oil pressure gauge. If necessary, install an adapter fitting. Use Teflon tape or thread sealant on the threads of the adapter and/or the fitting on the end of your gauge's hose.

4   Connect an accurate tachometer to the engine, according to the tachometer manufacturer's instructions.

2.2b On 1998 and later models the oil-pressure sending unit is located at the front of the engine block, just above the oil filter

5   Check the oil pressure with the engine running (normal operating temperature) at the specified engine speed, and compare it to this Chapter's Specifications. If it's extremely low, the bearings and/or oil pump are probably worn out.

3   Cylinder compression check

Refer to illustration 3.6

1   A compression check will tell you what mechanical condition the upper end of your engine (pistons, rings, valves, head gaskets) is in. Specifically, it can tell you if the compression is down due to leakage caused by worn piston rings, defective valves and seats or a blown head gasket. **Note:** *The engine must be at normal operating temperature and the battery must be fully charged for this check.*

2   Begin by cleaning the area around the spark plugs before you remove them (compressed air should be used, if available). The idea is to prevent dirt from getting into the cylinders as the compression check is being done.

3   Remove all of the spark plugs from the engine (see Chapter 1).

4   Block the throttle wide open.

5   Disable the fuel pump circuit by removing the circuit opening relay from the fuse/relay centre in the engine compartment (see Chapter 4).

6   Install a compression gauge in the spark plug hole **(see illustration)**.

7   Crank the engine over at least seven compression strokes and watch the gauge. The compression should build up quickly in a healthy engine. Low compression on the first stroke, followed by gradually increasing pressure on successive strokes, indicates worn piston rings. A low compression reading on the first stroke, which doesn't build up during successive strokes, indicates leaking valves or a blown head gasket (a cracked head could

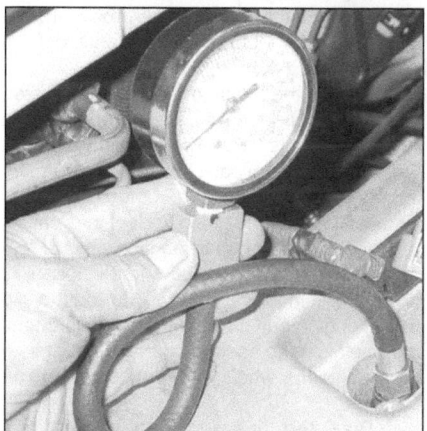

3.6 Use a compression gauge with a threaded fitting for the spark plug hole, not the type that requires hand pressure to maintain the seal - be sure to open the throttle valve as far as possible during the test

also be the cause). Deposits on the undersides of the valve heads can also cause low compression. Record the highest gauge reading obtained.

8   Repeat the procedure for the remaining cylinders and compare the results to this Chapter's Specifications.

9   Add some engine oil (about three squirts from a plunger-type oil can) to each cylinder, through the spark plug hole, and repeat the test.

10   If the compression increases after the oil is added, the piston rings are definitely worn. If the compression doesn't increase significantly, the leakage is occurring at the valves or head gasket. Leakage past the valves may be caused by burned valve seats and/or faces or warped, cracked or bent valves.

11   If two adjacent cylinders have equally low compression, there's a strong possibility that the head gasket between them is blown. The appearance of coolant in the combustion chambers or the crankcase would verify this condition.

12   If one cylinder is slightly lower than the others, and the engine has a slightly rough idle, a worn lobe on the camshaft could be the cause.

13   If the compression is unusually high, the combustion chambers are probably coated with carbon deposits. If that's the case, the cylinder head(s) should be removed and decarbonized.

14   If compression is way down or varies greatly between cylinders, it would be a good idea to have a leak-down test performed by an automotive repair shop. This test will pinpoint exactly where the leakage is occurring and how severe it is.

4   Vacuum gauge diagnostic checks

Refer to illustrations 4.4 and 4.6

A vacuum gauge provides inexpensive but valuable information about what is going on in the engine. You can check for worn rings or cylinder walls, leaking head or intake manifold gaskets, incorrect carburettor adjustments, restricted exhaust, stuck or burned valves, weak valve springs, improper ignition or valve timing and ignition problems.

Unfortunately, vacuum gauge readings are easy to misinterpret, so they should be used in conjunction with other tests to confirm the diagnosis.

Both the absolute readings and the rate of needle movement are important for accurate interpretation. Most gauges measure vacuum in kPa. As a point of reference, normal atmospheric pressure at sea level is about 100 kPa. As vacuum increases (or atmospheric pressure decreases), the reading will decrease. For every 300 meter increase in elevation above sea level; the gauge readings will decrease about three kPa.

Connect the vacuum gauge directly to the intake manifold vacuum, not to ported (throttle body) vacuum **(see illustration)**. Be

sure no hoses are left disconnected during the test or false readings will result.

Before you begin the test, allow the engine to warm up completely. Block the wheels and set the parking brake. With the transmission in Park, start the engine and allow it to run at normal idle speed. **Warning:** *Keep your hands and the vacuum gauge clear of the fans.*

Read the vacuum gauge; an average, healthy engine should normally produce about 51 to 71 kPa of vacuum with a fairly steady needle **(see illustration)**. Refer to the following vacuum gauge readings and what they indicate about the engine's condition:

1   A low steady reading usually indicates a leaking gasket between the intake manifold and throttle body, a leaky vacuum hose, late ignition timing or incorrect camshaft timing. Check ignition timing with a timing light and eliminate all other possible causes, utilizing the tests provided in this Chapter before you remove the timing belt cover to check the timing marks.

2   If the reading is 76 to 203 mm below normal and it fluctuates at that low reading, suspect an intake manifold gasket leak at an intake port or a faulty injector.

3   If the needle has regular drops of about 50 to 100 mm at a steady rate the valves are probably leaking. Perform a compression or leak-down test to confirm this.

4   An irregular drop or down-flick of the needle can be caused by a sticking valve or an ignition misfire. Perform a compression or leak-down test and read the spark plugs.

5   A rapid vibration of about seven kPa vibration at idle combined with exhaust smoke indicates worn valve guides. Perform a leak-down test to confirm this. If the rapid vibration occurs with an increase in engine speed, check for a leaking intake manifold gasket or head gasket, weak valve springs, burned valves or ignition misfire.

6   A slight fluctuation, say 25 mm up and down, may mean ignition problems. Check all the usual tune-up items and, if necessary, run the engine on an ignition analyzer.

4.4 A simple vacuum gauge can be handy in diagnosing engine condition and performance

Low, steady reading   Low, fluctuating needle   Regular drops

Irregular drops   Rapid vibration

Large fluctuation   Slow fluctuation

STD-O-OBR HAYNES

4.6 Typical vacuum gauge readings

7   If there is a large fluctuation, perform a compression or leak-down test to look for a weak or dead cylinder or a blown head gasket.

8   If the needle moves slowly through a wide range, check for a clogged PCV system, incorrect idle fuel mixture, throttle body or intake manifold gasket leaks.

9   Check for a slow return after revving the engine by quickly snapping the throttle open until the engine reaches about 2,500 rpm and let it shut. Normally the reading should drop to near zero, rise above normal idle reading (about 10 kPa over) and then return to the previous idle reading. If the vacuum returns slowly and doesn't peak when the throttle is snapped shut, the rings may be worn. If there is a long delay, look for a restricted exhaust system (often the muffler or catalytic converter). An easy way to check this is to temporarily disconnect the exhaust ahead of the suspected part and redo the test.

5   Engine rebuilding alternatives

The do-it-yourselfer is faced with a number of options when purchasing a rebuilt engine. The major considerations are cost,

warranty, parts availability and the time required for the rebuilder to complete the project. The decision to replace the engine block, piston/connecting rod assemblies and crankshaft depends on the final inspection results of your engine. Only then can you make a cost effective decision whether to have your engine overhauled or simply purchase an exchange engine for your vehicle.

Some of the rebuilding alternatives include:

Individual parts - If the inspection procedures reveal that the engine block and most engine components are in reusable condition, purchasing individual parts and having a rebuilder rebuild your engine may be the most economical alternative. The block, crankshaft and piston/connecting rod assemblies should all be inspected carefully by a machine shop first.

Short block - A short block consists of an engine block with a crankshaft and piston/connecting rod assemblies already installed. All new bearings are incorporated and all clearances will be correct. The existing camshafts, valve train components, cylinder head and external parts can be bolted to the short block with little or no machine shop necessary.

Long block - A long block consists of a short block plus an oil pump, sump, cylinder head, valve cover, camshaft and valve train components, timing sprockets and chain or gears and timing cover. All components are installed with new bearings, seals and gaskets incorporated throughout. The installation of manifolds and external parts is all that's necessary.

Low kilometre used engines - Some companies now offer low kilometre used engines which is a very cost effective way to get your vehicle up and running again. These engines often come from vehicles that have been in totaled in accidents or come from other countries that have a higher vehicle turn over rate. A low kilometre used engine also usually has a similar warranty like the newly remanufactured engines.

Give careful thought to which alternative is best for you and discuss the situation with local automotive machine shops, auto parts dealers and experienced rebuilders before ordering or purchasing replacement parts.

6   Engine removal - methods and precautions

Refer to illustrations 6.1, 6.2, 6.3, 6.4 and 6.5

If you've decided that an engine must be removed for overhaul or major repair work, several preliminary steps should be taken. Read all removal and installation procedures carefully prior to committing to this job. Some engines are removed by lowering to the floor and then raising the vehicle sufficiently to slide it out; this will require a vehicle hoist.

Locating a suitable place to work is extremely important. Adequate work space, along with storage space for the vehicle, will be needed. If a shop or garage isn't available, at the very least a flat, level, clean work surface made of concrete or asphalt is required. Cleaning the engine compartment and engine before beginning the removal procedure will help keep tools clean and organized **(see illustrations 6.1 and 6.2)**.

An engine hoist or A-frame will also be necessary. Make sure the equipment is rated in excess of the combined weight of the engine and transaxle. Safety is of primary importance, considering the potential hazards involved in lifting the engine out of the vehicle.

If you're a novice at engine removal, get at least one helper. One person cannot easily do all the things you need to do to lift a big heavy engine out of the engine compartment. Also helpful is to seek advice and assistance from someone who's experienced in engine removal.

Plan the operation ahead of time. Arrange for or obtain all of the tools and equipment you'll need prior to beginning the job **(see illustrations 6.3, 6.4 and 6.5)**. Some of the equipment necessary to perform engine removal and installation safely and with relative ease are (in addition to an engine hoist)

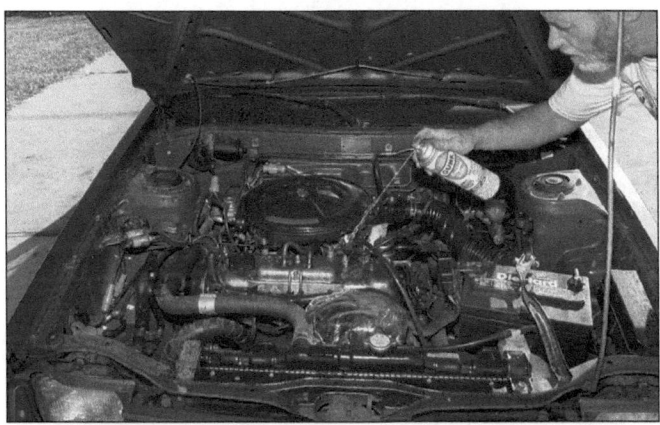

6.1 After tightly wrapping water-vulnerable components, use a spray cleaner on everything, with particular concentration on the greasiest areas, usually around the valve cover and lower edges of the block. If one section dries out, apply more cleaner

6.2 Depending on how dirty the engine is, let the cleaner soak in according to the directions and then hose off the grime and cleaner. Get the rinse water down into every area you can get at; then dry important components with a hair dryer or paper towels

6.3 Get an engine hoist that's strong enough to easily lift your engine in and out of the engine compartment; an adapter, like the one shown here, can be used to change the angle of the engine as it's being removed or installed

6.4 Get an engine stand sturdy enough to firmly support the engine while you're working on it. Stay away from three-wheeled models; they have a tendency to tip over more easily, so get a four-wheeled unit

6.5 A clutch alignment tool is necessary if you plan to install a rebuilt engine mated to a manual transaxle

a heavy duty floor jack, complete sets of wrenches and sockets as described in the front of this manual, wooden blocks, plenty of rags and cleaning solvent for mopping up spilled oil, coolant and gasoline. If the hoist must be rented, make sure that you arrange for it in advance and have everything disconnected and/or removed before bringing the hoist home. This will save you money and time.

Plan for the vehicle to be out of use for quite a while. A machine shop can do the work that is beyond the scope of the home mechanic. Machine shops often have a busy schedule, so before removing the engine, consult the shop for an estimate of how long it will take to rebuild or repair the components that may need work.

7   Engine - removal and installation

Refer to illustrations 7.17a, 7.17b, 7.27 and 7.30

Warning 1: *The models covered by this manual are equipped with Supplemental Restraint systems (SRS), more commonly known as airbags. Always disable the airbag system before working in the vicinity of the impact sensors, steering column or instrument panel to avoid the possibility of accidental deployment of the airbag, which could cause personal injury (see Chapter 12).*

Warning 2: *Gasoline is extremely flammable, so take extra precautions when you work on any part of the fuel system. Don't smoke or allow open flames or bare light bulbs near the work area, and don't work in a garage where a gas-type appliance (such as a water heater or a clothes dryer) is present. Since gasoline is carcinogenic, wear latex gloves when there's a possibility of being exposed to fuel, and, if you spill any fuel on your skin, rinse it off immediately with soap and water. Mop up any spills immediately and do not store fuel-soaked rags where they could ignite. The fuel system is under constant pressure, so, if any fuel lines are to be disconnected, the fuel pressure in the system must be relieved first (see Chapter 4 for more information). When you perform any kind of work on the fuel system, wear safety glasses and have a Class B type fire extinguisher on hand.*

Warning 3: *Wait until the engine is completely cool before beginning this procedure*

7.17a Unplug these electrical connectors (A) from the underbonnet fuse/relay box, then slide the harness up and out of the slot in the side of the box (B)

7.17b Label both ends of each wire and hose before disconnecting it - do the same for vacuum hoses

Note 1: *Engine removal on these vehicles is a difficult job, especially for the do-it-yourself mechanic working at home. Because of the vehicle's design, the manufacturer states that the engine and transaxle have to be removed as a unit from the bottom of the vehicle, not the top. With a floor jack and jackstands, the vehicle can't be raised high enough or supported safely enough for the engine/transaxle assembly to slide out from underneath. The manufacturer recommends that removal of the engine/transaxle assembly only be performed with the use of a frame-contact type vehicle hoist.*

Note 2: *Keep in mind that during this procedure you'll have to adjust the height of the vehicle with the vehicle hoist to perform certain operations.*

Removal

1   Park the vehicle on a frame-contact type vehicle hoist, then engage the arms of the hoist with the jacking points of the vehicle. Raise the hoist arms until they contact the vehicle, but not so much that the wheels come off the ground.

2   Loosen the wheel lug nuts and the driveaxle/hub nuts (see Chapter 8).

3   Relieve the fuel system pressure (see Chapter 4).

4   Remove the battery and battery tray (see Chapter 5).

5   Remove the air filter housing and air intake duct (see Chapter 4).

6   Drain the engine coolant (see Chapter 1).

7   Drain the engine oil (see Chapter 1).

8   Drain the transaxle lubricant or fluid (see Chapter 1).

9   Remove the engine cooling fan. Also remove the radiator (see Chapter 3).

10   If equipped with an automatic transaxle, disconnect the fluid cooler lines from the transaxle.

11   Disconnect the fuel feed hose from the rigid line on the left (passenger's) side of the engine compartment (see Chapter 4). Plug the line and fitting. Remove the EVAP canister from the engine compartment on 1ZZ-FE engines (see Chapter 4).

12   If equipped with cruise control, detach the cable from the throttle body, then remove the cruise control actuator.

13   Detach the heater hoses from the heater core tubes at the firewall (see Chapter 3).

14   Detach the shift cable(s) from the transaxle (see Chapter 7A or 7B).

15   If equipped with a manual transaxle, remove the clutch release cylinder (see Chapter 8).

16   Remove the air conditioning compressor without disconnecting the refrigerant lines (see Chapter 3). Tie the compressor out of the way.

17   Disconnect the engine wiring harness from the underbonnet fuse/relay box **(see illustration)**. Also label and detach any other electrical connectors/wiring harnesses and vacuum hoses between the engine and the vehicle **(see illustration)**.

18   Remove the glove box door, then disconnect the electrical connectors from the PCM (see Chapter 6) and the junction block. Dislodge the grommet from the firewall and pull the harness into the engine compartment.

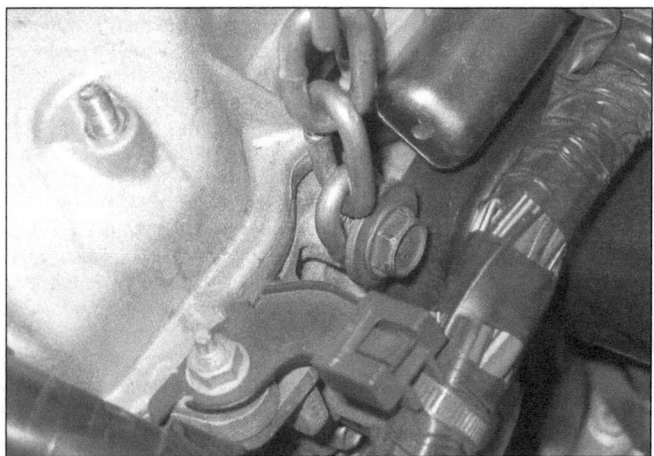

7.27 This engine was equipped with one lifting hook, at the back of the cylinder head near the transaxle. At the other end of the head there was no hook, but there was a large threaded hole that we used for connecting the lifting chain

7.30 Locations of the front suspension crossmember and longitudinal crossmember-to-vehicle bolts

19   Using a suction gun, remove as much fluid as possible from the power steering fluid reservoir. Unscrew the nut securing the power steering gear pressure line to the right side of the engine compartment (near the strut tower), then disconnect the hose from the line. Also, disconnect the supply (large diameter) hose from the power steering fluid reservoir.

20   Disconnect the steering column intermediate shaft from the steering gear (see Chapter 10).

21   Raise the vehicle on the hoist, then remove the front wheels. Detach the tie-rod ends from the steering knuckles (see Chapter 10).

22   Unbolt the exhaust pipe from the exhaust manifold (see Chapter 2A or 2B, Section 10).

23   Remove the driveaxle/hub nuts.

24   Unscrew the fasteners and separate the balljoints from the control arms (see Chapter 10).

25   Remove the driveaxles (see Chapter 8).

26   Disconnect the stabilizer bar links from the stabilizer bar (see Chapter 10).

27   Support the engine/transaxle assembly from above with an engine hoist. Attach the hoist chain to the lifting brackets. If no lifting brackets or hooks are present, lifting hooks may be available from your local auto parts store or dealer parts department. If not, you will have to fasten the chains to some substantial parts of the engine - ones that are strong enough to take the weight, but in locations that will provide good balance. If you're attaching a chain to a stud on the engine, or are using a bolt passing through the chain and into a threaded hole, place a washer between the nut or bolt head and the chain and tighten the nut or bolt securely **(see illustration)**. **Warning:** *Do not place any part of your body under the engine/transaxle when it's supported only by a hoist or other lifting device.*

28   Take up the slack until there is slight tension on the engine hoist. Position the chain on the hoist so it balances the engine and the transaxle level with the vehicle. **Note 1:** *Depending on the design of the engine hoist, it may be helpful to position the hoist from the side of the vehicle, so that when the engine/transaxle assembly is lowered, it will fit between the legs of the hoist.* **Note 2:** *The sling or chain must be long enough to allow the engine hoist to lower the engine/transaxle assembly to the ground, without letting the hoist arm contact the vehicle.*

29   Support the front suspension crossmember with a pair of floor jacks. Recheck to be sure that there aren't any hoses or wiring harnesses between the engine, crossmember and the vehicle.

30   Remove the bolts securing the front suspension crossmember and the longitudinal crossmember to the vehicle **(see illustration)**.

31   Remove the through-bolt from the powertrain mount securing the transaxle to the left (passenger's) side of the engine compartment, and the mount-to-engine bracket fasteners on the right-side mount (see Chapter 2A or 2B).

32   Recheck to be sure nothing is still connecting the engine or transaxle to the vehicle. Disconnect and label anything still remaining.

33   Lower the engine/transaxle/crossmember assembly. Once the assembly is on the floor, disconnect the engine lifting hoist and raise the vehicle until it clears the engine/transaxle assembly.

34   Reconnect the chain or sling to support the engine and transaxle.

35   Raise the engine/transaxle assembly, remove the fasteners connecting the remaining powertrain mounts to the crossmember, then move the crossmember out of the way. Support the engine with blocks of wood or another floor jack, while leaving the sling or chain attached. Support the transaxle with another floor jack, preferably one with a transaxle jack head adapter. At this point the transaxle can be unbolted and removed from the engine. Be very careful to ensure that the components are supported securely so they won't topple off their supports during disconnection.

36   Reconnect the lifting chain to the engine, then raise the engine and attach it to an engine stand.

Installation

37   Installation is the reverse of removal, noting the following points:

a) *Check the powertrain mounts. If they're worn or damaged, replace them.*

b) *Attach the transaxle to the engine following the procedure described in Chapter 7.*

c) *When installing the crossmember, tighten the mounting bolts to the torque listed in the Chapter 10 Specifications.*

d) *Tighten the driveaxle/hub nuts to the torque listed in the Chapter 8 Specifications. Tighten all steering and suspension fasteners to the torque listed in the Chapter 10 Specifications. Tighten the wheel lug nuts to the torque listed in the Chapter 1 Specifications.*

e) *Refill the engine coolant, oil, power steering and transaxle fluids (see Chapter 1).*

f) *Run the engine and check for proper operation and leaks. Shut off the engine and recheck fluid levels.*

8   Engine overhaul - disassembly sequence

1   It's much easier to remove the external components if it's mounted on a portable engine stand. A stand can often be rented quite cheaply from an equipment rental yard. Before the engine is mounted on a stand, the flywheel/driveplate should be removed from the engine.

2   If a stand isn't available, it's possible to remove the external engine components with it blocked up on the floor. Be extra careful not to tip or drop the engine when working without a stand.

3   If you're going to obtain a rebuilt engine, all external components must come off first, to be transferred to the replacement engine. These components include:

> *Clutch and flywheel (models with manual transaxle)*
> *Driveplate (models with automatic transaxle)*
> *Ignition system components*
> *Emissions-related components*
> *Engine mounts and mount brackets*
> *Fuel injection components*
> *Intake/exhaust manifolds*
> *Oil filter*
> *Thermostat and housing assembly*
> *Water pump*

Note: *When removing the external components from the engine, pay close attention to details that may be helpful or important during installation. Note the installed position of gaskets, seals, spacers, pins, brackets, washers, bolts and other small items.*

4   If you're going to obtain a short block (assembled engine block, crankshaft, pistons and connecting rods), then you should remove the timing belt, cylinder head, sump, oil pump pick-up tube, oil pump and water pump from your engine so that you can turn in your old short block to the rebuilder as a core. See *Engine rebuilding alternatives* for additional information regarding the different possibilities to be considered.

9   Initial start-up and break in after overhaul

Warning: *Have a fire extinguisher handy when starting the engine for the first time.*

1   Once the engine has been installed in the vehicle, double-check the engine oil and coolant levels.

2   Connect the remote starter used to check engine compression (see Section 3) and crank the engine for several seconds to allow engine oil pressure to build. Double check that there is no oil leaking from the oil filter or anywhere else on the engine.

3   Start the engine. It may take a few moments for the fuel system to build up pressure, but the engine should start without a great deal of effort.

4   After the engine starts, it should be allowed to warm up to normal operating temperature. While the engine is warming up, make a thorough check for fuel, oil and coolant leaks.

5   Shut the engine off and recheck the engine oil and coolant levels.

6   Drive the vehicle to an area with minimum traffic, accelerate from 40 to 80 Km/h, then allow the vehicle to slow to 20 km/h with the throttle closed. Repeat the procedure 10 or 12 times. This will load the piston rings and cause them to seat properly against the cylinder walls. Check again for oil and coolant leaks.

7   Drive the vehicle gently for the first 1,000 km (no sustained high speeds) and keep a constant check on the oil level. It is not unusual for an engine to use oil during the break-in period.

8   At approximately 1,000 km, change the oil and filter.

9   For the next few hundred kilometres, drive the vehicle normally. Do not pamper it or abuse it.

10   After 5,000 km, change the oil and filter again and consider the engine broken in.

Chapter 3
Cooling, heating and air conditioning systems

Contents

Specifications

General

Radiator cap pressure rating	73.7 to 103 kPa
Thermostat rating	
1997 models	84 to 95 degrees C
1998 to 2002 models	78 to 90 degrees C
2003 and later models	80 to 83.8 degrees C
Refrigerant type	R-134a
Refrigerant capacity	17 ounces

Torque specifications

	Nm
Thermostat housing bolts	11
Water pump-to-block bolts	
Smaller bolts	9
Larger bolts	11

1   General information

Engine cooling system

Refer to illustration 1.2

All vehicles covered by this manual employ a pressurized engine cooling system with thermostatically-controlled coolant circulation. An impeller type water pump mounted on the front of the block pumps coolant through the engine. The coolant flows around each cylinder and toward the rear of the engine. Cast-in coolant passages direct coolant around the intake and exhaust ports, near the spark plug areas and in proximity to the exhaust valve guides.

A wax-pellet type thermostat is located in the thermostat housing at the timing chain end of the engine **(see illustration)**. During warm up, the closed thermostat prevents

1.2 Typical thermostat

1   Flange
2   Piston
3   Jiggle valve
4   Main coil spring
5   Valve seat
6   Valve
7   Frame
8   Secondary coil spring

1.6 Under-dash arrangement of the blower unit (A) and evaporator/heater core housing (B)

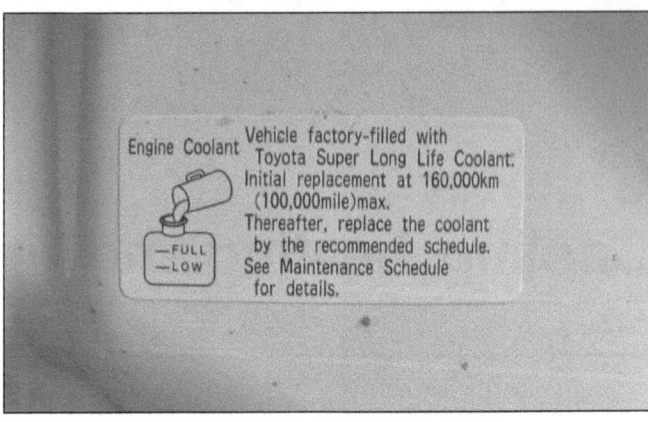

2.2 On later models a service sticker is located in the engine compartment for longer life service intervals

coolant from circulating through the radiator. When the engine reaches normal operating temperature, the thermostat opens and allows hot coolant to travel through the radiator, where it is cooled before returning to the engine.

The cooling system is sealed by a pressure-type radiator cap. This raises the boiling point of the coolant, and the higher boiling point of the coolant increases the cooling efficiency of the radiator. If the system pressure exceeds the cap pressure-relief value, the excess pressure in the system forces the spring-loaded valve inside the cap off its seat and allows the coolant to escape through the overflow tube into a coolant reservoir. When the system cools, the excess coolant is automatically drawn from the reservoir back into the radiator.

The coolant reservoir serves as both the point at which fresh coolant is added to the cooling system to maintain the proper fluid level and as a holding tank for overheated coolant.

This type of cooling system is known as a closed design because coolant that escapes past the pressure cap is saved and reused.

Heating system

Refer to illustration 1.6

The heating system consists of a blower fan and heater core located within the heater box under the right end of the dashboard, the inlet and outlet hoses connecting the heater core to the engine cooling system and the heater/air conditioning control head on the dashboard **(see illustration)**. Hot engine coolant is circulated through the heater core. When the heater mode is activated, a flap door opens to expose the heater box to the passenger compartment. A fan switch on the control head activates the blower motor, which forces air through the core, heating the air.

Air conditioning system

The air conditioning system consists of a condenser mounted in front of the radiator, an evaporator mounted adjacent to the heater core, a compressor mounted on the engine, a filter-drier which contains a high pressure

relief valve and the plumbing connecting all of the above.

A blower fan forces the warmer air of the passenger compartment through the evaporator core (sort of a radiator-in-reverse), transferring the heat from the air to the refrigerant. The liquid refrigerant boils off into low pressure vapor, taking the heat with it when it leaves the evaporator. The compressor keeps refrigerant circulating through the system, pumping the warmed coolant through the condenser where it is cooled and then circulated back to the evaporator.

2   Antifreeze - general information

Refer to illustrations 2.2 and 2.4

Warning: *Do not allow antifreeze to come in contact with your skin or painted surfaces of the vehicle. Rinse off spills immediately with plenty of water. Antifreeze is highly toxic if ingested. Never leave antifreeze lying around in an open container or in puddles on the floor; children and pets are attracted by its sweet smell and may drink it. Check with local authorities about disposing of used antifreeze. Many communities have collection centers that will see that antifreeze is disposed of safely. Never dump used antifreeze on the ground or into drains.*

Note: *Non-toxic antifreeze is now manufactured and available at local auto parts stores, but even these types should be disposed of properly.*

The cooling system should be filled with a water/ethylene-glycol based antifreeze solution, which will prevent freezing down to at least -28 degrees C, or lower if local climate requires it. It also provides protection against corrosion and increases the coolant boiling point.

The cooling system should be drained, flushed and refilled every 48,000 kilometres or every two years (see Chapter 1). **Note:** *On later models the system service requirements are longer* **(see illustration)**. The use of antifreeze solutions for periods of longer than two years is likely to cause damage and encour-

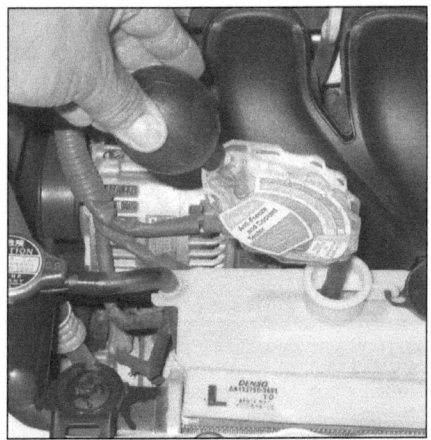

2.4 An inexpensive hydrometer can be used to test the condition of your coolant

age the formation of rust and scale in the system. If your tap water is hard, i.e. contains a lot of dissolved minerals, use distilled water with the antifreeze.

Before adding antifreeze to the system, check all hose connections, because antifreeze tends to leak through very minute openings. Engines do not normally consume coolant. Therefore, if the level goes down, find the cause and correct it.

The exact mixture of antifreeze-to-water you should use depends on the relative weather conditions. The mixture should contain at least 50 percent antifreeze, but should never contain more than 70 percent antifreeze. Consult the mixture ratio chart on the antifreeze container before adding coolant. Hydrometers are available at most auto parts stores to test the ratio of antifreeze to water **(see illustration)**. Use antifreeze that meets the vehicle manufacturer's specifications.

3   Thermostat - check and replacement

Warning: *Do not attempt to remove the radiator cap, coolant or thermostat until the engine has cooled completely.*

3.8 Thermostat housing mounting nuts – later model shown earlier models similar

3.9 The thermostat is installed with the spring end towards the engine, and the jiggle pin in the 12 o'clock position

3.10 The thermostat gasket, which is actually a grooved sealing ring, fits around the edge of the thermostat

Check

1   Before assuming the thermostat is responsible for a cooling system problem, check the coolant level (see Chapter 1), drivebelt tension (see Chapter 1) and temperature gauge (or light) operation.

2   If the engine takes a long time to warm up (as indicated by the temperature gauge or heater operation), the thermostat is probably stuck open. Replace the thermostat with a new one.

3   If the engine runs hot, use your hand to check the temperature of the lower radiator hose. If the hose is not hot, but the engine is, the thermostat is probably stuck in the closed position, preventing the coolant inside the engine from traveling through the radiator. Replace the thermostat. **Caution:** *Do not drive the vehicle without a thermostat. The computer may stay in open loop and emissions and fuel economy will suffer.*

4   If the lower radiator hose is hot, it means that the coolant is flowing and the thermostat is open. Consult the *Troubleshooting* Section at the front of this manual for further diagnosis.

Replacement

Refer to illustrations 3.8, 3.9 and 3.10

5   Disconnect the negative cable from the battery.

6   Drain the coolant from the radiator (see Chapter 1).

7   Remove the engine drivebelt (see Chapter 1) and the alternator (see Chapter 5).

8   Detach the thermostat housing from the engine **(see illustration)**. Be prepared for some coolant to spill as the gasket seal is broken. The radiator hose can be left attached to the housing, unless the housing itself is to be replaced.

9   Remove the thermostat, noting the direction in which it was installed in the housing, and thoroughly clean the sealing surfaces **(see illustration)**.

10   Fit a new gasket onto the thermostat **(see illustration)**. Make sure it is evenly fitted all the way around.

11   Install the thermostat and housing, positioning the jiggle pin at the highest point.

12   Tighten the housing fasteners to the torque listed in this Chapter's Specifications and reinstall the remaining components in the reverse order of removal.

13   Refill the cooling system (see Chapter 1), run the engine and check for leaks and proper operation.

---

4   Engine cooling fan and relay - check and replacement

Warning: *To avoid possible injury, keep clear of the fan blades, as they may start turning at any time!*

Check

Refer to illustration 4.2

1   On these models the engine cooling fan is controlled by the Powertrain Control Module (PCM) through the inputs it receives from the coolant temperature sensor. Refer to Chapter 6 for coolant temperature sensor information. The following fan motor and relay checks still apply to these models.

2   To test an inoperative fan motor (one that doesn't come on when the engine gets hot or when the air conditioner is on), first check the fuses and/or fusible links (see Chapter 12). Then disconnect the electrical connector at the motor and use fused jumper wires to connect the fan directly to the battery **(see illustration)**. If the fan still does not work, replace the fan motor. **Warning:** *Do not allow the test clips to contact each other or any metallic part of the vehicle.*

3   If the motor tested OK in the previous test but is still inoperative, then the fault lies in the relays, fuse, wiring or PCM.

Replacement

Refer to illustrations 4.7a, 4.7b, 4.8 and 4.9

4   Disconnect the negative battery cable.

5   Disconnect the wiring connector at the fan motor.

6   Disconnect the coolant overflow hose from the top of the radiator.

7   Unbolt the fan shroud from the radia-

4.2 Disconnect the fan wiring connector and connect jumper wires directly to the positive and negative terminals of the battery - this view is from the driver's side

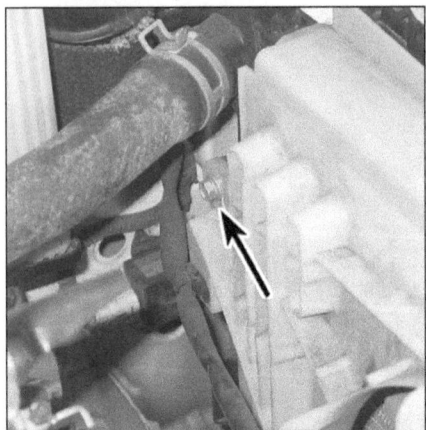

4.7a Remove the left-side mounting bolt for the fan assembly . . .

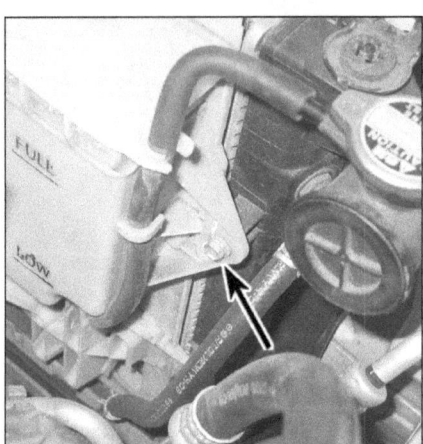

4.7b . . . and the right-side fan assembly bolt

4.8 Remove this nut to detach the fan blades from the motor

4.9 Remove the motor from the shroud

5.6 Remove the automatic transaxle cooler lines and the lower radiator hose from the left side of the radiator

1   Disconnect the negative battery cable.
2   Drain the engine coolant (see Chapter 1).
3   Detach the upper and lower radiator hoses from the radiator.
4   Disconnect the reservoir hose from the radiator filler neck.
5   Remove the cooling fan (see Section 4).
6   If equipped with an automatic transaxle, disconnect the cooler lines from the radiator **(see illustration)**. Place a drip pan to catch the fluid and cap the fittings.
7   Remove the two upper radiator mounting brackets **(see illustration)**. **Note:** *The bottom of the radiator is retained by grommeted projections that fit into holes in the body.*
8   Lift out the radiator **(see illustration)**. Be aware of dripping fluids and the sharp fins.
9   With the radiator removed, it can be inspected for leaks, damage and internal blockage. If in need of repairs, have a professional radiator shop or dealer service department perform the work as special techniques are required.
10   Bugs and dirt can be cleaned from the radiator with compressed air and a soft brush. Don't bend the cooling fins as this is done.

tor and lift the fan/shroud/coolant reservoir assembly from the vehicle **(see illustrations)**.
8   Hold the fan blades and remove the fan retaining nut (and spacer, if equipped) **(see illustration)**.
9   Unbolt the fan motor from the shroud **(see illustration)**.
10   Installation is the reverse of removal.

5   Radiator - removal and installation

Refer to illustrations 5.6, 5.7 and 5.8
Warning: *Do not start this procedure until the engine is completely cool.*

5.7 Remove the upper hold-down clamps (A) from each end of the radiator support - the other bolts (B) are for the air conditioning condenser

5.8 Remove the radiator carefully, and do not lose the rubber mounts - they must be in place on the bottom projections when the radiator is reinstalled

7.4 Water pump bolt locations (rear and lower bolts not visible in this photo)

6   Install a new O-ring in the timing chain cover and place the water pump in position. Install the bolts in their original positions and tighten them to the torque listed in this Chapter's Specifications.

7   Install the remaining parts in the reverse order of removal. Refill the cooling system (see Chapter 1), run the engine and check for leaks and proper operation.

Warning: *Wear eye protection when using compressed air.*

11   Installation is the reverse of the removal procedure. Be sure the rubber mounts are in place on the bottom of the radiator.

12   After installation, fill the cooling system with the proper mixture of antifreeze and water. Refer to Chapter 1 if necessary.

13   Start the engine and check for leaks. Allow the engine to reach normal operating temperature, indicated by both radiator hoses becoming hot. Recheck the coolant level and add more if required.

14   On automatic transmission equipped models, check and add fluid as needed.

6   Water pump - check

1   A failure in the water pump can cause serious engine damage due to overheating.

2   With the engine running and warmed to normal operating temperature, squeeze the upper radiator hose. If the water pump is working properly, a pressure surge should be felt as the hose is released. **Warning:** *Keep hands away from fan blades!*

3   Water pumps are equipped with weep or vent holes. If a failure occurs in the pump seal, coolant will leak from this hole. In most cases it will be necessary to use a flashlight

to find the hole on the water pump by looking through the space behind the pulley just below the water pump shaft.

4   If the water pump shaft bearings fail there may be a howling sound at the front of the engine while it is running. Bearing wear can be felt if the water pump pulley is rocked up and down. Do not mistake drivebelt slippage, which causes a squealing sound, for water pump failure. Spray automotive drivebelt dressing on the belt to eliminate the belt as a possible cause of the noise.

7   Water pump - removal and installation

Refer to illustration 7.4

Warning: *Do not start this procedure until the engine is completely cool.*

1   Disconnect the cable from the negative terminal of the battery. (see Chapter 1).

2   Referring to Chapter 1, drain the cooling system and remove the engine drivebelt (see Chapter 1).

3   Remove the alternator (see Chapter 5).

4   Remove the bolts retaining the water pump to the engine block and remove the water pump **(see illustration)**. Note the length and the position of the bolts as they were originally installed before removing them.

5   Thoroughly clean all sealing surfaces, removing the O-ring from the groove in the timing chain cover.

8   Coolant temperature sensor - replacement

On these vehicles there is only one coolant temperature sensor - the Engine Coolant Temperature (ECT) sensor, which provides information to the PCM for engine management and also for the temperature gauge on the instrument panel. Refer to Chapter 6 for the ECT sensor replacement procedure.

9   Blower motor - removal and installation

Refer to illustrations 9.2 and 9.3

Warning: *These models are equipped with a Supplemental Restraint System (SRS), more commonly known as airbags. Always disable the airbag system before working in the vicinity of any airbag system component to avoid the possibility of accidental deployment of the airbag(s), which could cause personal injury (see Chapter 12).*

1   The blower unit is located in the passenger compartment under the glove box area. If the blower doesn't work, check the fuse and all connections in the circuit for looseness and corrosion. Make sure the battery is fully charged.

2   If the blower motor operates at High speed, but not at one or more of the lower speeds, check the blower motor resistor, located under the instrument panel on the passenger side **(see illustration)**.

3   If the blower motor must be replaced, disconnect the wiring connector to the blower, then remove the three mounting screws and lower the blower assembly from the housing **(see illustration)**. The fan can be removed

9.2 Blower motor resistor location - the resistor is retained by two screws

9.3 Disconnect the electrical connector (A) then remove the three screws (B) and lower the blower motor from the housing

and reused on the new blower motor.

4   Installation is the reverse of removal.

10   Heater core - removal and installation

Refer to illustrations 10.3, 10.6, 10.8a, 10.8b, 10.8c, 10.9, 10.10, 10.11, 10.12a, 10.12b and 10.13

Warning 1: *These models are equipped with a Supplemental Restraint System (SRS), more commonly known as airbags. Always disable the airbag system before working in the vicinity of any airbag system component to avoid the possibility of accidental deployment of the airbag(s), which could cause personal injury (see Chapter 12).*

Warning 2: *Wait until the engine is completely cool before beginning this procedure.*

Note: *This procedure requires the removal of the instrument panel, and the cross-cowl support tube and steering column. This involves disconnecting numerous electrical connectors and there is the potential for breakage of delicate plastic tabs on various components. This is a difficult job for the average home mechanic.*

1   Disconnect the negative cable from the battery.

10.3 Disconnect the heater hoses at the firewall

10.6 Remove the pinch bolt at the bottom of the steering column

2   Drain the cooling system (see Chapter 1). It's not necessary to have the refrigerant recovered because, for heater core removal, the two refrigerant connections at the firewall do not have to be disconnected. However, moving the heat/AC unit away from the firewall for heater core removal is made easier by removing the screw securing the two refrigerant lines to the right fenderwell in the engine compartment.

3   Working in the engine compartment, disconnect the heater hoses at the firewall **(see illustration)**.

4   Refer to Chapters 11 and 12 and remove the centre console, glove compartment, glove compartment liner, ashtray, radio and centre dash bezels.

5   Refer to Section 11 to remove the heater/air conditioning controls and the instrument panel.

6   Remove the steering column pinch-bolt at the joint near the firewall **(see illustration)**.

7   Major electrical harnesses are attached to the body and the cross-cowl support tube. Disconnect the main electrical connectors at either end of the instrument panel (near the kick panels), and at the centre area below the instrument panel. Disconnect all harness connectors from the body side, but leave all harnesses attached to the cross-cowl tube. Use tape to tag and identify all connectors before separating them and take photos for later reference.

8   Remove all the fasteners securing the cross-cowl support tube to the cowl and the tube-to-floor brace **(see illustrations)**. When the tube is loose, you can drop the cowl tube down to the floor with the steering column still attached.

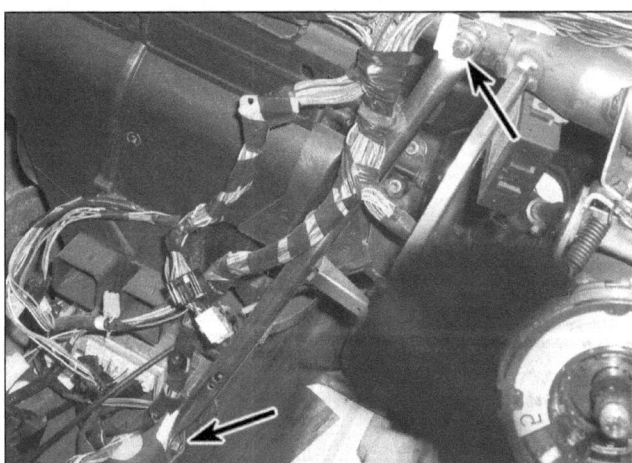

10.8a Remove the fasteners and the cowl-tube-to-floor brace(s)

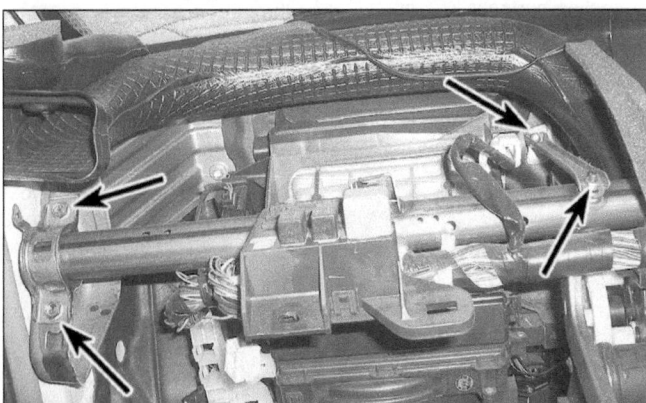

10.8b The cross-cowl support tube is secured to the vehicle at each side - remove the bolts and clamp at each end (right side shown)

10.8c Remove this screw in the centre of the cross-cowl tube

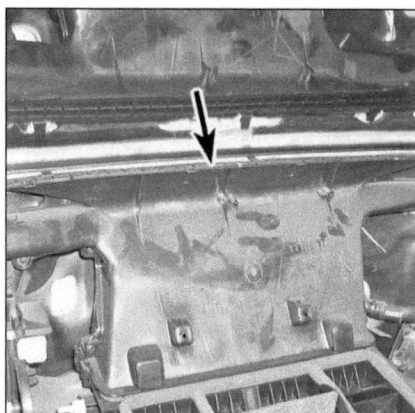

10.9 Shown with the cowl tube and steering column removed for clarity, remove the fasteners/clips and the number 1 duct

10.10 Remove the defroster duct from the top of the heat/AC housing

9   The heating/air-conditioning components are in several large plastic housings connected together and secured to the interior side of the firewall. To service the heater core, the entire assembly does not have to be removed from the vehicle, but the assembly must be unbolted and pulled out far enough for the heater core tubes to come through the firewall into the interior. Remove the number 1 air duct **(see illustration)**.

10   Remove the defroster duct above the heat/air housing **(see illustration)**.

11   Remove the fasteners securing the complete HVAC housing unit to the firewall **(see illustrations)**.

12   Disconnect the clips securing the tubes to the housing **(see illustrations)**.

13   Pull the heater unit out away from the firewall just enough for the heater core tubes to come through the firewall all the way, then remove the heater core from the housing **(see illustration)**. Keep plenty of towels or rags on

the carpeting to catch any coolant that may drip. **Caution:** *Work slowly and carefully to avoid breaking any plastic components during removal. The assembly must be pulled out (toward the rear of the vehicle) far enough for the tubes to clear the brake assembly at the firewall.*

14   Installation is the reverse order of removal.

15   Refill the cooling system, reconnect the battery and run the engine. Check for leaks and proper system operation.

11   Heater and air conditioning control assembly - removal and installation

Refer to illustrations 11.2, 11.3, 11.4a and 11.4b

Warning: *These models are equipped with a Supplemental Restraint System (SRS), more commonly known as airbags. Always disable the airbag system before working in the vicinity of any airbag system component to avoid the possibility of accidental deployment of the airbag(s), which could cause personal injury (see Chapter 12).*

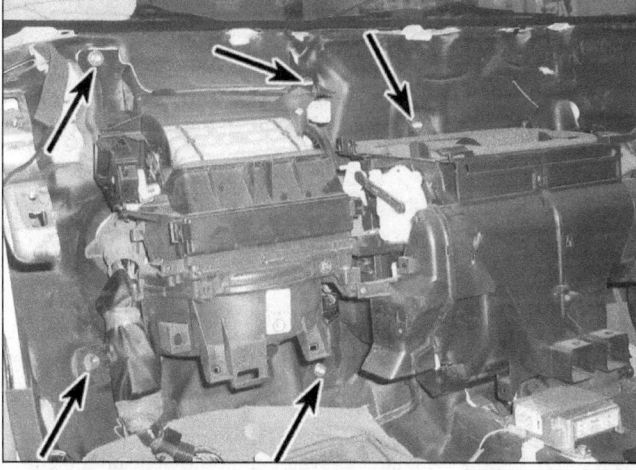

10.11 Remove the four nuts and one bolt securing the HVAC assembly to the firewall

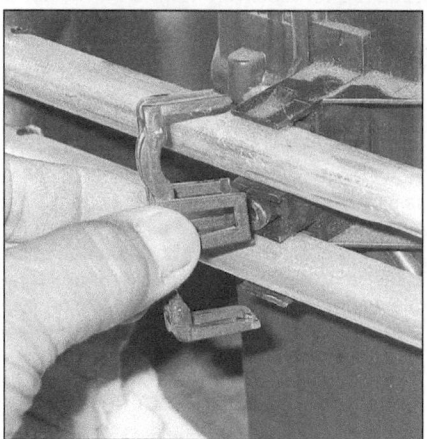

10.12a Release this clip securing the heater core tubes to the side of the case

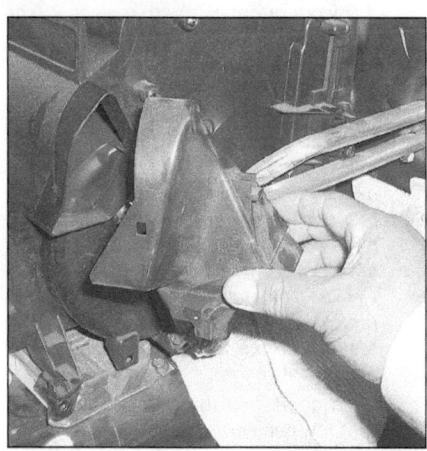

10.12b Remove the plastic cover over the left end of the heater core

10.13 Slide the heater core out of the left side of the housing, making sure the pipes clear obstructions on the firewall

11.2 Remove the centre knob from the heat/AC control panel and remove the screw holding the trim panel

11.3 Pry the centre instrument panel trim panel out, then disconnect the electrical connectors

11.4a Release the control panel from two claw-clips by pulling it straight out

11.4b Behind the control panel, disconnect the electrical connectors and use a screwdriver to open the clips holding the two control cables

1   Disconnect the negative cable from the battery.

2   Pull off the centre knob from the heat/AC control unit **(see illustration)**. This exposes a screw securing the top of the centre trim panel, the rest of the panel is retained by clips.

3   Remove the centre cluster trim panel (see Chapter 11). Pull the centre trim panel out far enough to mark the electrical connectors, then disconnect them **(see illustration)**.

4   Pull the control unit out enough to disconnect the heater control cables from the rear of the control unit. Disconnect the electrical connectors from the blower speed switch and the A/C switch **(see illustrations)**.

5   Installation is the reverse of the removal procedure.

6   Run the engine and check for proper functioning of the heater (and air conditioning, if equipped).

---

12   Air conditioning and heating system - check and maintenance

---

Air conditioning system

Warning: *The air conditioning system is under high pressure. Do not loosen any hose fittings or remove any components until the*

system has been discharged. Air conditioning refrigerant should be properly discharged by a dealer service department or an automotive air conditioning repair facility. Always wear eye protection when disconnecting air conditioning system fittings.

1   The following maintenance checks should be performed on a regular basis to ensure that the air conditioner continues to operate at peak efficiency **(see illustration)**:

a) *Inspect the condition of the drivebelt. If it is worn or deteriorated, replace it (see Chapter 1).*

b) *Inspect the system hoses. Look for cracks, bubbles, hardening and deterioration. Inspect the hoses and all fittings for oil bubbles or seepage. If there is any evidence of wear, damage or leakage, replace the hose(s).*

c) *Inspect the condenser fins for leaves, bugs and any other foreign material that may have embedded itself in the fins. Use a "fin comb" or compressed air to remove debris from the condenser.*

d) *Make sure the system has the correct refrigerant charge.*

2   It's a good idea to operate the system for about ten minutes at least once a month. This is particularly important during the winter months because long term non-use can cause hardening, and subsequent failure, of

the seals.

3   Leaks in the air conditioning system are best spotted when the system is brought up to operating temperature and pressure, by running the engine with the air conditioning ON for five minutes. Shut the engine off and inspect the air conditioning hoses and connections. Traces of oil usually indicate refrigerant leaks.

4   Because of the complexity of the air conditioning system and the special equipment required to effectively work on it, accurate troubleshooting of the system should be left to a professional technician.

5   If the air conditioning system doesn't operate at all, check the fuse panel and the air conditioning relay, located in the fuse/relay box in the engine compartment.

6   The most common cause of poor cooling is simply a low system refrigerant charge. If a noticeable drop in cool air output occurs, the following quick check will help you determine if the refrigerant level is low. For more complete information on the air conditioning system, refer to the *Haynes Automotive Heating and Air Conditioning Manual.*

Checking the refrigerant charge

Refer to illustrations 12.9 and 12.10

7   Warm the engine up to normal operating temperature.

12.9 With the system operating, the evaporator outlet line ("A" large tubing) should feel colder than the smaller line (arrow)

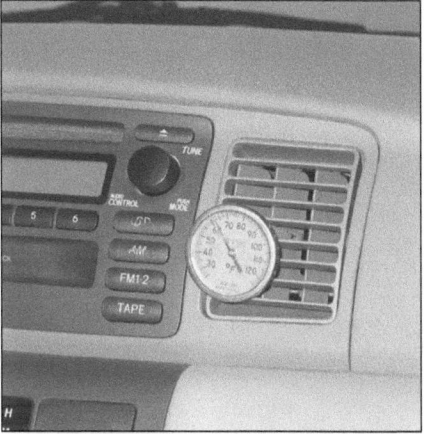

12.10 Check the temperature of the output air in the centre register with a thermometer - it should be 35-40 degrees below the ambient air temperature

12.12 A basic charging kit is available at most auto parts stores - it must say R-134a and so must the cans of refrigerant you buy

8   Place the air conditioning temperature selector at the coldest setting and put the blower at the highest setting. Open the doors (to make sure the air conditioning system doesn't cycle off as soon as it cools the passenger compartment.
9   With the compressor engaged - the clutch will make an audible click and the centre of the clutch will rotate - feel the large pipe exiting from the evaporator at the firewall **(see illustration)**.
10   The large evaporator outlet pipe should feel cold. If the evaporator outlet is warm or moderately warm, the system needs a charge. Insert a thermometer in the centre air distribution duct while operating the air conditioning system **(see illustration)** - the temperature of the output air should be 2 to 5 degrees C below the ambient air temperature (down to approximately 5 degrees C). If the ambient (outside) air temperature is very high, say 43 degrees C, the duct air temperature may be as high as 15 degrees C, but generally the air conditioning is 2 to 5 degrees C cooler than the ambient air. If the air isn't as cold as it used to be, the system probably needs a charge. Further inspection or testing of the system is beyond the scope of the home mechanic and should be left to a professional.
11   Before any components are replaced, the refrigerant should be discharged and recovered by a licensed air conditioning technician first. After your repairs, the shop can recharge your system, giving you credit for the amount they removed originally.

Adding refrigerant

Refer to illustrations 12.12 and 12.15

Caution: *All models covered by this manual use environmentally-friendly R-134a refrigerant. When replacing entire components, additional refrigerant oil should be added equal to the amount that is removed with the component being replaced. Be sure to read the can before adding any oil to the system, to make sure it is compatible with an R-134a system.*
12   Buy an automotive charging kit at an

auto parts store. A charging kit includes a can of R-134a refrigerant, a tap valve and a short section of hose that can be attached between the tap valve and the system low side service valve **(see illustration)**.
13   Connect the charging kit by following the manufacturer's instructions.
14   Back off the valve handle on the charging kit and screw the kit onto the refrigerant can, making sure first that the O-ring or rubber seal inside the threaded portion of the kit is in place. **Warning:** *Wear protective eyewear when dealing with pressurized refrigerant cans.*
15   Remove the dust cap from the low-side charging port and attach the quick-connect fitting on the kit hose **(see illustration)**. **Warning:** *DO NOT hook the charging kit hose to the system high side! The fittings on the charging kit are designed to fit only on the low side of the system.*
16   Warm the engine to normal operating temperature and turn on the air conditioner. Keep the charging kit hose away from the fan and other moving parts.
17   Turn the valve handle on the kit until the stem pierces the can, then back the handle out to release the refrigerant. You should be able to hear the rush of gas. Add refrigerant to the low side of the system until both the outlet and the evaporator inlet pipe feel about the same temperature. Allow stabilization time between each addition. **Warning:** *Never add more than two cans of refrigerant to the system. The can may tend to frost up, slowing the procedure. Wrap a shop towel wet with hot water around the bottom of the can to keep it from frosting.*
18   If you have an accurate thermometer, you can place it in the centre air conditioning duct inside the vehicle to monitor the air temperature. A charged system that is working properly, should output air down to approximately 5 degrees C.
19   When the can is empty, turn the valve handle to the closed position and release the connection from the low-side port. Replace

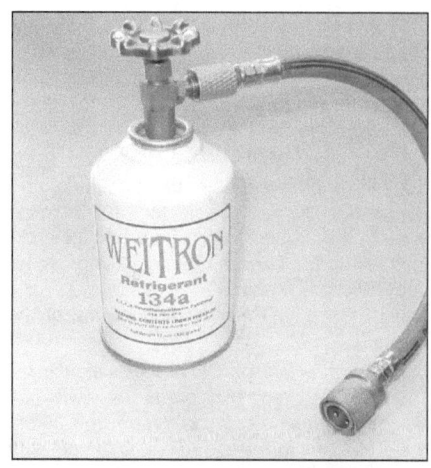

12.15 Add R-134a refrigerant to the low-side port only - the procedure will go faster if you wrap the can with a warm wet towel to prevent icing

the dust cap.
20   Remove the charging kit from the can and store the kit for future use with the piercing valve in the UP position, to prevent inadvertently piercing the can on the next use.

Heating systems

Refer to illustration 12.25

21   If the air coming out of the heater vents isn't hot, the problem could stem from any of the following causes:

a)   *The thermostat is stuck open, preventing the engine coolant from warming up enough to carry heat to the heater core. Replace the thermostat (see Section 3).*

b)   *A heater hose is blocked, preventing the flow of coolant through the heater core. Feel both heater hoses at the firewall. They should be hot. If one of them is cold, there is an obstruction in one of the hoses or in the heater core, or the heater control valve is shut. Detach the hoses and back flush the heater core with a*

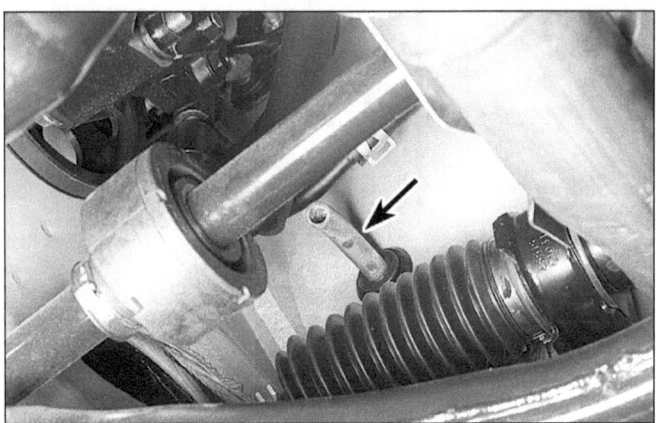

12.25 The drain hose from the heater/air-conditioning unit (arrow) should be kept clear to allow drainage of condensation - shown here from underneath, the hose is on the right side, below the power steering pump

12.29 Remove the cabin air filter, then insert the disinfectant spray nozzle - be sure to support the nozzle so it doesn't get tangled in the blower fan

water hose. If the heater core is clear but circulation is impeded, remove the two hoses and flush them out with a water hose.

c) If flushing fails to remove the blockage from the heater core, the core must be replaced. (see Section 10).

22   If the blower motor speed does not correspond to the setting selected on the blower switch, the problem could be a bad fuse, circuit, switch, blower motor resistor or motor (see Sections 9 and 11).

23   If there isn't any air coming out of the vents:

a) Turn the ignition ON and activate the fan control. Place your ear at the heating/air conditioning register (vent) and listen. Most motors are audible. Can you hear the motor running?

b) If you can't (and have already verified that the blower switch and the blower motor resistor are good), the blower motor itself is probably bad (see Section 9).

24   If the carpet under the heater core is damp, or if antifreeze vapor or steam is coming through the vents, the heater core is leaking. Remove it (see Section 10) and install a new unit (most radiator shops will not repair a leaking heater core).

25   Inspect the drain hose from the heater/air conditioning assembly at the right side of the firewall, making sure it is not clogged **(see illustration).**

Eliminating air-conditioning odors

Refer to illustration 12.29

26   Unpleasant odors that often develop in air-conditioning systems are caused by the growth of a fungus, usually on the surface of the evaporator core. The warm, humid environment there is a perfect breeding ground for mildew to develop. The evaporator core in your Corolla has been factory-treated with an anti-bacterial coating to reduce this, but

climactic conditions can still cause odors to develop.

27   Dealerships have a lengthy and often expensive process for eliminating the fungus by opening up the evaporator case and using a powerful disinfectant and rinse on the core until the fungus is gone. You can service your own system at home, but it takes something much stronger than basic household germ-killers or deodorizers.

28   Aerosol disinfectants for automotive air-conditioning systems are available in most auto parts stores, but remember when shopping for them that the most effective treatments are also the most expensive. The basic procedure for using these sprays is to start by running the system in the RECIRC mode for ten minutes with the blower on its highest speed. Use the highest heat mode to dry out the system and keep the compressor from engaging by disconnecting the wiring connector at the compressor (see Section 14).

29   The disinfectant can usually comes with a long spray hose. Remove the cabin air filter, point the nozzle inside the hole and to the left towards the evaporator core, and spray according to the manufacturer's recommendations **(see illustration).** Follow the manufacturer's recommendations for the length of spray and waiting time between applications.

30   Once the evaporator has been cleaned, the best way to prevent the mildew from coming back again is to make sure your evaporator housing drain tube is clear **(see illustration 12.25)** and to run the defrost cycle briefly to dry the evaporator out after a long drive with the air conditioning on.

---

13   Air conditioning receiver-drier - removal and installation

Refer to illustration 13.3

Warning: *The air conditioning system is under high pressure. Do not loosen any hose fittings or remove any components until the*

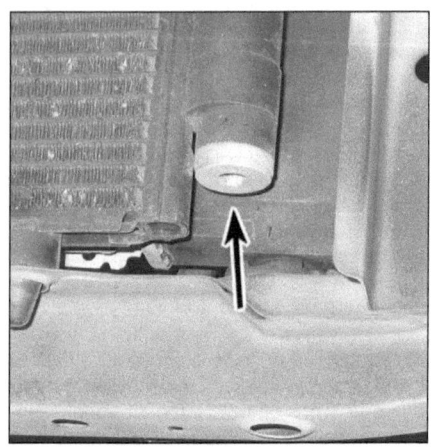

13.3 After the system has been discharged, remove the Allen plug at the bottom of the receiver-drier

system has been discharged. Air conditioning refrigerant should be properly discharged by a dealer service department or an automotive air conditioning repair facility. Always wear eye protection when disconnecting air conditioning system fittings.

1   Have the refrigerant discharged and recovered by an air conditioning technician.

2   The receiver-drier is mounted on the passenger's side of the vehicle, at the end of the condenser.

3   Using a Allen wrench, remove the large plug at the bottom of the receiver-drier **(see illustration).** Use needle-nose pliers to grip and remove the filter-drier element inside the receiver.

4   Installation is the reverse of removal. Install a new filter-drier element and lubricate the plug's O-ring with a touch of refrigerant oil.

5   Have the system evacuated, charged and leak tested by the shop that discharged it. If the receiver-drier or condenser was replaced, have them add new refrigeration oil to the system. Use only refrigerant oil compatible with R-134a refrigerant.

14.4 Air conditioning compressor mounting details

A   Electrical connector (unplugged)
B   Refrigerant line flange bolts
C   Compressor mounting bolts

15.3 Disconnect the refrigerant connections on the right (passenger's) side of the condenser by removing the flange bolts

14   Air conditioning compressor - removal and installation

Refer to illustration 14.4

Warning: *The air conditioning system is under high pressure. Do not loosen any hose fittings or remove any components until the system has been discharged. Air conditioning refrigerant should be properly discharged by a dealer service department or an automotive air conditioning repair facility. Always wear eye protection when disconnecting air conditioning system fittings.*

Caution: *The receiver-drier element should be replaced whenever a new compressor is installed* (see Section 13).

1   Have the refrigerant discharged by an automotive air conditioning technician.

2   Disconnect the negative cable from the battery.

3   Raise the front of the vehicle and support it securely on jackstands. Remove the engine under cover (if equipped). Remove the drivebelt from the compressor (see Chapter 1).

4   Detach the wiring connector and disconnect the refrigerant lines **(see illustration)**.

5   Unbolt the compressor and lift it from the vehicle.

6   If a new or rebuilt compressor is being installed, follow the directions supplied with the compressor regarding the proper level of oil prior to installation.

7   Installation is the reverse of removal. Replace any O-rings with new ones specifically made for R-134a refrigerant and lubricate them with the same oil.

8   Have the system evacuated, recharged and leak tested by the shop that discharged it.

15   Air conditioning condenser - removal and installation

Refer to illustration 15.3

Warning 1: *The air conditioning system is under high pressure. Do not loosen any hose fittings or remove any components until the system has been discharged. Air conditioning refrigerant should be properly discharged by a dealer service department or an automotive air conditioning repair facility. Always wear eye protection when disconnecting air conditioning system fittings.*

Warning 2: *These models are equipped with a Supplemental Restraint System (SRS), more commonly known as airbags. Always disable the airbag system before working in the vicinity of any airbag system component to avoid the possibility of accidental deployment of the airbag(s), which could cause personal injury* (see Chapter 12).

Warning 3: *Wait until the engine is completely cool before beginning this procedure.*

Caution: *The receiver-drier element should be replaced if the condenser is being replaced due to leakage* (see Section 13).

1   Have the refrigerant discharged and recovered by an air conditioning technician.

2   Remove the radiator as described in Section 5.

3   Disconnect the condenser inlet and outlet fittings **(see illustration)**. Cap the open fittings immediately to keep moisture and contamination out of the system.

4   Remove the condenser mounting bolts **(see illustration 5.7)**, angle the condenser back and lift it out.

5   Install the condenser, brackets and bolts, making sure the rubber cushions fit on the mounting points properly.

6   Reconnect the refrigerant lines, using new O-rings where needed. If a new condenser has been installed, add approximately 1.5 to 2.0 fluid ounces of new, R-134a-compatible refrigerant oil.

7   Reinstall the remaining parts in the reverse order of removal.

8   Refill the cooling system (see Chapter 1).

9   Have the system evacuated, charged and leak tested by the shop that discharged it.

Notes

Chapter 4
Fuel and exhaust systems

Contents

Specifications

Fuel system

Fuel pressure (key On, engine Off)	303 to 344 kPa
Fuel injector resistance (at 20-degrees C)	
2004 and earlier models	13.4 to 14.2 ohms
2005 and later models	11.6 to 12.4 ohms

Torque specifications

	Nm
Inlet manifold mounting bolts	30
Fuel rail mounting bolts	
2004 and early models	19
2005 and later models	28
Throttle body mounting bolts/nuts	
2004 and early models	30
2005 and later models	9
Throttle body upper bracket bolts with manual transaxle only	13

1   General information

The fuel system consists of a fuel tank, an electric fuel pump (located in the fuel tank), an EFI/fuel pump relay, fuel injectors, a fuel pressure regulator, an air filter assembly and a throttle body unit. All models covered by this manual are equipped with a multi port fuel injection system.

Multi port fuel injection system

Multi port fuel injection uses timed impulses to sequentially inject the fuel directly into the inlet port of each cylinder. The injec-tors are controlled by the Powertrain Control Module (PCM). The PCM monitors various engine parameters and delivers the exact amount of fuel, in the correct sequence, into the inlet ports. The throttle body serves only to control the amount of air passing into the system. Because each cylinder is equipped with an injector mounted immediately adjacent to the inlet valve, much better control of the fuel/air mixture ratio is possible.

Fuel pump and lines

Fuel is delivered from the fuel tank to the fuel injection system through a metal line running along the underside of the vehicle by an electric fuel pump inside the fuel tank. On 1997 models, excessive pressure is bled off by the fuel pressure regulator located on the fuel rail and fuel is returned to the fuel tank through a separate return line. On 1998 and later models, the fuel pressure regulator is located in the fuel tank with the fuel pump, and excessive fuel pressure is bled-off directly into the fuel tank.

The fuel pump will operate as long as the engine is cranking or running and the ECM is receiving ignition reference pulses from the electronic ignition system (see Chapter 5). If there are no reference pulses, the fuel pump will shut off after 2 or 3 seconds.

3.3a A fuel pressure testing kit like this should contain all the necessary fittings and adapters, along with the fuel pressure gauge, to test most automotive systems

3.3b Attach the fuel pressure gauge with fuel hose and clamps between the fuel rail and the fuel feed line - turn the ignition key ON and check the fuel pressure

Exhaust system

The exhaust system includes an exhaust manifolds, a catalytic converter, an exhaust pipe, and a muffler.

The catalytic converter is an emission control device added to the exhaust system to reduce pollutants. A three-way (reduction) catalyst is used to reduce hydrocarbons (HC), carbon monoxide (CO) and oxides of nitrogen (NOx). Refer to Chapter 6 for more information regarding the catalytic converter.

2   Fuel pressure relief procedure

Warning: *Petrol is extremely flammable, so take extra precautions when you work on any part of the fuel system. Don't smoke or allow open flames or bare light bulbs near the work area, and don't work in a garage where a gas-type appliance is present. Since petrol is carcinogenic, wear fuel-resistant gloves when there's a possibility of being exposed to fuel, and, if you spill any fuel on your skin, rinse it off immediately with soap and water. Mop up any spills immediately and do not store fuel-soaked rags where they could ignite. The fuel system is under constant pressure, so, if any fuel lines are to be disconnected, the fuel pressure in the system must be relieved first. When you perform any kind of work on the fuel system, wear safety glasses and have a Class B type fire extinguisher on hand.*

1   Before servicing any fuel system component, you must relieve the fuel pressure to minimize the risk of fire or personal injury.
2   Remove the fuel filler cap - this will relieve any pressure built up in the tank.
3   Remove the rear seat cushion (see Chapter 11), then remove the cover and unplug the fuel pump electrical connector **(see illustrations 5.4 and 5.5a)**.
4   Attempt to start the engine - the engine will stall. Crank the engine for 3 or 4

seconds, then turn the ignition key to Off.
5   The fuel system is now depressurized. **Note:** *Place a rag around the fuel line before removing any hose clamp or fitting to prevent any residual fuel from spilling onto the engine.*
6   Before working on the fuel system, disconnect the cable from the negative terminal of the battery.

3   Fuel pump/fuel pressure - check

Warning: *Petrol is extremely flammable, so take extra precautions when you work on any part of the fuel system. See the* **Warning** *in Section 2.*

General checks

1   Check that there is adequate fuel in the fuel tank.
2   Verify the fuel pump actually runs. Have an assistant turn the ignition switch to ON - you should hear a brief whirring noise (for approximately two seconds) as the pump comes on and pressurizes the system. **Note:** *The fuel pump is easily heard through the gas tank filler neck.* If there is no response from the fuel pump (makes no sound) proceed to Step 8 and check the fuel pump electrical circuit. If the fuel pump runs, but a fuel system problem is suspected, continue with the fuel pump pressure check.

Fuel pump pressure check

Refer to illustration 3.3a and 3.3b
Note: *In order to perform the fuel pressure test, you will need to obtain a fuel pressure gauge capable of measuring high fuel pressure and the proper adapter set for the specific fuel injection system.*
3   Relieve the fuel system pressure (see Section 2). Remove the fuel line from the fuel

rail and where this line attaches to a steel line near the master cylinder. A simple special tool is used to separate the quick-connect fittings (see Section 4). The fuel pressure test hose temporarily replaces this factory hose **(see illustrations)**. Make sure the clamps are tight on the hoses.
4   Turn all the accessories Off and switch the ignition key On. The fuel pump should run for about two seconds; note the reading on the gauge. After the pump stops running, the pressure should hold steady. After five minutes it should not drop below the minimum listed in this Chapter's Specifications.
5   Start the engine and let it idle at normal operating temperature. The pressure should remain the same. If all the pressure readings are within the limits listed in this Chapter's Specifications, the system is operating properly.
6   If the fuel pressure is not within specifications, check the following:

   a) *If the pressure is higher than specified, replace the fuel pressure regulator (see Section 6).*
   b) *If the pressure is lower than specified, the fuel filter could be clogged, the fuel line from the fuel rail to the fuel tank could be restricted, the fuel injectors could be leaking, or the fuel pressure regulator and/or the fuel pump could be defective (this is probably the most likely cause). In this situation, it is recommended that both the fuel pressure regulator and fuel pump be replaced to prevent any future fuel pressure problems.* **Note:** *The fuel filter is part of the fuel pump assembly. Check with your local auto parts store or dealer parts department regarding parts availability.*

7   After the testing is done, relieve the fuel pressure (see Section 2) and remove the fuel pressure gauge.

4.12a To disconnect a plastic type fitting, squeeze the retaining tabs in and pull the lines apart

4.12b To disconnect a metal collar type quick-connect fitting, remove the safety tether and place the tool squarely over the fuel line; push the tool into the fitting and pull the lines apart (the tool is not required to connect the fitting)

Fuel pump electrical circuit check

8   If the pump does not turn on (makes no sound) with the ignition switch in the ON position, check the EFI fuse located in the engine compartment fuse centre. If the fuse is blown, replace the fuse and see if the pump works. If the pump now works, check for a short in the circuit between the fuel pump relay (circuit opening relay) and the fuel pump. Also check the EFI relay and the circuit opening relay (C/OPN).

9   If the relays are good and the fuel pump does not operate, check the wiring from the underbonnet fuse/relay box to the fuel pump.

4.12c A special tool (available at most auto parts stores) is required to disconnect the metal collar type quick-connect fitting

4   Fuel lines and fittings - general information and replacement

Warning: *Petrol is extremely flammable, so take extra precautions when you work on any part of the fuel system. See the* **Warning** *in Section 2.*

1   Always relieve the fuel pressure before servicing fuel lines or fittings (see Section 2).
2   The fuel line extends from the fuel tank to the engine compartment. The line is secured to the underbody with clip and screw assemblies. This line must be occasionally inspected for leaks, kinks and dents.
3   If evidence of dirt is found in the system or fuel filter during disassembly, the line should be disconnected and blown out. Check the fuel strainer on the fuel gauge sending unit (see Section 5) for damage and deterioration.

Steel tubing

4   If replacement of a fuel line or emission line is called for, use welded steel tubing meeting the manufacturer's specifications or its equivalent.
5   Don't use copper or aluminum tubing to replace steel tubing. These materials cannot withstand normal vehicle vibration.
6   Because fuel lines used on fuel-injected

vehicles are under high pressure, they require special consideration.

7   Some fuel lines have threaded fittings with O-rings. Any time the fittings are loosened to service or replace components:

a) *Use a backup wrench while loosening and tightening the fittings.*
b) *Check all O-rings for cuts, cracks and deterioration. Replace any that appear hardened, worn or damaged.*
c) *If the lines are replaced, always use original equipment parts, or parts that meet the original equipment standards specified in this Section.*

Flexible hose

Warning: *Use only original equipment replacement hoses or their equivalent. Others may fail from the high pressures of this system.*

8   Don't route fuel hose within 10 mm of any part of the exhaust system or within 25 cm of the catalytic converter. Metal lines and rubber hoses must never be allowed to chafe against the frame. A minimum of 6 mm clearance must be maintained around a line or hose to prevent contact with the frame.
9   Some models may be equipped with nylon fuel line and quick-connect fittings at the fuel filter and/or fuel pump. The quick-connect fittings cannot be serviced separately. Do not attempt to service these types of fuel

lines in the event the retainer tabs or the line becomes damaged. Replace the entire fuel line as an assembly.

Replacement

Refer to illustrations 4.12a, 4.12b and 4.12c

10   In the event of any fuel line damage (metal or flexible lines) it is necessary to replace the damaged lines with factory replacement parts. Others may fail from the high pressures of this system.
11   Relieve the fuel pressure.
12   Remove all fasteners attaching the lines to the vehicle body. On fuel lines so equipped, detach the clamp(s) that attach the fuel hoses to the metal lines, then pull the hose off the fitting. Twisting the hoses back and forth will allow them to separate more easily. To separate quick-connect fittings, hold the connector with one hand and depress the retaining tabs with the other hand, then separate the connector from the pipe **(see illustrations)**. Some fittings require the use of a dedicated, yet simple tool **(see illustrations)**.
13   Installation is the reverse of removal, making sure to use new O-rings. On plastic quick-connect fittings, align the retainer locking pawls with the connector grooves. Push the connector onto the pipe until both retaining pawls lock with a clicking sound, then reinstall the covers.

5.4 On early models, the cover is secured by four screws. On later models prise the fuel pump access cover off (it's secured by butyl tape).

5.5a Disconnect both of the electrical connectors

5.5b Use needle-nose pliers to release the quick-release fitting securing the fuel return line

5.5c Slide out the retaining clip and remove the fuel pressure hose from the assembly

5.6 Remove the fuel pump/sending unit assembly mounting screws (2003 and 2004 models)

5   Fuel pump and fuel filter - removal and installation

Refer to illustrations 5.4, 5.5a, 5.5b, 5.5c, 5.6, 5.7, 5.8, 5.9a and 5.9b

Warning: *Petrol is extremely flammable, so take extra precautions when you work on any part of the fuel system. See the* **Warning** *in Section 2.*

1   Relieve the fuel system pressure (see Section 2), then disconnect the cable from the negative terminal of the battery. Remove the fuel tank cap.

2   Disconnect the cable from the negative terminal of the battery.

3   Remove the rear seat from inside the passenger compartment (see Chapter 11).

4   Remove the fuel pump/sending unit access cover **(see illustration)**.

5   Unplug the electrical connectors **(see illustration)**, then disconnect the fuel lines **(see illustrations)**. **Note:** *On 2005 and later models, the quick-release fitting on the pressure line can be squeezed by hand, without pliers.*

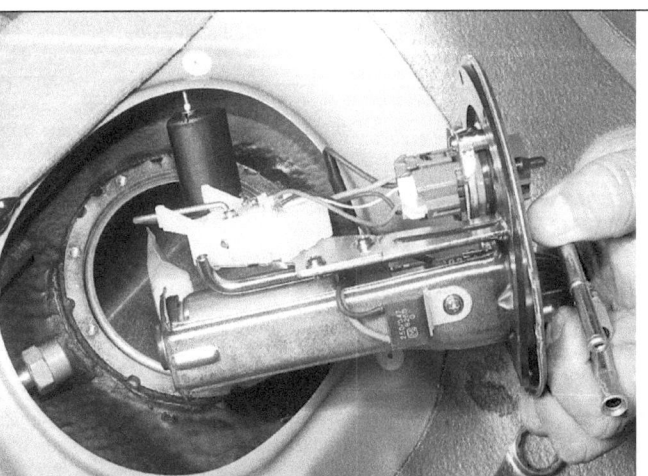

5.7 Lift the fuel pump/sending unit assembly from the fuel tank at an angle so as not to damage the inlet screen or float arm

6   Remove the fuel pump/sending unit retaining screws and remove the mounting flange **(see illustration)**. **Note:** *On some later models, the fuel pump assembly is retained to the tank by a large screw-on ring. A special tool (available at most auto parts stores) is available which makes loosening and tight-* *ening this ring very easy, but a large pair of water pump pliers will work.*

7   Carefully withdraw the fuel pump/fuel level sending unit assembly from the fuel tank **(see illustration)**.

8   The components of the fuel pump assembly are modular and all attach to the

5.8 Exploded view of the fuel pump assembly

A *Fuel filter*
B *Fuel pressure regulator*
C *Fuel pump*
D *Sock (inlet) filter*
E *Fuel level sending unit*

5.9a After removing the plastic support, carefully use a screwdriver to remove the clip securing the sock filter to the pump

main housing **(see illustration)**.
9   Remove the plastic support on the bottom of the pump by releasing the clips with a screwdriver, the pull off the rubber isolator, the fuel sock filter clip, then the electrical connector **(see illustrations)**.
10   Withdraw the pump from the housing.
11   Inspect the strainer for contamination. If it is dirty, replace it.
12   Reassemble the fuel pump/sending unit in the reverse order of disassembly.
13   Install the fuel pump/sending unit assembly in the fuel tank. Connect the fuel line and electrical connectors.
14   The remainder of installation is the reverse of removal.

6   Fuel pressure regulator - removal and installation

Warning: *Petrol is extremely flammable, so take extra precautions when you work on any part of the fuel system. See the* **Warning** *in Section 2.*

6.5 To remove the fuel pressure regulator from the fuel rail on a 1997 models, detach the fuel return hose, remove the two regulator bolts and separate the regulator from the fuel rail (fuel rail removed for clarity)

1   Relieve the fuel pressure (see Section 2) and detach the cable from the negative terminal of the battery. **Caution:** *If the stereo in your vehicle is equipped with an anti-theft system, make sure you have the correct activation code before disconnecting the battery.*

1997 models

Refer to illustrations 6.5 and 6.6
2   Detach the vacuum hose from the regulator.
3   Place a metal container or shop towel under the fuel return hose.
4   Slide the clamp down the hose and remove the fuel return hose from the regulator.
5   Remove the pressure regulator mounting bolts (see illustration) and detach the pressure regulator from the fuel rail.
6   Use a new O ring and make sure that the pressure regulator is installed properly on the fuel rail (see illustration).
7   The remainder of installation is the reverse of removal.

1998 and later models

Refer to illustration 6.10
8   Remove the fuel tank cap.
9   Remove the fuel pump assembly (see Section 5).

6.6 If the fuel pressure regulator is cocked during installation, it will not seal properly

5.9b Release the electrical connector at the top of the fuel pump assembly

10   Twist the fuel pressure regulator from the assembly **(see illustration)**.
11   Installation is the reverse of removal. Be sure to install a new O-ring on the fuel pressure regulator.

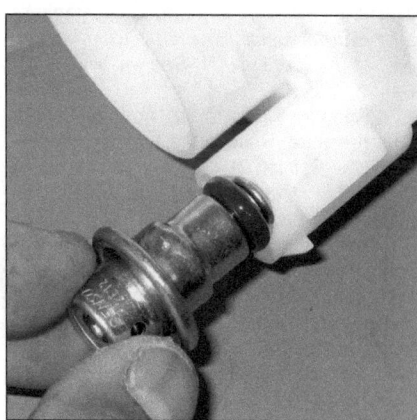

6.10 The fuel pressure regulator is a push-fit in the fuel pump/sending unit assembly; make sure the old O-ring comes out with it

7.4 Disconnect the electrical connector (A) and prise the fuel-level sending unit from the clips (B)

8.8 Remove the clamp that retains the fuel filler hose (A) and separate the fuel hose disconnects (B)

7   Fuel level sending unit - replacement

Refer to illustration 7.4

Warning: *Petrol is extremely flammable, so take extra precautions when you work on any part of the fuel system. See the* **Warning** *in Section 2.*

1   Remove the fuel pump/fuel level sending unit assembly from the fuel tank (see Section 5).

2   Carefully angle the sending unit out of the opening without damaging the fuel level float located at the bottom of the assembly.

3   Disconnect the electrical connector from the sending unit.

4   Prise the sending unit from the retaining clips **(see illustration)** and separate it from the assembly.

5   Installation is the reverse of removal.

8   Fuel tank - removal and installation

Refer to illustrations 8.8 and 8.9

Warning: *Petrol is extremely flammable, so take extra precautions when you work on any part of the fuel system. See the* **Warning** *in Section 2.*

1   Remove the fuel filler cap to relieve fuel tank pressure. Relieve the fuel system pressure (see Section 2).

2   Detach the cable from the negative terminal of the battery.

3   Siphon or pump the fuel into an approved container using a siphoning kit or hand operated pump (available at most auto parts stores). **Warning:** *Do not start the siphoning action by mouth!*

4   Remove the fuel pump access cover and disconnect the fuel pump electrical connector and fuel lines from the fuel pump unit (see Section 5).

5   Raise the vehicle and support it securely on jackstands.

6   Remove the centre exhaust pipe and

the heat insulator from the vehicle (see Section 16).

7   Detach the parking brake cables from the underbody and position them aside.

8   Disconnect the fuel lines, the vapor return line and the fuel filler hose **(see illustration)**. **Note:** *Be sure to plug the hoses to prevent leakage and contamination of the fuel system.*

9   Support the fuel tank with a floor jack. Place a sturdy plank between the jack head and the fuel tank to protect the tank. Remove the bolts from the fuel tank retaining straps **(see illustration)**.

10   Lower the tank enough to disconnect the electrical connector and ground strap from the fuel pump/fuel gauge sending unit, if you have not already done so.

11   Remove the tank from the vehicle.

12   Installation is the reverse of removal.

9   Fuel tank cleaning and repair - general information

1   Any repairs to the fuel tank or filler neck should be carried out by a professional who has experience in this critical and potentially dangerous work. Even after cleaning and flushing of the fuel system, explosive fumes can remain and ignite during repair of the tank.

2   If the fuel tank is removed from the vehicle, it should not be placed in an area where sparks or open flames could ignite the fumes coming out of the tank. Be especially careful inside garages where a gas-type appliance is located, because it could cause an explosion.

10   Air filter housing - removal and installation

Refer to illustration 10.3

1   Disconnect the air inlet hose and breather hose from the housing cover. Disconnect the electrical connector from the inlet

8.9 Remove the tank strap bolts (shown for clarity without supports required for tank removal)

air temperature sensor.

2   Detach the clips and remove the air filter housing cover and the air filter element (see Chapter 1).

3   Remove the three bolts and remove the air filter housing from the engine compartment **(see illustration)**.

4   Installation is the reverse of removal.

10.3 Remove the bolts that retain the air filter housing to the engine compartment

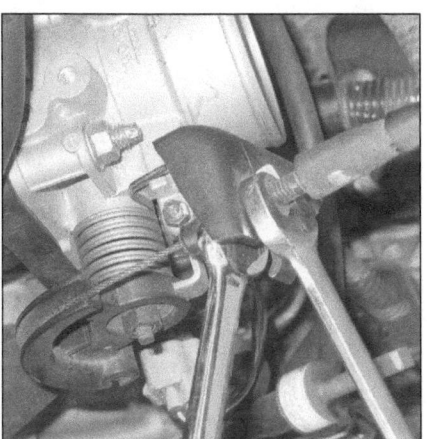

11.2 Loosen the locknuts on the accelerator cable

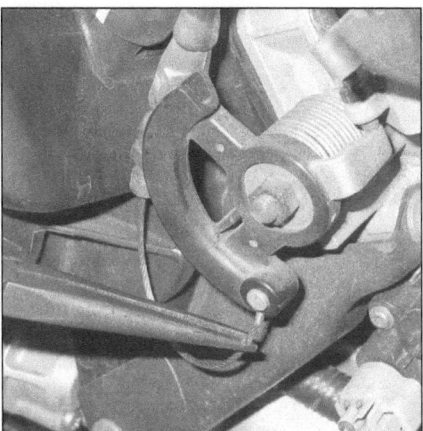

11.3a Rotate the throttle lever and remove the cable end from the slot in the throttle lever . . .

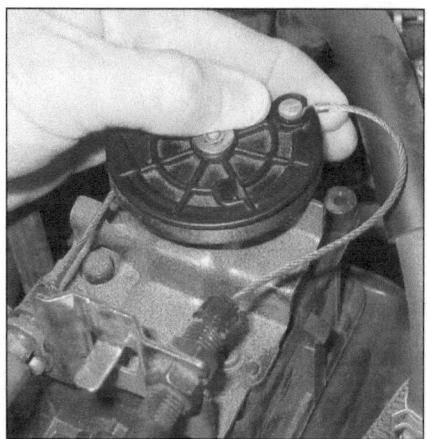

11.3b . . . or the cruise control actuator

11 Accelerator cable - removal, installation and adjustment

Refer to illustrations 11.2, 11.3a, 11.3b and 11.4

Note 1: *2005 and later models do not have an accelerator cable. Instead, the throttle body has an electric motor that operates the throttle and is controlled by the PCM.*

Note 2: *Models with cruise control have two accelerator cables - one from the accelerator pedal to the cruise control actuator and one from the cruise control actuator to the throttle body.*

Removal

1   Detach the cable from the negative terminal of the battery. On models with cruise control, remove the cover from the cruise control actuator.

2   Loosen the locknut on the threaded portion of the throttle cable at the throttle body or cruise control actuator **(see illustration)**.

3   Rotate the throttle lever or cruise control actuator and slip the throttle cable end out of the slot in the lever **(see illustration)**.

4   Detach the throttle cable from the accelerator pedal **(see illustration)**. Remove the two bolts securing the cable retainer to the firewall.

5   From inside the vehicle, pull the cable through the firewall.

Installation and adjustment

6   Installation is the reverse of removal. Make sure the cable casing grommet seats properly in the firewall.

7   To adjust the cable, fully depress the accelerator pedal and check that the throttle is fully opened.

8   If not fully opened, loosen the locknuts, depress the accelerator pedal and adjust the cable until the throttle is fully open.

9   Tighten the locknuts and recheck the adjustment. Make sure the throttle closes fully when the pedal is released.

12 Fuel injection system - general information

1   All models are equipped with a multi port fuel injection system. The fuel injection system is composed of three basic subsystems: fuel system, air induction system and electronic engine control system.

Fuel system

2   An electric fuel pump located inside the fuel tank supplies fuel under constant pressure to the fuel rail, which distributes fuel evenly to all injectors. From the fuel rail, fuel is injected into the intake ports, just above the intake valves, by fuel injectors. The amount of fuel supplied by the injectors is precisely controlled by an electronic Engine Control Modulo (ECM). On 1997 models, a pressure regulator controls system pressure in relation to inlet manifold vacuum. A fuel filter between the fuel pump and the fuel rail filters fuel to protect the components of the system. On 1998 and later models, the fuel pressure regulator maintains a constant pressure to the fuel rail regardless of engine load. The fuel pressure regulator and fuel filter are located in the fuel tank along with the fuel pump.

Air induction system

3   The air induction system consists of an air filter housing, the throttle body and the duct connecting the two. The throttle plate inside the throttle body is controlled by the driver. As the throttle plate opens, additional air is drawn into the cylinders. The information provided by the various sensors allows the PCM to determine the exact amount of fuel to be injected by the injectors during the various operating conditions.

Electronic engine control system

4   The electronic engine control system controls the fuel injection, ignition and emissions systems by means of a Powertrain Control Module (PCM), which employs a micro-

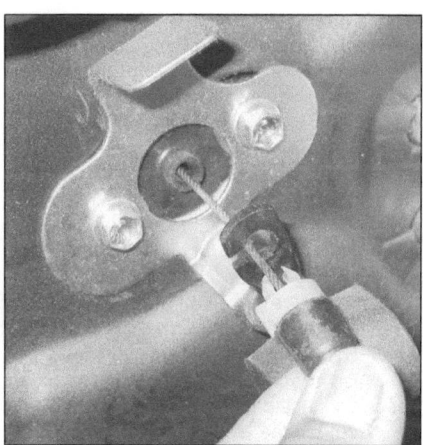

11.4 Separate the cable from the accelerator pedal arm and slide the cable end out of the slot in the arm

processor. The PCM receives signals from a number of information sensors, which monitor such variables as inlet air temperature, throttle angle, coolant temperature, engine rpm, engine load, vehicle speed and exhaust oxygen content. These signals help the PCM determine the injection duration necessary for the optimum air/fuel ratio. The sensors and their corresponding PCM-controlled relays, are located throughout the engine compartment. For further information regarding the PCM and its relationship to the fuel injection and ignition systems, see Chapter 6.

13 Fuel injection system - check

Refer to illustrations 13.7, 13.8 and 13.9

Note: *The following procedure is based on the assumption that the fuel pump is working and the fuel pressure is adequate (see Section 3).*

1   Check the ground wire connections for tightness. Check all wiring and electrical connectors that are related to the system. Loose electrical connectors and poor grounds can cause many problems that resemble more

13.7 Use a stethoscope or a screwdriver to determine if the injectors are working properly - they should make a steady clicking sound that rises and falls with engine speed changes

13.8 Install the "noid" light into the fuel injector electrical connector and check to see that it flashes with the engine running

serious malfunctions.

2   Check to see that the battery is fully charged, as the control unit and sensors depend on an accurate supply voltage in order to properly meter the fuel.

3   Check the air filter element - a dirty or partially blocked filter will severely impede performance and economy (see Chapter 1).

4   Check the fuses. If a blown fuse is found, replace it and see if it blows again. If it does, search for a grounded wire in the fuel injection system wiring harness.

5   Check the air inlet duct from the air cleaner housing to the inlet manifold for leaks, which will result in an excessively lean mixture. Also check the condition of the vacuum hoses connected to the inlet manifold.

6   Remove the air inlet duct from the throttle body and check for dirt, carbon, varnish, or other residue in the throttle body, particularly around the throttle plate. If it's dirty, refer to Chapter 6 and troubleshoot the PCV system for the cause of excessive varnish buildup.

7   With the engine running, place a stethoscope against each injector, one at a time, and listen for a clicking sound, indicating operation **(see illustration)**. If you don't have an automotive stethoscope you can use a long screwdriver; just place the tip of the screw-

driver against the injector body and press your ear against the handle.

8   If there is a problem with an injector, purchase a special injector test light (noid light) and install it into the injector electrical connector **(see illustration)**. Start the engine and make sure that each injector connector flashes the noid light. This will test for the proper voltage signal to the injector.

9   With the engine OFF and the fuel injector electrical connectors disconnected, measure the resistance of each injector **(see illustration)**. Compare your measurement with the value listed in this Chapter's Specifications. If the injector resistance is excessive or an open or short circuit is indicated, replace the injector (see Section 15).

10   Additional fuel injection control system component checks can be found in Chapter 6.

14   Throttle body - removal and installation

Refer to illustrations 14.6 and 14.7

Warning: *Wait until the engine is completely cool before beginning this procedure.*

1   Detach the cable from the negative terminal of the battery.

2   Loosen the hose clamps and remove the air inlet duct.

3   On 2004 and earlier models, detach the accelerator cable from the throttle lever (see Section 11).

4   Detach the throttle cable bracket and set it aside (it's not necessary to detach the throttle cable from the bracket).

5   Clearly label, then detach, all vacuum and coolant hoses from the throttle body. Plug the coolant hoses to prevent coolant loss.

6   Disconnect the electrical connectors from the throttle position sensor, idle air control valve, manifold absolute pressure sensor and/or mass airflow sensor, as required. On 2005 and models, disconnect the electrical connector at the throttle body motor **(see illustration)**.

7   Remove the throttle body mounting bolts/nuts **(see illustration)**.

8   Detach the throttle body and gasket from the inlet manifold.

9   Using a soft brush and carburettor cleaner, thoroughly clean the throttle body casting, then blow out all passages with com-

13.9 Using an ohmmeter, measure the resistance across the terminals of the injector

14.6 On 2005 and later models, disconnect the throttle body motor electrical connector (arrow)

14.7 Throttle-body mounting details - disconnect the electrical connectors and hoses, then remove the two mounting nuts and two bolts

15.5 Remove the two mounting bolts and pull up the fuel rail from the cylinder head

pressed air. **Caution:** *Do not clean the throttle position sensor with anything. Just wipe it off carefully with a clean, soft cloth.*

10   Installation of the throttle body is the reverse of removal.

11   Tighten the throttle body mounting bolts/nuts to the torque listed in this Chapter's Specifications.

12   Check the coolant level, adding as necessary (see Chapter 1).

15   Fuel rail and injectors - removal and installation

Refer to illustrations 15.5, 15.6a, 15.6b and 15.7

Warning: *Petrol is extremely flammable, so take extra precautions when you work on any part of the fuel system. See the* **Warning** *in Section 2.*

Caution: *If the stereo in your vehicle is equipped with an anti-theft system, make sure you have the correct activation code before disconnecting the battery.*

1   Relieve the fuel pressure (see Section 2) and detach the cable from the negative terminal of the battery.

2   Detach the PCV hose from the valve cover and remove the engine cover (over the valve cover).

3   Disconnect the electrical connectors from the fuel injectors. Open the wiring harness clamps and position the wiring harness aside.

4   Disconnect the fuel line leading to the fuel rail (see Section 4 for fuel line disconnect procedures).

5   Remove the fuel rail mounting bolts and carefully withdraw the fuel rail and injectors from the cylinder head **(see illustration)**.

6   Replace the O-ring and grommet on each injector **(see illustrations)**.

7   Remove the insulators in the cylinder head and replace them with new ones **(see illustration)**.

8   Lubricate the O-rings with clean engine oil and install the fuel injectors onto the fuel rail. Make sure the spacers are in place and install the fuel rail/injector assembly onto the cylinder head. Install the fuel rail mounting bolts and tighten the bolts to the torque listed in this Chapter's Specifications.

9   The remainder of installation is the reverse of removal.

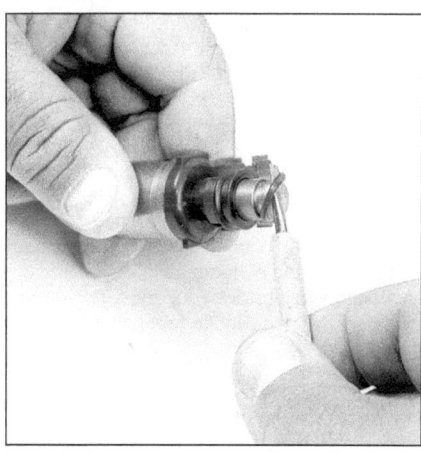

15.6a Remove the O-ring from the injector

16   Exhaust system servicing - general information

Refer to illustration 16.1

Warning: *Inspection and repair of exhaust system components should be done only after the system components have cooled completely.*

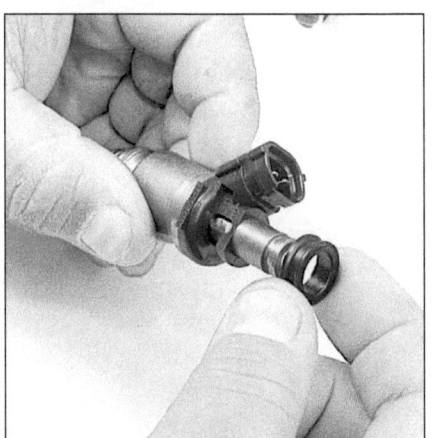

15.6b Remove the grommet from the injector

15.7 Install new insulators in the cylinder head holes (A), and position the two spacers (B) before installing the fuel rail

1   The exhaust system consists of the exhaust manifold, catalytic converter, the muffler, the tailpipe and all connecting pipes, brackets, hangers and clamps. The exhaust system is attached to the body with mounting brackets and rubber hangers **(see illustration)**. If any of these parts are damaged or deteriorated, excessive noise and vibration will be transmitted to the body.

2   Conducting regular inspections of the exhaust system will keep it safe and quiet. Look for any damaged or bent parts, open seams, holes, loose connections, excessive corrosion or other defects which could allow exhaust fumes to enter the vehicle. Deteriorated exhaust system components should not be repaired - they should be replaced with new parts.

3   If the exhaust system components are extremely corroded or rusted together, they will probably have to be cut from the exhaust system. The convenient way to accomplish this is to have a muffler repair shop remove the corroded sections with a cutting torch. If, however, you want to save money by doing it yourself and you don't have an oxy/acetylene welding outfit with a cutting torch, simply cut off the old components with a hack-saw. If you have compressed air, special pneumatic cutting chisels can also be used. If you do decide to tackle the job at home, be sure to wear eye protection to protect your eyes from metal chips and work gloves to protect your hands.

16.1 Check all of the exhaust system rubber hangers for cracking, replacing them as necessary

4   Here are some simple guidelines to apply when repairing the exhaust system:

a) *Work from the back to the front when removing exhaust system components.*

b) *Apply penetrating oil to the exhaust system component fasteners to make them easier to remove.*

c) *Use new gaskets, hangers and clamps when installing exhaust system components.*

d) *Apply anti-seize compound to the threads of all exhaust system fasteners during reassembly.*

e) *Be sure to allow sufficient clearance between newly installed parts and all points on the underbody to avoid overheating the floor pan and possibly damaging the interior carpet and insulation. Pay particularly close attention to the catalytic converter and its heat shield.* **Warning:** *The catalytic converter operates at very high temperatures and takes a long time to cool. Wait until it's completely cool before attempting to remove the converter. Failure to do so could result in serious burns.*

Chapter 5
Engine electrical systems

Contents

Specifications

Ignition timing (1997 models)
With test terminals TE1 and E1 earthed .... 10-degrees BTDC

Ignition coil resistance (cold)
1997 models
  Distributors with internal igniter
    Primary resistance .... 1.11 to 1.75 ohms
    Secondary resistance .... 9.0 to 15.7K ohms
  Distributors with external igniter
    Primary resistance .... 0.36 to 0.55 ohms
    Secondary resistance .... 9.0 to 15.4K ohms
1998 and 1999
  Primary resistance .... Not applicable
  Secondary resistance .... 9.7 to 16.7K ohms
2000 and later .... Not applicable

Distributor
Air gap .... 0.20 to 0.40 mm
Pick-up coil resistance
  Distributors with internal igniter
    Cold (below 39-degrees C)
      Terminals G+ and G- .... 185 to 275 ohms
      Terminals NE+ and NE- .... 370 to 550 ohms
    Hot (above 40-degrees C)
      Terminals G+ and G- .... 240 to 325 ohms
      Terminals NE+ and NE- .... 475 to 650 ohms
  Distributors with external igniter
    Cold (below 39-degrees C)
      Terminals G+ and G- .... 185 to 275 ohms
      Terminals NE+ and NE- .... 1,630 to 2,740 ohms
    Hot (above 40-degrees C)
      Terminals G+ and G- .... 240 to 325 ohms
      Terminals NE+ and NE- .... 2,065 to 3,225 ohms

Charging system

Charging voltage	12.9 to 14.9 volts
Standard amperage	
All lights and accessories turned off.................................	Less than 10 amps
Headlights (hi-beam) and heater blower motor turned on.................	30 amps or more
Alternator brush length	
Standard...	10.3 mm
Minimum..	1.58 mm

1   General information

The engine electrical systems include all ignition, charging and starting components. Because of their engine-related functions, these components are discussed separately from chassis electrical devices such as the lights, the instruments, etc. (which are included in Chapter 12).

Always observe the following precautions when working on the electrical systems:

a) *Be extremely careful when servicing engine electrical components. They are easily damaged if checked, connected or handled improperly.*

b) *Never leave the ignition switch on for long periods of time (10 minutes maximum) with the engine off.*

c) *Don't disconnect the battery cables while the engine is running.*

d) *Maintain correct polarity when connecting a battery cable from another vehicle during jump-starting.*

e) *Always disconnect the negative cable first and hook it up last or the battery may be shorted by the tool being used to loosen the cable clamps.*

It's also a good idea to review the safety-related information regarding the engine electrical systems located in the *Safety first* section near the front of this manual before beginning any operation included in this Chapter.

2   Battery - emergency jump starting

Refer to the *Booster battery (jump) starting* procedure at the front of this manual.

3   Battery - check and replacement

Warning: *Hydrogen gas is produced by the battery, so keep open flames and lighted cigarettes away from it at all times. Always wear eye protection when working around a battery. Rinse off spilled electrolyte immediately with large amounts of water.*

Check

Refer to illustrations 3.2 and 3.3

1   The battery's surface charge must be removed before accurate voltage measurements can be made. Turn On the high beams for ten seconds, then turn them Off, and let the vehicle stand for two minutes. Remove the battery from the vehicle (see Steps 4 through 10).

2   Check the battery state of charge. Visually inspect the indicator eye on the top of the battery, if the indicator eye is clear, charge the battery as described in Chapter 1. Next perform an open voltage circuit test using a digital voltmeter **(see illustration)**. With the engine and all accessories Off, connect the negative probe of the voltmeter to the negative terminal of the battery and the positive probe to the positive terminal of the battery. The battery voltage should be 12.4 volts or more. If the battery is less than the specified voltage, charge the battery before proceeding to the next test. Do not proceed with the battery load test unless the battery charge is correct.

3   Perform a battery load test. An accurate check of the battery condition can only be performed with a load tester (available at most auto parts stores). This test evaluates the ability of the battery to operate the starter and other accessories during periods of heavy amperage draw (load). Install a special battery load-testing tool onto the terminals **(see illustration)**. Load test the battery according to the tool manufacturer's instructions. This tool utilizes a carbon pile to increase the load demand (amperage draw) on the battery. Maintain the load on the battery for 15 seconds or less and observe that the battery voltage does not drop below 9.6 volts. If the battery condition is weak or defective, the tool will indicate this condition immediately. **Note:** *Cold temperatures will cause the minimum voltage requirements to drop slightly. Follow the chart given in the tool manufacturer's instructions to compensate for cold climates. Minimum load voltage for freezing temperatures (0-degrees C) should be approximately 9.1 volts.*

3.2 To test the open circuit voltage of the battery, connect a voltmeter to the battery - a fully charged battery should measure at least 12.4 volts (depending on outside air temperature)

3.3 Connect a battery load tester to the battery and check the battery condition under load following the tool manufacturer's instructions

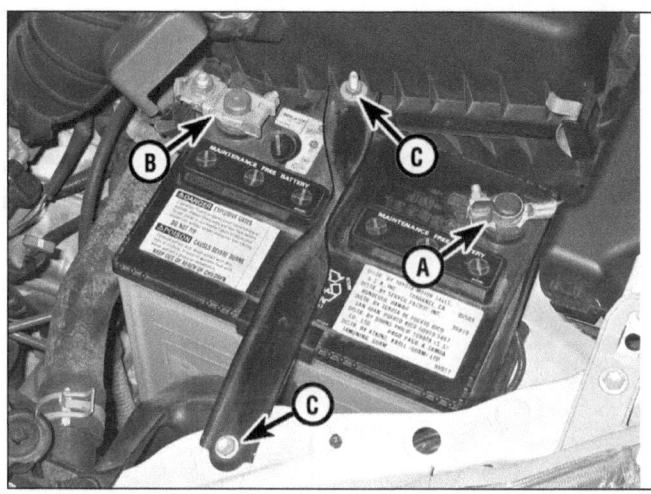

3.6 To remove the battery, detach the negative battery cable first, then the positive cable, remove the hold-down clamp nut and bolt (arrows) and remove the hold-down clamp

Replacement

Refer to illustration 3.6

4   Disconnect the cable from the negative battery terminal.

5   Disconnect the positive battery cable.

6   Remove the battery hold-down clamp **(see illustration)**.

7   Remove the battery and place it on a workbench. **Note:** *Battery handling tools are available at most auto parts stores for a reasonable price. They make it easier to remove and carry the battery.*

8   While the battery is removed, inspect the tray, retainer brackets and related fasteners for corrosion or damage.

9   If corrosion is evident, remove the battery tray and use a baking soda/water solution to clean the corroded area to prevent further oxidation. Repaint the area as necessary using rust resistant paint.

10   Clean and service the battery and cables (see Chapter 1).

11   If you are replacing the battery, make sure you purchase one that is identical to yours, with the same dimensions, amperage rating, cold cranking amps rating, etc. Make sure it is fully charged prior to installation in the vehicle.

12   Installation is the reverse of removal. Connect the positive cable first and the negative cable last.

13   After connecting the cables to the battery, apply a light coating of battery terminal corrosion inhibitor to the connections to help prevent corrosion.

---

4   Battery cables - replacement

1   Periodically inspect the entire length of each battery cable for damage, cracked or burned insulation and corrosion. Poor battery cable connections can cause starting problems and decreased engine performance.

2   Check the cable-to-terminal connections at the ends of the cables for cracks, loose wire strands and corrosion. The presence of white, fluffy deposits under the insulation at the cable terminal connection is a sign that the cable is corroded and should be replaced. Check the terminals for distortion, missing mounting bolts and corrosion.

3   When removing the cables, always disconnect the negative cable first and hook it up last or the battery may be shorted by the tool used to loosen the cable clamps. Even if only the positive cable is being replaced, be sure to disconnect the negative cable from the battery first (see Chapter 1 for further information regarding battery cable removal).

4   Disconnect the old cables from the battery, then trace each of them to their opposite ends and detach them from the starter solenoid and earth terminals. Note the routing of each cable to ensure correct installation.

5   If you are replacing either or both of the old cables, take them with you when buying new cables. It is vitally important that you replace the cables with identical parts. Cables have characteristics that make them easy to identify: positive cables are usually red, larger in cross-section and have a larger diameter battery post clamp; earth cables are usually black, smaller in cross-section and have a slightly smaller diameter clamp for the negative post.

6   Clean the threads of the solenoid or earth connection with a wire brush to remove rust and corrosion. Apply a light coat of battery terminal corrosion inhibitor, or petroleum jelly, to the threads to prevent future corrosion.

7   Attach the cable to the solenoid or earth connection and tighten the mounting nut/bolt securely.

8   Before connecting a new cable to the battery, make sure that it reaches the battery post without having to be stretched.

9   Connect the positive cable first, followed by the negative cable.

---

5   Ignition system - general information and precautions

1   There are two types of ignition systems used on the models covered by this manual - 1997 models are equipped with a conven-tional distributor ignition system and 1998 and later models are equipped with a distributor-less ignition system.

1997 models only

2   The distributor ignition system includes the ignition switch, the battery, the igniter, the pick-up coil, the ignition coil, the primary (low voltage) and secondary (high voltage) wiring circuits, the distributor and the spark plugs. The ignition system is controlled by the Engine Control Module (ECM). Using data provided by information sensors which monitor various engine functions (such as rpm, intake air volume, engine temperature, etc.), the ECM ensures a perfectly timed spark under all conditions.

3   The distributor ignition system is divided into two groups; distributor with external igniter and distributor with internal igniter. On the latter ignition system, the igniter is located within the distributor housing. On both systems the ignition coil is mounted inside the distributor. When diagnosing these units, be sure to make all the necessary ignition system checks before replacing any components, as they are expensive and usually non-returnable.

1998 and later models

4   1998 and later models are equipped with a distributorless ignition system. The ignition system consists of the battery, ignition coils, spark plugs, camshaft position sensor, crankshaft position sensor and the Engine Control Module (ECM). The ECM controls the ignition timing and spark advance characteristics for the engine. The ignition timing is not adjustable.

5   The crankshaft position sensor and camshaft position sensor generate pulses that are input to the Engine Control Module. The ECM determines piston position and engine speed from these two sensors. The ECM calculates injector sequence and ignition timing from the piston position. Refer to Chapter 6 for testing and replacement procedures for the crankshaft position sensor and camshaft position sensor.

6   1998 and 1999 models utilize a coil pack consisting of two ignition coils with an igniter incorporated into each unit. This type of ignition system uses a "waste spark" method of spark distribution. Each cylinder is paired with its opposing cylinder in the firing order (1-4, 2-3) so one cylinder under compression fires simultaneously with its opposing cylinder, where the piston is on the exhaust stroke. Since the cylinder on the exhaust stroke requires very little of the available voltage to fire its plug, most of the voltage is used to fire the plug of the cylinder on the compression stroke. In a conventional ignition system, one end of the ignition coil secondary winding is connected to engine earth. In a waste spark system, neither end of the secondary winding is earthed - instead, one end of the coil secondary winding is directly attached to the spark plug and the other end is attached to the spark plug of the companion cylinder.

6.2 To use a calibrated ignition tester (available at most auto parts stores), remove a spark plug wire from a spark plug, connect the spark plug boot to the tester and clip the tester to a good earth connection, then crank the engine over - if there is enough voltage to fire the plug, bright blue spark will be clearly visible between the electrode tip and the tester body

7   2000 and later models utilize an individual ignition coil/igniter unit for each cylinder. The unit is positioned directly over each spark plug. The ECM fires each coil sequentially in the firing order sequence.

8   The ECM controls the ignition system by opening and closing the primary ignition coil control circuit. The computerized ignition system provides complete control of the ignition timing by determining the optimum timing in response to engine speed, coolant temperature, throttle position and engine load. These parameters are relayed to the ECM by the camshaft position sensor, crankshaft position sensor, throttle position sensor, coolant temperature sensor and manifold absolute pressure sensor or mass airflow sensor. Refer to Chapter 6 for additional information on the various sensors.

9   The ignition system is also integrated with a knock sensor system. The system uses a knock sensor in conjunction with the ECM to control spark timing. The knock sensor system allows the engine to use maximum spark advance without spark knock, which improves driveability and fuel economy.

10   When working on the ignition system, take the following precautions:

a) *Do not keep the ignition switch on for more than 10 seconds if the engine will not start.*

b) *Always connect a tachometer in accordance with the manufacturer's instructions. Some tachometers may be incompatible with this ignition system. Consult the tachometer manufacturer before buying a tachometer for use with this vehicle.*

c) *Never allow the ignition coil terminals to touch earth. Earthing the coil could result*

6.7 Check for battery voltage to the positive side (+) of the ignition coil

in damage to the igniter and/or the ignition coil.

d) *Do not disconnect the battery when the engine is running.*

e) *Make sure the igniter is properly earthed.*

---

6   Ignition system - check

Warning: *Because of the high voltage generated by the ignition system, extreme care should be taken whenever an operation is performed involving ignition components.*

1   If a malfunction occurs and the vehicle won't start, do not immediately assume that the ignition system is causing the problem. First, check the following items:

a) *Make sure the battery cable clamps, where they connect to the battery, are clean and tight.*

b) *Test the condition of the battery (see Section 3). If it does not pass all the tests, replace it with a new battery.*

c) *Check the ignition system wiring and connections.*

d) *Check the related fuses inside the fuse box (see Chapter 12). If they're burned, determine the cause and repair the circuit.*

1997 models only

Refer to illustrations 6.2, 6.7 and 6.8

2   If the engine turns over but won't start, disconnect the spark plug wire from any spark

plug and attach it to a calibrated tester (available at most auto parts stores) **(see illustration).** Connect the clip on the tester to a bolt or metal bracket on the engine.

3   Crank the engine and watch the end of the tester or spark plug wire to see if a bright blue, well-defined spark occurs (weak spark or intermittent spark is the same as no spark).

4   If spark occurs, sufficient voltage is reaching the plug to fire it (repeat the check at the remaining plug wires to verify that the distributor cap and rotor are OK).

5   If the ignition system is operating properly the problem lies elsewhere; i.e. a mechanical or fuel system problem. However, the plugs themselves may be fouled, so remove and check them as described in Chapter 1.

6   If no sparks or intermittent sparks occur, remove the distributor cap and check the cap, rotor and spark plug wires as described in Chapter 1. If moisture is present, dry out the cap and rotor, then reinstall the cap and repeat the spark test. If sparks now occur, the distributor cap, rotor or plug wire(s) may be defective.

7   If no sparks occur, check the primary wire connections at the coil to make sure they're clean and tight. Check for voltage to the coil on the primary circuit from the ignition switch **(see illustration).** Check the ignition coil (see Section 7) and the distributor pick-up coil (see Section 11). Make any necessary repairs, then repeat the check again.

8   Check for battery voltage to the igniter and ignition coil with the ignition key On (engine not running) **(see illustration).** If volt-

6.8 Disconnect the igniter electrical connector and with the ignition key ON (engine not running), check for battery voltage to the igniter (external igniter shown - on models with an internal igniter, check for voltage on the brown wire to the igniter)

6.9 To use a calibrated ignition tester (available at most auto parts stores), or an old spark plug, remove one coil and plug the tester into the boot, clip the tester to a good earth connection, then crank the engine over

age is available and there is still no spark, the igniter or the ECM may be defective. Have the system diagnosed by a dealer service department or other qualified repair shop.

1998 and later models

Refer to illustrations 6.9 and 6.12

9   If the engine turns over but won't start, make sure there is sufficient secondary ignition voltage to fire the spark plug. On 1998 and 1999 models, disconnect a spark plug wire from one of the spark plugs and attach a calibrated ignition system tester (available at most auto parts stores) to the spark plug boot. Connect the clip on the tester to a bolt or metal bracket on the engine **(see illustration 6.2)**. On 2000 and later models, remove an ignition coil (see Section 7) and attach the calibrated ignition system tester to the spark plug boot **(see illustration)**. Reconnect the electrical connector to the coil and clip the tester to a good earth connection. Crank the engine and watch the end of the tester to see if a bright blue, well-defined spark occurs (weak spark or intermittent spark is the same as no spark).

10   If spark occurs, sufficient voltage is reaching the plug to fire it (repeat the check at the remaining spark plug wires or ignition coils to verify that the spark plug wires, connectors and ignition coils are good). If the ignition system is operating properly the problem lies elsewhere; i.e. a mechanical or fuel system problem. However, the plugs themselves may be fouled, so remove and check them as described in Chapter 1.

11   If no spark occurs, remove the spark plug wire or boot from the suspected ignition coil and check the terminals for damage. Using an ohmmeter, check the wire or boot for an open or high resistance (on 1998 and 1999 models, the spark plug wire resistance should not be greater than 25,000 ohms). On 1998 and 1999 models, disconnect the spark plug wires from all the ignition coil towers and check the ignition coil secondary resistance across each pair of coil towers (see Section 7). Compare

6.12 Disconnect the electrical connector from the ignition coil and check for battery voltage at terminal no. 1 with the ignition key On - also check for continuity to a good engine earth point at terminal no. 4

your measurement with the values listed in this Chapter's Specifications. Replace the ignition coil assembly if either coil is not within specifications.

12   Check for battery voltage to the ignition coil with the ignition key On (engine not running). Disconnect the coil electrical connector and check for power at the indicated terminal of the coil connector **(see illustration)**.

13   Battery voltage should be available with the ignition key On. If there is no battery voltage present, check the wiring and/or circuit between the fuse box and ignition coil (don't forget to check the fuses). Also check the earth circuit for continuity. **Note:** *Refer to the wiring diagrams at the end of Chapter 12 for wire colour identification for testing and additional information on the circuits.*

14   If battery voltage is available to the ignition coil, check the ignition coil control circuits as follows **(see illustration 6.12): Caution:** *Use only an LED test light to avoid damaging the ECM.*

a) *Remove the EFI fuse from the fuse box (this disables the fuel injectors so the engine will not start or flood).*

b) *On 1998 and 1999 models, connect an LED test light to terminal no. 2 of one of the coil harness connectors. Perform the remainder of the test, then connect the LED test light to terminal no. 2 of the*

other coil harness connector and perform the test.

c) *On 2000 and later models, connect an LED test light to terminal no. 3 of one of the coil harness connectors. Perform the remainder of the test at each coil connector in turn.*

d) *Crank the engine with the starter and confirm that the LED test light flashes as the engine rotates. A flashing LED test light indicates the ECM, camshaft position sensor and crankshaft position sensor are functioning properly.*

15   If a control signal is not present at the ignition coil, refer to Chapter 6 and use a code-reading tool to check for Diagnostic Trouble Codes relating to the ignition system, the PCM, or the camshaft and crankshaft position sensors.

16   If battery voltage and a control signal exist at the ignition coil and there is no spark, replace the ignition coil.

---

7   Ignition coils - check and replacement

Note: *Toyota does not publish primary or secondary resistance specifications for the ignition coils units used on these models. The only way to check them is to substitute a known good unit. But this option isn't feasible for a home mechanic because you can't return electrical components to a parts department once you have purchased them. If you have already eliminated all other possible causes of an ignition malfunction, a defective ignition coil/igniter unit is the likely cause of the problem, but the only way to verify this is to substitute a known good unit.*

1   Detach the cable from the negative terminal of the battery. **Caution:** *If the stereo in your vehicle is equipped with an anti-theft system, make sure you have the correct activation code before disconnecting the battery.*

1997 and earlier models
Check

Refer to illustrations 7.2, 7.4a and 7.4b

2   Remove the plastic shield from the coil **(see illustration)**.

7.2 Carefully prise the plastic shield at the locking tab to release it from the ignition coil

7.4a   To check the primary resistance of the coil, measure the resistance between the positive and the negative terminals

7.4b   To check the secondary resistance of the coil, measure the resistance between the positive terminal and the high tension terminal

3   Remove the nuts from the coil electrical terminals and pull the wires back off the terminals.

4   Using an ohmmeter, measure the primary and secondary resistance (**see illustrations**):

a)   *Measure the resistance between the positive and negative terminals of the coil. Compare your reading with the specified coil primary resistance listed in this Chapter's Specifications.*

b)   *Measure the resistance between the positive terminal and the high tension terminal. Compare your reading with the specified coil secondary resistance listed in this Chapter's Specifications.*

5   If either of the above tests yield resistance values outside the specified amount, replace the coil.

Replacement

Refer to illustration 7.9

6   Detach the cable from the negative terminal of the battery (see the **Caution** above).

7   Remove the heat shield from the coil.

8   Label and disconnect the wires from the coil terminals.

9   Remove the coil mounting screws (**see illustration**).

10   Installation is the reverse of removal.

1998 and 1999 models

Check

11   If the spark plug wires are not marked, label them corresponding to the cylinder numbers. Detach the spark plug wires from the ignition coils.

12   Using an ohmmeter, measure the resistance across each pair of spark plug wire terminals. Compare your measurement with the secondary resistance value listed in this Chapter's Specifications.

13   If the test yields a resistance value outside the specified amount, replace the coil.

Replacement

14   If the spark plug wires are not marked, label them corresponding to the cylinder numbers. Detach the spark plug wires from the ignition coils.

15   Disconnect the electrical connectors

from the ignition coils.

16   Remove the mounting bolts/nuts and remove the coils. If reinstalling the original coils, label the coils so they may be installed in their original locations.

17   Installation is the reverse of removal.

2000 and later models

Refer to illustration 7.21

Note: *Coil resistance cannot be measured on 2000 and later models; refer to Section 6 to check the ignition coil.*

18   Remove the engine cover.

19   Disconnect the electrical connectors from the coils.

20   Remove the nuts and position the wire harness aside if necessary.

21   Remove the mounting bolts and carefully withdraw the coil from the cylinder head (**see illustration**).

22   Installation is the reverse of removal.

7.9   Remove the retaining screws (arrows) and lift the coil from the distributor housing

7.21   Ignition coil mounting bolts (arrows) - 2000 and later models

8.5 Paint or scribe a mark (arrow) on the edge of the distributor housing immediately below the rotor tip to ensure that the rotor is pointing in the same direction when the distributor is reinstalled - also, paint or scribe another mark across the cylinder head and the distributor body (arrow) to ensure that the distributor is aligned correctly when it is reinstalled

8.7 Remove the hold-down bolt from the distributor body and pull the distributor straight out

9.3 Tools needed to check and adjust the ignition timing

1 **Vacuum plugs** - *Vacuum hoses will, in most cases, have to be disconnected and plugged. Molded plugs in various shapes and sizes are available for this*
2 **Inductive pick-up timing light** - *Flashes a bright, concentrated beam of light when the number one spark plug fires. Connect the leads according to the instructions supplied with the light*
3 **Distributor spanner** - *On some models, the hold-down bolt for the distributor is difficult to reach and turn with conventional spanner or sockets. A special spanner like this must be used*

8 Distributor (1997 models only) - removal and installation

Removal

Refer to illustrations 8.5 and 8.7

1 Detach the cable from the negative battery terminal. **Caution:** *If the stereo in your vehicle is equipped with an anti-theft system, make sure you have the correct activation code before disconnecting the battery.*
2 Disconnect the electrical connectors from the distributor.
3 Look for a raised "1" on the distributor cap. This marks the location for the number one cylinder spark plug wire terminal. If the cap does not have a mark for the number one terminal, locate the number one spark plug and trace the wire back to the terminal on the cap.
4 Remove the distributor cap (see Chapter 1) and turn the engine over until the rotor is pointing toward the number one spark plug terminal (see locating TDC procedure in Chapter 2A).
5 Make a mark on the edge of the distributor base directly below the rotor tip and in line with it. Also, mark the distributor base and the engine block to ensure that the distributor is installed correctly **(see illustration)**.
6 If equipped with collar bolts, loosen but do not remove the two bolts in the distributor collar. This will give the distributor shaft clearance.
7 Remove the distributor hold-down bolt **(see illustration)**, then pull the distributor straight out to remove it. **Caution:** *DO NOT turn the crankshaft while the distributor is out of the engine, or the alignment marks will be useless.*

Installation

Note: *If the crankshaft has been moved while the distributor is out, locate Top Dead Centre (TDC) for the number one piston (see Chapter 2A) and position the distributor and the rotor accordingly.*

8 Install a new O-ring onto the distributor housing.
9 Align the cut-out portion of the coupling with the groove in the housing.
10 Insert the distributor into the engine in exactly the same relationship to the block that it was in when removed.
11 If the distributor does not seat completely, recheck the alignment marks between the distributor base and the block to verify that the distributor is in the same position it was in before removal. Also check the rotor to see if it's aligned with the mark you made on the edge of the distributor base.
12 Loosely install the distributor hold-down bolt(s).
13 Installation is the reverse of removal.
14 Check the ignition timing (see Section 9) and tighten the distributor hold-down bolt securely.

9 Ignition timing (1997 models only) - check and adjustment

Refer to illustration 9.3

Note: *Ignition timing is not adjustable on 1998 and later models.*

1 Connect a tachometer according to the manufacturer's instructions.
2 Locate the diagnostic test connector and insert a jumper wire between terminals E1 and TE1.
3 With the ignition switch off, connect a timing light according to the manufacturer's instructions **(see illustration)**. Most timing lights are powered by the battery. Also, an inductive pick-up is installed onto the number one cylinder spark plug wire.
4 Locate the timing marks on the front

cover and the crankshaft pulley.
5 Start the engine and allow it to warm up to normal operating temperature (upper radiator hose hot). Verify that the engine idle is correct (750 rpm with an automatic transaxle and 700 rpm with a manual transaxle). Aim the timing light at the timing scale on the front cover. The mark on the crankshaft pulley should line up with the 10-degree mark on the scale. If necessary, loosen the distributor hold-down bolt and slowly rotate the distributor until the timing marks align. Tighten the hold-down bolt and recheck the timing.
6 Remove the jumper wire from the test connector.
7 Turn the engine off and remove the tachometer and the timing light.

10 Igniter (1997 models only) - replacement

1 Detach the cable from the negative terminal of the battery. **Caution:** *If the stereo in your vehicle is equipped with an anti-theft system, make sure you have the correct activation code before disconnecting the battery.*

Externally mounted igniter

2 Disconnect the electrical connector from the igniter.
3 Remove the screws from the bracket

11.1 Check the resistance between the terminals on the pick-up coil indicated in this Chapter's Specifications

11.5 Measure the air gap between the signal rotor and the pick-up coil projection - if the gap is not within specification, replace the distributor

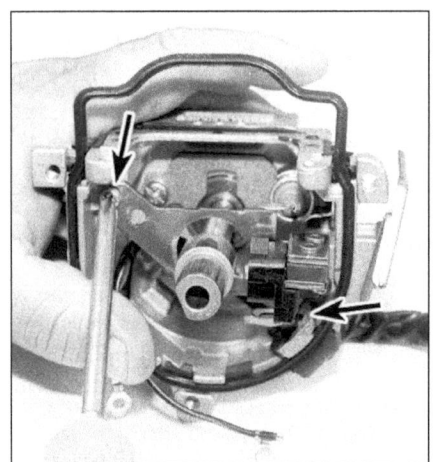

11.9 Remove the pick-up coil set screws (arrows)

assembly and pull the igniter/bracket assembly out of the engine compartment.
4   Installation is the reverse of removal.

Internally mounted igniter

5   Remove the ignition coil from the distrib-

utor (see Section 7).
6   Disconnect the electrical connector from the igniter.
7   Remove the screws from the igniter assembly and pull the igniter/bracket assembly out of the engine compartment.
8   Installation is the reverse of removal.

---

11   Pick-up coil (1997 models only) - check and replacement

Pick-up coil check

Refer to illustration 11.1

1   Disconnect the electrical connector at the distributor and using an ohmmeter, measure the resistance between the pick-up coil terminals **(see illustration)**.
2   Compare the measurements to the values listed in this Chapter's Specifications. If the resistance is not as specified, replace the pick-up coil.

Air gap check

Refer to illustration 11.5

3   Detach the cable from the negative ter-

minal of the battery. **Caution:** *If the stereo in your vehicle is equipped with an anti-theft system, make sure you have the correct activation code before disconnecting the battery.*
4   Remove the distributor from the engine (see Section 8).
5   Using a brass feeler gauge, measure the gap between the signal rotor and the pick-up coil projection **(see illustration)**. Compare your measurement to the air gap listed in this Chapter's Specifications. If the air gap is not as specified, replace the distributor, as the air gap is not adjustable. Excessive air gap is usually a sign of wear in the distributor shaft bushing.

Replacement

Refer to illustrations 11.9, 11.10 and 11.11

6   Detach the cable from the negative terminal of the battery. **Caution:** *If the stereo in your vehicle is equipped with an anti-theft system, make sure you have the correct activation code before disconnecting the battery.*
7   Remove the distributor from the engine (see Section 8).
8   Remove the coil from the distributor (see Section 7).

11.10 Remove the pick-up coil from the distributor

11.11 Remove the ignition condenser from the distributor

13.3 Connect a voltmeter to the battery terminals and check the battery voltage with the engine Off, and then again with the engine running

9   Remove the set screws that retain the pick-up coil to the distributor **(see illustration)**.
10   Remove the pick-up coil from the distributor **(see illustration)**.
11   Remove the condenser from the distributor **(see illustration)** and replace it.
12   Installation is the reverse of removal.

12   Charging system - general information and precautions

The charging system includes the alternator, an internal voltage regulator, a charge indicator, the battery, a fusible link and the wiring between all the components. The charging system supplies electrical power for the ignition system, the lights, the radio, etc. The alternator is driven by a drivebelt at the front of the engine.

The purpose of the voltage regulator is to limit the alternator's voltage to a preset value. This prevents power surges, circuit overloads, etc., during peak voltage output.

The fusible link is a short length of insulated wire integral with the engine compartment wiring harness. The link is several wire gauges smaller in diameter than the circuit it protects. See Chapter 12 for additional information regarding fusible links.

The charging system doesn't ordinarily require periodic maintenance. However, the drivebelt, battery and wires and connections should be inspected at the intervals outlined in Chapter 1.

The dashboard warning light should come on when the ignition key is turned to Start, then should go off immediately. If it remains on, there is a malfunction in the charging system. Some vehicles are also equipped with a voltage gauge. If the voltage gauge indicates abnormally high or low voltage, check the charging system (see Section 9).

Be very careful when making electrical circuit connections to a vehicle equipped with an alternator and note the following:

a)   *When reconnecting wires to the alternator from the battery, be sure to note the polarity.*
b)   *Before using welding equipment to repair any part of the vehicle, disconnect the wires from the alternator and the battery terminals.*
c)   *Never start the engine with a battery charger connected.*
d)   *Always disconnect both battery leads before using a battery charger.*
e)   *The alternator is driven by an engine drivebelt that could cause serious injury if your hand, hair or clothes become entangled in it with the engine running.*
f)   *Because the alternator is connected directly to the battery, it could arc or cause a fire if overloaded or shorted out.*
g)   *Wrap a plastic bag over the alternator and secure it with rubber bands before steam cleaning the engine.*

13   Charging system - check

Refer to illustration 13.3

1   If a malfunction occurs in the charging circuit, don't automatically assume that the alternator is causing the problem. First check the following items:

a)   *Check the drivebelt tension and its condition. Replace it if worn or deteriorated.*
b)   *Make sure the alternator mounting bolts are tight.*
c)   *Inspect the alternator wiring harness and the electrical connectors at the alternator and voltage regulator. They must be in good condition and tight.*
d)   *Check the fusible link located at the positive battery cable or the large main fuses in the engine compartment. If it's burned, determine the cause, repair the circuit and replace the link or fuse (the vehicle won't start and/or the accessories won't work if the fusible link or fuse blows).*
e)   *Check all the fuses that are in series with the charging system circuit. The location of these fuses and fusible links may vary from year and model but the designations are the same; main fusible link, Alt fuse (100 amp), AM1 (25 amp), AM2 (15 amp), Main fuse (30A), Gauge (10A), and ALT-S (5 amp).*
f)   *Start the engine and check the alternator for abnormal noises (a shrieking or squealing sound indicates a bad bushing).*
g)   *Check the specific gravity of the battery electrolyte. If it's low, charge the battery (doesn't apply to maintenance free batteries).*
h)   *Make sure that the battery is fully charged (one bad cell in a battery can cause overcharging by the alternator).*
i)   *Disconnect the battery cables (negative first, then positive). Inspect the battery posts and the cable clamps for corrosion. Clean them thoroughly if necessary (see Section 4 and Chapter 1). Reconnect the positive cable, then the negative cable.*

2   With the ignition key off, check the battery voltage with no accessories operating. It should be approximately 12.5 volts. It may be slightly higher if the engine had been operating within the last hour.
3   Connect a multimeter to the charging system following the tool manufacturer's instructions. Start the engine, and check the battery voltage and amperage. It should now be approximately 13.2 to 15.0 volts at 10 amps or less **(see illustration)**.
4   Load the battery by turning on the high beam headlights and the air conditioning (if equipped) and place the blower fan on HIGH. Raise the engine speed to 2,000 rpm and check the voltage and amperage. If the charging system is working properly the voltage should stay above 13.5 volts and the amperage should be 30 amps or more (depending on the condition of the battery - it could be less than 30 amps).
5   If the voltage rises above 15.0 volts in either test, the regulator is defective.
6   If the indicated voltage reading is less than the specified charge voltage, the alternator is probably defective. Have the charging system checked at a dealer service department or other properly equipped repair facility. **Note:** *Many auto parts stores will bench test an alternator off the vehicle. Refer to your local auto parts store regarding their policy (many stores will perform this service free of charge).*

14   Alternator - removal and installation

Refer to illustrations 14.2 and 14.3

1   Detach the cable from the negative terminal of the battery. Remove the drivebelt (see Chapter 1).

14.2 Disconnect the electrical connections from the alternator

14.3 Alternator mounting bolts

2   Disconnect the electrical connectors from the alternator **(see illustration)**.

3   Remove the alternator mounting bolts **(see illustration)**.

4   Remove the alternator from the engine.

5   If you are replacing the alternator, take the old alternator with you when purchasing a replacement unit. Make sure that the new/rebuilt unit is identical to the old alternator. Look at the terminals - they should be the same in number, size and locations as the terminals on the old alternator. Finally, look at the identification markings - they will be stamped in the housing or printed on a tag or plaque affixed to the housing. Make sure that these numbers are the same on both alternators.

6   Many new/rebuilt alternators do not have a pulley installed, so you may have to switch the pulley from the old unit to the new/rebuilt one. When buying an alternator, find out the shop's policy regarding installation of pulleys - some shops will perform this service free of charge.

7   Installation is the reverse of removal.

8   After the alternator is installed, install the drivebelt.

9   Check the charging voltage to verify proper operation of the alternator (see Section 9).

15   Starting system - general information and precautions

The starting system consists of the battery, the starter motor, the starter solenoid and the electrical circuit connecting the components. The solenoid is mounted directly on the starter motor.

The starter motor assembly is installed on the front (radiator) side of the engine on the lower section of transaxle bellhousing.

When the ignition key is turned to the START position, the starter solenoid is actuated through the starter control circuit. The starter solenoid then connects the battery to the starter. The battery supplies the electrical energy to the starter motor, which does the actual work of cranking the engine.

The starter motor on a vehicle equipped with a manual transaxle can be operated only when the clutch pedal is depressed; the starter on a vehicle equipped with an automatic transaxle can be operated only when the transaxle selector lever is in Park or Neutral.

Always observe the following precautions when working on the starting system:

a)   *Excessive cranking of the starter motor can overheat it and cause serious damage. Never operate the starter motor for more than 15 seconds at a time without pausing to allow it to cool for at least two minutes.*

b)   *The starter is connected directly to the battery and could arc or cause a fire if mishandled, overloaded or short-circuited.*

c)   *Always detach the cable from the negative terminal of the battery before working on the starting system.*

16   Starter motor and circuit - check

Refer to illustration 16.3

Note: *Before diagnosing starter problems, make sure the battery is fully charged.*

1   If a malfunction occurs in the starting circuit, do not immediately assume that the starter is causing the problem. First, check the following items:

a)   *Make sure the battery cable clamps, where they connect to the battery, are clean and tight.*

b)   *Check the condition of the battery cables (see Section 4). Replace any defective battery cables with new parts.*

c)   *Test the condition of the battery (see Section 3). If it does not pass all the tests, replace it with a new battery.*

d)   *Check the starter solenoid wiring and connections. Refer to the wiring diagrams at the end of Chapter 12.*

e)   *Check the starter mounting bolts for tightness.*

f)   *Check the fusible links near the positive battery terminal. If they're burned, determine the cause and repair the circuit. Also, check the ignition switch circuit for correct operation (see Chapter 12).*

g)   *Check the operation of the transmission range sensor (automatic transaxle) or clutch start switch (manual transaxle). Make sure the shift lever is in PARK or NEUTRAL (automatic transaxle) or the clutch pedal is pressed (manual transaxle). Refer to Chapter 7 for the transmission range sensor check and adjustment procedure. Refer to Chapter 12 wiring diagrams, if necessary, when performing circuit checks. These systems must operate correctly to provide battery voltage to the ignition solenoid.*

2   If the starter does not actuate when the ignition switch is turned to the start position, check for battery voltage to the solenoid. This will determine if the solenoid is receiving the correct voltage signal from the ignition switch. Connect a test light or voltmeter to the starter solenoid positive terminal while an assistant turns the ignition switch to the start position. If voltage is not available, refer to the wiring diagrams in Chapter 12 and check all the fuses and relays in series with the starting system. If voltage is available but the starter motor does not operate, remove the starter from the engine compartment (see Section 13) and bench test the starter (see Step 4).

3   If the starter turns over slowly, check the starter cranking voltage and the current draw from the battery. This test must be performed with the starter assembly on the engine. Crank the engine over (for 10 seconds or less) and observe the battery voltage. It should not drop below 8.0 volts on manual transaxle models or 8.5 volts on automatic transaxle models. Also, observe the current draw using an ammeter **(see illustration)**. It should not exceed 400 amps or drop below 250 amps. If the starter motor cranking amp values are not within the correct range, replace it with a new unit. There are several conditions that may affect the starter cranking potential. The battery must be in good condition and the battery

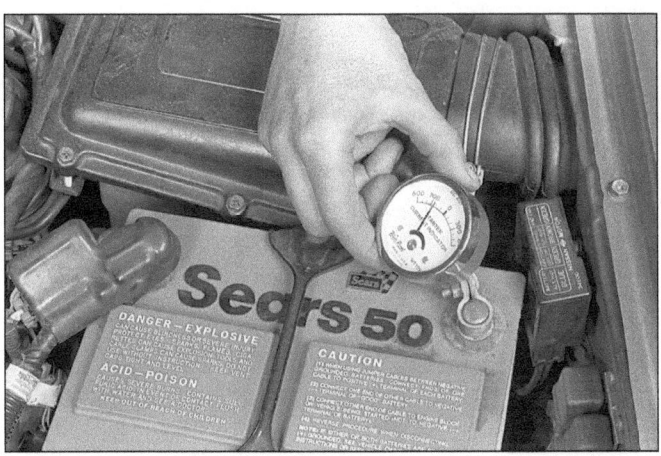

16.3 To use an inductive ammeter, simply hold the ammeter over the positive or negative cable (whichever is more accessible)

17.4 Disconnect the electrical connector (A), then remove the nut securing the starter cable (B)

cold-cranking rating must not be under-rated for the particular application. Be sure to check the battery specifications carefully. The battery terminals and cables must be clean and not corroded. Also, in cases of extreme cold temperatures, make sure the battery and/or engine block is warmed before performing the tests.

4   If the starter is receiving voltage but does not activate, remove and check the starter/solenoid assembly on the bench. Most likely the solenoid is defective. In some rare cases, the engine may be seized so be sure to try

and rotate the crankshaft pulley (see Chapter 2A) before proceeding. With the starter/solenoid assembly mounted in a vise on the bench, install one jumper cable from the negative battery terminal to the body of the solenoid. Install the other jumper cable from the positive battery terminal to the B+ terminal on the solenoid. Install a starter switch and apply battery voltage to the solenoid S terminal (for 10 seconds or less) and see if the solenoid plunger, shift lever and overrunning clutch extends and rotates the pinion drive. If the pinion drive extends but does not rotate,

the solenoid is operating but the starter motor is defective. If there is no movement but the solenoid clicks, the solenoid and/or the starter motor is defective. If the solenoid plunger extends and rotates the pinion drive, the starter/solenoid assembly is working properly.

---

17   Starter motor - removal and installation

Refer to illustrations 17.4 and 17.5

Note: *The starter motor and solenoid assembly cannot be repaired using separate components. In the event of failure, exchange the starter/solenoid assembly for a new or rebuilt complete unit.*

1   Detach the cable from the negative terminal of the battery (see Chapter 1).
2   Raise the vehicle and support it securely on jackstands.
3   Remove the splash shield from under the engine.
4   Disconnect the electrical connector from the starter solenoid, then remove the nut and disconnect the battery cable from the solenoid, too **(see illustration)**.
5   Remove the starter motor mounting bolts and remove the starter from the vehicle **(see illustration)**.
6   Installation is the reverse of removal.

17.5 Remove the starter mounting bolts (lower bolt shown)

Notes

Chapter 6
Emissions and engine control systems

Contents

1 General information

Refer to illustrations 1.1a, 1.1b and 1.1c

To prevent pollution of the atmosphere from incompletely burned and evaporating gases, and to maintain good driveability and fuel economy, a number of emission control systems are incorporated (**see illustrations**). They include the:

*On-Board Diagnostic (OBD) II system
Electronic Fuel Injection (EFI) system
Evaporative Emissions Control (EVAP) system*

*Positive Crankcase Ventilation (PCV) system
Catalytic converter*

The Sections in this Chapter include general descriptions, checking procedures within the scope of the home mechanic and component replacement procedures (when possible)

1.1a Emissions and engine control components - 1998 and earlier models

1	Crankshaft position sensor	5	EGR valve	9	IAC valve
2	MAP sensor	6	Throttle Position Sensor	10	Oxygen sensor
3	EGR vacuum switching valve	7	Test connector	11	PCV valve
4	EGR vacuum modulator	8	Air intake resonator		

1.1b Emissions and engine control components - 1999 to 2002 models

1	Positive Crankcase Ventilation valve	5	Throttle body with Throttle Position Sensor and IAC valve
2	EVAP purge and vent valves	6	Camshaft position sensor
3	Mass Airflow sensor and intake air temperature sensor	7	Knock sensor
4	Engine coolant temperature sensor	8	Crankshaft position sensor

1.1c Emissions and engine control components - 2003 and later models

1	Positive Crankcase Ventilation valve	3	EVAP purge and vent valves	5	Throttle body motor and Throttle Position Sensor
2	EVAP canister	4	Mass Airflow sensor		

for each of the systems listed above.

Before assuming that an emissions control system is malfunctioning, check the fuel and ignition systems carefully. The diagnosis of some emission control devices requires specialized tools, equipment and training. If checking and servicing become too difficult or if a procedure is beyond your ability, consult a dealer service department or other repair shop. Remember, the most frequent cause of emissions problems is simply a loose or broken wire or vacuum hose, so always check the hose and wiring connections first.

This doesn't mean, however, that emissions control systems are particularly difficult to maintain and repair. You can quickly and easily perform many checks and do most of the regular maintenance at home with common tune-up and hand tools. Pay close attention to any special precautions outlined in this Chapter. It should be noted that the illustrations of the various systems may not exactly match the system installed on your vehicle because of changes made by the manufacturer during production or from year-to-year.

2 On-Board Diagnostic (OBD) system and trouble codes

Scan tool information

Refer to illustration 2.2

1   Hand-held scanners are the most powerful and versatile tools for analyzing engine management systems used on later model vehicles. Early model scanners handle codes and some diagnostics for many systems. Each brand scan tool must be examined carefully to match the year, make and model of the vehicle you are working on. Often, interchangeable cartridges are available to access the particular manufacturer (Ford, Holden, Toyota etc.). Some manufacturers will specify by continent (Asia, Europe, USA, etc.).

2   With the arrival of the (OBD-II), a spe-

2.2 Scanners like this G-Scan are powerful diagnostic aids - programmed with comprehensive diagnostic information, they can tell you just about anything you want to know about your engine management system

cially designed scanner has been developed. Several tool manufacturers have released OBD-II scan tools for the home mechanic **(see illustration)**.

OBD system general description

3   All models are equipped with the second generation OBD-II system. This system consists of an on-board computer known as the Powertrain Control Module (PCM), and information sensors, which monitor various functions of the engine and send data to the PCM. This system incorporates a series of diagnostic monitors that detect and identify fuel injection and emissions control systems faults and store the information in the computer memory. This updated system also tests sensors and output actuators, diagnoses drive cycles, freezes data and clears codes. This powerful diagnostic computer must be accessed using the new OBD-II scan tool and 16 pin Data Link Connector (DLC) located under the driver's dash area. The PCM is the "brain" of the electronically controlled fuel and emissions system. It receives data from a number of sensors and other electronic components (switches, relays, etc.). Based on the information it receives, the PCM generates output signals to control various relays, solenoids (i.e. fuel injectors) and other actuators. The PCM is specifically calibrated to optimize the emissions, fuel economy and driveability of the vehicle.

4   It isn't a good idea to attempt diagnosis or replacement of the PCM or emission control components at home while the vehicle is under warranty. Take the vehicle to a dealer service department if the PCM or a system component malfunctions.

Information sensors

5   **Oxygen sensors (O2S)** - The O2S generates a voltage signal that varies with the difference between the oxygen content of the exhaust and the oxygen in the surrounding air.

6   **Crankshaft Position (CKP) sensor** - The crankshaft sensor provides information on crankshaft position and the engine speed signal to the PCM.

7   **Camshaft Position (CMP) sensor** - The camshaft sensor produces a signal in which the PCM uses to identify number 1 cylinder and to time the sequential fuel injection.

8   **Air/Fuel Sensor** - Some vehicles are equipped with an air/fuel ratio sensor mounted upstream of the catalytic converter. These sensors work similar to the O2 sensors.

9   **Engine Coolant Temperature (ECT) sensor** - The coolant temperature (ECT) sensor monitors engine coolant temperature and sends the PCM a voltage signal that affects PCM control of the fuel mixture, ignition timing, and EGR operation (if equipped).

10   **Throttle Position Sensor (TPS)** - The TPS senses throttle movement and position, then transmits a voltage signal to the PCM.

This signal enables the PCM to determine when the throttle is closed, in a cruise position, or wide open. On the 2005 and later models, the TPS is part of the electronic throttle control on the throttle body.

11   **Mass Airflow sensor (MAF)** - The MAF sensor measures the mass of the intake air by detecting volume and weight of the air from samples passing over the hot wire element.

12   **Knock sensor** - The knock sensor is a "piezoelectric" crystal that oscillates in proportion to engine vibration. (The term *piezoelectric* refers to the property of certain crystals that produce a voltage when subjected to a mechanical stress.) The oscillation of the piezoelectric crystal produces a voltage output that is monitored by the PCM, which retards the ignition timing when the oscillation exceeds a certain threshold. When the engine is operating normally, the knock sensor oscillates consistently and its voltage signal is steady. When detonation occurs, engine vibration increases, and the oscillation of the knock sensor exceeds a design threshold. (Detonation is an uncontrolled explosion, after the spark occurs at the spark plug, which spontaneously combusts the remaining air/fuel mixture, resulting in a "pinging" or "knocking" sound.) If allowed to continue, the engine can be damaged. The knock sensor is located on the engine block.

13   **Vehicle Speed Sensor (VSS)** - The vehicle speed sensor provides information to the PCM to indicate vehicle speed.

14   **Vapor pressure sensor** - The vapor pressure sensor is part of the evaporative emission control system and is used to monitor vapor pressure in the EVAP system. The PCM uses this information to turn on and off the vacuum switching valves (VSV) of the evaporative emission system.

15   **Power Steering Pressure (PSP) switch** - The PSP switch is used to increase engine idle speed during low-speed vehicle maneuvers.

16   **Transaxle sensors** - In addition to the vehicle speed sensor, the PCM receives input signals from the following sensors inside the transaxle or connected to it: (a) the direct clutch speed sensor (b) the vehicle speed sensor.

17   **Accelerator pedal position sensor** - 2005 models do not have a throttle cable, but rather "drive-by-wire" system with an electronically-controlled throttle body. This sensor informs the PCM of the driver's pedal input, which is compared to the operation of the throttle body to check for malfunctions.

18   **Intake air temperature sensor** - The PCM uses information from this sensor to control fuel flow and timing functions. The IAT sensor is part of the MAF sensor module.

Output actuators

19   **EFI main relay** - The EFI main relay activates power to the fuel pump relay (circuit opening relay). It is activated by the ignition

switch and supplies battery power to the PCM and the EFI system when the switch is in the Start or Run position. It's located in the under-bonnet fuse/relay box.

20   **Fuel injectors** - The PCM opens the fuel injectors individually in firing order sequence. The PCM also controls the time the injector is open, called the "pulse width." The pulse width of the injector (measured in millisec-onds) determines the amount of fuel deliv-ered. For more information on the fuel deliv-ery system and the fuel injectors, including injector replacement, refer to Chapter 4.

21   **EVAP vacuum switching valve (VSV)** - The EVAP vacuum switching valve is a sole-noid valve, operated by the PCM to purge the fuel vapor canister and route fuel vapor to the intake manifold for combustion. This valve is also called the purge control valve.

Obtaining trouble codes

Refer to illustration 2.23

22   The PCM will illuminate the CHECK ENGINE light (also called the Malfunction

2.23 16-pin Data Link Connector (DLC)

Indicator Light) on the dash if it recognizes a component fault for two consecutive drive cycles. It will continue to set the light until the PCM does not detect any malfunction for three or more consecutive drive cycles.

23   The diagnostic codes for the OBD-II sys-tem can be extracted from the PCM by plug-ging a generic OBD-II scan tool **(see illustra-tion 2.2)** into the PCM's data link connector

(see illustration), which is located under the left end of the dash.

24   Plug the scan tool into the 16-pin data link connector (DLC), and then follow the instructions included with the scan tool to extract all the diagnostic codes.

25   After repairs have been made, use your code reader or scan tool to erase the trouble code(s).

Diagnostic Trouble Codes

Trouble code	Code identification
P0010	Oil control valve circuit fault
P0011	VVT camshaft timing system over-advanced
P0012	VVT camshaft timing system over-retarded
P0016	VVT camshaft timing system, chain stretch or failure
P0031	Open in A/F sensor heater circuit
P0032	Short in A/F sensor heater circuit
P0037	Open in HO2 sensor heater circuit
P0038	Short in HO2 sensor heater circuit
P0100	Mass airflow sensor or circuit fault
P0101 - P0103	Mass airflow sensor range or performance problem
P0110 - P0113	Intake air temperature sensor or circuit fault
P0115 - P0118	Engine coolant temperature sensor or circuit fault
P0120 - P0123	Throttle position sensor or circuit fault
P0125	Insufficient coolant temperature for closed loop; oxygen sensor heater malfunction
P0128	Thermostat malfunction
P0130	Heated oxygen sensor circuit (sensor 1), circuit malfunction
P0133	Heated oxygen sensor, slow response (sensor 1)

Trouble code	Code identification
P0135	Heated oxygen sensor heater, circuit malfunction (sensor 1)
P0136 - P0138	Heated oxygen sensor circuit malfunction (sensor 2)
P0141	Heated oxygen sensor heater or circuit fault (sensor 2)
P0171	Fuel injection system lean
P0172	Fuel injection system rich
P0220 - P0223	Throttle Position Sensor circuit
P0300	Multiple cylinder misfire detected
P0301	Cylinder no. 1 misfire detected
P0302	Cylinder no. 2 misfire detected
P0303	Cylinder no. 3 misfire detected
P0304	Cylinder no. 4 misfire detected
P0325 - P0328	Knock sensor or circuit fault
P0335	Crankshaft position sensor or circuit fault
P0340 - P0341	Camshaft position sensor or circuit fault
P0351	Ignition coil #1 or circuit fault
P0352	Ignition coil #2 or circuit fault
P0353	Ignition coil #3 or circuit fault
P0354	Ignition coil #4 or circuit fault
P0420	Catalytic converter system fault
P0440	EVAP system malfunction
P0441	EVAP system incorrect purge flow detected
P0450	EVAP system pressure sensor or circuit fault
P0451- P0453	EVAP system pressure sensor range or performance problem
P0455	EVAP system gross leakage (leak or loose gas cap)
P0500	Vehicle speed sensor or circuit fault
P0504	Brake light switch circuit fault
P0505	Idle air control valve or circuit fault
P0560	Voltage supply problem to PCM
P0601	PCM internal memory problem
P0604	PCM random-access memory problem

Diagnostic Trouble Codes (continued)

Trouble code	Code identification
P0606	PCM processor problem
P0607	PCM input signal problem
P0617	Starter relay circuit fault
P0657	PCM actuator supply voltage fault
P0705	Automatic transmission range sensor circuit fault
P0710	Automatic transaxle fluid temperature sensor or circuit fault
P0711	Automatic transaxle fluid temperature sensor range performance or circuit fault
P0724	Automatic transaxle, brake light circuit fault
P0741	Automatic transaxle, torque converter clutch solenoid
P0750 - P0751	Automatic transaxle shift solenoid A performance
P0753	Automatic transaxle shift solenoid A circuit fault
P0755 - P0756	Automatic transaxle shift solenoid B performance
P0765	Automatic transaxle shift solenoid D stuck open or closed
P0850	Park/Neutral switch input circuit fault
P0973 - P0974	Automatic transaxle shift solenoid A control circuit
P0976 - P0977	Automatic transaxle shift solenoid B control circuit
P1300	Ignition system malfunction (#1 coil/igniter circuit fault)
P1305	Ignition system malfunction (#2 coil/igniter circuit fault)
P1310	Ignition system malfunction (#3 coil/igniter circuit fault)
P1315	Ignition system malfunction (#4 coil/igniter circuit fault)
P1335	Crankshaft position sensor or circuit fault
P1346	VVT sensor circuit fault
P1349	VVT system malfunction
P1520	Brake light signal malfunction
P1600	PCM battery supply malfunction
P1656	OCV (oil control valve) circuit malfunction
P1780	Park/Neutral position switch malfunction
P2102	Throttle actuator control motor, circuit low (2005 and later models)
P2103	Throttle actuator control motor, circuit high (2005 and later models)

Trouble code	Code identification
P2111	Throttle actuator control motor, stuck open (2005 and later models)
P2112	Throttle actuator control motor, stuck closed (2005 and later models)
P2118	Throttle actuator control motor, performance range (2005 and later models)
P2119	Throttle control system error (2005 and later models)
P2120 - P2123	Throttle pedal position sensor, D circuit (2005 and later models)
P2125 - P2128	Throttle pedal position sensor, E circuit (2005 and later models)
P2135	Throttle pedal position sensor, switch A/B voltage (2005 and later models)
P2138	Throttle pedal position sensor, switch D/E voltage (2005 and later models)
P2195	Oxygen sensor 1, stuck lean
P2196	Oxygen sensor 1, stuck rich
P2238	Oxygen sensor 1, circuit current low
P2239	Oxygen sensor 1, circuit current high
P2252	Oxygen sensor 1, reference earth low
P2253	Oxygen sensor 1, reference earth high
P2401	EVAP leak detection pump circuit low
P2402	EVAP leak detection pump circuit high
P2419	EVAP switching valve control circuit low
P2420	EVAP switching valve control circuit high
P2610	PCM timer performance off
P2716	Automatic transaxle, pressure control solenoid D
P2769	Automatic transaxle, DSL solenoid circuit low
P2770	Automatic transaxle, DSL solenoid circuit high

3 Powertrain Control Module (PCM) - removal and installation

Refer to illustration 3.1

Warning: *The models covered by this manual are equipped with Supplemental Restraint systems (SRS), more commonly known as airbags. Always disable the airbag system before working in the vicinity of any airbag system components to avoid the possibility of accidental deployment of the airbag, which could cause personal injury (see Chapter 12).*
Caution 1: *To avoid electrostatic discharge damage to the PCM, handle the PCM only by its case. Do not touch the electrical terminals during removal and installation. If available,*
earth yourself to the vehicle with an anti-static earth strap, available at computer supply stores.
Caution 2: If the stereo in your vehicle is equipped with an anti-theft system, make sure you have the correct activation code before disconnecting the battery.

1   The PCM is located inside the passenger compartment under the glove box **(see illustration)**.
2   Disconnect the cable from the negative battery terminal (see Chapter 1).
3   Remove the glove box (see Chapter 11).
4   Use a trim tool to prise up the two clips securing the plastic cover over the PCM.
5   Unplug the electrical connectors from

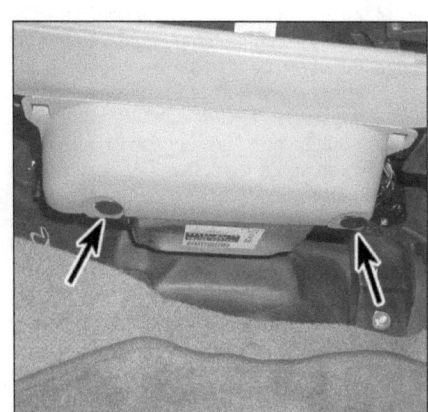

3.1 Typical PCM mounting location under the glove box (there are two push-fasteners securing the cover)

4.1 The TPS is mounted on the firewall-side of the throttle body (2003 and 2004 models)

4.5 On 2005 and later models, the TPS is part of throttle motor assembly and cannot be replaced separately (arrow)

the PCM. **Caution:** *The ignition switch must be turned OFF when pulling out or plugging in the electrical connectors to prevent damage to the PCM.*

6   Remove the two mounting screws, accessing them from the glove box area.

7   Release the two claw-clips and carefully remove the PCM. **Note:** *Avoid any static electricity damage to the computer by earthing yourself to the body before touching the PCM and using a special anti-static pad to store the PCM on once it is removed.*

8   Installation is the reverse of removal.

4   Throttle Position Sensor (TPS) and throttle control motor - replacement

Refer to illustrations 4.1 and 4.5

Caution: If the stereo in your vehicle is equipped with an anti-theft system, make sure you have the correct activation code before disconnecting the battery.

1   The Throttle Position Sensor (TPS) on 2004 and earlier models is attached to the firewall side of the throttle body **(see illustration)**. Problems with the TPS and/or motor can cause intermittent bursts of fuel from the injectors and an unstable idle because the PCM thinks the throttle is moving. The PCM is constantly comparing the driver's input from the accelerator pedal position sensor to the actual throttle position at the throttle body. A problem with the TPS circuits will set a diagnostic trouble code (see Section 2).

2   To replace a defective TPS, disconnect the negative battery cable (see Chapter 1).

3   Disconnect the electrical connector at the TPS and remove the two mounting screws.

4   Installation is the reverse of removal.

5   On 2005 and later models, the throttle body is operated by an electric throttle control motor instead of a cable. One these models, the TPS is part of throttle motor assembly and cannot be replaced separately **(see illustration)**. If there are problems with the throttle control motor or the TPS, the complete throttle body must be replaced (see Chapter 4).

5   Mass Airflow (MAF) sensor - replacement

Refer to illustration 5.3

1   The Mass Airflow (MAF) sensor is located on the air filter housing. The MAF system circuit consists of a platinum hot wire, a thermistor and a control circuit inside a plastic housing. The sensor uses a hot-wire sensing element to measure the molecular mass (weight) of air entering the engine. As the throttle opens, increasing volume of air passes over the hot wire, which cools the wire. The MAF sensor circuit is designed to maintain the hot wire at a constant preset temperature by controlling the current flow through the hot wire. So, as the wire cools, the PCM increases the flow of current through the hot wire in order to maintain the wire at a constant temperature. The output voltage signal of the MAF sensor varies in accordance with this current flow. This voltage signal is measured by the PCM, which converts this signal into a digital waveform, calculates the fuel injector pulse width (duration) and turns the injectors on and off accordingly. A problem in the MAF sensor circuit will set a diagnostic trouble code (see Section 2).

2   Make sure the ignition key is in the OFF position.

3   Disconnect the electrical connector from

the MAF sensor **(see illustration)**.

4   Remove the two sensor retaining screws and remove the MAF sensor and O-ring from the air filter housing.

5   Installation is the reverse of removal. Be sure to install a new O-ring between the MAF sensor and the filter housing.

6   Engine Coolant Temperature (ECT) sensor - replacement

Refer to illustration 6.4

Warning: *Wait until the engine has cooled completely before beginning this procedure.*

1   The engine coolant temperature (ECT) sensor is a thermistor (a resistor which varies the value of its resistance in accordance with temperature changes). The change in the resistance values will directly affect the voltage signal from the sensor to the PCM. As the sensor temperature DECREASES, the resistance values will INCREASE. As the sensor temperature INCREASES, the resistance values will DECREASE. A problem in the ECT sensor circuit will set a diagnostic trouble code.

2   Make sure the ignition key is in the OFF position.

5.3 The MAF sensor is located on the air intake housing - note the two mounting screws (A) and the electrical connector (B)

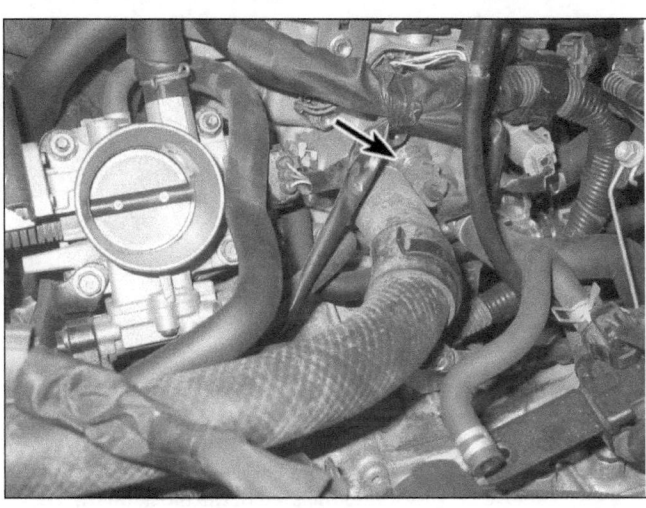

6.4 Location of
the Engine Coolant
Temperature sensor

7.4 The Crankshaft Position sensor is
mounted on the timing chain cover

3   Drain approximately one gallon from the cooling system.
4   Disconnect the electrical connector and carefully unscrew the sensor (see illustration).
5   Wrap the threads of the new sensor with Teflon sealing tape to prevent leakage and thread corrosion.
6   Installation is the reverse of removal. Caution: *Handle the coolant sensor with care. Damage to this sensor will affect the operation of the entire fuel injection system.*

7   Crankshaft Position (CKP) sensor - replacement

Refer to illustration 7.4

1   The crankshaft position sensor (CKP) determines the timing for the fuel injection and ignition on each cylinder. The crankshaft sensor is mounted on the timing chain cover next to the crankshaft pulley. A problem in the crankshaft sensor circuit will set a diagnostic trouble code (see Section 2).
2   Loosen the right front wheel lug nuts. Disconnect the cable from the negative battery terminal (see Chapter 1).

3   Raise the front of the vehicle and support it securely on jackstands. Remove the wheel and the inner fender shield (see Chapter 11).
4   Remove the two bolts (one secures the sensor, the other is close by and secures the harness) and detach the sensor (see illustration).
5   At the upper part of the timing chain cover, disconnect the harness connector and remove the harness and sensor.
6   Installation is the reverse of removal. Be sure to use a new O-ring on the sensor, lightly coated with engine oil.

8   Camshaft Position (CMP) sensor - replacement

Refer to illustration 8.1

1   The camshaft position sensor determines the position of the cylinder for sequential fuel injection signals to each cylinder. The camshaft sensor is mounted on the cylinder head near the intake runner for cylinder no. 4 (see illustration). A problem in the camshaft sensor circuit will set a diagnostic trouble code (see Section 2).
2   Make sure the ignition key is in the OFF position.
3   Remove the engine cover (see Chapter 2).

4   Disconnect the harness connector, remove the mounting bolt and remove the camshaft sensor from the cylinder head.
5   Installation is the reverse of the removal. Use a new O-ring, lightly coated with engine oil.

9   Oxygen sensor and air/fuel sensor - general information and replacement

General information

Refer to illustrations 9.2a and 9.2b

1   All vehicles covered by this manual have On-Board Diagnostics II (OBD-II) engine management systems, which means that they have the ability to verify the accuracy of the basic feedback loop between the oxygen sensor and the PCM. They accomplish this by using an oxygen sensor or air/fuel sensor ahead of the catalytic converter and an oxygen sensor behind the catalytic converter. By sampling the exhaust gas before and after the catalytic converter, the PCM can determine the efficiency of the converter and can even predict when it will fail.
2   The primary (upstream) oxygen sensor (sensor 1) is located in the exhaust manifold

8.1 The camshaft position sensor
mounts with one bolt to the cylinder head
(connector removed for clarity)

9.2a The upstream
oxygen sensor (A)
is located in the
exhaust manifold,
B is the sensor
harness connector

9.2b Location of the downstream oxygen sensor

9.6 Use a slotted socket to remove the oxygen sensors

10.5 The knock sensor is screwed into the side of the block below the intake manifold

and the secondary (downstream) oxygen sensor (sensor 2) is located behind the catalytic converter **(see illustrations)**.

3   Special care must be taken whenever a sensor is serviced.

a) *Oxygen sensors and air/fuel sensors have a permanently attached pigtail and electrical connector, which should not be removed from the sensor. Damage or removal of the pigtail or electrical connector can adversely affect operation of the sensor.*

b) *Grease, dirt and other contaminants should be kept away from the electrical connector and the louvered end of the sensor.*

c) *Do not use cleaning solvents of any kind on an oxygen sensor or air/fuel ratio sensor.*

d) *Do not drop or roughly handle an oxygen sensor or air/fuel ratio sensor.*

e) *The silicone boot must be installed in the correct position to prevent the boot from being melted and to allow the sensor to operate properly.*

Replacement

Refer to illustration 9.6

Note: *Because it is installed in the exhaust manifold or pipe, which contracts when cool, the oxygen sensor may be very difficult to loosen when the engine is cold. Rather than risk damage to the sensor (assuming you are planning to reuse it in another manifold or pipe), start and run the engine for a minute or two, then shut it off. Be careful not to burn yourself during the following procedure.*

4   If you're replacing the downstream sensor, raise the vehicle and secure it on jackstands. Follow the oxygen sensor harness through the floor pan, then unplug the electrical connector inside the vehicle.

5   The upstream sensor can be replaced without raising the vehicle. Follow the harness from the sensor (mounted in the exhaust manifold) to the electrical connector, then unplug the connector.

6   Unscrew the sensor from the exhaust

manifold or exhaust pipe **(see illustration)**.
Note: *The best tool for removing an oxygen sensor is a special slotted socket, especially if you're planning to reuse a sensor. If you don't have this tool, and you plan to reuse the sensor, be extremely careful when unscrewing the sensor.*

7   Apply anti-seize compound to the threads of the sensor to facilitate future removal. The threads of new sensors should already be coated with this compound, but if you're planning to reuse an old sensor, recoat the threads. Install the sensor and tighten it securely. **Caution:** *Do not get anti-seize compound on the sensor tip or it could be ruined.*

8   Reconnect the electrical connector of the pigtail lead to the main wiring harness.

9   Lower the vehicle (if it was raised), test drive the car and verify that no trouble codes have been set.

10   Knock sensor - replacement

Refer to illustration 10.5

Warning: *Wait for the engine to cool completely before performing this procedure.*

1   The knock control system is designed to reduce spark knock during periods of heavy detonation. This allows the engine to use optimal spark advance to improve driveability. The knock sensor detects abnormal vibration in the engine and produces a voltage output that increases with the severity of the knock. The voltage signal is monitored by the PCM, which retards ignition timing until the detonation ceases. The knock sensor is located on the backside of the engine block, directly below the cylinder head (facing toward the rear of the engine compartment).

2   Disconnect the cable from the negative terminal of the battery.

3   Drain the cooling system (see Chapter 1).

4   Remove the inlet manifold (see Chapter 2).

5   Disconnect the electrical connector and remove the knock sensor **(see illustration)**.

6   If you're going to reuse the old sensor,

coat the threads with thread sealant. New sensors are pre-coated with thread sealant; do not apply any additional sealant or the operation of the sensor may be affected.

7   Install the knock sensor and tighten it securely (approximately 40 Nm). Don't over-tighten the sensor or damage may occur. Plug in the electrical connector, refill the cooling system (see Chapter 1) and check for leaks.

11   Vehicle Speed Sensor (VSS) - replacement

Refer to illustration 11.1

1   The Vehicle Speed Sensor (VSS) **(see illustration)** is located on top of the transaxle. This sensor is an electronic component that produces a pulsing voltage signal whenever the sensor shaft is rotated. These voltage pulses are monitored by the PCM, which uses this information to help control the fuel and ignition systems and transaxle shifting.

2   Disconnect the electrical connector from the VSS.

11.1 The VSS is located on top of the transaxle (viewed here looking straight down on the transaxle in the engine compartment)

12.1 PCV valve location at the valve cover

13.1 The EVAP canister is located above the rear crossmember, near the fuel tank

3   Remove the VSS from the transaxle.
4   Replace the O-ring.
5   Installation is the reverse of removal.

12   Positive Crankcase Ventilation (PCV) system

Refer to illustration 12.1

1   The Positive Crankcase Ventilation (PCV) system reduces hydrocarbon emissions by scavenging crankcase vapors. It does this by circulating fresh air from the air cleaner through the crankcase, where it mixes with blow-by gases and is then rerouted through a PCV valve to the intake manifold **(see illustration)**.
2   The main components of the PCV system are the PCV valve and the vacuum hose connecting the valve to the intake manifold.
3   To maintain idle quality, the PCV valve restricts the flow when the intake manifold vacuum is high. If abnormal operating conditions (such as piston ring problems) arise, the system is designed to allow excessive amounts of blow-by gases to flow back through the crankcase vent tube into the air cleaner to be consumed by normal combustion.
4   Checking and replacement of the PCV valve is covered in Chapter 1.

13   Evaporative emissions control (EVAP) system

General description

Refer to illustrations 13.1 and 13.6

1   The fuel evaporative emissions control (EVAP) system absorbs fuel vapors and, during engine operation, releases them into the engine intake where they mix with the incoming air-fuel mixture. The charcoal canister is mounted in the engine compartment in the front of the vehicle **(see illustration)**.
2   When the engine is not operating, fuel vapors are transferred from the fuel tank,

13.6 Two EVAP system vacuum switching valves (purge valve shown) are mounted in the engine compartment

throttle body and intake manifold to the charcoal canister where they are stored. When the engine is running, the fuel vapors are purged from the canister by the purge control valve. The gasses are consumed in the normal combustion process. The electronic purge control valve is directly controlled by the PCM.
3   The fuel filler cap is fitted with a two-way valve as a safety device. The valve vents fuel vapors to the atmosphere if the EVAP system fails.
4   The EVAP system also incorporates a vapor pressure sensor. This sensor detects abnormal vapor pressure in the system. The vapor pressure sensor is mounted in the fuel pump/sending unit assembly on top of the fuel tank.
5   After the engine has been running and warmed up to a pre-set temperature, the vacuum switching valve (VSV) opens. The vacuum switching valve (purge control valve) allows intake manifold vacuum to draw the fuel vapors from the canister to the intake manifold, where they are mixed with intake air before being burned with the air/fuel mixture inside the combustion chambers.
6   The fuel tank vapor pressure sensor monitors changes in pressure inside the tank and, when the pressure exceeds a pre-set threshold, opens a vacuum switching valve (VSV) **(see illustration)**, which allows

a purge port in the canister to admit fuel tank vapors into the canister. These models have three VSV valves, two in the engine compartment and one on the charcoal canister. Also on 2005 and later models, there is a timer in the PCM that operates the pump module to check for fuel vapor leakage five hours after the vehicle has been turned off.

Replacement

7   Disconnect the cable from the negative battery terminal (see Chapter 1).
8   Unplug all electrical connectors and clearly label and disconnect the vent hoses to the charcoal canister, remove the bolts and separate the canister from the vehicle.
9   Installation is the reverse of removal.

14   Catalytic converters

General description

1   The catalytic converter is an emission control device added to the exhaust system to reduce pollutants from the exhaust gas stream. There are two types of converters. The conventional oxidation catalyst reduces the levels of hydrocarbon (HC) and carbon monoxide (CO). The three-way catalyst lowers the levels of oxides of nitrogen (NOx) as

well as hydrocarbons (HC) and carbon monoxide (CO). These models are equipped only with three-way catalytic converters.

Check

2   The test equipment for a catalytic converter is expensive and highly sophisticated. If you suspect that the converter on your vehicle is malfunctioning, take it to a dealer or authorized emissions inspection facility for diagnosis and repair.

3   Whenever the vehicle is raised for servicing of underbody components, check the converter for leaks, corrosion, dents and other damage. Check the welds/flange bolts that attach the front and rear ends of the converter to the exhaust system. If damage is discovered, the converter should be replaced.

4   Although catalytic converters don't break too often, they can become plugged. The easiest way to check for a restricted converter is to use a vacuum gauge to diagnose the effect of a blocked exhaust on intake vacuum.

  a) Connect a vacuum gauge to an inlet manifold vacuum source (see Chapter 2C).

  b) Warm the engine to operating temperature, place the transaxle in Park (automatic) or Neutral (manual) and apply the parking brake.

  c) Note and record the vacuum reading at idle.

  d) Quickly open the throttle to near full throttle and release it shut. Note and record the vacuum reading.

  e) Perform the test three more times, recording the reading after each test.

  f) If the reading after the fourth test is more than 3.3 kPa lower than the reading recorded at idle, the exhaust system may be restricted (the catalytic converter could be plugged or an exhaust pipe or muffler could be restricted).

Replacement

Refer to illustration 14.6

5   Be sure to spray the nuts on the exhaust flange studs before removing them from the front of the catalytic converter.

6   Remove the nuts and separate the catalytic converter from the exhaust manifold **(see illustration)**. The rear of the converter is welded to the exhaust pipe and must be cut off for replacement. A new converter must be welded in.

7   Installation is the reverse of removal. Install new gaskets where required.

14.6 Remove the two spring-loaded bolts at the front of the catalytic converter

Chapter 7 Part A
Manual transaxle

Contents

Specifications

Torque specifications

Nm (unless otherwise indicated)

Back-up light switch	41
Drain and filler plugs	39
Exhaust manifold brace	32
Floor pan brace nuts	30
Transaxle-to-engine bolts	
1999 and earlier models	
Upper mounting bolts	64
Lower mounting bolts	
1.6L engine	46
1.8L engine **(see illustration 6.32b)**	
Bolts A	23
Bolt B	46
2000 and later models **(see illustration 5.24)**	
Bolt A	64
Bolt B	47
Bolt C	23
Stiffener plate bolts	23
Shift lever mounting bolts	12.2
Subframe crossmember **(see illustration 5.22)**	
Bolt A	157
Bolt B	114
Bolts/nuts C	51
Balljoint bolts/nuts D	90

2.1 To disconnect the shift cables from the transaxle linkage, remove these two clips and washers (arrows)

2.2 To detach the shift cable assembly from the cable bracket, remove these two retainers (arrows) with a pair of pliers

1   General information

The vehicles covered by this manual are equipped with a 5-speed manual transaxle or a 3- or 4-speed automatic transaxle. Information on the manual transaxle is included in this Part of Chapter 7. Service procedures for the automatic transaxle are contained in Chapter 7, Part B.

The manual transaxle is a compact, two-piece, lightweight aluminum alloy housing containing both the transmission and differential assemblies.

Because of the complexity, unavailability of replacement parts and special tools necessary, internal repair procedures for the manual transaxle are beyond the scope of this manual. For readers who wish to tackle a transaxle rebuild, exploded views and a brief *Manual transaxle overhaul - general information* Section are provided. The bulk of information in this Chapter is devoted to removal and installation procedures.

2   Shift and select cables - removal and installation

Refer to illustrations 2.1, 2.2 and 2.7

Caution: *If the stereo in your vehicle is equipped with an anti-theft system, make sure you have the correct activation code before disconnecting the battery.*

1   In the engine compartment, remove the retaining clips and washers and disconnect the shift cables from the selecting bellcrank **(see illustration)**.
2   Remove the cable retainers from the cable bracket **(see illustration)**.
3   On 2002 and later models, disconnect the cable from the negative terminal of the battery.
4   Inside the vehicle, remove the floor console (see Chapter 11).
5   On 2002 and later models, pull back the carpeting and remove the three bolts securing

the airbag ECU to the floor and set the ECU aside.
6   Remove the cable retainers from the shift lever base.
7   Remove the retaining clips and washers from the cable ends **(see illustration)** and disconnect the cables from the shift lever assembly.
8   Under the vehicle, remove the two nuts securing the cable bracket to the floor, then pull the cables/grommet through the floor and out.
9   Installation is the reverse of removal.

3   Shift lever - removal and installation

1   Remove the centre console (see Chapter 11).
2   Remove the shift and select cable retainers and disconnect both cables from the shift lever (see Section 2).
3   Remove the retaining bolts and detach the shift lever assembly from the floor.
4   Installation is the reverse of removal.

2.7 To disconnect the shift cables from the shift lever, remove these clips and washers (arrow)

4   Back-up light switch - check and replacement

Check

1   The back-up light switch is located on top of the transaxle.
2   Turn the ignition key to the On position and move the shift lever to the Reverse position. The switch should close the back-up light circuit and turn on the back-up lights.
3   If it doesn't, check the back-up light fuse (see Chapter 12).
4   If the fuse is okay, verify that there's voltage available on one side of the switch (with the ignition turned to On).
5   If there's no voltage to the switch, check the wire between the fuse and the switch; if there is voltage, put the shift lever in reverse and see if there's voltage on the other side of the switch.
6   If there's no voltage on the other side of the switch, replace the switch (see below); if there is voltage, note whether one or both back-up lights are out.
7   If only one bulb is out, replace it; if they're both out, the bulbs could be the problem, but it's more likely that the wire between the switch and the bulbs has an open somewhere.

Replacement

Refer to illustration 4.8

8   Disconnect the electrical connector from the back-up light switch **(see illustration)**.
9   Unscrew and remove the switch.
10   To test the new switch before installation, simply check continuity across the switch terminals: with the plunger depressed, there should be continuity; with the plunger free, there should be no continuity.
11   Screw in the new switch and tighten it securely.
12   Connect the electrical connector.
13   Check the operation of the back-up lights.

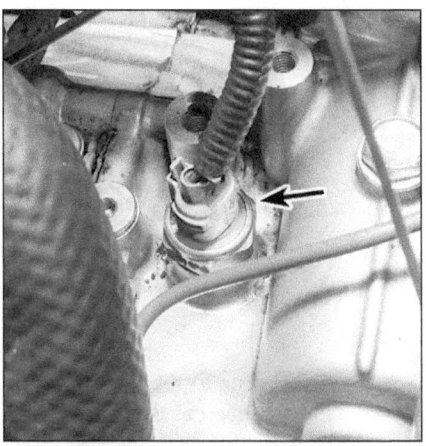

4.8 Unplug the electrical connector from the back-up light switch (arrow)

5.11a Remove the left engine mount stay

5.11b Remove the left engine mount retaining bolt

5 Manual transaxle - removal and installation

2001 and earlier models

Caution: *If the stereo in your vehicle is equipped with an anti-theft system, make sure you have the correct activation code before disconnecting the battery.*

Removal

Refer to illustrations 5.11a, 5.11b, 5.18, 5.19, 5.20, 5.22, 5.23 and 5.24

1   Disconnect the negative cable from the battery.
2   Remove the air filter housing (see Chapter 4). Remove the coolant reservoir (see Chapter 3).
3   Loosen the driveaxle/hub nuts (see Chapter 8).
4   Remove the clutch release cylinder and the clutch hydraulic line (see Chapter 8).
5   Unplug the electrical connectors from the back-up light switch (see Section 4) and the speed sensor (see Chapter 6).
6   Locate the earth cable on top of the transaxle. Remove the cable retaining bolt and detach the earth cable from the transaxle.
7   Disconnect the shift cables from the transaxle (see Section 2).
8   Detach any wire harness clamps from

5.18 Disconnect the front engine mount

the engine and/or transaxle and set the harnesses aside.
9   Remove the upper starter mounting bolt (see Chapter 5).
10   Remove the two upper and the single front transaxle-to-engine mounting bolts. Note the location of any earth connectors or brackets, so that they may be installed in their original location.
11   Remove the left engine mount stay and the left engine mount retaining bolt **(see illustrations)**.
12   Loosen the wheel lug nuts. Raise the vehicle and support it securely on jackstands. Remove the wheels.
13   Support the engine. This can be done from above by using an engine support fixture or an engine hoist, or by placing a jack (with a wood block as an insulator) under the engine

5.19 Remove the rear engine mount

oil pan. The engine must be supported at all times while the transaxle is out of the vehicle.
14   Remove the under-vehicle splash shields (see Chapter 2).
15   Drain the transaxle fluid (see Chapter 1).
16   Remove the driveaxles (see Chapter 8).
17   Remove the front exhaust pipe (see Chapter 4).
18   Disconnect the front engine mount **(see illustration)**.
19   Remove the rear engine mount **(see illustration)**.
20   Remove the centre support member **(see illustration)**.
21   Remove the starter motor (see Chapter 5).
22   On 1.6L models, remove the stiffener plate **(see illustration)**.
23   On 1.8L models, remove the engine rear end plate **(see illustration)**.

5.20 Remove the centre support member

5.22 On 1.6L models, remove the stiffener plate

5.23 On 1.8L models, remove the engine rear end plate

5.24 Remove the left engine mount

5.32a Tighten bolts A and B to the torque listed in this Chapter's Specifications (1997 models with a 1.8L engine)

5.32b Tighten bolts A and B to the torque listed in this Chapter's Specifications (1998 through 2001 models)

24   Remove the left engine mount **(see illustration)**. Also remove the mount bracket.
25   Support the transaxle with a jack (preferably a special jack made for this purpose; these jacks are available at most equipment rental yards). Safety chains will help steady the transaxle on the jack.
26   Remove the rest of the bolts securing the transaxle to the engine.
27   Make a final check that all wires and hoses have been disconnected from the transaxle.
28   Lower the left (passenger's) end of the engine, then roll the transaxle and jack toward the side of the vehicle. Once the input shaft is clear of the splines in the clutch hub, lower the transaxle and remove it from under the vehicle. Try to keep the transaxle as level as possible. **Caution:** *Do not depress the clutch pedal while the transaxle is removed from the vehicle.*
29   The clutch components can now be inspected (see Chapter 8). In most cases, new clutch components should be routinely installed whenever the transaxle is removed.

Installation

Refer to illustrations 5.32a and 5.32b

30   If removed, install the clutch components (see Chapter 8).
31   With the transaxle secured to the jack as on removal, raise it into position and then carefully slide it forward, engaging the input shaft with the splines in the clutch hub. Do not use excessive force to install the transaxle - if the input shaft does not slide into place, readjust the angle of the transaxle so it is level and/or turn the input shaft so the splines engage properly with the clutch.
32   Install the transaxle-to-engine bolts **(see illustrations)**. Tighten the bolts to the torque listed in this Chapter's Specifications.
33   Install the transaxle mount nuts and bolts. Tighten all nuts and bolts securely.
34   Install any suspension components which were detached or removed. Tighten all nuts and bolts to the torque listed in the Chapter 10 Specifications.
35   Remove the jacks supporting the transaxle and the engine.
36   Install the various items removed previously. Refer to Chapter 4 for information

regarding the exhaust pipe, Chapter 5 for the starter motor and Chapter 8 for the driveaxles.
37   Make sure that the wiring harness connectors for the back-up light switch and the speed sensor, and any other electrical devices, are plugged in. And make sure that all harness clamps are reattached to the engine and/or transaxle.
38   If the transaxle was drained, fill it with the specified lubricant to the proper level (see Chapter 1) and lower the vehicle.
39   Connect the shift cables (see Section 2).
40   Connect the negative battery cable. Road test the vehicle to check for proper transaxle operation and check for leakage.

2002 and later models

Caution: *If the stereo in your vehicle is equipped with an anti-theft system, make sure you have the correct activation code before disconnecting the battery.*

Removal

Refer to illustrations 5.55, 5.62 and 5.64

41   Place protective covers on the fenders and cowl and remove the bonnet (see Chapter 11).
42   Relieve the fuel system pressure (see Chapter 4).
43   Disconnect the negative cable from the

battery and drain the transaxle lubricant (see Chapter 1).
44   If the vehicle is equipped with cruise control, unplug the electrical connector for the actuator and remove the actuator (see Chapter 12).
45   Remove the battery and the battery tray (see Chapter 5).
46   Remove the air intake duct and the air cleaner housing (see Chapter 4).
47   Release the residual fuel pressure in the tank by removing the gas cap, then disconnect the fuel lines connecting the engine to the chassis (see Chapter 4). Plug or cap all open fittings.
48   Remove the starter (see Chapter 5).
49   Disconnect the earth cable from the transaxle.
50   Disconnect the clutch release cylinder mounting bolts from the transaxle but do NOT disconnect the hydraulic line. Remove the two mounting bolts from the clutch line bracket.
51   Clearly label, then disconnect all vacuum lines, coolant and emissions hoses, wiring harness connectors (VSS and back-up light switch) and earth straps.
52   Masking tape and/or a touch-up paint applicator work well for marking items. Take instant photos or sketch the locations of components and brackets.
53   Disconnect the shift and select cables (see Section 2).

5.55 Support the engine with an engine support fixture (these are available at most tool rental yards and some auto parts stores)

5.62 Remove the front suspension subframe bolts (with an overhead support for the engine and a floorjack under the transaxle) - refer to the letter designations for torque specs when installing fasteners for the subframe (A and B), engine mount crossmember (C) and the lower control arm balljoint bolts (D) - 2005 models shown other models similar

54   Remove the exhaust manifold brace.
55   Loosen but do NOT remove the front wheel lug nuts. Also loosen the driveaxle/hub nuts (see Chapter 8). Raise the vehicle and support it securely on jackstands. Secure the engine using an engine support fixture that is installed above the engine compartment **(see illustration)**. If an engine support fixture is not available, install an engine lift and a lifting chain assembly. This will keep the engine stable during the transaxle removal procedure. Remove the front wheels.
56   Detach the exhaust pipe from the manifold and separate the front exhaust pipe from the underside of the vehicle (see Chapter 4). Remove the floorpan brace to allow the exhaust to drop out of the way.
57   Remove the splash shields.
58   Remove the driveaxles (see Chapter 8).
59   Disconnect the two power steering fluid lines from the steering gear. Also detach the tie-rod ends from the steering knuckles (see Chapter 10).

60   Disconnect the stabilizer bar from the links (see Chapter 10).
61   Remove the mounting bolts from the engine/transaxle mounts to the subframe. Refer to Chapter 2A for engine and transaxle mount replacement procedures.
62   Remove the subframe mounting bolts from the chassis, using a floor jack to lower the subframe **(see illustration)**. Be sure to note exactly the size and location of each nut and bolt to insure correct reassembly. **Note:** *The transaxle should be supported by a floor jack immediately after the subframe is removed from the vehicle. The transaxle will tilt slightly but should remain steady if the engine is properly secured with the engine support fixture.*
63   Support the transaxle with a floor jack, preferably a floor jack with a transmission adapter head. Safety chains will help steady the transaxle on the jack.
64   Remove the transaxle-to-engine bolts **(see illustration)**.

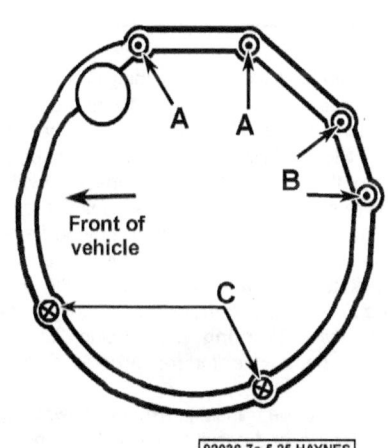

5.64 Refer to these letter designations for torque specs on the transaxle-to-engine bolts - 2002 and later models

Clutch Release Bearing

Clutch Release Fork Assembly

Clutch Release Fork Boot

Vehicle Speed Sensor

Vehicle Speed Sensor Driven Gear

Control Lever Housing Support Bracket

Oil Seal

Transaxle Case

Transaxle Case Receiver

Clutch Release Bearing Retainer

Plate Washer

Magnet

Differential Side Bearing Outer Race

Oil Seal

Input Shaft Front Bearing

Output Shaft Cover

Output Shaft Front Bearing

Differential Case Assembly

6.4a An exploded view of the manual transaxle assembly (1 of 3)

65   Recheck to be sure nothing is connecting the engine to the vehicle or to the transaxle. Disconnect and label anything still remaining.
66   Slowly lower the transaxle assembly out of the vehicle. Keep the transaxle level as you're separating it from the engine to prevent damage to the input shaft. It may be necessary to prise the mounts away from the frame brackets. **Caution:** *Do not depress the clutch pedal while the transaxle is removed from the vehicle.* **Warning:** *Do not place any part of your body under the transaxle as it's being removed.*
67   Move the transaxle assembly away from the vehicle and carefully place the transaxle assembly on the floor onto wood blocks. Leave enough room for a floor jack underneath the transaxle.
68   The clutch components can now be inspected (see Chapter 8). In most cases, new clutch components should be routinely installed whenever the transaxle is removed.

69   Check the engine and transaxle mounts and the transaxle shock absorber. If any of these components are worn or damaged, replace them.

Installation

70   If removed, install the clutch components (see Chapter 8). Apply a thin film of high temperature grease to the input shaft splines and the surface of the input shaft bearing retainer.
71   With the transaxle secured to the jack as on removal, raise it into position and then carefully slide it forward, engaging the input shaft with the clutch splines. Do not use excessive force to install the transaxle - if the input shaft does not slide into place, readjust the angle of the transaxle so it is level and/or turn the input shaft so the splines engage properly with the clutch. **Caution:** *Do NOT use transaxle-to-engine bolts to force the engine and transaxle into alignment. Doing so could crack or damage major components.*

If you experience difficulties, have an assistant help you line up the dowel pins on the block with the transaxle. Some wiggling of the engine and/or the transaxle will probably be necessary to secure proper alignment of the two.
72   Install the transaxle-to-engine bolts and the engine-to-transaxle bolt. Tighten the bolts to the torque listed in this Chapter's Specifications **(see illustration 5.64)**.
73   Install the right engine mount, the front engine mount, the left transaxle mount and the rear engine mount. Tighten all mounting bolts and nuts securely.
74   Reinstall the remaining components in the reverse order of removal. When installing the subframe, use a rod of the same diameter as the four subframe to-chassis bolts to align each side until that side's bolts can be inserted one at a time. Do not tighten any of the bolts until all have been installed finger tight, then tighten to the Specifications

No. 1 Shift Fork

Reverse Shift Fork

Snap Ring

Screw Plug

Spring Seat

Spring

Ball

No. 1 Shift Fork Shaft

Reverse Shift Arm Bracket

No. 3 Shift Fork Shaft

No. 3 Shift Fork

Reverse Idler Gear

Thrust Washer

Idler Gear Shaft

Shift Head

Output Shaft Assembly

No. 2 Shift Fork

No. 2 Shift Fork Shaft

Input Shaft Assembly

5th Driven Gear

Snap Ring

Rear Bearing Retainer

Snap Ring

Spacer

Needle Roller Bearing

5th Gear

Synchronizer Ring

No. 3 Hub Sleeve

Key Spring

Snap Ring

No. 3 Clutch Hub

6.4b An exploded view of the manual transaxle assembly (2 of 3)

---

in this Chapter.
75   Remove the jack and support fixture and lower the vehicle. Tighten the wheel lug nuts to the torque listed in the Chapter 1 Specifications. Tighten the driveaxle/hub nuts to the torque listed in the Chapter 8 Specifications.
76   Refill the transaxle with the proper lubricant (see Chapter 1).
77   Road test the vehicle to check for proper transaxle operation and check for leakage.

6   Manual transaxle overhaul - general information

Refer to illustrations 6.4a, 6.4b and 6.4c
1   Overhauling a manual transaxle is a difficult job for the do-it-yourselfer. It involves the disassembly and reassembly of many small parts. Numerous clearances must be precisely measured and, if necessary, changed with select-fit spacers and snap-rings. As a

result, if transaxle problems arise, it can be removed and installed by a competent do-it-yourselfer, but overhaul should be left to a transmission repair shop. Rebuilt transaxles may be available - check with your dealer parts department and auto parts stores. At any rate, the time and money involved in an overhaul is almost sure to exceed the cost of a rebuilt unit.
2   Nevertheless, it's not impossible for an inexperienced mechanic to rebuild a transaxle

Reverse Restrict Pin
Slotted Spring Pin
Screw Plug
No. 2 Oil Receiver Pipe
Lock Ball Assembly
Screw Plug
Outer Race
Plate Washer
No. 1 Oil Receiver Pipe
Plug
Shift and Select Lever Assembly
Selecting Bellcrank
Oil Seal
Transmission Case Cover
Transmission Case
Plug

6.4c An exploded view of the manual transaxle assembly (3 of 3)

if the special tools are available and the job is done in a deliberate step-by-step manner so nothing is overlooked.

3   The tools necessary for an overhaul include internal and external snap-ring pliers, a bearing puller, a slide hammer, a set of pin punches, a dial indicator and possibly a hydraulic press. In addition, a large, sturdy workbench and a vise or transaxle stand will be required.

4   During disassembly of the transaxle, make careful notes of how each piece comes off, where it fits in relation to other pieces and what holds it in place. Exploded views are included **(see illustrations)** to show where the parts go - but actually noting how they are installed when you remove the parts will make it much easier to get the transaxle back together.

5   Before taking the transaxle apart for repair, it will help if you have some idea what area of the transaxle is malfunctioning. Certain problems can be closely tied to specific areas in the transaxle, which can make component examination and replacement easier. Refer to the Troubleshooting section at the front of this manual for information regarding possible sources of trouble.

Chapter 7 Part B
Automatic transaxle

Contents

Specifications

Shift lock system

Shift lock solenoid resistance	21 to 27 ohms
Key interlock solenoid resistance	12.5 to 16.5 ohms

Torque specifications

Nm (unless otherwise indicated)

Park/Neutral Position switch	5.4
Torque converter-to-driveplate bolts	24
Transaxle-to-engine bolts	
Upper bolts	64
Lower bolts	
Bolts A	47
Bolts B	23
Valve body bolts	9.5
Manual valve retaining bolts (A131L)	9.5
Wire retainer bolt (A245E)	6.5
Detent spring bolt(s)	9.5

1   General information

All vehicles covered in this manual are equipped with either a 5-speed manual transaxle or a 3- or 4-speed automatic transaxle. All information on the automatic transaxle is included in this Part of Chapter 7. Information for the manual transaxle can be found in Part A of this Chapter.

The A131L is a three-speed automatic transaxle. Its shift points are controlled by the governor and the throttle valve. The A245E is an electronically controlled four-speed automatic transaxle with fourth gear being an overdrive gear. Shifts are attained by the use of shift solenoids, which are controlled by the Engine Control Module (ECM). Both transaxles utilize a lock-up torque converter.

Because of the complexity of the automatic transaxles and the specialized equipment necessary to perform most service operations, this Chapter contains only those procedures related to general diagnosis, routine maintenance, adjustment and removal and installation.

If the transaxle requires major repair work, it should be left to a dealer service department or an automotive or transmission repair shop. You can, however, remove and install the transaxle yourself and save the expense, even if the repair work is done by a transmission shop.

2   General diagnosis and trouble codes

Note: *Automatic transaxle malfunctions may be caused by five general conditions: poor engine performance, improper adjustments, hydraulic malfunctions, mechanical malfunctions or malfunctions in the computer or its signal network. Diagnosis of these problems should always begin with a check of the easily repaired items: fluid level and condition (see Chapter 1), shift linkage adjustment and throttle linkage adjustment. Next, perform a road test to determine if the problem has been corrected or if more diagnosis is necessary. If the problem persists after the preliminary tests and corrections are completed, additional diagnosis should be done by a dealer service department or transmission repair shop. Refer to the Troubleshooting section at the front of this manual for information on symptoms of transaxle problems.*

Preliminary checks

1   Drive the vehicle to warm the transaxle to normal operating temperature.
2   Check the fluid level as described in Chapter 1:

   a) *If the fluid level is unusually low, add enough fluid to bring the level within the designated area of the dipstick, then*
       check for external leaks (see below).
   b) *If the fluid level is abnormally high, drain off the excess, then check the drained fluid for contamination by coolant. The presence of engine coolant in the automatic transmission fluid indicates that a failure has occurred in the internal radiator walls that separate the coolant from the transmission fluid (see Chapter 3).*
   c) *If the fluid is foaming, drain it and refill the transaxle, then check for coolant in the fluid, or a high fluid level.*

3   Check the engine idle speed. **Note:** *If the engine is malfunctioning, do not proceed with the preliminary checks until it has been repaired and runs normally.*
4   Check the throttle valve cable for freedom of movement. Adjust it if necessary (see Section 4). **Note:** *The throttle valve cable may function properly when the engine is shut off and cold, but it may malfunction once the engine is hot. Check it cold and at normal engine operating temperature.*
5   Inspect the shift cable (see Section 5). Make sure that it's properly adjusted and that the cable operates smoothly.

Fluid leak diagnosis

6   Most fluid leaks are easy to locate visually. Repair usually consists of replacing a seal or gasket. If a leak is difficult to find, the following procedure may help.
7   Identify the fluid. Make sure it's transmission fluid and not engine oil or brake fluid (automatic transmission fluid is a deep red colour).
8   Try to pinpoint the source of the leak. Drive the vehicle several miles, then park it over a large sheet of cardboard. After a minute or two, you should be able to locate the leak by determining the source of the fluid dripping onto the cardboard.
9   Make a careful visual inspection of the suspected component and the area immediately around it. Pay particular attention to gasket mating surfaces. A mirror is often helpful for finding leaks in areas that are hard to see.
10   If the leak still cannot be found, clean the suspected area thoroughly with a degreaser or solvent, then dry it.
11   Drive the vehicle for several miles at normal operating temperature and varying speeds. After driving the vehicle, visually inspect the suspected component again.
12   Once the leak has been located, the cause must be determined before it can be properly repaired. If a gasket is replaced but the sealing flange is bent, the new gasket will not stop the leak. The bent flange must be straightened.
13   Before attempting to repair a leak, check to make sure that the following conditions are corrected or they may cause another leak.
Note: *Some of the following conditions cannot be fixed without highly specialized tools and*
expertise. Such problems must be referred to a transmission shop or a dealer service department.

Gasket leaks

14   Check the pan periodically. Make sure the bolts are tight, no bolts are missing, the gasket is in good condition and the pan is flat (dents in the pan may indicate damage to the valve body inside).
15   If the pan gasket is leaking, the fluid level may be too high, the vent may be plugged, the pan bolts may be too tight, the pan sealing flange may be warped, the sealing surface of the transaxle housing may be damaged, the gasket may be damaged or the transaxle casting may be cracked or porous. If sealant instead of gasket material has been used to form a seal between the pan and the transaxle housing, it may be the wrong sealant.

Seal leaks

16   If a transaxle seal is leaking, the fluid level or pressure may be too high, the vent may be plugged, the seal bore may be damaged, the seal itself may be damaged or improperly installed, the surface of the shaft protruding through the seal may be damaged or a loose bearing may be causing excessive shaft movement.
17   Make sure the dipstick tube seal is in good condition and the tube is properly seated. Periodically check the area around the speedometer gear or sensor for leakage. If transmission fluid is evident, check the O-ring for damage.

Case leaks

18   If the case itself appears to be leaking, the casting is porous and will have to be repaired or replaced.
19   Make sure the oil cooler hose fittings are tight and in good condition.

Fluid comes out vent pipe or fill tube

20   If this condition occurs, the transaxle is overfilled, there is coolant in the fluid, the case is porous, the dipstick is incorrect, the vent is plugged or the drain-back holes are plugged.

Self-diagnosis system and trouble codes

21   The electronic control system for the transaxle has some self-diagnostic capabilities. If certain kinds of system malfunctions occur, the PCM stores the appropriate diagnostic trouble code in its memory and the CHECK ENGINE indicator light illuminates to inform the driver. The diagnostic trouble codes can only be extracted from the PCM using a SCAN tool that can be linked to the On Board Diagnostic (OBD II) computer via the 16-pin diagnostic link. Codes are listed below for reference (refer to Chapter 6 for additional information).

Trouble Code identification

P0500	Vehicle speed sensor or circuit fault
P0705	Transmission range sensor circuit fault
P0710	Transmission fluid temperature sensor fault
P0711	Transmission fluid temperature sensor, range or performance fault
P0724	Brake light switch circuit fault
P0741	Torque converter clutch solenoid performance
P0750 - P0751	Shift solenoid A fault
P0756	Shift solenoid B performance
P0850	Park/Neutral function performance
P0973 - P0974	Shift solenoid A control circuit
P0976 - P0977	Shift solenoid B control circuit
P2716	Pressure control solenoid D circuit
P02769	Torque converter clutch solenoid circuit, low
P02770	Torque converter clutch solenoid circuit, high

Other Electronic Control System checks

Preliminary checks

22   Check the fluid level and condition. If the fluid smells burned, replace it (see Chapter 1).
23   Check for fluid leaks (see Section 2).
24   Check and, if necessary, adjust the shift cable (see Section 3).
25   Check and, if necessary, adjust the transmission range sensor (see Section 5).

O/D OFF indicator light check

26   Turn the ignition switch to ON.
27   Verify that the O/D OFF indicator light comes on when the O/D main switch is in the Off (up) position, and goes out when the O/D main switch is pushed to the On position.
28   If the O/D OFF indicator light does not light up, or remains on all the time, have the circuit checked out by a dealer service department or other qualified repair shop.

3   Shift cable - adjustment and replacement

Adjustment

Refer to illustrations 3.3 and 3.4

1   When the shift lever inside the vehicle is moved from the Neutral position to other positions, it should move smoothly and accurately to each position and the shift indicator should indicate the correct gear position.
2   If the indicator isn't aligned with the correct position, adjust the shift cable as follows:
3   Loosen the nut on the manual shift lever at the transaxle (see illustration).
4   Move the manual lever down into Park (anticlockwise), then return it (clockwise) two notches to the Neutral position (see illustration).

3.3 Before adjusting the shift cable, loosen the nut (A) that connects the shift cable to the manual lever on the transaxle - B is the clip securing the cable to the bracket on the transaxle

3.4 To adjust the shift cable, push the manual lever all the way DOWN, return it two clicks to the Neutral position, place the shift lever inside the vehicle at the Neutral position and tighten the swivel nut

3.11 Remove the three bolts at the airbag ECU (two are shown here) and set the unit aside - the shift cable is under the ECU

5   Move the shift lever inside the vehicle to the Neutral position.

6   While holding the lever with a slight force toward the REVERSE position, tighten the swivel nut securely.

7   Check the operation of the transaxle in each shift lever position (try to start the engine in each gear - the starter should operate in the Park and Neutral positions only).

Replacement

Refer to illustrations 3.11, 3.12 and 3.13

8   Disconnect the negative battery cable. **Warning:** *The models covered by this manual are equipped with Supplemental Restraint systems (SRS), more commonly known as airbags. Always disable the airbag system before working in the vicinity of the impact sensors, steering column or instrument panel to avoid the possibility of accidental deployment of the airbag, which could cause personal injury (see Chapter 12).*

9   Disconnect the cable from the manual lever and remove the large C-clip cable retainer from the bracket above the manual

lever **(see illustration 3.3)**.

10   Refer to Chapter 11 and remove the floor console, then pull back the carpeting at the front of the floor tunnel.

11   Remove the three bolts securing the airbag ECU to the floor and set it aside **(see illustration)**.

12   Remove the bolts from the cable-housing retainer on the floor inside the vehicle **(see illustration)**.

13   Prise off the cable ends from the shift housing and disconnect the cable eye from the shifter **(see illustration)**.

14   Pull the cable and grommet through the floor pan.

15   Installation is the reverse of removal.

16   Be sure to adjust the cable when you're done.

---

4   Transmission range sensor - replacement and adjustment

---

1   The transmission range sensor incorporates the Park/Neutral function as well as the back-up light switch and inputs transmission gear position information to the PCM. The

Park/Neutral function of the switch prevents the engine from starting in any gear other than Park or Neutral. If the engine starts with the shift lever in any position other than Park or Neutral, adjust the switch. The transmission position switch is also an information sensor for the Electronic Controlled Transaxle (ECT) Powertrain Control Module (PCM). When the shift lever is placed in position, the Park/Neutral position switch sends a voltage signal to the PCM.

Replacement

Refer to illustration 4.4

2   Raise the front of the vehicle and place it securely on jackstands.

3   Disconnect the electrical connector.

4   Remove the manual lever retaining nut and its lock plate **(see illustration)**. **Note:** *If equipped, bend the tabs flat on the lock plate before removing it.*

5   Disconnect the electrical connector from the switch.

6   Remove the retaining bolts and the switch **(see illustration 4.4)**.

7   Installation is the reverse of removal. Be sure to adjust the switch.

3.12 To detach the cable boot seal from the floor under the heater housing, remove the mounting bolts

3.13 To detach the shift cables from the shift lever assembly, twist the flange (A) to release its clips, then remove the clips and prise the cable eye (B) from the shifter arm

Adjustment

Refer to illustration 4.8

8   Loosen the switch retaining bolts and rotate the switch until the flat on the shaft and the neutral basic line on the switch are aligned **(see illustration)**. Hold the switch in this position and tighten the bolts. **Note:** *The pointer on the sheetmetal lock plate will indicate the alignment of the flat on the shaft with the Neutral line on the body of the switch.*

9   Refer to Section 3 for the cable adjustment procedure.

5   Shift lock system - description and component replacement

Description

1   The shift lock system prevents the shift lever from being shifted out of Park until the brake pedal is applied. The system consists of the brake light switch, a key interlock solenoid, a shift lock override button, a shift lock solenoid, and a shift lock control computer that incorporates a switch operated by the shift lever.

Component replacement

Refer to illustrations 5.3, 5.4 and 5.5

2   Remove the centre console (see Chapter 11).

3   To disconnect the cable, push in the locking tab and separate the cable end **(see illustration)**.

4   Refer to Chapter 11 and remove the steering column covers. Where the cable mounts at the steering column, disconnect the clip **(see illustration)**. **Note:** *Whenever this end of the cable is connected or disconnected, the ignition switch must be in the ACC position.*

5   The shift lock control computer is located at the bottom of the shift lever base on the right side **(see illustration)**. Disconnect the electrical connector and unclip the shift-lock computer from the shifter assembly.

6   The key interlock solenoid is located near the ignition switch (see Chapter 12).

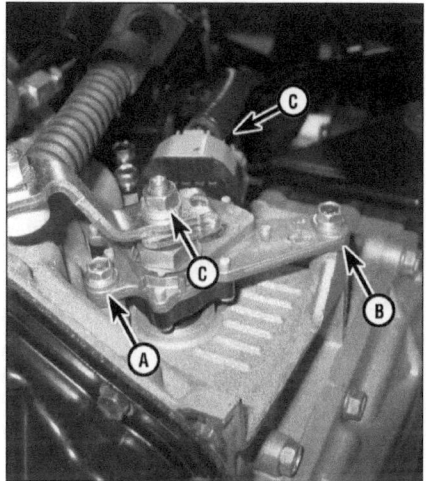

4.4 Remove the manual shift-lever retaining nut (A), disconnect the electrical connector (B), and remove the mounting bolts (C)

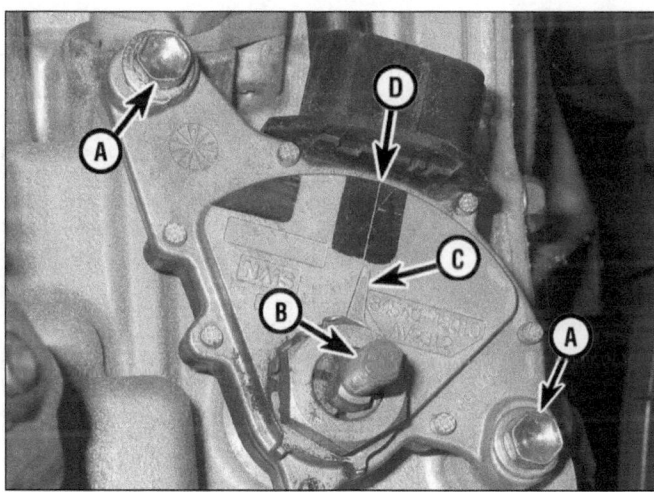

4.8 Detach the manual lever then loosen the switch retaining bolts (A) - the flat on the shaft (B) and the pointer (C) should align with the Neutral line on the switch (D) when installing the switch

5.3 Disconnect the shift lock cable at the shifter end - squeeze the clip (A), then lever the cable eye off the stud (B)

5.4 Use a screwdriver to release the clip securing the cable at the top of the ignition lock cylinder housing on the steering column

5.5 Shift lock system computer location

6.4 Carefully prise out the old driveaxle seal with a lever, screwdriver or a special seal removal tool; make sure you don't gouge or nick the surface of the seal bore

6.6 Drive in the new driveaxle seal with a large socket or a special seal installer

6.10 Remove the O-ring from the speed sensor

6   Oil seal replacement

1   Fluid leaks frequently occur due to wear of the driveaxle oil seals and/or the speedometer drive gear oil seal and O-rings. Replacement of these seals is relatively easy, since the repairs can usually be performed without removing the transaxle from the vehicle.

Driveaxle seals

Refer to illustrations 6.4 and 6.6

2   The driveaxle oil seals are located in either sides of the transaxle, where the driveaxle shaft is splined into the differential. If leakage at the seal is suspected, raise the vehicle and support it securely on jackstands. If the seal is leaking, fluid will be found on the side of the transaxle.

3   Remove the driveaxle assembly (see Chapter 8).

4   Using a screwdriver or lever, carefully prise the oil seal out of the transaxle bore **(see illustration)**.

5   If the oil seal cannot be removed with a screwdriver or lever, a special oil seal removal tool (available at auto parts stores) will be required.

6   Using a seal driver (preferably) or a large deep socket as a drift, install the new oil seal. Drive it into the bore squarely and make sure that it is completely seated **(see illustration)**. Lubricate the lip of the new seal with multi-purpose grease.

7   Install the driveaxle assembly (see Chapter 8). Be careful not to damage the lip of the new seal.

Speed sensor

Refer to illustration 6.10

8   The vehicle speed sensor is located on the case of the transaxle. Look for lubricant around the sensor housing to determine if an O-ring is leaking.

9   Disconnect the electrical connector from the vehicle or transmission speed sensor and

remove it from the transaxle (see Chapter 6 for VSS location).

10   Remove the O-ring **(see illustration)**.

11   Install a new O-ring and reinstall the vehicle speed sensor. Tighten the hold-down bolt securely.

7   Automatic transaxle - removal and installation

Removal

Refer to illustrations 7.12, 7.21 and 7.22

1   Place protective covers on the fenders and cowl and remove the bonnet (see Chapter 11).

2   Relieve the fuel system pressure (see Chapter 4), and drain the transaxle fluid (see Chapter 1).

3   Disconnect the negative cable from the battery.

4   Remove the battery and the battery tray (see Chapter 5).

5   Remove the air filter housing (see Chapter 4).

6   Remove the starter (see Chapter 5).

7   Remove the fluid cooler hoses from the rigid lines at the transaxle. Be sure to posi-

tion a pan below the line connections to catch any residual fluid. From the fluid cooler lines, remove the bolts and bracket securing the transmission fluid filler pipe to the cooler lines, then pull the filler tube from the transmission case.

8   Disconnect the transmission range sensor electrical connector (see Section 4).

9   Disconnect the vehicle speed sensor (VSS) electrical connector.

10   Clearly label, then disconnect all vacuum lines, coolant and emissions hoses, wiring harness connectors and earth straps. Masking tape and/or a touch-up paint applicator works well for marking items. Take instant photos or sketch the locations of components and brackets.

11   Disconnect the shift cable (see Section 3) from the transaxle.

12   Loosen but do NOT remove the front wheel lug nuts. Also loosen the driveaxle/hub nuts (see Chapter 8). Secure the engine using an engine support fixture that is installed above the engine compartment **(see illustration)**. If an engine support fixture is not available, install an engine lift and a lifting chain assembly. This will keep the engine stable during the transaxle removal procedure. Raise the vehicle and support it securely on jackstands, then remove the front wheels.

7.12 Support the engine with an engine support fixture (these are available at most tool rental yards and some auto parts stores)

7.21 Remove the torque converter-to-driveplate bolts - rotate the engine by hand to gain access to successive bolts - also seen clearly here are the lower transaxle-to-engine bolts

Front of vehicle

92036-7a-5.25 HAYNES

7.22 Transaxle-to-engine mounting bolts

Warning: *Be sure the engine/transaxle is securely supported by the brace or hoist. If it is not securely supported, it could fall during the removal procedure, causing injury or death.*

13   Detach the exhaust pipe from the manifold (see Chapter 4). Remove the floor pan brace under the car and lower the exhaust system out of the way.
14   Remove the under-vehicle splash shields.
15   Disconnect the two power steering fluid lines from the steering gear and unbolt the power steering gear from the suspension crossmember. Disconnect the stabilizer bar from the links (see Chapter 10).
16   Remove the stabilizer bar bracket bolts (see Chapter 10).
17   Use wire to tie the power steering gear to the chassis and remove the mounting bolts. The steering gear should remain suspended but out of the way during the transaxle removal procedure.
18   Remove the mounting bolts from the engine/transaxle mounts to the subframe. Refer to Chapter 2A for engine and transaxle mount replacement procedures.
19   Remove the subframe mounting bolts from the chassis, using a floor jack to lower the subframe **(see illustration 5.23 in Chapter 7, Part A)**. Be sure to note exactly the size and location of each nut and bolt to insure correct reassembly. **Note:** *The transaxle should be supported by a floor jack immediately after the subframe is removed from the vehicle. The transaxle will tilt slightly but should remain steady if the engine is properly secured with the engine compartment brace.*
20   Support the transaxle with an approved transaxle jack and safety chains. Floor jacks are often not stable enough to support and lower the transaxle from the vehicle.
21   Remove the access cover in the bell-housing and rotate the engine until all of the six converter-to-driveplate bolts can be removed **(see illustration)**. Have an assis-

tant keep the engine from turning by using a socket and breaker bar on the crankshaft pulley bolt. **Note:** *One of the converter bolts will be coloured green.*
22   Remove the transaxle-to-engine bolts **(see illustration)**.
23   Recheck to be sure nothing is connecting the engine to the vehicle or to the transaxle. Disconnect and label anything still remaining.
24   Slowly lower the transaxle assembly out of the vehicle. Keep the transaxle level as you're separating it from the engine to prevent damage to the input shaft. **Caution:** *Do not allow the transaxle to tilt forward very much (toward the engine) or the converter may slide out.* **Warning:** *Do not place any part of your body under the transaxle assembly when it's supported only by a hoist or other lifting device.*
25   Move the transaxle assembly away from the vehicle and carefully place the transaxle assembly on the floor onto wood blocks. Leave enough room for a floor jack underneath the transaxle.
26   Check the engine and transaxle mounts and the transaxle shock absorber. If any of these components are worn or damaged, replace them.

Installation

27   If removed, install the torque converter on the transaxle input shaft. Make sure the converter hub splines are properly engaged with the splines on the transaxle input shaft.
28   With the transaxle secured to the jack as on removal, and with an assistant holding the torque converter in place, raise the transaxle into position and turn the converter to align the bolt holes in the converter with the bolt holes in the driveplate. Install the converter-to-driveplate bolts, starting with the green bolt. **Note:** *Install all of the bolts before tightening any of them.* Do not use excessive force to install the transaxle - if something binds and the transaxle won't mate with the engine, alter the angle of the transaxle slightly

until it does mate. **Caution:** *Do NOT use transaxle-to-engine bolts to force the engine and transaxle into alignment. Doing so could crack or damage major components. If you experience difficulties, have an assistant help you line up the dowel pins on the block with the transaxle. Some wiggling of the engine and/or the transaxle will probably be necessary to secure proper alignment of the two.*
29   Install the transaxle-to-engine bolts. Tighten the bolts to the torque listed in this Chapter's Specifications **(see illustration 7.22)**.
30   Install the right engine mount, the front engine mount, the transaxle shock absorber, the left transaxle mount and the rear engine mount. Tighten all mounting bolts and nuts securely.
31   Reinstall the remaining components in the reverse order of removal. When installing the subframe, use a rod of the same diameter as the four subframe-to-chassis bolts to align each side until that side's bolts can be inserted and started. Do not tighten any of the four bolts until all have been installed finger tight, then tighten to the Specifications in this Chapter **(see illustration 5.23 in Chapter 7, Part A)**.
32   Remove all jacks and hoists and lower the vehicle. Tighten the wheel nuts to the torque listed in the Chapter 1 Specifications.
33   Add the specified amount of new transaxle fluid (see Chapter 1).
34   Connect the negative battery cable. Road test the vehicle to check for proper transmission operation and check for leakage.
35   Run the engine and check for proper operation and leaks. Shut off the engine and recheck the fluid levels. **Note:** *Since this an electronically-controlled transaxle, the manufacturer recommends that when a transaxle has been replaced, you should take the vehicle to a dealer or other service facility with a scan tool to perform a "reset memory" procedure for optimum transmission performance.*

8　Transaxle mount - check and replacement

Refer to illustration 8.1

1　Insert a large screwdriver or lever between the transaxle mount and the body and try to prise it away from the body (see illustration).

2　The transaxle mount should not move excessively. If it does, replace the mount.

3　To replace a mount, support the transaxle with a jack, remove the nuts and bolts and remove the mount. It may be necessary to raise the transaxle slightly to provide enough clearance to remove the mount.

4　Installation is the reverse of removal.

8.1 To check any of the three transaxle mounts, insert a large screwdriver or lever between the mount and the body as shown, and try to prise the mount from side to side or up and down - there should be a little movement, but it should be firm; if the mount moves too easily or looks cracked and torn, replace it (upper left transaxle mount shown)

Chapter 8
Clutch and driveaxles

Contents

Specifications

Clutch

Fluid type	See Chapter 1
Pedal freeplay	See Chapter 1
Driveaxle standard length	
Left driveaxle	56.3 to 57.3 cm
Right driveaxle	84.3 to 85.3 cm

Torque specifications

	Nm (unless otherwise indicated)
Clutch master cylinder mounting nuts	12.2
Clutch pressure plate-to-flywheel bolts	19
Clutch release cylinder mounting bolts	12.2
Clutch release cylinder line fitting	15
Driveaxle/hub nut	215
Wheel lug nuts	See Chapter 1

1   General information

The information in this Chapter deals with the components from the rear of the engine to the front wheels, except for the transaxle, which is dealt with in Chapters 7A and 7B. For the purposes of this Chapter, these components are grouped into two categories: clutch and driveaxles. Separate Sections within this Chapter offer general descriptions and checking procedures for both groups.

Since nearly all the procedures covered in this Chapter involve working under the vehicle, make sure it's securely supported on sturdy jackstands or a hoist where the vehicle can be easily raised and lowered.

2   Clutch - description and check

Refer to illustration 2.1

1   All vehicles with a manual transaxle use a single dry plate, diaphragm spring type clutch **(see illustration)**. The clutch disc has a splined hub that allows it to slide along the splines of the transaxle input shaft. The clutch and pressure plate are held in contact by spring pressure exerted by the diaphragm in the pressure plate.

2   The clutch release system is operated by hydraulic pressure. The hydraulic release system consists of the clutch pedal, a master cylinder and fluid reservoir, the hydraulic line, a slave cylinder which actuates the clutch release lever and the clutch release (or throwout) bearing.

3   When pressure is applied to the clutch pedal to release the clutch, hydraulic pressure is exerted against the outer end of the clutch release lever. As the lever pivots, the shaft fingers push against the release bearing. The bearing pushes against the fingers of the diaphragm spring of the pressure plate assembly, which in turn releases the clutch plate.

4   Terminology can be a problem regarding the clutch components because common names have in some cases changed from that used by the manufacturer. For example, the driven plate is also called the clutch plate or disc, the pressure plate assembly is sometimes referred to as the clutch cover, the clutch release bearing is sometimes called a throwout bearing, and the release cylinder is sometimes called the operating or slave cylinder.

5   Other than replacing components that have obvious damage, some preliminary checks should be performed to diagnose a clutch system failure.

a) *The first check should be of the fluid level in the clutch master cylinder (see Chapter 1). If the fluid level is low, add fluid as necessary and inspect the hydraulic clutch system for leaks. If the master cylinder reservoir has run dry, bleed the system (see Section 7) and retest the clutch operation.*

2.1 Typical clutch disc

1   *Lining* - this will wear down in use
2   *Springs or dampers* - check for cracking and deformation
3   *Splined hub* - the splines must not be worn and should slide smoothly on the transaxle input shaft splines
4   *Rivets* - these secure the lining and will damage the flywheel or pressure plate if allowed to contact the surfaces

b) *To check "clutch spin down time," run the engine at normal idle speed with the transaxle in Neutral (clutch pedal up - engaged). Disengage the clutch (pedal down), wait several seconds and shift the transaxle into Reverse. No grinding noise should be heard. A grinding noise would most likely indicate a problem in the pressure plate or the clutch disc.*

c) *To check for complete clutch release, run the engine (with the parking brake applied to prevent movement) and hold the clutch pedal approximately 13 mm from the floor. Shift the transaxle between 1st gear and Reverse several times. If the shift is not smooth, component failure is indicated. Check the release cylinder pushrod travel. With the clutch pedal depressed completely the release cylinder pushrod should extend substantially. If it doesn't, check the fluid level in the clutch master cylinder.*

d) *Visually inspect the clutch pedal bushing at the top of the clutch pedal to make sure there is no sticking or excessive wear.*

e) *Under the vehicle, check that the clutch release lever is solidly mounted on the ball stud.*

3   Clutch components - removal, inspection and installation

Warning: *Dust produced by clutch wear and deposited on clutch components is hazardous to your health. DO NOT blow it out with compressed air and DO NOT inhale it. DO NOT use petrol or petroleum based solvents to remove the dust. Brake system cleaner should be used to flush the dust into a drain pan. After the clutch components are wiped clean with a rag, dispose of the contaminated rags and cleaner in a labeled, covered container.*

Removal

Refer to illustration 3.6

1   Access to the clutch components is normally accomplished by removing the transaxle, leaving the engine in the vehicle. If, of course, the engine is being removed for major overhaul, then the opportunity should always be taken to check the clutch for wear and replace worn components as necessary. However, the relatively low cost of the clutch components compared to the time and labor involved in gaining access to them warrants their replacement any time the engine or transaxle is removed, unless they are new or in near-perfect condition. The following procedures assume that the engine will stay in place.

2   Remove the release cylinder (see Section 6). Hang it out of the way with a piece of wire - it isn't necessary to disconnect the hose.

3   Remove the transaxle from the vehicle (see Chapter 7A). Support the engine while the transaxle is out. Preferably, an engine hoist or support fixture should be used to support it from above. However, if a jack is used underneath the engine, make sure a piece of wood is used between the jack and oil pan to spread the load. **Caution:** *The pick-up for the oil pump is very close to the bottom of the oil pan. If the pan is bent or distorted in any way, engine oil starvation could occur.*

4   The release fork and release bearing can remain attached to the transaxle for the time being.

5   To support the clutch disc during removal, install a clutch alignment tool through the clutch disc hub.

6   Carefully inspect the flywheel and pressure plate for indexing marks. The marks are usually an X, an O or a white letter. If they cannot be found, scribe marks yourself so the pressure plate and the flywheel will be in the same alignment during installation **(see illustration)**.

7   Slowly loosen the pressure plate-to-fly-

3.6 Mark the relationship of the pressure plate to the flywheel (in case you're going to reuse the same pressure plate)

3.10 Examine the clutch disc for evidence of excessive wear, such as smeared friction material, loose rivets, worn hub splines and distorted damper cushions or springs

wheel bolts. Work in a diagonal pattern and loosen each bolt a little at a time until all spring pressure is relieved. Then hold the pressure plate securely and completely remove the bolts, followed by the pressure plate and clutch disc.

Inspection

Refer to illustrations 3.10, 3.12a and 3.12b

8   Ordinarily, when a problem occurs in the clutch, it can be attributed to wear of the clutch driven plate assembly (clutch disc). However, all components should be inspected at this time.

9   Inspect the flywheel for cracks, heat checking, score marks and other damage. If the imperfections are slight, a machine shop can resurface it to make it flat and smooth. Refer to Chapter 2 for the flywheel removal procedure.

10   Inspect the lining on the clutch disc. There should be at least 0.8 mm of lining above the rivet heads **(see illustration 2.1)**. Check for loose rivets, distortion, cracks, broken springs and other obvious damage **(see illustration)**. As mentioned above, ordinarily the clutch disc is replaced as a matter of course, so if in doubt about the condition, replace it with a new one.

11   The release bearing should be replaced along with the clutch disc (see Section 4).

12   Check the machined surface and the diaphragm spring fingers of the pressure plate **(see illustrations)**. If the surface is grooved or otherwise damaged, replace the pressure plate assembly. Also check for obvious damage, distortion, cracking, etc. Light glazing can be removed with emery cloth or sandpaper. If a new pressure plate is indicated, new or factory rebuilt units are available.

Installation

Refer to illustration 3.14

13   Before installation, carefully wipe the flywheel and pressure plate machined surfaces clean. It's important that no oil or grease is on these surfaces or the lining of the clutch disc. Handle these parts only with clean hands.

14   Position the clutch disc and pressure plate with the clutch held in place with an alignment tool **(see illustration)**. Make sure it's installed properly (most replacement clutch plates will be marked "flywheel side" or something similar - if not marked, install the clutch disc with the damper springs or cushion toward the transaxle).

15   Tighten the pressure plate-to-flywheel bolts only finger tight, working around the pressure plate.

16   Centre the clutch disc by ensuring the alignment tool is through the splined hub and into the recess in the crankshaft. Wiggle the tool up, down or side-to-side as needed to bottom the tool. Tighten the pressure plate-to-flywheel bolts a little at a time, working in a criss-cross pattern to prevent distortion of the cover. After all of the bolts are snug, tighten them to the torque listed in this Chapter's Specifications. Remove the alignment tool.

NORMAL FINGER WEAR

EXCESSIVE WEAR →

3.12a Replace the pressure plate if excessive wear or damage are noted

EXCESSIVE FINGER WEAR

BROKEN OR BENT FINGERS

3.12b Examine the pressure plate friction surface for score marks, cracks and evidence of overheating (blue spots)

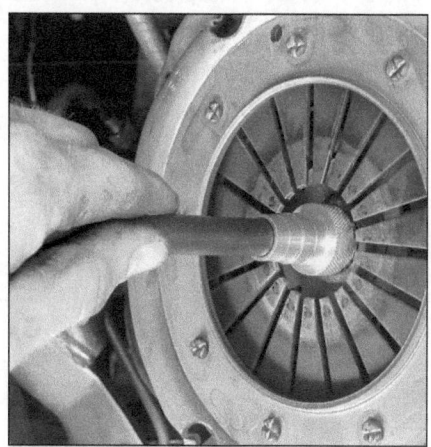

3.14 Centre the clutch disc in the pressure plate with a clutch alignment tool

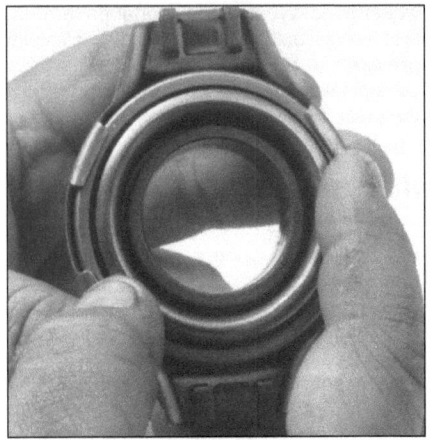

4.4 To check the operation of the bearing, hold it by the outer race and rotate the inner race while applying pressure - the bearing should turn smoothly - if it doesn't, replace it

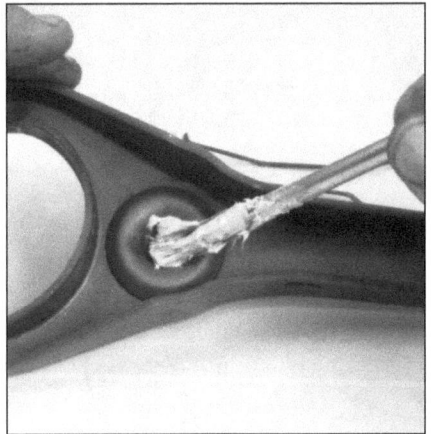

4.6a Using high temperature grease, lubricate the ball stud socket in the back of the release lever . . .

4.6b . . . the lever ends and the depression for the cylinder pushrod

17   Using high-temperature grease, lubricate the inner groove of the release bearing (see Section 4). Also place grease on the release lever contact areas and the transaxle input-shaft bearing retainer.

18   Install the clutch release bearing (see Section 4).

19   Install the transaxle, release cylinder and all components removed previously, tightening all fasteners to the proper torque specifications.

---

4   Clutch release bearing and lever - removal, inspection and installation

---

Warning: *Dust produced by clutch wear and deposited on clutch components is hazardous to your health. DO NOT blow it out with compressed air and DO NOT inhale it. DO NOT use petrol or petroleum-based solvents to remove the dust. Brake system cleaner should be used to flush it into a drain pan. After the clutch components are wiped clean with a rag, dispose of the contaminated rags and cleaner in a labeled, covered container.*

Removal

1   Disconnect the negative cable from the battery.

2   Remove the transaxle (see Chapter 7).

3   Remove the clutch release lever from the ball stud by pulling on the retention spring, then remove the bearing and the lever.

Inspection

Refer to illustration 4.4

4   Hold the bearing by the outer race and rotate the inner race while applying pressure **(see illustration)**. If the bearing doesn't turn smoothly or if it's noisy, replace the bearing/hub assembly with a new one. Wipe the bearing with a clean rag and inspect it for damage, wear and cracks. Don't immerse the bearing

in solvent - it's sealed for life and to do so would ruin it. Also check the release lever for cracks and bends.

Installation

Refer to illustrations 4.6a and 4.6b

5   Fill the inner groove of the release bearing with high-temperature grease. Also apply a light coat of the same grease to the transaxle input shaft splines and the front bearing retainer.

6   Lubricate the release lever ball socket, lever ends and release cylinder pushrod socket with high-temperature grease **(see illustrations)**.

7   Attach the release bearing to the release lever. On models that use a retaining clip, make sure it engages properly with the lever.

8   Slide the release bearing onto the transaxle input shaft front bearing retainer while passing the end of the release lever through the opening in the clutch housing. Push the clutch release lever onto the ball stud until it's firmly seated.

9   Apply a light coat of high-temperature grease to the face of the release bearing where it contacts the pressure plate diaphragm fingers.

10   The remainder of installation is the reverse of the removal procedure.

---

5   Clutch master cylinder - removal and installation

Removal

Refer to illustration 5.2

1   Disconnect the negative cable from the battery.

2   Remove the driver's side knee bolster (see Chapter 11). Under the dashboard, disconnect the pushrod from the top of the clutch pedal. It's held in place with a clevis pin. To remove the clevis pin, remove the clip **(see illustration)**.

3   Remove the brake master cylinder and the power brake booster (see Chapter 9).

4   Disconnect the hydraulic line at the clutch master cylinder. If available, use a flare-nut wrench on the fitting, to protect the fitting from being rounded off. Have rags handy as some fluid will be lost as the line is removed. **Caution:** *Don't allow brake fluid to come into contact with paint, as it will damage the finish.*

5   From under the dash, remove the

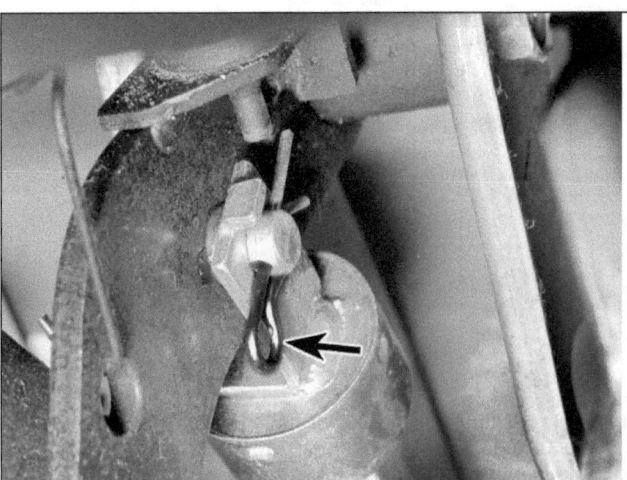

5.2 To release the clutch pushrod from the clutch pedal, remove this clip and the clevis pin

nuts which attach the master cylinder to the firewall. Remove the master cylinder, again being careful not to spill any of the fluid.

Installation

6   Position the master cylinder on the firewall, installing the mounting nuts finger-tight.

7   Connect the hydraulic line to the master cylinder, moving the cylinder slightly as necessary to thread the fitting properly into the bore. Don't cross-thread the fitting as it's installed.

8   Tighten the mounting nuts and the hydraulic line fitting securely.

9   Connect the pushrod to the clutch pedal.

10   Install the power brake booster and master cylinder (see Chapter 9). Connect the clutch fluid feed line to the brake fluid reservoir.

11   Fill the brake fluid reservoir with the proper brake fluid (see Chapter 1) and bleed the clutch system (see Section 7) and the brake system (see Chapter 9).

12   Check the clutch pedal height and free-play (see Chapter 1).

6.3 Use a flare-nut wrench when disconnecting the hydraulic line fitting (left) to prevent rounding off the corners of the tubing nut, then remove the mounting bolts (typical installation)

6   Clutch release cylinder - removal and installation

Removal

Refer to illustration 6.3

1   Disconnect the negative cable from the battery.

2   Raise the vehicle and support it securely on jackstands.

3   Disconnect the hydraulic line at the release cylinder. If available, use a flare-nut wrench on the fitting, which will prevent the fitting from being rounded off **(see illustration)**. Have a small can and rags handy, as some fluid will be spilled as the line is removed.

4   Remove the release cylinder mounting bolts.

5   Remove the release cylinder.

Installation

6   Install the release cylinder on the clutch housing. Make sure the pushrod is seated in the release fork pocket.

7   Connect the hydraulic line to the release cylinder. Tighten the connection securely.

8   Fill the brake master cylinder with the proper brake fluid (see Chapter 1).

9   Bleed the system (see Section 7).

10   Lower the vehicle and connect the negative battery cable.

7   Clutch hydraulic system - bleeding

1   The hydraulic system should be bled of all air whenever any part of the system has been removed or if the fluid level has been allowed to fall so low that air has been drawn into the master cylinder. The procedure is

similar to bleeding a brake system.

2   Fill the brake master cylinder with new brake fluid of the proper type (see Chapter 1). **Caution:** *Do not re-use any of the fluid coming from the system during the bleeding operation or use fluid which has been inside an open container for an extended period of time.*

3   Raise the vehicle and place it securely on jackstands to gain access to the release cylinder, which is located on the left side of the clutch housing.

4   Locate the bleeder valve on the clutch release cylinder (right above the fitting for the hydraulic fluid line). Remove the dust cap that fits over the bleeder valve and push a length of clear tubing over the valve. Place the other end of the hose into a clear container with about two inches of brake fluid in it. The hose end must be submerged in the fluid.

5   Have an assistant depress the clutch pedal and hold it. Open the bleeder valve on the release cylinder, allowing fluid to flow through the hose. Close the bleeder valve when fluid stops flowing from the hose. Once closed, have your assistant release the pedal.

6   Continue this process until all air is evacuated from the system, indicated by a full, solid stream of fluid being ejected from the bleeder valve each time and no air bubbles in the hose or container. Keep a close watch on the fluid level inside the clutch master cylinder reservoir; if the level drops too low, air will be sucked back into the system and the process will have to be started all over again.

7   Install the dust cap and lower the vehicle. Check carefully for proper operation before placing the vehicle in normal service.

8   Clutch start switch - check and replacement

1   Check the pedal height, pedal freeplay and pushrod play (see Chapter 1).

2   Verify that the engine will not start when the clutch pedal is released.

3   Verify that the engine will start when the clutch pedal is depressed all the way.

4   The clutch start switch is located on a

bracket forward of the clutch pedal (under the dash).

5   If the switch fails either of the tests, replace it. This is accomplished by removing the nut nearest the plunger end of the switch and unscrewing the switch. Disconnect the wire harness. Installation is the reverse of removal.

6   To adjust the clutch start switch, depress the clutch pedal completely and turn the switch in or out to achieve the spacing of the original switch.

7   Verify that the switch operates properly by performing Steps 2 and 3 again.

9   Driveaxles - general information and inspection

1   Power is transmitted from the transaxle to the wheels through a pair of driveaxles. The inner end of each driveaxle is splined into the differential side gears. The outer ends of the driveaxles are splined to the axle hubs and locked in place by a large nut.

2   The inner ends of the driveaxles are equipped with sliding constant velocity joints, which are capable of both angular and axial motion. Each inner joint assembly consists of a tripod bearing and a joint housing (outer race) in which the joint is free to slide in and out as the driveaxle moves up and down with the wheel. The joints can be disassembled and cleaned in the event of a boot failure (see Section 11), but if any parts are damaged, the joints must be replaced as a unit. When buying parts for a driveaxle, or a complete replacement driveaxle assembly, make sure you get the right components. Some Corollas may have Toyota-made axles, and some may have axles from other suppliers to Toyota.

3   The outer CV joints consist of ball bearings running between an inner race and an outer cage, and are capable of angular but not axial movement. The outer joints should be cleaned, inspected and repacked, but they cannot be disassembled. If an outer joint is damaged, it must be replaced along with the axleshaft (the outer joint and axleshaft are sold as a single component).

10.4 Using a hammer and punch, unstake the driveaxle/hub nut

10.5 Use a large lever to immobilize the hub while loosening the driveaxle/hub nut

4   The boots should be inspected periodically for damage and leaking lubricant. Torn CV joint boots must be replaced immediately or the joints can be damaged. Boot replacement involves removal of the driveaxle (see Section 10). **Note:** *Some auto parts stores carry split-type replacement boots, which can be installed without removing the driveaxle from the vehicle. This is a convenient alternative; however, the driveaxle should be removed and the CV joint disassembled and cleaned to ensure the joint is free from contaminants such as moisture and dirt which will accelerate CV joint wear.* The most common symptom of worn or damaged CV joints, besides lubricant leaks, is a clicking noise in turns, a clunk when accelerating after coasting and vibration at highway speeds. To check for wear in the CV joints and driveaxle shafts, grasp each axle (one at a time) and rotate it in both directions while holding the CV joint housings, feeling for play indicating worn splines or sloppy CV joints. Also check the driveaxle shafts for cracks, dents and distortion.

10 Driveaxle - removal and installation

Caution: *The manufacturer states that a new driveaxle/hub nut must be installed whenever it is removed.*

Removal

Refer to illustrations 10.4, 10.5, 10.6, 10.9 and 10.10

1   Disconnect the cable from the negative terminal of the battery.
2   Set the parking brake.
3   Loosen the front wheel lug nuts, raise the vehicle and support it securely on jackstands. Remove the wheel.
4   Unstake the driveaxle/hub nut **(see illustration)**.
5   Remove the driveaxle/hub nut. To prevent the hub from turning, wedge a lever between two of the wheel studs and allow the lever to rest against the ground or the floor pan of the vehicle **(see illustration)**.

6   To loosen the driveaxle from the hub splines, tap the end of the driveaxle with a soft-faced hammer or a hammer and a brass punch **(see illustration)**. **Note:** *Don't attempt to push the end of the driveaxle through the hub yet. Applying force to the end of the driveaxle, beyond just breaking it loose from the hub, can damage the driveaxle or transaxle.* If the driveaxle is stuck in the hub splines and won't move, it may be necessary to remove the brake disc (see Chapter 9) and push it from the hub with a two-jaw puller after Step 8 is performed.
7   Remove the engine splash shields (see Chapter 1). Place a drain pan underneath the transaxle to catch any lubricant that may spill out when the driveaxle is removed.
8   Remove the nuts and bolt securing the balljoint to the control arm, then prise the control arm down to separate the components (see Chapter 10).
9   Pull out on the steering knuckle and detach the driveaxle from the hub **(see illustration)**. Don't let the driveaxle hang by the

10.6 Using a brass punch, strike the end of the driveaxle sharply with a hammer; when it breaks free, it will move noticeably

10.9 Pull the steering knuckle out and slide the end of the driveaxle out of the hub

10.10 To separate the inner end of the driveaxle from the transaxle, prise on the CV joint housing like this with a large screwdriver or lever - you may need to give the lever a sharp rap with a brass hammer

11.3 Lift the tabs on all the boot clamps with a screwdriver, then open the clamps

inner CV joint after the outer end has been detached from the steering knuckle, as the inner joint could become damaged. Support the outer end of the driveaxle with a piece of wire, if necessary.

10   Carefully prise the inner CV joint out of the transaxle **(see illustration)**.

11   If necessary, refer to Chapter 7 for the driveaxle oil seal replacement procedure.

Installation

12   Installation is the reverse of the removal procedure, but with the following additional points:

a) *Push the driveaxle sharply in to seat the retaining ring on the inner CV joint in the groove in the differential side gear.*

b) *Tighten the **new** driveaxle/hub nut to the torque listed in this Chapter's Specifications, then stake the collar of the nut into the groove in the driveaxle.*

c) *Tighten the lug nuts to the torque listed in the Chapter 1 Specifications.*

d) *Check the transaxle lubricant and add, if necessary, to bring it to the proper level (see Chapter 1).*

11   Driveaxle boot replacement

Note: *If the CV joint boots must be replaced, explore all options before beginning the job. Complete rebuilt driveaxles are available on an exchange basis, which eliminates much time and work. Whichever route you choose to take, check on the cost and availability of parts before disassembling the vehicle.*

1   Remove the driveaxle (see Section 10).

Disassembly

Refer to illustrations 11.3, 11.4 and 11.6

2   Mount the driveaxle in a vise with wood lined jaws (to prevent damage to the axleshaft). Check the CV joint for excessive play in the radial direction, which indicates worn

parts. Check for smooth operation throughout the full range of motion for each CV joint. If a boot is torn, disassemble the joint, clean the components and inspect for damage due to loss of lubrication and possible contamination by foreign matter.

3   Using a small screwdriver, prise the retaining tabs on the clamps up to loosen them and slide them off **(see illustration)**.

4   Using a screwdriver, carefully prise up on the edge of the outer boot and push it away from the CV joint. Old and worn boots can be cut off. Pull the inner CV joint boot back from the housing and slide the housing from the tripod **(see illustration)**.

5   Mark the tripod and axleshaft to ensure that they are reassembled properly.

6   Remove the tripod joint snap-ring with a pair of snap-ring pliers **(see illustration)**.

7   Remove the tripod joint from the driveaxle, then remove the inner stop-ring from its groove on the shaft.

8   If you haven't already cut them off, remove both boots. If you're working on a right-side driveaxle, you'll also have to cut off

the clamp for the dynamic damper and slide the damper off. **Note:** *Before removing the damper, measure its distance from the end of the driveaxle - when reassembling, it must be returned to the same spot.*

Check

9   Thoroughly clean all components, including the outer CV joint assembly, with solvent until the old CV joint grease is completely removed. Inspect the bearing surfaces of the inner tripods and housings for cracks, pitting, scoring and other signs of wear. It's very difficult to inspect the bearing surfaces of the inner and outer races of the outer CV joint, but you can at least check the surfaces of the ball bearings themselves. If they're in good shape, the races probably are too; if they're not, neither are the races. If the inner CV joint is worn, you can buy a new inner CV joint and install it on the old axleshaft; if the outer CV joint is worn, you'll have to purchase a new outer CV joint *and* axleshaft (they're sold preassembled).

11.4 Remove the boot from the inner CV joint and slide the joint housing from the tripod

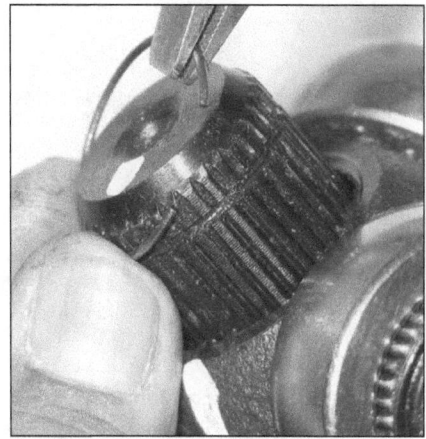

11.6 Remove the snap-ring with a pair of snap-ring pliers

11.10a Wrap the splined area of the axleshaft with tape to prevent damage to the boots when removing or installing them

11.10b Place grease at the bottom of the CV joint housing

Reassembly

Refer to illustrations 11.10a, 11.10b, 11.10c, 11.12a and 11.12b

10   Wrap the splines on the end the axleshaft with electrical tape to protect the boots from the sharp edges of the splines **(see illustration)**. Slide the clamps and boot(s) onto the axleshaft, then place the inner stop-ring and the tripod on the shaft, aligning the marks made before removal. **Note:** *If you removed the dynamic damper, be sure to install it in its original location and secure it with a new clamp before installing the inner boot.* Pack the CV joint(s) with CV joint grease, and also apply some to the inside of the boot(s). Insert the tripod into the housing and pack the remainder of the grease around the tripod **(see illustrations)**. **Caution:** *Use CV joint grease only.*

11   Slide the boot into place, making sure both ends seat in their grooves. When installing the inner boot, position the CV joint midway through its travel, then proceed to the next Step.

12   Equalize the pressure in the boot, then tighten and secure the boot clamps **(see illustrations)**.

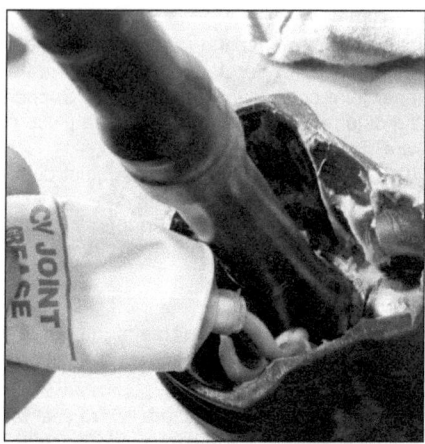

11.10c Install the boot and clamps onto the axleshaft, then insert the tripod into the housing, followed by the rest of the grease

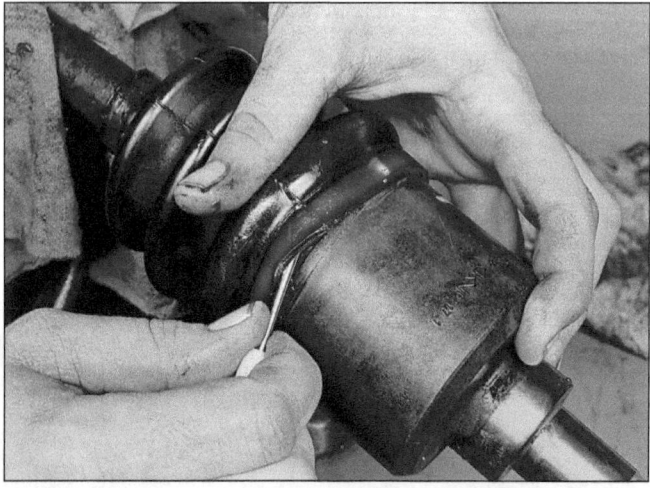

11.12a Equalize the pressure inside the boot by inserting a small screwdriver between the boot and the outer race

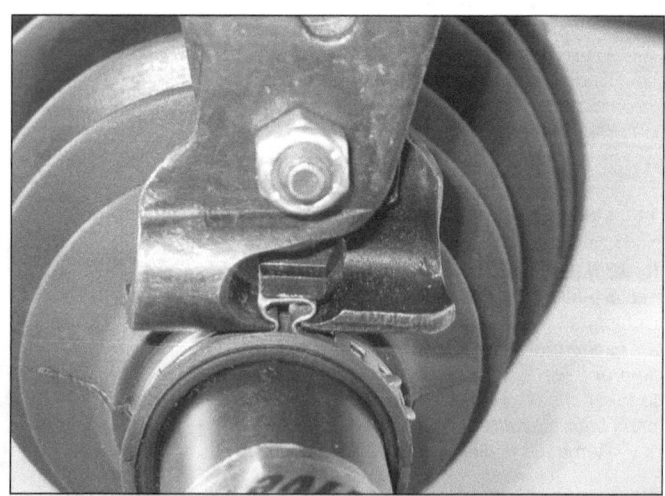

11.12b You'll need a special boot clamp installation tool like this one to tighten the new clamps; follow the instructions provided by the tool manufacturer

Chapter 9
Brakes

Contents

Specifications

General

Brake fluid type	See Chapter 1
Brake pedal height	131.6 to 141.6 mm
Brake pedal freeplay	1 to 6 mm
Power brake booster pushrod-to-master cylinder piston clearance	0.0 mm
Brake light switch plunger protrusion (from threaded portion of switch)	0.5 to 2.4 mm

Disc brakes

Minimum brake pad thickness	See Chapter 1
Front disc thickness	
Standard	25.0 mm
Minimum*	23.0 mm
Rear disc thickness	
Standard	9.0 mm
Minimum*	8.0 mm
Disc runout limit	0.05 mm
Parking brake shoe minimum thickness	1.0 mm

Drum brakes

Brake shoe minimum lining thickness	See Chapter 1
Drum inside diameter	
Standard	200.0 mm
Maximum*	201.0 mm

* **Note:** *If different specifications are cast into the disc or drum, they supersede information printed here.*

Parking brake

Parking brake lever travel

  Drum brakes... 4 to 7 clicks
  Disc brakes .... 5 to 8 clicks

Torque specifications   **Nm** (unless otherwise indicated)

Caliper mounting bolts

  Front... 34
  Rear 47
Caliper torque plate bolts... 106.8
Brake hose-to-caliper banjo bolt... 30
Wheel cylinder mounting bolt 10
Master cylinder-to-brake booster nuts 13
Power brake booster mounting nuts.. 13
Wheel lug nuts... 103

1   General information

The vehicles covered by this manual are equipped with hydraulically operated front and rear brake systems. The front brakes are disc type and the rear brakes are either disc or drum type. Both the front and rear brakes are self-adjusting. The disc brakes automatically compensate for pad wear, while the drum brakes incorporate an adjustment mechanism that is activated as the parking brake is applied.

Hydraulic system

The hydraulic system consists of two separate circuits. The master cylinder has separate reservoirs for the two circuits, and, in the event of a leak or failure in one hydraulic circuit, the other circuit will remain operative. A dual proportioning valve on the firewall provides brake balance between the front and rear brakes.

Power brake booster

The power brake booster, utilizing engine manifold vacuum and atmospheric pressure to provide assistance to the hydraulically operated brakes, is mounted on the firewall in the engine compartment.

Parking brake

The parking brake lever operates the rear brakes only, through cable actuation. It's mounted in the centre console.

Service

After completing any operation involving disassembly of any part of the brake system, always test-drive the vehicle to check for proper braking performance before resuming normal driving. When testing the brakes, perform the tests on a clean, dry, flat surface. Conditions other than these can lead to inaccurate test results.

Test the brakes at various speeds with both light and heavy pedal pressure. The vehi-

cle should stop evenly without pulling to one side or the other. Avoid locking the brakes, because this slides the tyres and diminishes braking efficiency and control of the vehicle.

Tyres, vehicle load and wheel alignment are factors which also affect braking performance.

2   Anti-lock Brake System (ABS) - general information

1   The Anti-lock Brake System (ABS) is designed to maintain vehicle steerabilty, directional stability and optimum deceleration under severe braking conditions and on most road surfaces. It does so by monitoring the rotational speed of each wheel and controlling the brake line pressure to each wheel during braking. This prevents the wheel from locking up.

The ABS system is primarily designed to prevent wheel lockup during heavy braking, but the information provided by the wheel speed sensors of the ABS system is shared with an optional system that uses the data to control vehicle handling. EBD (Electronic Brakeforce Distribution), varies the front-to-rear and side-to-side braking balance under different vehicle loads.

Components

Actuator assembly

2   The actuator assembly is mounted in the right front corner of the engine compartment (behind the headlight housing), and consists of the master cylinder, an electric hydraulic pump and four solenoid valves. **Note:** *The actuator assembly for ABS brakes and ABS with EBD are similar, but the configuration of the actuator and ECU differ.*

a) *The electric pump provides hydraulic pressure to charge the reservoirs in the actuator, which supplies pressure to the braking system. The pump and reservoirs are housed in the actuator assembly.*

b) *The solenoid valves modulate brake line pressure during ABS operation. The body contains four valves - one for each wheel.*

Speed sensors

3   These sensors are located at each wheel and generate small electrical pulsations when the toothed sensor rings are turning, sending a signal to the electronic controller indicating wheel rotational speed.

4   The front speed sensors are mounted to the front steering knuckle in close relationship to the toothed sensor rings, which are integral with the front driveaxle outer CV joints.

5   The rear wheel sensors are bolted to the axle carriers. The sensor rings are integral with the rear hub assemblies.

ABS computer

6   The ABS computer is mounted with the actuator and is the "brain" for the ABS system. The function of the computer is to accept and process information received from the wheel speed sensors to control the hydraulic line pressure, avoiding wheel lock up. The computer also constantly monitors the system, even under normal driving conditions, to find faults within the system.

Diagnosis and repair

7   If a problem develops within the system, an "ABS" light will glow on the dashboard. If the dashboard warning light comes on and stays on while the vehicle is in operation, the ABS system requires attention. Here are few simple checks you can perform:

a) *Check the brake fluid level in the master cylinder reservoir.*

b) *Check that all electrical connectors are securely connected.*

c) *Check all the applicable fuses.*

If the above preliminary checks do not rectify the problem, the vehicle should be diagnosed and repaired by a dealer service department or other qualified repair shop.

3.5 Before removing the caliper, be sure to depress the piston into its bore in the caliper with a large G-clamp to make room for the new pads

3.6a Always wash the brakes with brake cleaner before disassembling anything

3   Disc brake pads - replacement

Refer to illustration 3.5

Warning: *Disc brake pads must be replaced on both front wheels at the same time - never replace the pads on only one wheel. Also, the dust created by the brake system is harmful to your health. Never blow it out with compressed air and don't inhale any of it. An approved filtering mask should be worn when working on the brakes. Do not, under any circumstances, use petroleum-based solvents to clean brake parts. Use brake system cleaner only!*

1   Remove the cap from the brake fluid reservoir.

2   Loosen the wheel lug nuts, raise the vehicle and support it securely on jackstands. Block the wheels at the opposite end.

3   Remove the wheels. Work on one brake assembly at a time, using the assembled brake for reference if necessary.

4   Inspect the brake disc carefully as out-lined in Section 5. If machining is necessary, follow the information in that Section to remove the disc, at which time the pads can be removed as well.

5   Push the piston back into its bore to provide room for the new brake pads. A G-clamp can be used to accomplish this **(see illustration)**. As the piston is depressed to the bottom of the caliper bore, the fluid in the master cylinder will rise. Make sure that it doesn't overflow. If necessary, siphon off some of the fluid.

Front brakes

Refer to illustrations 3.6a through 3.6r

6   Follow the accompanying photos **(Illustrations 3.6a through 3.6r)**, for the actual pad replacement procedure. Be sure to stay in order and read the caption under each illustration. **Note:** *Several different types of pads, springs and supports are used. Take note of all of these parts before removing any of them.*

3.6b To remove the caliper, remove the bolts indicated by the upper and lower arrows (the centre arrow points to the brake hose banjo bolt, which shouldn't be unscrewed unless the caliper is being completely removed from the vehicle)

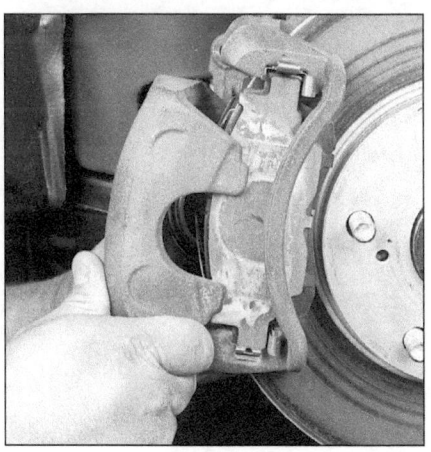

3.6c Remove the caliper . . .

3.6d . . . and hang it from the strut coil spring with a piece of wire; do not allow the caliper to hang by the flexible brake hose

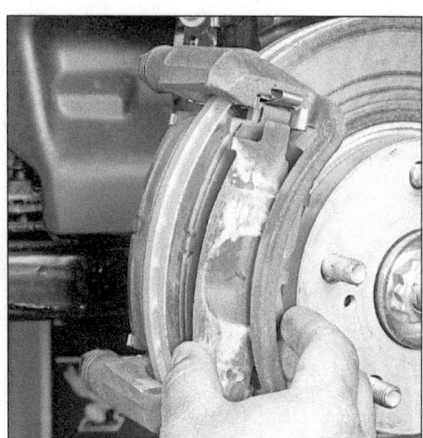

3.6e Remove the outer shim . . .

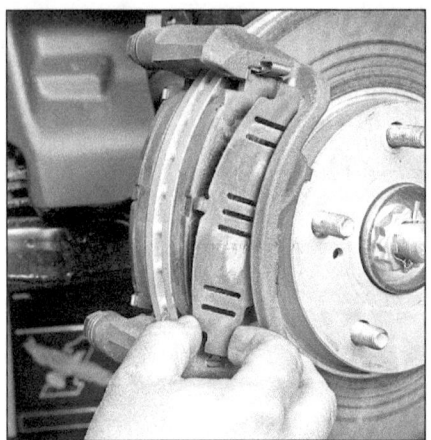

3.6f . . . and the inner shim from the outer brake pad

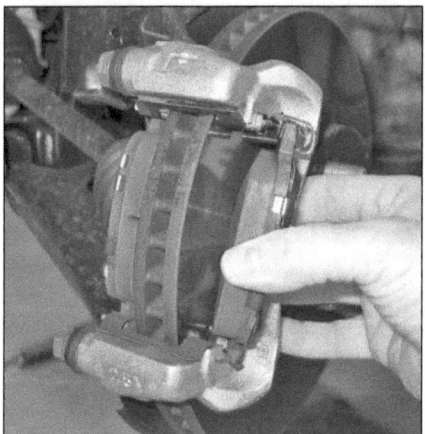

3.6g Remove the outer brake pad

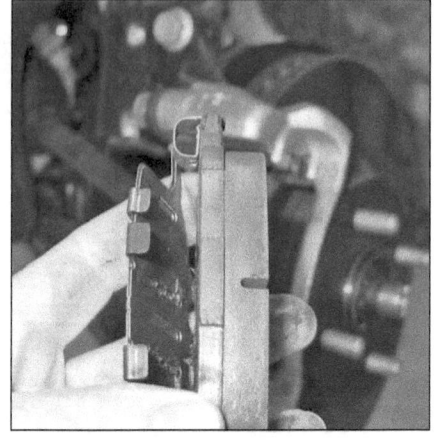

3.6h Remove the outer shim . . .

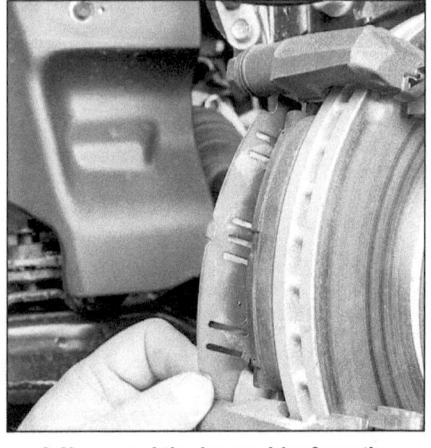

3.6i . . . and the inner shim from the inner brake pad

3.6j Remove the inner brake pad

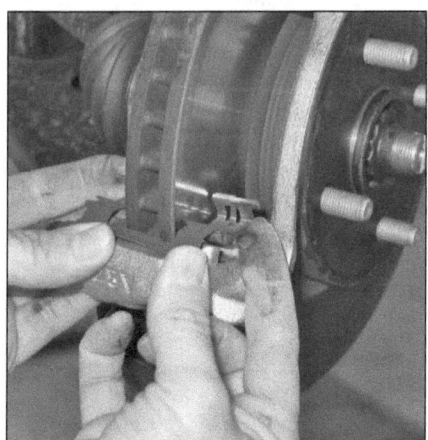

3.6k Remove the upper and lower pad support plates; inspect them for damage and replace as necessary (the supports should "snap" into place in the torque plate; if they're weak or distorted, they should be replaced)

7   When reinstalling the caliper, be sure to tighten the mounting bolts to the torque listed in this Chapter's Specifications. After the job has been completed, firmly depress the brake pedal a few times to bring the pads into con-tact with the disc. Check the level of the brake fluid, adding some if necessary. Check the operation of the brakes carefully before plac-ing the vehicle into normal service.

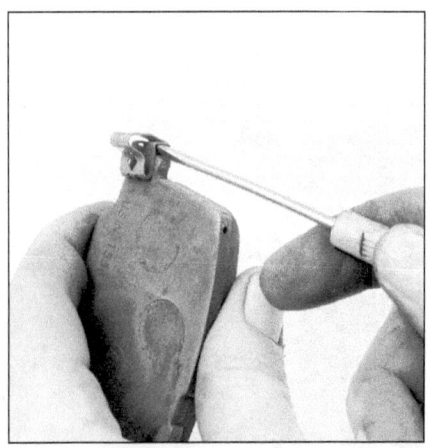

3.6l If equipped, prise the wear indicator off the old inner brake pad and transfer it to the new inner pad (if the wear indicator is worn or bent, replace it)

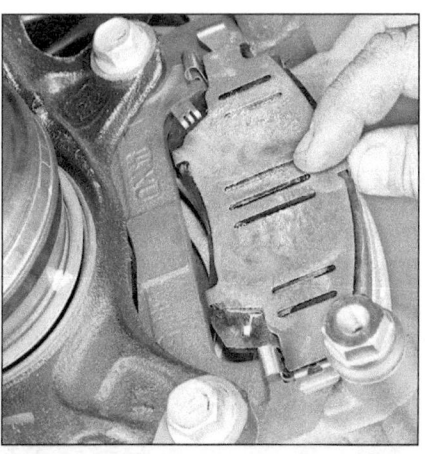

3.6m Install the upper and lower pad support plates, the new inner brake pad and the shims; make sure the ears on the pad are properly engaged with the pad support plate as shown

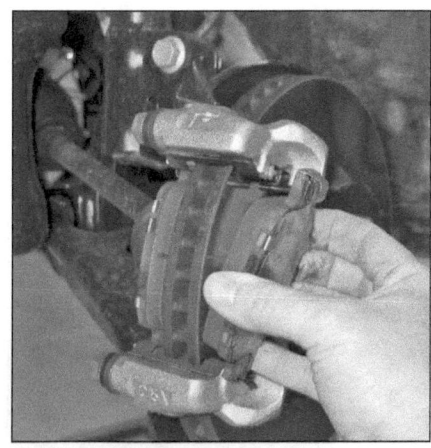

3.6n Install the outer pad and the shims, engaging the pad with the support plates

3.6o Pull out the upper and lower sliding pins and clean them off
(if either rubber boot is damaged, remove it by levering the flange
of the metal bushing that retains the boot) . . .

3.6p . . . apply a coat of high-temperature grease to the
pins and install them

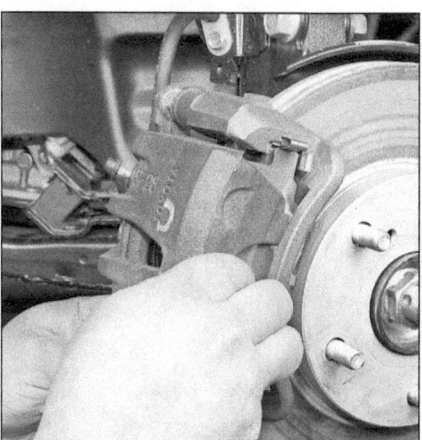

3.6q Install the caliper and tighten the
caliper bolts to the torque listed in this
Chapter's Specifications

3.6r If you have difficulty installing the
caliper over the new pads, use a G-clamp
to bottom the piston in its bore, then try
again - it should now slip over the pads

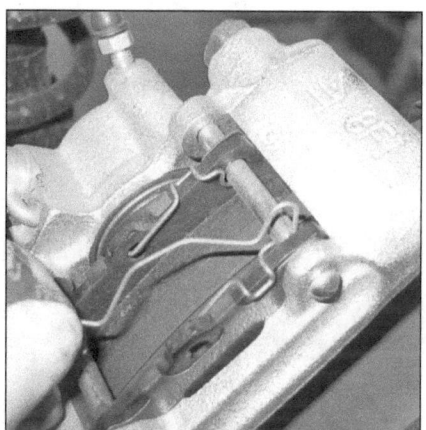

3.8a Remove the pin lock . .

Rear brakes

Refer to illustrations 3.8a through 3.8k

8   Follow the accompanying photos **(illustrations 3.8a through 3.8k),** for the actual
pad replacement procedure. Be sure to stay
in order and read the caption under each illustration. **Note:** *Several different types of pads,
springs and supports are used. Take note
of all of these parts before removing any of
them.*

9   After the job has been completed, firmly
depress the brake pedal a few times to bring
the pads into contact with the disc. Check the
level of the brake fluid, adding some if necessary. Check the operation of the brakes carefully before placing the vehicle into normal
service.

3.8b . . . outer anti-rattle clip . .

3.8c . . and inner anti-rattle clip

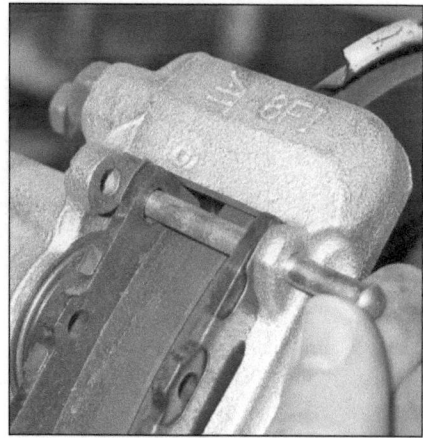

3.8d Remove the upper and lower
mounting pins

3.8e Using a G-clamp depress the piston into the bore to make room for the new pads and make it easier to remove the old pads

3.8f Remove the outer pad and shim . . .

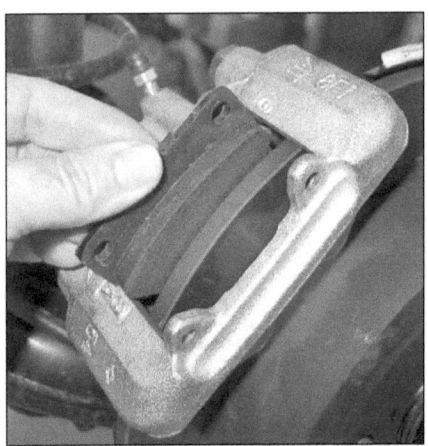

3.8g . . then remove the inner pad and shim

3.8h Remove the shim from the old pad and fit it to the new pad

3.8i Fit the new inboard pad and shim . .

3.8j . . . and outboard pad and shim into the caliper assembly

3.8k Carefully check that the spring pin lock is correctly fitted into the pins

A   Spring pins lock
B   Outboard anti-rattle spring
C   Inboard anti-rattle spring
D   Lower mounting pin
E   Upper mounting pin

4.2 Using a piece of rubber hose of the appropriate size, plug the brake line banjo fitting to prevent brake fluid from leaking out and to prevent dirt and moisture from contaminating the fluid in the hose

---

4   Disc brake caliper - removal and installation

Warning: *Dust created by the brake system is harmful to your health. Never blow it out with compressed air and don't inhale any of it. An approved filtering mask should be worn when working on the brakes. Do not, under any circumstances, use petroleum-based solvents to clean brake parts. Use brake system cleaner only!*

Note: *Always replace the calipers in pairs - never replace just one of them.*

Removal

Refer to illustrations 4.2 and 4.3

1   Loosen the wheel lug nuts, raise the vehicle and support it securely on jackstands. Remove the wheels.

2   Remove the brake hose banjo bolt and disconnect the hose from the caliper. Plug the hose to keep contaminants out of the brake system and to prevent losing any more brake

5.2 To remove the caliper torque plate from the steering knuckle, remove these two bolts

---

4.3 On rear disc brake models remove the caliper mounting bolts (arrows) and remove the caliper - for front brake calipers (see illustration 3.6b)

fluid than is necessary **(see illustration)**. **Note:** *If you're just removing the caliper for access to other components, don't disconnect the hose.*

3   Remove the caliper mounting bolts **(see illustration)**.

4   Remove the caliper. If necessary, remove the caliper torque plate from the steering knuckle **(see illustration 5.2)**.

Installation

5   Install the caliper by reversing the removal procedure. Remember to install new sealing washers on either side of the brake hose banjo fitting (they should be included with the rebuild kit). Tighten the caliper mounting bolts (and torque plate bolts, if removed) to the torque listed in this Chapter's Specifications.

6   If the hose was disconnected, bleed the brake system (see Section 10).

7   Install the wheels and lug nuts. Lower the vehicle and tighten the lug nuts to the torque listed in the Chapter 1 Specifications.

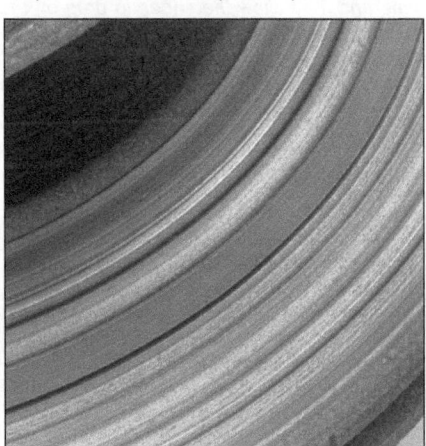

5.3 The brake pads on this vehicle were obviously neglected, as they wore down completely and cut deep grooves into the disc - wear this severe means the disc must be replaced

---

5   Brake disc - inspection, removal and installation

Inspection

Refer to illustrations 5.2, 5.3, 5.4a, 5.4b, 5.5a and 5.5b

1   Loosen the wheel lug nuts, raise the vehicle and support it securely on jackstands. Remove the wheel and install the lug nuts to hold the disc in place.

2   Remove the brake caliper as outlined in Section 4. It isn't necessary to disconnect the brake hose. After removing the caliper bolts, suspend the caliper out of the way with a piece of wire **(see illustration 3.6d)**. Remove the torque plate mounting bolts and detach the torque plate **(see illustration)**.

3   Visually inspect the disc surface for score marks and other damage. Light scratches and shallow grooves are normal after use and may not always be detrimental to brake operation, but deep scoring requires disc removal and refinishing by an automotive machine shop. Be sure to check both sides of the disc **(see illustration)**. If pulsating has been noticed during application of the brakes, suspect disc runout.

4   To check disc runout, place a dial indicator at a point about 13 mm from the outer edge of the disc **(see illustration)**. Set the indicator to zero and turn the disc. The indicator reading should not exceed the specified allowable runout limit. If it does, the disc should be refinished by an automotive machine shop. **Note:** *The discs should be resurfaced regardless of the dial indicator reading, as this will impart a smooth finish and ensure a perfectly flat surface, eliminating any brake pedal pulsation or other undesirable symptoms related to questionable discs. At the very least, if you elect not to have the discs resurfaced, remove the glaze from the surface with sandpaper or emery cloth using a swirling motion* **(see illustration)**.

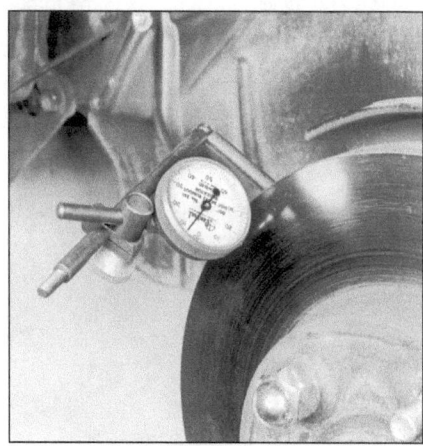

5.4a Use a dial indicator to check disc runout; if the reading exceeds the maximum allowable runout limit, the disc will have to be machined or replaced

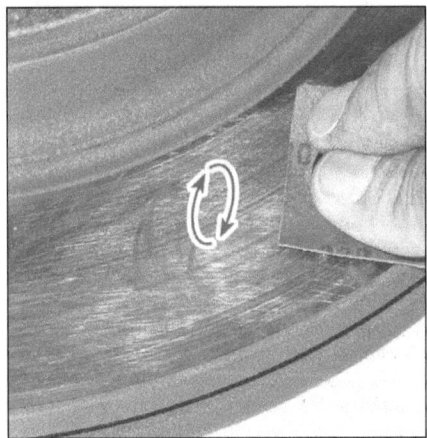

5.4b Using a swirling motion, remove the glaze from the disc surface with sandpaper or emery cloth

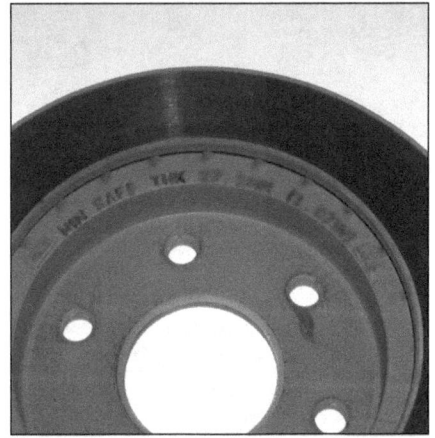

5.5a The minimum wear dimension is cast into the back side of the disc (typical)

5.5b Use a micrometer to measure disc thickness

5   It's absolutely critical that the disc not be machined to a thickness under the specified minimum allowable refinish thickness. The minimum wear (or discard) thickness is cast into the inside of the disc **(see illustration)**. The disc thickness can be checked with a micrometer **(see illustration)**.

Removal

6   Remove the lug nuts that were put on to hold the disc in place and slide the disc from the hub.

Installation

7   Place the disc in position over the threaded studs.

8   Install the torque plate, tightening the bolts to the torque listed in this Chapter's Specifications.

9   Install the caliper, tightening the bolts to the torque listed in this Chapter's Specifications. Bleeding won't be necessary unless the brake hose was disconnected from the caliper.

10   Install the wheel and lug nuts. Lower the vehicle and tighten the lug nuts to the torque listed in the Chapter 1 Specifications. Depress the brake pedal a few times to bring the brake

pads into contact with the disc. Check the operation of the brakes carefully before driving the vehicle.

---

6   Drum brake shoes - replacement

Refer to illustrations 6.4a through 6.4y and 6.5

Warning: *Drum brake shoes must be replaced on both wheels at the same time - never replace the shoes on only one wheel. Also, the dust created by the brake system is harmful to your health. Never blow it out with compressed air and don't inhale any of it. An approved filtering mask should be worn when working on the brakes. Do not, under any circumstances, use petroleum-based solvents to clean brake parts. Use brake system cleaner only!*

Caution: *Whenever the brake shoes are replaced, the return and hold-down springs should also be replaced. Due to the continuous heating/cooling cycle the springs are subjected to, they lose tension over a period of time and may allow the shoes to drag on the drum and wear at a much faster rate than normal.*

Note: *The accompanying photo sequence illustrates a drum brake shoe replacement*

procedure on a NUMMI/TMMC-manufactured drum brake, which is the most common type of drum brake on the models covered by this manual. Some 2005 and later models are equipped with a TMC-manufactured drum brake. The differences lie in the adjuster mechanism and the upper return spring.

1   Loosen the wheel lug nuts, raise the rear of the vehicle and support it securely on jackstands. Block the front wheels to keep the vehicle from rolling.

2   Release the parking brake.

3   Remove the wheel. **Note:** *All four rear brake shoes must be replaced at the same time, but to avoid mixing up parts, work on the brake assembly for only one side at a time.*

4   Follow the accompanying illustrations for the brake shoe replacement procedure **(see illustrations 6.4a through 6.4y)**. Be sure to stay in order and read the caption under each illustration. **Note:** *If the brake drum cannot be easily removed, make sure the parking brake is completely released. If the drum still cannot be pulled off, the brake shoes will have to be retracted. This is done by first removing the plug from the backing plate. With the plug removed, push the lever off the adjuster star wheel with a narrow screwdriver while turning the adjuster wheel with another screwdriver, moving the shoes away from the drum. The drum should now come off.*

6.4a Mark the relationship of the drum to the hub to insure that the dynamic balance is unaltered

6.4b Before removing anything, clean the brake assembly with brake cleaner and allow it to dry (position a drain pan under the brake to catch the fluid and residue); DO NOT USE COMPRESSED AIR TO BLOW OFF BRAKE DUST!

6.4c This is the complete rear brake assembly, refer to this photo during your disassembly/assembly procedure (NUMMI/TMMC-manufactured brake)

6.4d Unhook the return spring from the adjuster lever.
Note: *This is a NUMMI/TMMC brake - on 2005 and later models with a TMC brake, the return spring is wound around the adjuster screw assembly, and the adjuster lever is on the front shoe*

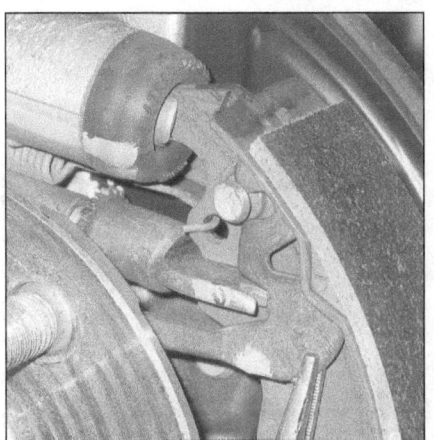

6.4e Remove the brake adjuster lever from the stud at the top of the rear shoe.
Note: *This is a NUMMI/TMMC brake - on 2005 and later models with a TMC brake, the adjuster lever is on the front shoe*

6.4f Remove the lower spring between the primary and secondary shoes

6.4g Depress the hold-down spring and turn the retainer 90-degrees, then release it; a pair of pliers will work, but a special hold-down spring removal tool makes the job easier (these inexpensive tools are available at most auto parts stores)

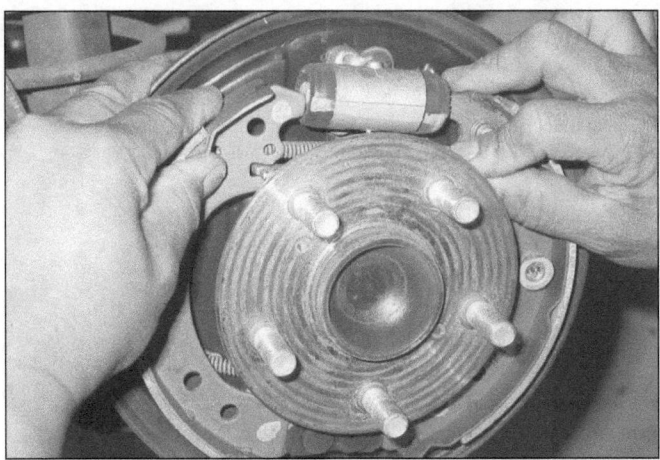

6.4h Pull the front shoe away from the adjuster mechanism and the wheel cylinder while holding the adjuster mechanism back - twist the shoe until the spring end comes free of the shoe

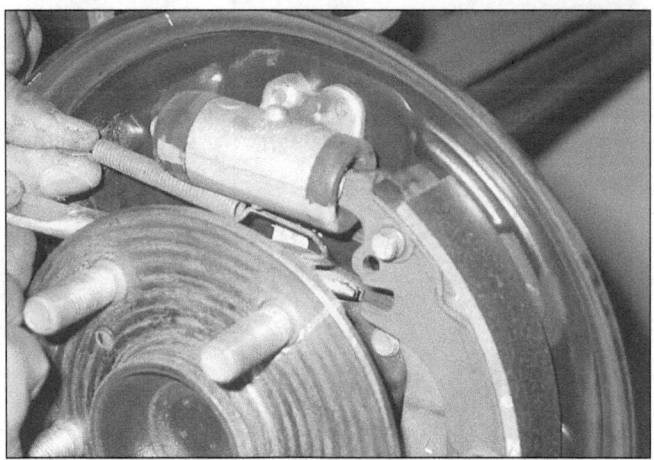

6.4i With the front shoe removed, disconnect the other end of the upper return spring and remove it.
Note: *On 2005 and later models with a TMC brake, the spring comes out with the adjuster screw assembly*

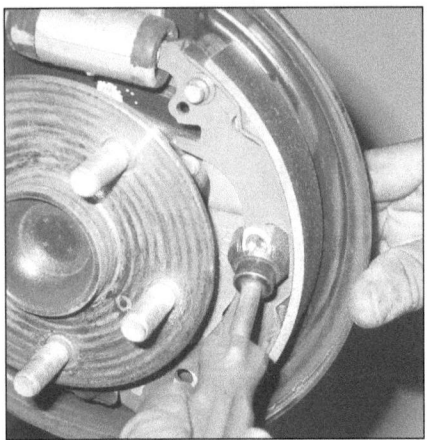

6.4j Remove the hold-down spring from the rear shoe

6.4k Remove the rear shoe and adjuster assembly from the backing plate, then use pliers to remove the clip holding the park brake lever to the stud on the rear shoe

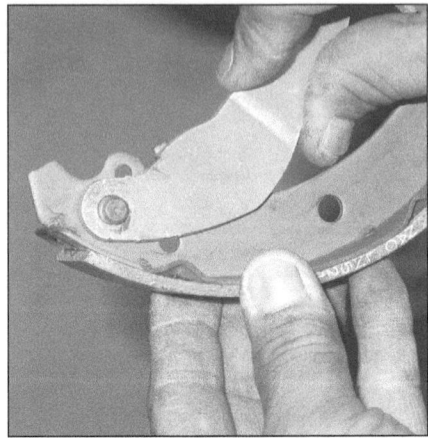

6.4l Remove the parking brake lever from the rear shoe

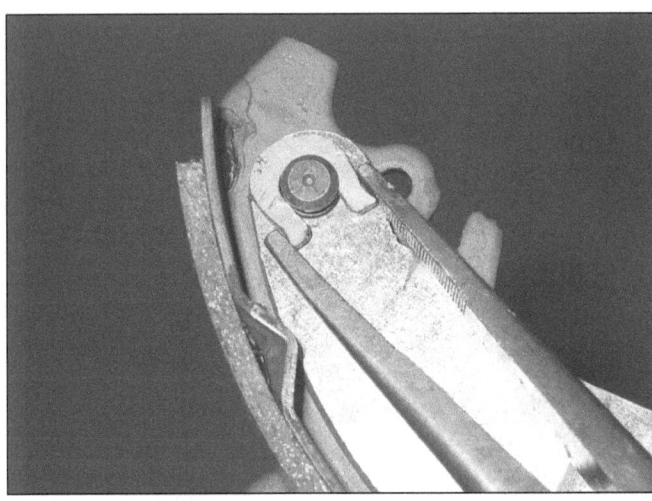

6.4m Assemble the parking brake lever to the new rear shoe and crimp the C-washer closed with a pair of pliers (always use a new C-washer)

6.4n These points of shoe contact on the backing plate should receive a small dab of high-temperature grease before installing the new shoes

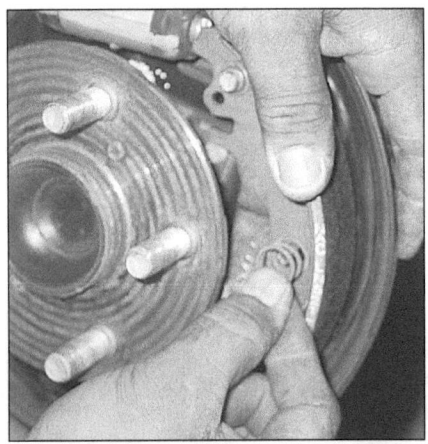

6.4o Guide the hold-down pin through while positioning the rear shoe

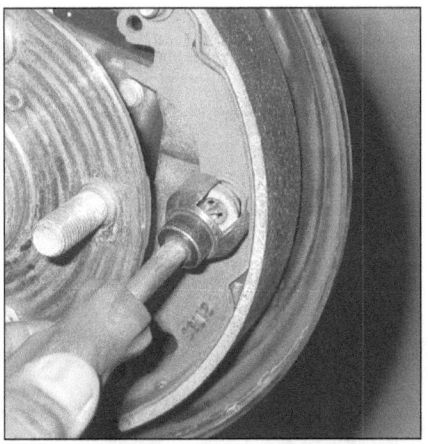

6.4p Secure the rear shoe with the hold-down cup/spring/outer cup over the pin

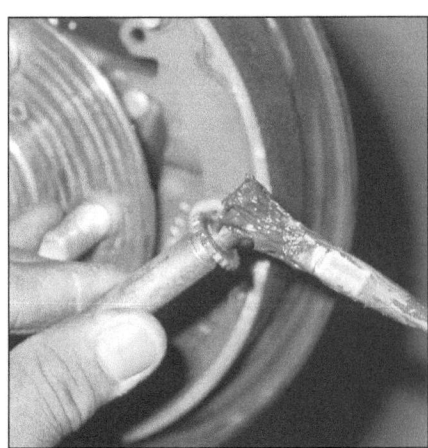

6.4q Lubricate the moving parts of the adjuster screw with a light coat of high-temperature grease; the screw portion of the adjuster will need to be threaded in further than before to allow the drum to fit over the new shoes

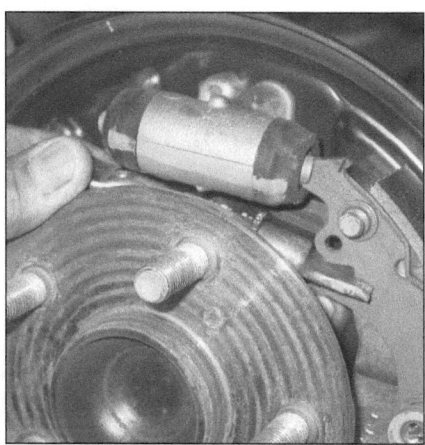

6.4r Install the adjuster assembly on the rear shoe (make sure the end fits properly into the slot in the shoe)

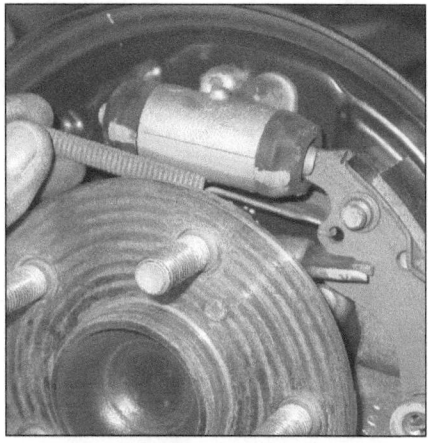

6.4s Hook the spring into the hole in the rear shoe.
Note: *NUMMI/TMMC brake shown; on 2005 and later models with a TMC brake, the spring is installed with the adjuster and connects to the shoe from the front side*

6.4t Hold the front end of the spring with pliers while guiding it through the front shoe. Note: *NUMMI/TMMC brake shown; on 2005 and later models with a TMC brake, the spring connects to the shoe from the front side*

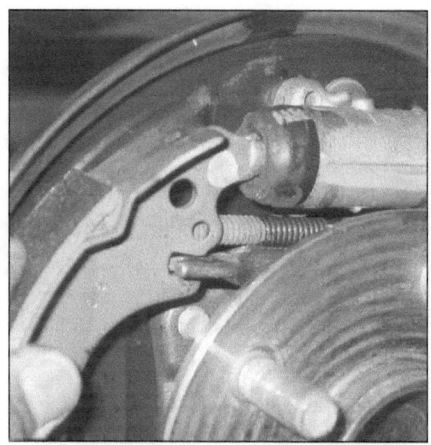

6.4u Align the top of the front shoe with the adjuster and the slot in the piston on the wheel cylinder

6.4v Wiggle the shoe to make sure it's seated properly against the backing plate, then secure it with the hold-down spring

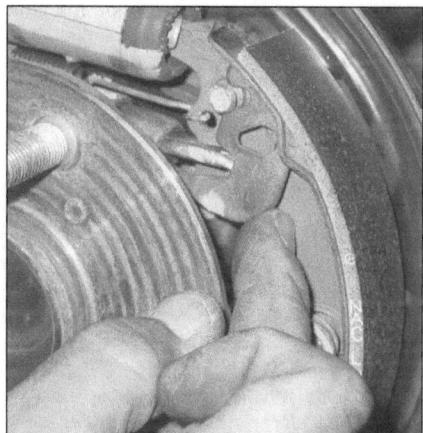

6.4w Install the lever for the automatic adjuster. Note: *NUMMI/TMMC brake shown; on 2005 and later models with a TMC brake, the adjuster lever is on the front shoe*

6.4x Install the upper spring and connect it to the adjuster lever.
Note: *NUMMI/TMMC brake shown; on 2005 and later models with a TMC brake, the adjuster lever is on the front shoe*

6.4y Install the lower spring between the two shoes

6.5 The maximum drum diameter is cast into the inside of the rear drums (typical)

7.4 To remove the wheel cylinder, unscrew the hydraulic line-to-wheel cylinder threaded fitting (1), then remove the mounting bolt (2)

5   Before reinstalling the drum, it should be checked for cracks, score marks, deep scratches and hard spots, which will appear as small discoloured areas. If the hard spots cannot be removed with fine emery cloth or if any of the other conditions listed above exist, the drum must be taken to an automotive machine shop to have it resurfaced. **Note:** *Professionals recommend resurfacing the drums each time a brake job is done. Resurfacing will eliminate the possibility of out-of-round drums. If the drums are worn so much that they can't be resurfaced without exceeding the maximum allowable diameter (stamped into the drum), then new ones will be required* **(see illustration)**. *At the very least, if you elect not to have the drums resurfaced, remove the glaze from the surface with emery cloth using a swirling motion.*

6   Install the brake drum on the axle flange.

7   Install the wheel and lug nuts, then lower the vehicle. Tighten the lug nuts to the torque listed in the Chapter 1 Specifications.

8   Make a number of forward and reverse stops and operate the parking brake to adjust the brakes until satisfactory pedal action is obtained.

9   Check the operation of the brakes carefully before driving the vehicle.

7   Wheel cylinder - removal and installation

Note: *Never replace only one wheel cylinder - always replace both of them at the same time.*

Removal

Refer to illustration 7.4

1   Raise the rear of the vehicle and support it securely on jackstands. Block the front wheels to keep the vehicle from rolling.

2   Remove the brake shoe assembly (see Section 6).

3   Remove all dirt and foreign material from around the wheel cylinder.

4   Disconnect the brake line with a flare-nut wrench, if available **(see illustration)**. Don't pull the brake line away from the wheel cylinder.

5   Remove the wheel cylinder mounting bolt.

6   Detach the wheel cylinder from the brake backing plate and place it on a clean workbench. Immediately plug the brake line to prevent fluid loss and contamination.

Installation

7   Place the wheel cylinder in position and install the bolt finger tight. Connect the brake line to the cylinder, being careful not to cross-thread the fitting. Tighten the wheel cylinder bolt to the torque listed in this Chapter's Specifications.

8   Tighten the brake line fitting and install the brake shoes and drum.

9   Bleed the brakes (see Section 10). Install the wheel and lug nuts. Lower the vehicle to the ground and tighten the lug nuts to the torque listed in this Chapter's Specifications.

10   Check the operation of the brakes carefully before driving the vehicle.

8   Master cylinder - removal and installation

Removal

Refer to illustration 8.1

1   Remove the cover from the air filter housing. Unplug the electrical connector for the brake fluid level warning switch **(see illustration)**.

2   Remove as much fluid as possible from the reservoir with a syringe. If the vehicle is

equipped with a manual transaxle, clamp off the fluid feed hose to the clutch master cylinder, then detach the hose from the brake fluid reservoir.

3   Place rags under the fittings and prepare caps or plastic bags to cover the ends of the lines once they're disconnected. **Caution:** *Brake fluid will damage paint. Cover all body parts and be careful not to spill fluid during this procedure.*

4   Loosen the fittings at the ends of the brake lines where they enter the master cylinder. To prevent rounding off the flats, use a flare-nut wrench, which wraps around the fitting hex.

5   Pull the brake lines away from the master cylinder and plug the ends to prevent contamination.

6   Remove the nuts attaching the master cylinder to the power booster **(see illustration 8.1)**. Pull the master cylinder off the studs to remove it. Again, be careful not to spill the fluid as this is done.

8.1 Master cylinder installation details

A   *Electrical connector*
B   *Brake line fittings*
C   *Mounting nut (left side shown)*

8.8 The best way to bleed air from the master cylinder before installing it on the vehicle is with a pair of bleed tubes (typical master cylinder)

Installation

Refer to illustrations 8.8 and 8.16

7   Bench bleed the new master cylinder before installing it. Because it will be necessary to apply pressure to the master cylinder piston and, at the same time, control flow from the brake line outlets, it is recommended that the master cylinder be mounted in a vise, with the jaws of the vise clamping on the mounting flange.

8   Attach a pair of master cylinder bleeder tubes to the outlet ports of the master cylinder **(see illustration)**.

9   Fill the reservoir with brake fluid of the recommended type (see Chapter 1).

10   Slowly push the pistons into the master cylinder (a large Phillips screwdriver can be used for this) - air will be expelled from the pressure chambers and into the reservoir. Because the tubes are submerged in fluid, air can't be drawn back into the master cylinder when you release the pistons.

11   Repeat the procedure until no more air bubbles are present.

12   Remove the bleed tubes, one at a time,

and install plugs in the open ports to prevent fluid leakage and air from entering. If installing a new master cylinder, adjust the booster pushrod length (see Section 11). Also install a new O-ring on the master cylinder body.

13   Install the reservoir cover, then install the master cylinder over the studs on the power brake booster and tighten the attaching nuts only finger tight at this time.

14   Thread the brake line fittings into the master cylinder. Since the master cylinder is still a bit loose, it can be moved slightly in order for the fittings to thread in easily. Do not strip the threads as the fittings are tightened.

15   Fully tighten the mounting nuts, then the brake line fittings.

16   Fill the master cylinder reservoir with fluid, then bleed the master cylinder and the brake system as described in Section 10. To bleed the cylinder on the vehicle, have an assistant depress the brake pedal slowly and then hold the pedal to the floor. Loosen the fitting nut to allow air and fluid to escape **(see illustration)**. Repeat this procedure on both fittings until the fluid is clear of air bubbles. **Caution:** *Have plenty of rags on hand*

to catch the fluid - brake fluid will ruin painted surfaces.

17   Test the operation of the brake system carefully before placing the vehicle into normal service. **Warning:** *Do not operate the vehicle if you are in doubt about the effectiveness of the brake system.*

---

9   Brake hoses and lines - inspection and replacement

Inspection

1   About every six months, with the vehicle raised and supported securely on jackstands, the rubber hoses which connect the steel brake lines with the front and rear brake assemblies should be inspected for cracks, chafing of the outer cover, leaks, blisters and other damage. These are important and vulnerable parts of the brake system and inspection should be complete. A light and mirror will be helpful for a thorough check. If a hose exhibits any of the above conditions, replace it with a new one.

Replacement

Front brake hose

Refer to illustrations 9.3 and 9.4

2   Loosen the wheel lug nuts, raise the vehicle and support it securely on jackstands. Remove the wheel.

3   At the frame bracket, unscrew the brake line fitting from the hose **(see illustration)**. Use a flare-nut wrench to prevent rounding off the corners.

4   Remove the U-clip from the female fitting at the bracket with a pair of pliers **(see illustration)**, then pass the hose through the bracket.

5   At the caliper end of the hose, remove the banjo fitting bolt **(see illustration 3.6b)**, then separate the hose from the caliper. Note

8.16 Have an assistant depress the brake pedal and hold it down, then loosen the fitting nut, allowing the air and fluid to escape; repeat this procedure on both fittings until the fluid is clear of air bubbles

9.3 Unscrew the brake line threaded fitting with a flare-nut spanner to protect the fitting corners from being rounded off

9.4 Remove the brake hose-to-brake line U-clip (A) with a pair of pliers - B is the brake hose bracket bolt on the strut

that there are two copper sealing washers on either side of the fitting - they should be replaced with new ones during installation.

6   Remove the U-clip from the strut bracket, then feed the hose through the bracket.

7   To install the hose, pass the caliper fitting end through the strut bracket, then connect the fitting to the caliper with the banjo bolt and copper washers. Make sure the locating lug on the fitting is engaged with the hole in the caliper, then tighten the bolt to the torque listed in this Chapter's Specifications.

8   Push the metal support into the strut bracket and install the U-clip. Make sure the hose isn't twisted between the caliper and the strut bracket.

9   Route the hose into the frame bracket, again making sure it isn't twisted, then connect the brake line fitting, starting the threads by hand. Install the clip and E-ring, if equipped, then tighten the fitting securely.

10   Bleed the caliper (see Section 10).

11   Install the wheel and lug nuts, lower the vehicle and tighten the lug nuts to the torque specified in Chapter 1.

Rear brake hose

12   Perform Steps 2, 3 and 4 above, then repeat Steps 3 and 4 at the other end of the hose. Be sure to bleed the wheel cylinder (see Section 10).

Metal brake lines

13   When replacing brake lines, be sure to use the correct parts. Don't use copper tubing for any brake system components. Purchase genuine steel brake lines from a dealer or auto parts store.

14   Prefabricated brake line, with the tube ends already flared and fittings installed, is available at auto parts stores and dealer parts departments.

15   When installing the new line, make sure it's securely supported in the brackets and has plenty of clearance between moving or hot components.

16   After installation, check the master cylinder fluid level and add fluid as necessary. Bleed the brake system (see Section 10) and test the brakes carefully before driving the vehicle in traffic.

---

10   Brake hydraulic system - bleeding

Refer to illustration 10.8

Warning: *Wear eye protection when bleeding the brake system. If the fluid comes in contact with your eyes, immediately rinse them with water and seek medical attention.*

Note: *Bleeding the hydraulic system is necessary to remove any air that manages to find its way into the system when it's been opened during removal and installation of a hose, line, caliper or master cylinder.*

1   You'll probably have to bleed the system at all four brakes if air has entered it due to low fluid level, or if the brake lines have been

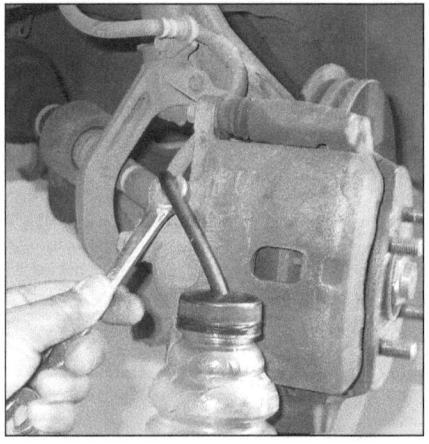

10.8 When bleeding the brakes, a hose is connected to the bleeder valve at the caliper or wheel cylinder and then submerged in brake fluid. Air will be seen as bubbles in the tube and container. All air must be expelled before moving to the next wheel

disconnected at the master cylinder.

2   If a brake line was disconnected only at a wheel, then only that caliper or wheel cylinder must be bled.

3   If a brake line is disconnected at a fitting located between the master cylinder and any of the brakes, that part of the system served by the disconnected line must be bled.

4   Remove any residual vacuum from the brake power booster by applying the brake several times with the engine off.

5   Remove the master cylinder reservoir cover and fill the reservoir with brake fluid. Reinstall the cover. **Note:** *Check the fluid level often during the bleeding operation and add fluid as necessary to prevent the fluid level from falling low enough to allow air bubbles into the master cylinder.*

6   Have an assistant on hand, as well as a supply of new brake fluid, a clear container partially filled with clean brake fluid, a length of tubing to fit over the bleeder valve and a wrench to open and close the bleeder valve.

7   Beginning at the right rear wheel, loosen the bleeder valve slightly, then tighten it to a point where it's snug but can still be loosened quickly and easily.

8   Place one end of the tubing over the bleeder valve and submerge the other end in brake fluid in the container **(see illustration)**.

9   Have the assistant depress the brake pedal slowly, then hold the pedal down firmly.

10   While the pedal is held down, open the bleeder valve just enough to allow a flow of fluid to leave the valve. Watch for air bubbles to exit the submerged end of the tube. When the fluid flow slows after a couple of seconds, close the valve and have your assistant release the pedal.

11   Repeat Steps 9 and 10 until no more air is seen leaving the tube, then tighten the bleeder valve and proceed to the left rear wheel, the right front wheel and the left front wheel, in that order, and perform the same

11.11 To disconnect the power brake booster pushrod from the brake pedal, remove the retaining clip and clevis pin (centre); to detach the booster from the firewall, remove the four mounting nuts (three seen here)

procedure. Be sure to check the fluid in the master cylinder reservoir frequently.

12   Never use old brake fluid. It contains moisture that will deteriorate the brake system components.

13   Refill the master cylinder with fluid at the end of the operation.

14   Check the operation of the brakes. The pedal should feel solid when depressed, with no sponginess. If necessary, repeat the entire process. **Warning:** *Do not operate the vehicle if you're in doubt about the effectiveness of the brake system.*

---

11   Power brake booster - check, removal and installation

Operating check

1   Depress the brake pedal several times with the engine off and make sure there's no change in the pedal reserve distance.

2   Depress the pedal and start the engine. If the pedal goes down slightly, operation is normal.

Airtightness check

3   Start the engine and turn it off after one or two minutes. Depress the brake pedal slowly several times. If the pedal depresses less each time, the booster is airtight.

4   Depress the brake pedal while the engine is running, then stop the engine with the pedal depressed. If there's no change in the pedal reserve travel after holding the pedal for 30 seconds, the booster is airtight.

Removal

Refer to illustration 11.11

5   Power brake booster units shouldn't be disassembled. They require special tools not normally found in most automotive repair stations or shops. They're fairly complex and,

11.14a Measure the distance that the pushrod protrudes from the brake booster at the master cylinder mounting surface (including the gasket)

11.14b Measure the distance from the mounting flange to the end of the master cylinder

because of their critical relationship to brake performance, should be replaced with a new or rebuilt one.

6   Remove the brake master cylinder (see Section 8).

7   Remove the air filter housing (see Chapter 4).

8   In the engine compartment, disconnect the vacuum hose from the booster.

9   On models with cruise control, remove the cruise control actuator and bracket.

10   Unclip and/or detach any brake lines around the booster, as necessary, to allow the booster to be removed without damaging the lines.

11   Using a flashlight, locate the clevis which connects the booster pushrod to the top of the brake pedal. Remove the clevis pin retaining clip with pliers and pull out the pin **(see illustration)**.

12   Remove the four nuts and washers holding the brake booster to the firewall (you may need a light to see them). Slide the booster straight out from the firewall until the studs clear the holes.

Installation

Refer to illustrations 11.14a, 11.14b, 11.14c and 11.14d

13   Installation procedures are basically the reverse of removal. Tighten the clevis locknut securely and the booster mounting nuts to the torque listed in this Chapter's Specifications.

14   If a new power brake booster unit is being installed, the booster pushrod-to-master cylinder piston clearance must be at zero - if there is interference between the two, the brakes may drag. If there is too much clearance, there will be excessive brake pedal travel. Check the pushrod clearance as follows:

a) *Measure the distance that the pushrod protrudes from the master cylinder mounting surface on the front of the power brake booster, including the gasket. Write down this measurement* **(see illustration)**. *This is "dimension A."*

b) *Measure the distance from the mounting flange to the end of the master cylinder* **(see illustration)**. *Write down this mea-*

surement. This is "dimension B."

c) *Measure the distance from the end of the master cylinder to the bottom of the pocket in the piston* **(see illustration)**. *Write down this measurement. This is "dimension C."*

d) *Subtract measurement B from measurement C, then subtract measurement A from the difference between B and C. This is the pushrod clearance.*

e) *Compare your calculated pushrod clearance to the pushrod clearance listed in this Chapter's Specifications. If necessary, adjust the pushrod length to achieve the correct clearance* **(see illustration 11.14d)**.

15   After the final installation of the master cylinder and brake hoses and lines, the brake pedal height and freeplay must be adjusted and the system must be bled. See the appropriate Sections of this Chapter for the procedures.

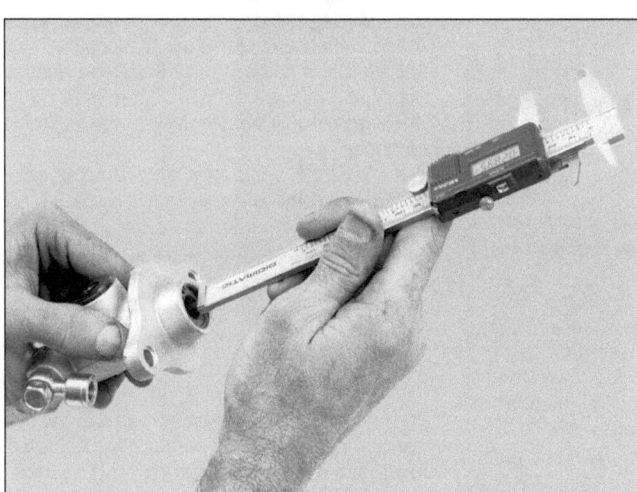

11.14c Measure the distance from the piston pocket to the end of the master cylinder

11.14d To adjust the length of the booster pushrod, hold the serrated portion of the rod with a pair of pliers and turn the adjusting screw in or out, as necessary, to achieve the desired setting

12 Parking brake - adjustment

Refer to illustration 12.3

1   The parking brake lever, when properly adjusted, should travel six to nine clicks when a moderate pulling force is applied. If it travels less than six clicks, there's a chance the parking brake might not be releasing completely and might be dragging on the drum or disc. If the lever can be pulled up more than nine clicks, the parking brake may not hold adequately on an incline, allowing the car to roll.

2   To gain access to the parking brake cable adjuster, remove the centre console (see Chapter 11).

3   Loosen the locknut (the upper nut) while holding the adjusting nut (lower nut) with a spanner **(see illustration)**. Tighten the adjusting nut until the desired travel is attained. Tighten the locknut.

4   Install the console.

13 Parking brake shoes (rear disc models) - adjustment and replacement

Warning: *Dust created by the brake system is harmful to your health. Never blow it out with compressed air and don't inhale any of it. An approved filtering mask should be worn when working on the brakes. Do not, under any circumstances, use petroleum-based solvents to clean brake parts. Use brake system cleaner only!*

Note: *Always service the brakes in pairs - never adjust or renew the shoe assembly in one brake. Always perform the procedure on one brake, then on the other.*

1   Raise the vehicle and support it securely on jackstands and remove the rear wheels

Adjustment

Refer to illustration 13.3

2   Remove the rubber plug from the brake disc rotor hub.

3   Using a small screw driver or brake

12.3 Loosen the locknut (A), then turn the adjusting nut (B) until the desired handle travel is obtained

spoon, turn the adjuster to bring this measurement within specification. Turning the adjuster clockwise increases the diameter **(see illustration)**. Refit the plug.

Replacement

Refer to illustration 13.7

4   Remove the brake caliper (see Section 3).

5   Remove the brake rotor (see Section 4).

6   Disconnect the cable from the parking brake lever at each rear wheel.

7   Inspect all parts, looking for any that are excessively worn or discoloured (see illustration).

8   Remove each hold-down spring by disconnecting them from the equilizer bar using a pair of pliers.

9   Unhook the return spring from the shoes using a pair of pliers.

10   Depress the hold-down spring and turn the retainer 90-degrees, then release it; a pair of pliers will work, but a special hold-down spring removal tool makes the job easier (these inexpensive tools are available at most auto parts stores).

13.3 Using a small screw driver or brake spoon, turn the adjuster clockwise to expand the shoes against the rotor hub/drum

11   Remove the star wheel adjuster and equalizer bar. **Note:** *The adjustable side of the star wheel should be connected to the back shoe or the shoe that has the parking brake lever attached to it.*

12   Lift the shoe over the axle flange.

13   Wipe the backing plate with a clean rag.

14   Turn the parking brake adjuster screw all the way in to its home position and then back the screw off 1/4 turn.

15   Fit the new shoes into place on the backing plate. Be sure the shoe tips engage the shoe at the top and in the adjuster at the bottom.

16   Secure the shoe in place with new hold-down springs and retaining pins.

17   Reassembly is the reverse of removal **(see illustration 13.7)**, as a guide.

18   Install the brake drum on the axle flange.

19   Adjust the brake shoe as described above.

Reassembly

20   Adjust the parking brake cable as described in Section 12.

21   Install the wheel and lug nuts, then lower the vehicle. Tighten the lug nuts to the torque listed in the Chapter 1 Specifications.

22   Make a number of forward and reverse stops and operate the parking brake to adjust the brakes until satisfactory pedal action is obtained.

23   Check the operation of the brakes carefully before driving the vehicle.

14 Brake pedal - adjustment

Pedal height

Refer to illustration 14.1

1   The height of the brake pedal is the distance the pedal sits off the floor **(see illustration)**. If the pedal height is not within Specifications, it must be adjusted.

13.7 Typical rear parking brake shoe assembly - axle flange removed for clarity

1   Brake shoe hold-down spring and pin
2   Parking brake shoe
3   Star wheel adjuster
4   Lower return spring
5   Parking brake lever
6   Upper spring (left)
7   Equilizer bar
8   Upper spring (right)

92037-9-13.1 HAYNES

14.1 Brake pedal adjusting details

A   *Pedal height adjusting point*
B   *Brake light switch locknut*
C   *Pedal height measurement point*
D   *Freeplay measurement point*

2   Loosen the locknut on the brake light switch and unscrew the switch until it doesn't contact the pedal arm. **(see illustration 15.1)**. Before measuring the brake pedal height, make sure the pedal is in the fully-returned position. Measure the pedal height and, if necessary, adjust it by loosening the locknut on the pedal pushrod and turning the pushrod to achieve the proper height. When the proper height has been obtained, tighten the locknut securely.
3   Adjust the brake light switch (see Section 15).

Pedal freeplay

4   The freeplay is the pedal slack, or the distance the pedal can be depressed before it begins to have any effect on the brake system **(see illustration 14.1)**. Before checking brake pedal freeplay, depress the brake pedal several times (with the engine off).
5   If the pedal freeplay is not within the specified range, check the adjustment of the brake light switch (see Section 15).

15.1 The brake light switch (A) is located at the top of the brake pedal - B is the adjusting locknut

6   If the brake light switch is properly adjusted, troubleshoot the brake system for the cause of excessive freeplay (suspect either air in the hydraulic system [see Section 10], excessive clearance between the booster pushrod and the master cylinder piston [see Section 11]), or excessive clearance between the rear brake shoes and the brake drums.

Brake pedal reserve distance

7   With the parking brake released and the engine running, depress the pedal with normal braking effort and have an assistant measure the distance from the centre of the pedal pad to the floor. If the distance is less than specified, troubleshoot the brake system (see Step 6).

15 Brake light switch - removal, installation and adjustment

Removal and installation

Refer to illustration 15.1

1   The brake light switch **(see illustration)** is located on a bracket at the top of the brake pedal.

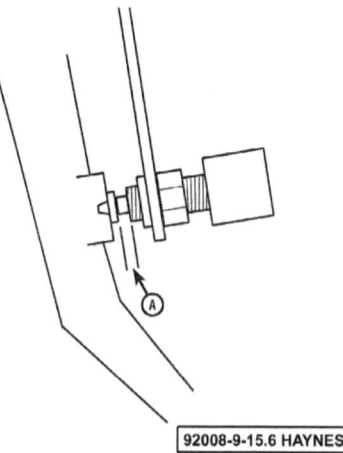

92008-9-15.6 HAYNES

15.6 To adjust the brake light switch, loosen the locknut and rotate the switch until the plunger distance (dimension A) is within the range listed in this Chapter's Specifications, then tighten the locknut

2   Disconnect the wiring harness at the brake light switch.
3   Loosen the locknut and unscrew the switch from the pedal bracket.
4   Installation is the reverse of removal.

Adjustment

Refer to illustration 15.6

5   Check and, if necessary, adjust brake pedal height (see Chapter 1).
6   Loosen the switch locknut, adjust the switch so that the distance the plunger protrudes **(see illustration)** is within the range listed in this Chapter's Specifications. (If you're unable to measure this distance, adjust the plunger so that it lightly contacts the pedal stop.) Tighten the locknut.
7   Plug the electrical connector into the switch and reconnect the battery. Make sure the brake lights come on when the brake pedal is depressed and go off when the pedal is released. If not, repeat the adjustment procedure until the brake lights function properly.

Notes

Chapter 10
Suspension and steering systems

Contents

Specifications

Torque specifications

Nm (unless otherwise indicated)

Front suspension

Balljoints

Balljoint-to-control arm bolt/nuts	90
Balljoint-to-steering knuckle nut	103
Control arm to crossmember	137

Stabilizer bar

Bracket-to-crossmember bolts	19
Link nuts	74

Struts

Strut-to-steering knuckle bolts/nuts	153
Strut upper mounting nuts	39
Damper shaft nut	47

Subframe crossmember

Bolt A	157
Bolt B	112
Bolts/nuts C	51

Torque specifications (continued)

Nm (unless otherwise indicated)

Rear suspension

Axle beam pivot bolts 90
Hub and bearing assembly-to-rear axle carrier bolts............................. 61
Stabilizer bar-to-axle bolts/nuts 195
Shock absorber/coil spring assembly
    Lower mounting nut.. 80
    Upper mounting nuts/bolt.. 80
    Damper shaft nut.. 55

Steering

Airbag module Torx screws 8.8
Steering gear-to-crossmember bolts 58
Steering wheel nut.. 70
Tie-rod end-to-steering knuckle nut... 49
Tie-rod end locknuts 74
U-joint-to-pinion shaft pinch bolt.. 35
Power steering pressure line fitting-to-pump 40
Power steering pump mounting bolts 36
Pressure lines to steering gear... 12

1.1a Typical 1999 and earlier front suspension and steering components

1	Front stabilizer bar	4	Balljoint	7	Support brace
2	Stabilizer bar bushing clamp	5	Strut/coil spring assembly	8	Suspension crossmember
3	Control arm	6	Rack-and-pinion steering gear		

1   General information

Refer to illustrations 1.1a, 1.1b, 1.2a and 1.2b

The front suspension **(see illustrations)** is a MacPherson strut design. The upper end of each strut/coil spring assembly is attached to the vehicle's body strut support. The lower end of the strut assembly is connected to the upper end of the steering knuckle. The steering knuckle is attached to a balljoint mounted on the outer end of the suspension control arm. A stabilizer bar reduces body roll.

The rear suspension on 1999 and earlier models **(see illustration)** also uses strut/coil spring assemblies. The upper end of each strut is attached to the vehicle body. The lower end of each strut is attached to an axle carrier. The carrier is located by a pair of suspension arms on each side, and a longitudinally mounted strut rod between the body and each carrier.

The rear suspension on 2000 and later models **(see illustration)** utilizes shock absorber/coil spring assemblies. The upper end of each assembly is attached to the vehicle body. The lower ends are attached to a beam axle. The axle has two integral forward arms located to the chassis by bolts through pivot bushings.

The rack-and-pinion steering gear is located behind the engine/transaxle assembly on the firewall and actuates the tie-rods, which are attached to the steering knuckles. The inner ends of the tie-rods are protected by rubber boots, which should be inspected periodically for secure attachment, tears and leaking lubricant.

The power assist system consists of a belt-driven pump and associated lines and hoses. The fluid level in the power steering pump reservoir should be checked periodically (see Chapter 1).

The steering wheel operates the steering shaft, which actuates the steering gear through universal joints. Looseness in the steering can be caused by wear in the steering shaft universal joints, the steering gear, the tie-rod ends and loose retaining bolts.

Precautions

Frequently, when working on the suspension or steering system components, you may come across fasteners that seem impossible to loosen. These fasteners on the underside of the vehicle are continually subjected to water, road grime, mud, etc., and can become rusted or "frozen," making them extremely difficult to remove. In order to unscrew these stubborn fasteners without damaging them (or other components), be sure to use lots of penetrating oil and allow it to soak in for a while. Using a wire brush to clean exposed threads will also ease removal of the nut or bolt and prevent damage to the threads. Sometimes a sharp blow with a hammer and punch will break the bond between a nut and bolt threads, but care must be taken to prevent the punch from slipping off the fastener and ruining the threads. Heating the stuck fastener and surrounding area with a torch sometimes helps too, but isn't recommended because of the obvious dangers associated with fire. Long breaker bars and extension, or "cheater," pipes will increase leverage, but never use an extension pipe on a ratchet - the ratcheting mechanism could be damaged. Sometimes tightening the nut or bolt first will help to break it loose. Fasteners that require drastic measures to remove should always be replaced with new ones.

Since most of the procedures dealt with in this Chapter involve jacking up the vehicle and working underneath it, a good pair of jackstands will be needed. A hydraulic floor jack is the preferred type of jack to lift the vehicle, and it can also be used to support certain components during various operations. **Warning:** *Never, under any circumstances, rely on a jack to support the vehicle while working on it. Whenever any of the suspension or steering fasteners are loosened or removed they*

1.1b Typical 2000 and later front suspension and steering components

1	Front stabilizer bar	3	Balljoint	5	Support brace
2	Control arm	4	Strut/coil spring assembly	6	Suspension crossmember

1.2a Typical 1999 and earlier rear suspension components

1 Rear lateral arm	5 Stabilizer bar bushing clamp	8 Strut/coil spring assembly
2 Rear arm toe adjuster	6 Stabilizer link	9 Rear axle carrier
3 Front lateral arm	7 Strut rod	10 Rear suspension crossmember
4 Rear stabilizer bar		

1.2b Typical 2000 and later rear suspension components

1 Rear axle beam	3 Shock absorber/coil spring assembly
2 Rear axle beam pivots	4 Rear stabilizer bar (inside axle beam)

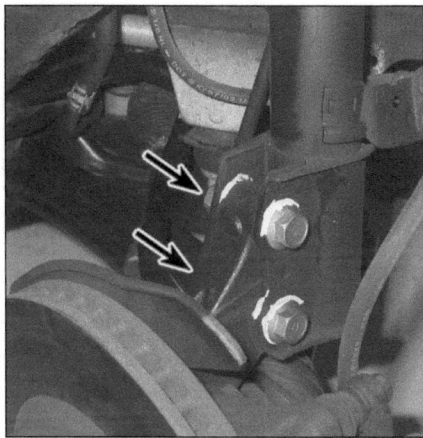

2.3 To detach the strut assembly from the steering knuckle, remove the two nuts, then knock out the bolts with a hammer and punch - note marks of bolt/strut relationship

must be inspected and, if necessary, replaced with new ones of the same part number or of original equipment quality and design. Torque specifications must be followed for proper reassembly and component retention. Never attempt to heat or straighten any suspension or steering components. Instead, replace any bent or damaged part with a new one.

2 Strut assembly (front) - removal, inspection and installation

Removal

Refer to illustrations 2.3 and 2.5

1   Loosen the wheel lug nuts, raise the vehicle and support it securely on jackstands. Remove the wheel.

2   Unbolt the brake hose bracket from the strut. If the vehicle is equipped with ABS, detach the speed sensor wiring harness from

3.3 Install the spring compressor according to the tool manufacturer's instructions and compress the spring until all pressure is relieved from the upper spring seat

the strut by removing the clamp bracket bolt. Refer to Section 4 and disconnect the stabilizer link from the strut.

3   Mark the relationship of the strut to the steering knuckle. **Note:** *Also mark the positions of the bolts, as special camber adjusting bolts may have been fitted at some point.* Remove the strut-to-knuckle nuts **(see illustration)** and knock the bolts out with a hammer and punch.

4   Separate the strut from the steering knuckle. Be careful not to overextend the inner CV joint. Also, don't let the steering knuckle fall outward and strain the brake hose.

5   Support the strut and spring assembly (an assistant would be helpful here) and remove the three strut-to-body nuts **(see illustration)**. Remove the assembly out from the fenderwell.

Inspection

6   Check the strut body for leaking fluid, dents, cracks and other obvious damage that would warrant repair or replacement.

7   Check the coil spring for chips or cracks in the spring coating (this will cause premature spring failure due to corrosion). Inspect the spring seat for cuts, hardness and general deterioration.

8   If any undesirable conditions exist, proceed to the strut disassembly procedure (see Section 3).

Installation

9   Guide the strut assembly up into the fenderwell and insert the upper mounting studs through the holes in the body. Once the studs protrude, install the nuts so the strut won't fall back through. This is most easily accomplished with the help of an assistant, as the strut is quite heavy and awkward.

10   Slide the steering knuckle into the strut flange and insert the two bolts. Install the nuts, align the previously made match-marks and tighten them to the torque listed in this Chapter's Specifications.

11   Connect the brake hose bracket to the strut and tighten the bolt securely. If the vehicle is equipped with ABS, install the speed sensor wiring harness bracket.

12   Install the wheel and lug nuts, then lower

the vehicle and tighten the lug nuts to the torque listed in the Chapter 1 Specifications.

13   Tighten the upper mounting nuts to the torque listed in this Chapter's Specifications.

14   Drive the vehicle to an alignment shop to have the front-end alignment checked, and if necessary, adjusted.

3 Strut or shock absorber/coil spring assembly - replacement

1   If the struts or coil springs exhibit the telltale signs of wear (leaking fluid, loss of damping capability, chipped, sagging or cracked coil springs) explore all options before beginning any work. The strut/shock absorber assemblies are not serviceable and must be replaced if a problem develops. However, strut assemblies complete with springs may be available on an exchange basis, which eliminates much time and work. Whichever route you choose to take, check on the cost and availability of parts before disassembling your vehicle. **Warning:** *Disassembling a strut is potentially dangerous and utmost attention must be directed to the job, or serious injury may result. Use only a high-quality spring compressor and carefully follow the manufacturer's instructions furnished with the tool. After removing the coil spring from the strut assembly, set it aside in a safe, isolated area.*

Disassembly

Refer to illustrations 3.3, 3.4, 3.5, 3.6 and 3.7

2   Remove the strut assembly following the procedure described in Section 2 (front) or if you're working on a rear shock absorber/ coil spring assembly, Section 11. Mount the assembly in a vise. Line the vise jaws with wood or rags to prevent damage to the unit and don't tighten the vise excessively.

3   Following the tool manufacturer's instructions, install the spring compressor (which can be obtained at most auto parts stores or equipment yards on a daily rental basis) on the spring and compress it sufficiently to relieve all pressure from the upper spring seat **(see illustration)**. This can be verified by wiggling the spring.

2.5 To detach the upper end of the strut assembly from the body, remove the upper mounting nuts

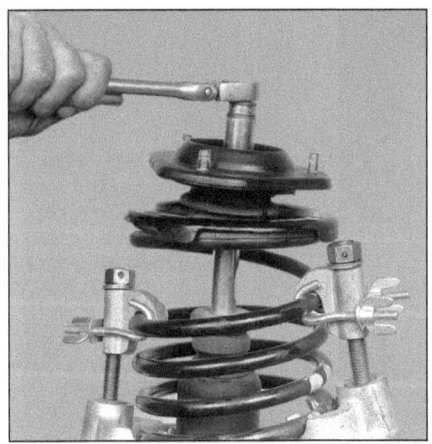

3.4 Remove the damper shaft nut - if the upper spring seat turns while loosening the nut, immobilize it with a chain wrench or strap wrench

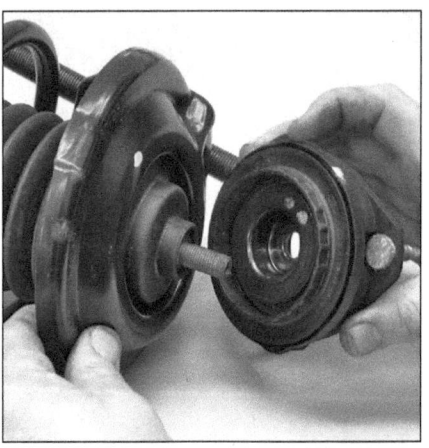

3.5 Lift the suspension support off the damper shaft

3.6 Remove the spring seat from the damper shaft

4   Mark the positions of the upper and lower spring seats and suspension support to each other. Loosen the damper shaft nut with a socket **(see illustration)**.

5   Remove the nut and suspension support **(see illustration)**. Inspect the bearing in the suspension support for smooth operation. If it doesn't turn smoothly, replace the suspension support. Check the rubber portion of the suspension support for cracking and general deterioration. If there is any separation of the rubber, replace it.

6   Lift the spring seat and upper insulator from the damper shaft **(see illustration)**. Check the rubber spring seat for cracking and hardness, replacing it if necessary.

7   Carefully lift the compressed spring from the assembly **(see illustration)** and set it in a safe place. **Warning:** *Never place your head near the end of the spring!*

8   Slide the rubber bumper off the damper shaft.

9   Check the lower insulator (if equipped) for wear, cracking and hardness and replace it if necessary.

Reassembly

Refer to illustrations 3.11 and 3.12

10   If the lower insulator is being replaced, set it into position with the dropped portion seated in the lowest part of the seat. Extend the damper rod to its full length and install the rubber bumper.

11   Carefully place the coil spring onto the lower insulator, with the end of the spring resting in the lowest part of the insulator **(see illustration)**.

12   Install the upper insulator and spring seat, making sure that the flats in the hole in the seat match up with the flats on the damper shaft **(see illustration)**.

13   Install the dust seal and suspension support to the damper shaft. Make sure all of the marks made in Step 4 are in alignment.

14   Install a new nut and tighten it to the torque listed in this Chapter's Specifications. **Warning:** *The manufacturer states that a new damper shaft nut must be installed.*

15   Install the strut assembly following the procedure outlined in Section 2 (front), or the rear shock absorber/coil spring as described in Section 10 or 11.

4   Stabilizer bar and bushings (front) - removal and installation

1999 and earlier models
Removal

Refer to illustrations 4.2, 4.3a and 4.3b

1   Loosen the front wheel lug nuts. Raise the front of the vehicle and support it securely on jackstands. Apply the parking brake and block the rear wheels to keep the vehicle from rolling off the stands. Remove the front wheels.

2   Detach the stabilizer bar link from the bar **(see illustration)**. If the ballstud turns with the nut, use an Allen wrench to hold the stud.

3   Unbolt the stabilizer bar bushing clamps **(see illustrations)**.

4   If you're working on a 1997 model, unbolt the front exhaust pipe from the flange in front of the catalytic converter (see Chapter 4) and pull it down far enough to remove the stabilizer bar.

5   While the stabilizer bar is off the vehicle, slide off the retainer bushings and inspect them. If they're cracked, worn or deteriorated,

3.7 Remove the compressed spring assembly - keep the ends of the spring pointed away from your body

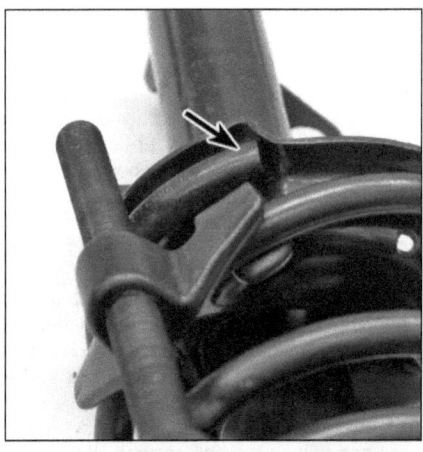

3.11 When installing the spring, make sure the end fits into the recessed portion of the lower seat

3.12 The flats on the damper shaft must match up with the flats in the spring seat

4.2 If you're removing the stabilizer bar, detach the bar from the link by removing the upper nut; if you're removing the control arm, remove the lower nut and detach the link from the arm

4.3a To detach the front stabilizer bar from the vehicle, remove this nut (left arrow) and these two bolts (arrows) from the bushing clamps (1997 models)

replace them. It's also a good idea to inspect the stabilizer bar link. To check it, flip the balljoint stud side-to-side five or six times, then install the nut. Using an inch-pound torque wrench, turn the nut continuously one turn every two to four seconds and note the torque reading on the fifth turn. It should be about 0.4 to 0.9 Nm. If it isn't, replace the link.

6   Clean the bushing area of the stabilizer bar with a stiff wire brush to remove any rust or dirt.

Installation

7   Lubricate the inside and outside of the new bushing with vegetable oil (used in cooking) to simplify reassembly. **Caution:** *Don't use petroleum or mineral-based lubricants or brake fluid - they will lead to deterioration of the bushings.*

8   Installation is the reverse of removal.

2000 and later models

Note: *This is a difficult procedure for the novice mechanic, since the engine/transaxle must be supported from above with an engine support fixture or hoist, while the front suspension crossmember is unbolted and lowered.*

Removal

Refer to illustrations 4.10, 4.14 and 4.15

9   Loosen the front wheel lug nuts. Raise the front of the vehicle and support it securely on jackstands. Apply the parking brake and block the rear wheels to keep the vehicle from rolling off the stands. Remove the front wheels.

10   Detach the stabilizer bar link from the bar **(see illustration)**. If the ballstud turns with the nut, use an Allen wrench to hold the stud.

11   Remove the steering shaft pinch bolt

(see Section 20).

12   Support the engine/transaxle assembly from above with an engine hoist or support fixture **(see illustration 20.3)**.

13   Remove the mounting bolts from the engine/transaxle mounts to the crossmember. Refer to Chapter 2 for engine and transaxle mount replacement procedures.

14   Remove the subframe/crossmember mounting bolts from the chassis, using a floor jack to lower the crossmember enough to access the stabilizer bar clamps **(see illustration)**. Be sure to note exactly the size and location of each nut and bolt to insure correct reassembly. **Note:** *The transaxle should be supported by a floor jack immediately after the subframe is removed from the vehicle. The transaxle will tilt slightly but should remain steady if the engine is properly secured with the engine compartment brace.*

4.3b If you're working on a 1998 or 1999 model, remove this nut and bolts and detach the bracket

4.10 If you're removing the stabilizer bar, detach the bar from the link by removing the lower nut; if you're removing the strut, remove the upper nut and detach the link from the strut

4.14 Remove the front suspension subframe bolts (with an overhead support for the engine/transaxle and a floor jack under the subframe - refer to the letter designations for torque specs when installing fasteners for the subframe (A and B), engine mount crossmember (C) and the lower control arm balljoint bolts (D)

15   Unbolt the stabilizer bar bushing clamps and remove the stabilizer bar **(see illustration)**.

16   While the stabilizer bar is off the vehicle, slide off the retainer bushings and inspect them. If they're cracked, worn or deteriorated, replace them. It's also a good idea to inspect the stabilizer bar link. To check it, flip the balljoint stud side-to-side five or six times, then install the nut. Using a beam type torque wrench, turn the nut continuously one turn every two to four seconds and note the torque reading on the fifth turn. It should be about 0.04 to 0.9 Nm. If it isn't, replace the link.

17   Clean the bushing area of the stabilizer bar with a stiff wire brush to remove any rust or dirt.

Installation

18   Lubricate the inside and outside of the new bushing with vegetable oil (used in cooking) to simplify reassembly. **Caution:** *Don't use petroleum or mineral-based lubricants or brake fluid - they will lead to deterioration of the bushings.*

19   Installation is the reverse of removal. Tighten all fasteners to the torque values listed in this Chapter's Specifications. **Note:** *When installing the subframe, use a rod of the same diameter as the four subframe-to-chassis bolts to align each side until that side's bolts can be inserted one at a time. Do not tighten any of the four bolts until all have been installed finger tight, then tighten to the Specifications in this Chapter.*

20   Install the wheel and lug nuts, lower the vehicle and tighten the lug nuts to the torque listed in the Chapter 1 Specifications.

21   It's a good idea to have the front wheel alignment checked, and if necessary, adjusted after this job has been performed.

4.15 Remove the bolts and the stabilizer clamps

5.2a To detach the control arm from the steering knuckle balljoint, remove this bolt and these two nuts . . .

5   Control arm - removal, inspection and installation

Removal

Refer to illustrations 5.2a and 5.2b

1   Loosen the wheel lug nuts on the side to be dismantled, raise the front of the vehicle, support it securely on jackstands and remove the wheel.

2   Remove the bolt and two nuts holding the control arm to the steering knuckle. Use a lever to disconnect the control arm from the steering knuckle **(see illustrations)**.

3   Refer to Section 4 and unbolt and lower the front suspension crossmember with a floor jack.

4   Remove the control arm front pivot bolt.

5   Remove the rear bushing bolt.

6   Remove the control arm.

Inspection

7   Check the control arm for distortion and the bushings for wear, replacing parts as necessary. Do not attempt to straighten a bent control arm.

Installation

8   Installation is the reverse of removal. Tighten all of the fasteners to the torque values listed in this Chapter's Specifications, but don't tighten the front pivot bolt until the outer end of the control arm has been raised with a floor jack to simulate normal ride height. **Note:** *When installing the subframe, use a rod of the same diameter as the four subframe-to-chassis bolts to align each side until that side's bolts can be inserted one at a time. Do not tighten any of the four bolts until all have been installed finger tight, then tighten to the Specifications in this Chapter.*

9   Install the wheel and lug nuts, lower the vehicle and tighten the lug nuts to the torque listed in the Chapter 1 Specifications.

10   It's a good idea to have the front wheel alignment checked, and if necessary, adjusted after this job has been performed.

6   Balljoint - replacement

Refer to illustration 6.3

1   Loosen the wheel lug nuts, raise the vehicle and support it securely on jackstands. Remove the wheel.

2   Remove the cotter pin from the balljoint stud and loosen the nut (but don't remove it yet).

3   Separate the balljoint from the steering knuckle with a picklefork-type balljoint separator **(see illustration)**. Remove the balljoint stud nut. The clearance between the balljoint stud and the CV joint is very tight. To remove the stud nut, you'll have to alternately back off the nut a turn or two, pull down the stud, turn the nut another turn or two, etc. until the nut is off.

4   Remove the bolt and nuts securing the balljoint to the control arm, then separate the balljoint from the control arm with a lever **(see illustrations 5.2a and 5.2b)**.

5   To install the balljoint, insert the balljoint stud through the hole in the steering knuckle and install the nut, but don't tighten it yet.

Don't push the balljoint stud all the way up into and through the hole; instead, thread the nut onto the stud as soon as the stud protrudes through the hole, then turn the nut to draw the stud up through the hole.

6   Attach the balljoint to the control arm and install the bolt and nuts, tightening them to the torque listed in this Chapter's Specifications.

7   Tighten the balljoint stud nut to the torque listed in this Chapter's Specifications and install a new cotter pin. If the cotter pin hole doesn't line up with the slots on the nut, tighten the nut additionally until it does line up - don't loosen the nut to insert the cotter pin.

8   Install the wheel and lug nuts. Lower the vehicle and tighten the lug nuts to the torque listed in the Chapter 1 Specifications.

7   Steering knuckle and hub - removal and installation

Warning: *Dust created by the brake system is harmful to your health. Never blow it out with compressed air and don't inhale any of it. Do not, under any circumstances, use petroleum-based solvents to clean brake parts. Use brake system cleaner only.*

Removal

Refer to illustration 7.8

1   Loosen the wheel lug nuts, raise the vehicle and support it securely on jackstands, then remove the wheel.

2   Remove the brake caliper (don't disconnect the hose) and the brake disc (see Chapter 9), and disconnect the brake hose from the strut. Hang the caliper from the coil spring with a piece of wire - don't let it hang by the brake hose.

3   If the vehicle is equipped with ABS, disconnect and remove the wheel speed sensor.

4   Mark the relationship of the strut to the steering knuckle **(see illustration 2.3)**. Loosen, but don't remove the strut-to-steering knuckle nuts and bolts (see Section 2).

5   Separate the tie-rod end from the steering knuckle arm (see Section 15).

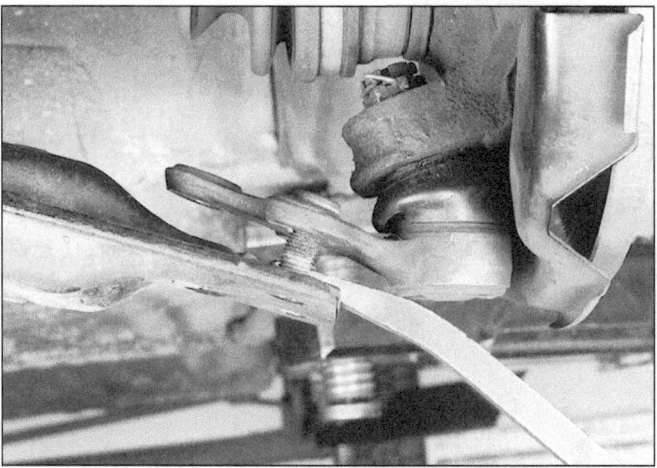

5.2b . . . and prise the control arm and balljoint apart with a large lever or screwdriver

6.3 Separate the balljoint from the steering knuckle with a picklefork-type balljoint separator

7.8 Use a balljoint removal tool or small puller to remove the balljoint

9.2 To detach a rear stabilizer bar link from the stabilizer bar, remove this nut (arrow) and pivot the link out of the way - remove the upper nut if you're removing the strut

6   Remove the balljoint-to-lower arm bolt and nuts **(see illustrations 5.2a and 5.2b)**.
7   Remove the driveaxle/hub nut and push the driveaxle from the hub as described in Chapter 8. Support the end of the driveaxle with a piece of wire.
8   Since the axle is out in this case, you can use a balljoint removal tool **(see illustration)** or a small puller to remove the balljoint from the steering knuckle. **Note:** *If you're removing the steering knuckle to replace the hub bearings, and the balljoint is in good condition, the balljoint can remain attached.*
9   The strut-to-knuckle bolts can now be removed.
10   Carefully separate the steering knuckle from the strut.

Installation

11   Guide the knuckle and hub assembly into position, inserting the driveaxle into the hub.
12   Push the knuckle into the strut flange and install the bolts and nuts, but don't tighten them yet.
13   If you removed the balljoint from the old knuckle, and are planning to use it with the new knuckle, connect the balljoint to the knuckle and tighten the balljoint stud nut to the torque listed in this Chapter's Specifications. Install a new cotter pin.
14   Attach the balljoint to the control arm, but don't tighten the bolt and nuts yet.
15   Attach the tie-rod to the steering knuckle arm (see Section 18). Tighten the strut bolt nuts, the balljoint-to-control arm bolt and nuts and the tie-rod nut to the torque listed in this Chapter's Specifications.
16   Place the brake disc on the hub and install the caliper as outlined in Chapter 9.
17   Install the driveaxle/hub nut and tighten it to the torque listed in the Chapter 8 Specifications.
18   Install the wheel and lug nuts. Lower the vehicle and tighten the lug nuts to the torque

listed in the Chapter 1 Specifications.
19   Have the front-end alignment checked and, if necessary, adjusted.

8   Hub and bearing assembly (front) - removal and installation

Due to the special tools and expertise required to press the hub and bearing from the steering knuckle, this job should be left to a professional shop. However, the steering knuckle and hub may be removed and the assembly taken to an automotive machine shop or other qualified repair facility equipped with the necessary tools. See Section 7 for the steering knuckle and hub removal procedure.

9   Stabilizer bar and bushings (rear) - removal and installation

1   Loosen the rear wheel lug nuts. Raise the rear of the vehicle and place it securely on jackstands. Remove the rear wheels.

1999 and earlier models

Refer to illustrations 9.2 and 9.3

2   Remove the stabilizer bar-to-link nut **(see illustration)**. If the ballstud turns with the nut, use a hex wrench to hold the stud.
3   Unbolt the stabilizer bar bushing clamps from the body **(see illustration)**.
4   The stabilizer bar can now be removed from the vehicle. Pull the retainers off the stabilizer bar (if they haven't fallen off already) using a rocking motion.
5   Check the bushings for wear, hardness, distortion, cracking and other signs of deterioration, replacing them if necessary. Also check the link bushings for these signs.
6   Using a wire brush, clean the areas of the bar where the bushings ride. Installation is the reverse of the removal procedure. If necessary, use a light coat of vegetable oil to ease bushing and U-bracket installation (don't use petroleum-based products or brake fluid, as these will damage the rubber).
7   To inspect the links, refer to Section 4.
8   Installation is the reverse of removal.

9.3 To detach the rear stabilizer bar from the vehicle body, remove the bolts (arrows) from the bushing clamps

9.9 To detach the rear stabilizer bar (A) from the axle beam, remove the bolts/nuts (B, right side shown)

10.3 Remove the clip (arrow) and pass the hose fitting through the slot in the bracket

2000 and later models

Refer to illustration 9.9

9   Remove the stabilizer bar-to-axle beam bolts/nuts **(see illustration)**.

10   The stabilizer bar is mounted inside the open back of the U-channel axle beam. Once the bolts are removed, you may have to use a lever to remove the stabilizer bar from the axle beam.

11   Installation is the reverse of the removal procedure. When reinstalling the bar to the axle beam, look for a distinctive mark on the top of the bar at one side. When properly installed, this mark will face up and be on the left side of the axle beam.

12   Tighten the bolts/nuts to the Specifications listed in this Chapter.

---

10 Strut assembly (rear) 1999 and earlier models - removal, inspection and installation

Removal

Refer to illustrations 10.3, 10.6 and 10.7

1   On models with a one-piece rear seat, remove the seat cushions and the rear seat back (see Chapter 11); on models with separate rear seat backs, lean the seat backs forward; on station wagon models, remove the rear strut cover (the plastic trim piece/cup holder on top of the side trim panel, attached by a single screw) (see Chapter 11).

2   Loosen the rear wheel lug nuts, raise the rear of the vehicle and support it securely on jackstands. Remove the wheel.

3   Remove the clip and detach the brake hose from the bracket on the strut **(see illustration)**. If the vehicle is equipped with ABS, detach the ABS sensor wire from the strut.

4   Disconnect the stabilizer bar link from the strut **(see illustration 9.2)**.

5   Support the axle carrier with a floor jack.

6   Loosen the strut-to-axle carrier bolt nuts **(see illustration)**.

10.6 To detach the rear strut from the axle carrier, remove these two nuts (arrows) and drive out the bolts with a hammer and punch

7   Remove the three upper strut-to-body mounting nuts **(see illustration)**.

8   Lower the axle carrier with the jack and remove the two strut-to-axle carrier bolts.

9   Remove the strut assembly.

Inspection

Refer to illustration 10.11

10   Follow the inspection procedures described in Section 3. If you determine that the strut assembly must be disassembled for replacement of the strut or the coil spring, refer to Section 3.

11   When reassembling the strut, make sure the suspension support is aligned as shown **(see illustration)**.

Installation

12   Maneuver the assembly up into the fenderwell and insert the mounting studs through the holes in the body. Install the nuts, but don't tighten them yet.

13   Push the axle carrier into the strut lower bracket and install the bolts and nuts, tightening them to the torque listed in this

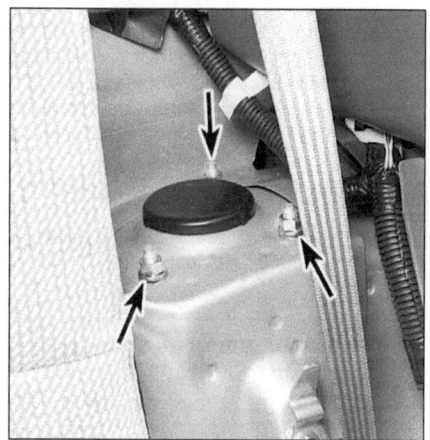

10.7 To detach the upper end of the rear strut from the vehicle, remove these three nuts (arrows)

10.11 Install the suspension support with the flat side facing forward and the strut-to-axle carrier bracket within 5-degrees of the middle of the distance between the two outer holes

---

Chapter's Specifications.

14   Connect the stabilizer bar link to the strut bracket.

15   Attach the brake hose to the strut bracket and install the clip. If the vehicle is equipped with ABS, attach the ABS wire to the strut.

11.4 Inside the boot, remove the two nuts (A) securing the upper part of the shock absorber - the bolt (B) is removed from below

11.6 To detach the rear shock absorber from the axle beam, remove the nut and washer then pull the shock off the stud

16   Install the wheel and lug nuts, lower the vehicle and tighten the lug nuts to the torque listed in the Chapter 1 Specifications.

17   Tighten the three strut upper mounting nuts to the torque listed in this Chapter's Specifications.

18   Repeat Steps 2 through 17 for the other strut.

19   Install the seat, rear side seat backs or rear strut covers (see Chapter 11).

11   Shock absorber/coil spring assembly (rear) 2000 and later models - removal, inspection and installation

Note: *Shock absorber/coil spring assemblies should only be replaced in pairs.*

Removal

Refer to illustrations 11.4 and 11.6

1   Open the boot and remove the spare tyre.

2   Refer to Chapter 11 and remove the left and right inner trim panels at the sides of the boot compartment, and the floor trim panel ahead of the spare tyre well.

3   Raise the rear of the vehicle and support it securely on jackstands. Support the axle beam with a floor jack, nearest the shock absorber being removed.

4   From inside the boot remove the two nuts at the upper mount **(see illustration)**. **Note:** *The shock absorber is still secured by one bolt, which is accessed from below.*

5   From below, remove the bolt securing the upper part of the shock absorber to the body.

6   Remove the shock absorber lower mounting nut and washer **(see illustration)**.

7   Remove the shock absorber assembly. It may be necessary to lower the floor jack far enough to disengage the upper mount before pulling the shock off the lower mounting stud.

Inspection

8   Follow the inspection procedures described in Section 3. If you determine that the shock absorber assembly must be disassembled for replacement of the shock body or the coil spring, refer to Section 3.

Installation

9   Manoeuvre the assembly up into the fenderwell and install the lower mount onto the stud and guide the upper mounting studs into the holes in the body. Install the bolt from below, tightening it to the torque listed in this Chapter's Specifications.

10   Install the lower washer and nut. Raise the axle beam with the floor jack to simulate normal ride height, then tighten the nut to the torque listed in this Chapter's Specifications.

11   Install the two upper mounting nuts and tighten them to the torque listed in this Chapter's Specifications.

12   Install the spare tyre and the trim panels in the boot.

12   Strut rod (1999 and earlier models) - removal and installation

Refer to illustrations 12.2 and 12.3

1   Loosen the wheel lug nuts, raise the vehicle and support it securely on jackstands. Remove the wheel.

2   Remove the strut rod-to-axle carrier bolt **(see illustration)**.

3   Remove the strut rod-to-body bracket bolt **(see illustration)** and detach the rod from the vehicle.

4   Installation is the reverse of the removal procedure, but don't tighten the bolts until the suspension is raised by a jack (placed under the axle carrier) to simulate normal ride height. Be sure to tighten the bolts to the torque listed in this Chapter's Specifications. Tighten the wheel lug nuts to the torque listed in the Chapter 1 Specifications.

12.2 To disconnect the strut rod from the axle carrier, remove this nut and bolt (arrows)

12.3 To disconnect the strut rod from the body, remove this nut and bolt (arrows)

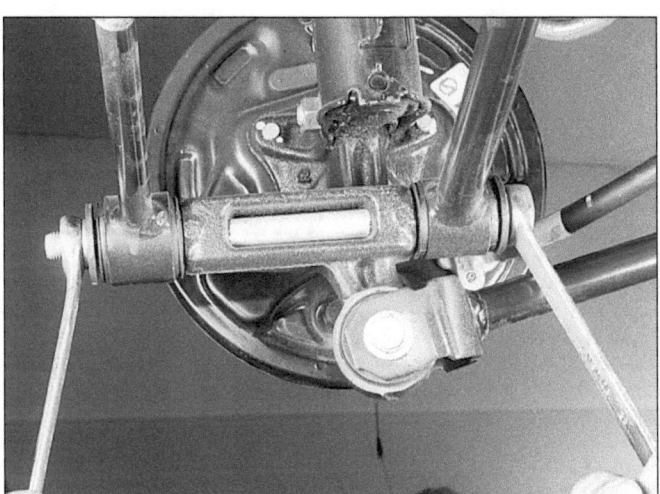

13.3 To detach the suspension arms from the axle carrier, remove this nut and bolt (if you're only removing the no. 2 arm, it isn't necessary to pull the bolt out)

13.4 To detach the No. 2 (rear) suspension arms from the suspension crossmember, remove the nut and washer; to remove the No. 1 (front) arms, remove the centre exhaust pipe and lower the suspension crossmember so the bolt can be pulled out

13 Suspension arms (1999 and earlier models) - removal and installation

Removal

1   Loosen the rear wheel lug nuts, raise the rear of the vehicle and support it securely on jackstands.

2   Block the front wheels and remove the rear wheel.

No. 2 (rear) suspension arms

Refer to illustrations 13.3 and 13.4

3   Remove the nut and washer from the outer end of the suspension arm at the axle carrier **(see illustration)**.

4   Remove the nut and washer from the inner end of the suspension arm at the suspension crossmember **(see illustration)**.

5   Remove the No. 2 suspension arm. **Caution:** *Do NOT loosen the locknuts and turn the adjusting tube; moving this tube will affect the rear wheel toe adjustment.*

No. 1 (front) suspension arms

6   Loosen the nut and bolt securing the inner end of the arms **(see illustration 13.4)**. Also loosen the nut and bolt attaching the outer ends of the arms to the axle carrier **(see illustration 13.3)**. Remove the exhaust system centre pipe and the exhaust pipe insulator (see Chapter 4).

7   Support the suspension crossmember with a floor jack. Remove the four bolts retaining the crossmember. Lower the crossmember far enough to allow the long through bolt at the inner end of the suspension arm to be pulled forward, out of the crossmember.

8   Remove the front suspension arm-to-rear axle carrier nut and bolt.

9   Remove the front suspension arm-to-suspension crossmember nut and bolt.

10   Remove the No. 1 suspension arm.

Installation

11   Installation is the reverse of removal. If you removed a No. 1 (front) suspension arm, be sure to tighten the crossmember-to-body bolts to the torque listed in this Chapter's Specifications. Don't tighten the bolts/nuts at either end of the arm until the suspension is raised by a jack (placed under the axle carrier) to simulate normal ride height. Be sure to tighten the bolts/nuts to the torque listed in this Chapter's Specifications.

12   Install the wheel and lug nuts, then lower the vehicle to the ground. Tighten the wheel lug nuts to the torque listed in the Chapter 1 Specifications.

13   Have the rear wheel alignment checked and, if necessary, adjusted.

14 Hub and bearing assembly (rear) - removal and installation

Warning: *Dust created by the brake system is harmful to your health. Never blow it out with compressed air and don't inhale any of it. Do not, under any circumstances, use petroleum-based solvents to clean brake parts. Use brake system cleaner only.*

Removal

Refer to illustration 14.3

1   Loosen the wheel lug nuts, raise the vehicle and support it securely on jackstands. Remove the wheel.

2   Remove the brake drum (see Chapter 9). On models with ABS, disconnect the wheel sensor.

3   Remove the four hub-to-axle beam bolts, accessed from behind the brake backing plate **(see illustration)**.

4   Remove the hub and bearing assembly from its seat, manoeuvre it out through the brake assembly.

5   If the hub exhibits looseness or excessive runout, the hub and bearing assembly must be replaced as a unit.

Installation

6   Position the hub and bearing assembly on the axle carrier and align the holes in the backing plate. After all four bolts have been installed, tighten them to the torque listed in this Chapter's Specifications.

7   Install the brake rotor (and ABS sensor if equipped) and the wheel. Lower the vehicle and tighten the lug nuts to the torque listed in the Chapter 1 Specifications.

15 Rear axle beam - removal and installation

Warning: *Dust created by the brake system is harmful to your health. Never blow it out with compressed air and don't inhale any of it. Do not, under any circumstances, use petroleum-based solvents to clean brake parts.*

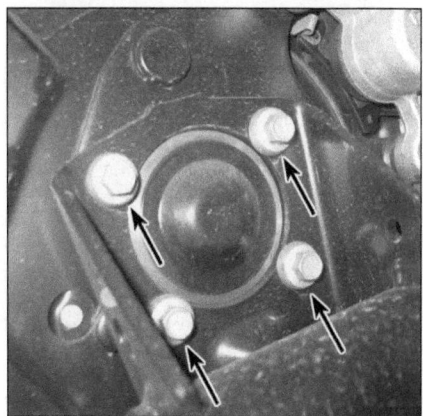

14.3 Remove the four bolts that attach the hub and bearing assembly to the rear axle beam

Use brake system cleaner only.
1   Loosen the wheel lug nuts, raise the vehicle and support it on jackstands. Block the front wheels and remove the rear wheel.

1999 and earlier models

Removal

2   Remove the rear brake rotor and detach the brake line from the bracket on the strut **(see illustration 10.3)**.
3   Remove the rear hub and bearing assembly (see Section 14).
4   Detach the backing plate and rear brake assembly from the axle carrier. It isn't necessary to disassemble the parking brake shoe assembly or disconnect the parking brake cable from the backing plate. Suspend the backing plate and brake assembly from the coil spring with a piece of wire. Be careful not to kink the brake line.
5   On models with ABS, remove the wheel speed sensor from the axle carrier.
6   Loosen, but don't remove the strut-to-axle carrier bolts **(see illustration 10.6)**.
7   Remove the suspension arm-to-axle carrier bolt, nut and washers **(see illustration 13.3)**. Also remove the rear strut rod-to-axle carrier bolt **(see illustration 12.2)**.
8   Remove the loosened strut-to-axle carrier bolts while supporting the carrier so it doesn't fall and detach the axle carrier from the strut bracket.

Installation

9   Inspect the carrier bushing for cracks, deformation and signs of wear. If it is worn out, take the carrier to a dealer service department or other repair shop to have the old one pressed out and a new one pressed in.
10   Push the axle carrier into the strut bracket, aligning the two bolt holes. Insert the two strut-to-carrier bolts and tighten them to the torque listed in this Chapter's Specifications.
11   Install the suspension arm-to-axle carrier bolt (from the front), washers and nut. Tighten the nut by hand.
12   Connect the strut rod to the axle carrier and tighten the nut and bolt finger tight.
13   Place a jack under the carrier and raise it to simulate normal ride height.
14   Tighten the suspension arm bolt/nut and the strut rod bolt/nut to the torque values listed in this Chapter's Specifications. Remove the floor jack from under the rear axle carrier.
15   On models with ABS, reattach the wheel speed sensor to the axle carrier.
16   Attach the brake backing plate to the axle carrier, install the hub and tighten the four bolts to the torque listed in this Chapter's Specifications.
17   Connect the brake line to the strut bracket and install the clip. Make sure the hose isn't twisted.
18   Install the rear brake drum and adjust the brake shoes (see Chapter 9).
19   Install the wheel and lug nuts. Lower the vehicle and tighten the lug nuts to the torque listed in the Chapter 1 Specifications.

2000 and later models

Removal

Refer to illustration 15.25
20   On models with ABS, disconnect the sensors and unbolt the ABS wire harness on each side from the axle beam.
21   Remove the rear stabilizer bar (see Section 9).
22   Remove the rear hub and bearing assembly on each side (see Section 14).
23   Detach the backing plate and rear brake assembly and brake lines from the axle beam. It isn't necessary to disassemble the parking brake shoe assembly or disconnect the parking brake cable from the backing plate. Suspend the backing plate and brake assembly from the coil spring with a piece of wire. Be careful not to kink the brake line.
24   Support the axle beam with a floor jack, then disconnect the shock absorbers from the studs on the axle beam (see Section 14).
25   Lower the axle beam down, then remove the two bolts/nuts through the pivot bushings and remove the axle beam **(see illustration)**.

Installation

26   Inspect the axle beam bushings for cracks, deformation and signs of wear. If either is worn out, take the beam to a dealer service department or other repair shop to have the old ones pressed out and new ones pressed in. **Note:** *Only replace the bushings as a pair.*
27   Push the axle beam up to the vehicle until the bolts can be inserted into the front bushings and body. Install the nuts, but do not tighten them yet.
28   Raise the axle beam and push the bottom of the shock absorbers onto the axle beam studs and secure with the washers and nuts.
29   Raise the axle beam to simulate normal ride height, then tighten the bushing bolts/nuts and the shock absorber lower mounting nuts to the torque listed in this Chapter's Specifications.
30   The remainder of the installation is the reverse of the removal procedure. Install the wheel and lug nuts. Lower the vehicle and tighten the lug nuts to the torque listed in the Chapter 1 Specifications.

16 Steering system - general information

All models are equipped with rack-and-pinion steering. The steering gear operates the steering knuckles via tie-rods. The inner ends of the tie-rods are protected by rubber boots that should be inspected periodically for secure attachment, tears and leaking lubricant.

The power assist system consists of a belt-driven pump and associated lines and hoses. The fluid level in the power steering pump reservoir should be checked periodically (see Chapter 1).

The steering wheel operates the steering shaft, which actuates the steering gear through universal joints. Looseness in the steering can be caused by wear in the steering shaft universal joints, the steering gear, the tie-rod ends, or loose retaining bolts.

17 Steering wheel - removal and installation

Warning: *These models are equipped with airbags. Always disable the airbag system before working in the vicinity of any airbag system component to avoid the possibility of accidental deployment of the airbag(s), which could cause personal injury (see Chapter 12).*

Removal

Refer to illustrations 17.2, 17.3, 17.5 and 17.6
1   Turn the ignition key to Off, then disconnect the cable from the negative terminal of the battery. Wait at least two minutes before proceeding.
2   Turn the steering wheel so the wheels are pointing straight ahead, then loosen the

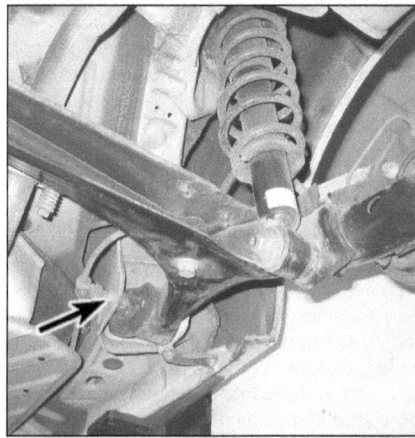

15.25 On each side, remove the bolt and nut securing the axle beam to the body (right side shown)

17.2 Back out the Torx screws until the airbag module is free, but don't try to remove them from the screw case (left side shown)

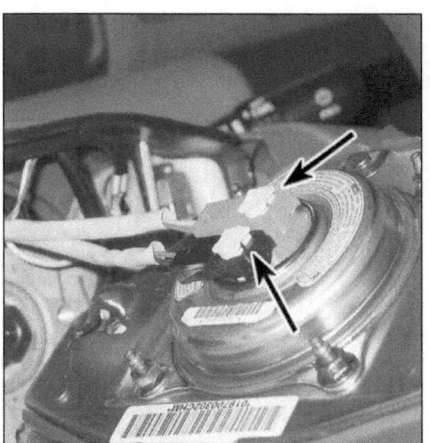

17.3 Lift the airbag module straight out from the steering wheel, then disconnect the electrical connectors at the back of the module

17.5 Mark the relationship of the steering wheel to the shaft before removing the wheel

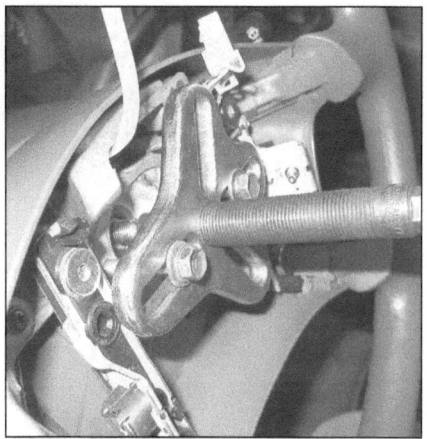

17.6 If the steering wheel is difficult to remove from the shaft, use a steering wheel puller to remove it

Torx screws that attach the airbag module to the steering wheel **(see illustration)**. Loosen each screw until the groove in the circumference of the screw catches on the screw case.

3   Pull the airbag module off the steering wheel and disconnect the module electrical connectors **(see illustration)**. To disconnect the connectors, use a small screwdriver to prise up the locks (centre part), then disconnect the connectors. Set the airbag module in a safe, isolated area. **Warning:** *Carry the airbag module with the trim side facing away from you, and set the airbag module down with the trim side facing up. Don't place anything on top of the airbag module.*

4   Unplug the electrical connector for the cruise control (if equipped).

5   Mark the relationship of the steering shaft to the hub (if marks don't already exist or don't line up) to simplify installation and ensure steering wheel alignment, then remove the steering wheel retaining nut **(see illustration)**.

6   Use a puller to disconnect the steering wheel from the shaft **(see illustration)**. **Warning:** *Do not hammer on the shaft or the puller in an attempt to loosen the wheel*

from the shaft. Also, don't allow the steering shaft to turn with the steering wheel removed. If the shaft turns, the airbag spiral cable will become uncentred, which may cause the wire inside to break when the vehicle is returned to service.

7   If it is necessary to remove the airbag spiral cable, follow the spiral cable wiring harness and unplug the electrical connector, then disengage the three claws and detach it from the combination switch.

Installation

Refer to illustration 17.8

8   Make sure that the front wheels are pointing straight ahead. Depress the lock tab or hub of the spiral cable and turn the spiral cable anticlockwise by hand until it stops (don't apply too much force). Rotate the cable clockwise about 2-1/2 turns and align the two pointers **(see illustration)**.

9   To install the wheel, align the mark on the steering wheel hub with the mark on the shaft and slip the wheel onto the shaft. Install the nut and tighten it to the torque listed in this Chapter's Specifications.

10   Plug in the cruise control connector.

11   Plug in the electrical connectors for the airbag module and press down the locking tab.

12   Make sure the airbag module electrical connector is positioned correctly and that the wires don't interfere with anything, then install the airbag module and tighten the retaining screws to the torque listed in this Chapter's Specifications.

13   Connect the negative battery cable.

18 Tie-rod ends - removal and installation

Removal

Refer to illustrations 18.2, 18.3a, 18.3b and 18.4

1   Loosen the wheel lug nuts. Raise the front of the vehicle, support it securely on jackstands, block the rear wheels and set the parking brake. Remove the front wheel.

2   Remove the cotter pin **(see illustration)** and loosen the nut on the tie-rod end stud.

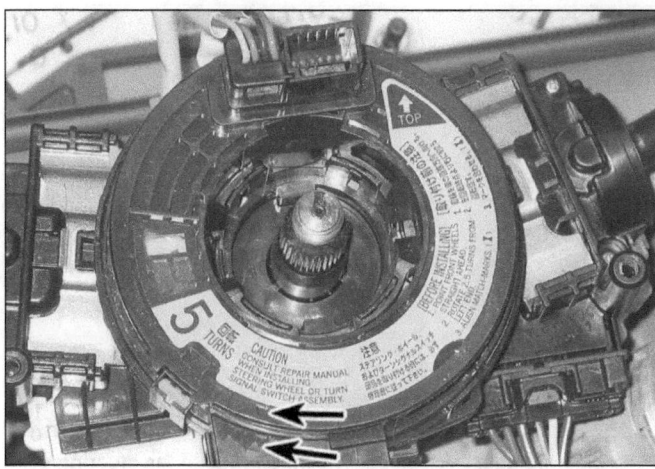

17.8 After properly centreing the spiral cable as described in the text, make sure the pointers are aligned

18.2 Remove the cotter pin from the castle nut and loosen - but don't remove - the nut

18.3a Loosen the jam nut . . .

18.3b . . . then mark the position of the tie-rod end in relation to the threads

3   Hold the tie-rod with a pair of locking pliers or spanner and loosen the jam nut enough to mark the position of the tie-rod end in relation to the threads **(see illustrations)**.
4   Disconnect the tie-rod from the steering knuckle arm with a puller **(see illustration)**. Remove the nut and detach the tie-rod.
5   Unscrew the tie-rod end from the tie-rod.

Installation

6   Thread the tie-rod end on to the marked position and insert the tie-rod stud into the steering knuckle arm. Tighten the jam nut securely.
7   Install the castle nut on the stud and tighten it to the torque listed in this Chapter's Specifications. Install a new cotter pin. If the hole for the cotter pin doesn't line up with one of the slots in the nut, turn the nut an additional amount until it does.
8   Install the wheel and lug nuts. Lower the vehicle and tighten the lug nuts to the torque listed in the Chapter 1 Specifications.
9   Have the alignment checked and, if necessary, adjusted.

19   Steering gear boots - replacement

Refer to illustrations 19.3a and 19.3b

1   Loosen the lug nuts, raise the vehicle and support it securely on jackstands. Remove the wheel.
2   Remove the tie-rod end and jam nut (see Section 18).
3   Remove the outer steering gear boot clamp with a pair of pliers **(see illustration)**. Cut off the inner boot clamp with a pair of diagonal cutters **(see illustration)**. Slide off the boot.
4   Before installing the new boot, wrap the threads and serrations on the end of the steering rod with a layer of tape so the small end of the new boot isn't damaged.
5   Slide the new boot into position on the steering gear until it seats in the groove in the steering rod and install new clamps.
6   Remove the tape and install the tie-rod end (see Section 18).

7   Install the wheel and lug nuts. Lower the vehicle and tighten the lug nuts to the torque listed in the Chapter 1 Specifications.

20   Steering gear - removal and installation

Refer to illustrations 20.3, 20.5, 20.6a and 20.6b

Warning: *These models are equipped with airbags. Always disable the airbag system before working in the vicinity of any airbag system component to avoid the possibility of accidental deployment of the airbag(s), which could cause personal injury (see Chapter 12).*
1   Disconnect the cable from the negative terminal of the battery.
2   Remove the steering wheel (see Section 17). **Note:** *This will prevent the spiral cable from being damaged in the event the steering gear is not centred when it is installed.*
3   Support the engine from above with an engine support fixture **(see illustration)**. This

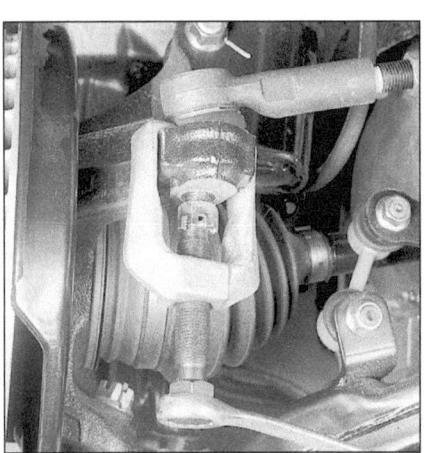

18.4 Disconnect the tie-rod from the steering knuckle arm with a puller

19.3a The outer ends of the steering gear boots are secured by spring-type clamps; they're easily released with a pair of pliers

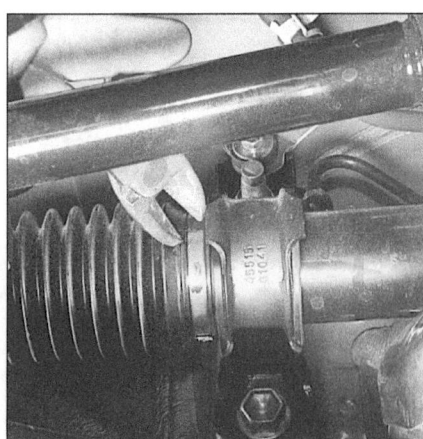

19.3b The inner ends of the steering gear boots are retained by boot clamps, which must be cut off and discarded

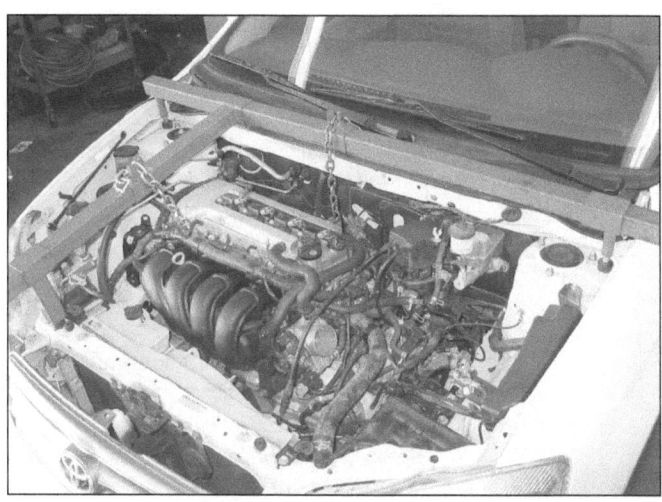

20.3 Support the engine from above with an engine support fixture

20.5 Disconnect the power steering line fittings

tool can be obtained at most equipment rental yards.

4   Loosen the front wheel lug nuts, raise the front of the vehicle and support it securely on jackstands. Apply the parking brake and remove the wheels. Remove the engine under covers.

5   Place a drain pan under the steering gear. Detach the power steering pressure and return lines **(see illustration)** and cap the ends to prevent excessive fluid loss and contamination. Also unbolt the line clamp from the top of the steering gear.

6   Remove the universal joint cover **(see illustration)**. Mark the relationship of the lower universal joint to the steering gear input shaft and remove the lower intermediate shaft pinch-bolt **(see illustration)**. Loosen the upper universal joint bolt, then slide the joint up and disconnect it from the steering gear input shaft.

7   Separate the tie-rod ends from the steering knuckle arms (see Section 18). Separate

the stabilizer bar links from the bar (see Section 4).

8   Disconnect the balljoints from the control arms **(see illustrations 5.2a and 5.2b)**.

9   Remove the front section of the exhaust pipe. Unbolt the suspension crossmember and lower it along with the control arms **(see illustration 4.6)**.

10   Remove the bolts securing the steering gear to the crossmember.

11   Installation is the reverse of removal, noting the following points:

a) *Tighten all steering and suspension fasteners to the torque listed in this Chapter's Specifications.*

b) *Install the wheels and lug nuts. Lower the vehicle and tighten the lug nuts to the torque listed in the Chapter 1 Specifications.*

c) *Set the front wheels in the straight-ahead position, then centre the spiral cable and install the steering wheel and airbag module (see Section 17).*

d) *Fill the power steering fluid reservoir with the recommended fluid (see Chapter 1). Bleed the steering system (see Section 22).*

---

21   Power steering pump - removal and installation

Refer to illustration 21.4

Removal

1   Disconnect the cable from the negative battery terminal.

2   Using a large syringe or suction gun, suck as much fluid out of the power steering fluid reservoir as possible. Place a drain pan under the vehicle to catch any fluid that spills out when the hoses are disconnected.

3   Remove the drivebelt (see Chapter 1). Loosen the right front wheel lug nuts, raise the front of the vehicle and support it securely on

20.6a Pull back the carpeting at the bottom of the steering column and remove the universal joint cover fasteners (arrows)

20.6b Mark the relationship of the universal joint to the steering gear input shaft, loosen the upper U-joint pinch bolt (A), then remove the lower bolt (B) and detach the joint from the steering gear input shaft

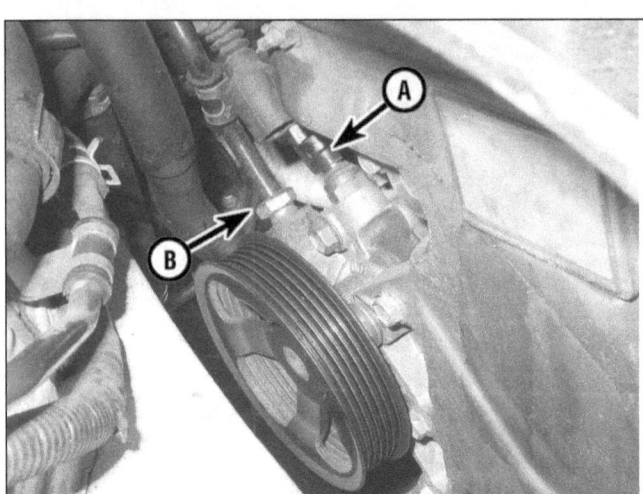

21.4 Power steering pump mounting details

A   *Power steering pressure switch connector*
B   *Pressure line fitting*

jackstands. Remove the wheel and the right side engine under cover.

4   Unplug the electrical connector from the power steering fluid pressure switch **(see illustration)**.

5   Unscrew the pressure line-to-pump fitting, using a flare-nut wrench, if available, to avoid rounding-off the corners of the fitting.

6   Loosen the hose clamp and detach the return hose from the pump.

7   Remove the two mounting nuts and detach the power steering pump from the engine. **Note:** *The pump-to-mounting bracket nuts are accessible through the holes in the pump pulley, using a short extension and socket.*

Installation

8   Installation is the reverse of removal. Be sure to tighten the mounting bolts/nuts and the pressure line fitting to the torque listed in this Chapter's Specifications.

9   Install the engine under cover, wheel and lug nuts. Lower the vehicle and tighten the lug nuts to the torque listed in the Chap-

ter 1 Specifications.

10   Install the drivebelt (see Chapter 1).

11   Top up the fluid level in the reservoir (see Chapter 1) and bleed the system (see Section 19).

22   Power steering system - bleeding

1   Following any operation in which the power steering fluid lines have been disconnected, the power steering system must be bled to remove all air and obtain proper steering performance.

2   With the front wheels in the straight ahead position, check the power steering fluid level and, if low, add fluid until it reaches the Cold mark on the reservoir.

3   Start the engine and allow it to run at fast idle. Recheck the fluid level and add more if necessary to reach the Cold mark.

4   Bleed the system by turning the wheels from side to side, without hitting the stops. This will work the air out of the system. Keep the reservoir full of fluid as this is done.

5   When the air is worked out of the system, return the wheels to the straight-ahead position and leave the vehicle running for several more minutes before shutting it off.

6   Road test the vehicle to be sure the steering system is functioning normally and noise free.

7   Recheck the fluid level to be sure it is up to the Hot mark on the reservoir while the engine is at normal operating temperature. Add fluid if necessary (see Chapter 1).

23   Wheel studs - replacement

Refer to illustrations 23.3 and 23.4

Note: *This procedure applies to both the front and rear wheel studs.*

1   Loosen the wheel lug nuts, raise the vehicle and support it securely on jackstands. Remove the wheel.

2   Remove the brake disc (see Chapter 9).

3   Install a lug nut part way onto the stud being replaced. Push the stud out of the hub flange with a press tool **(see illustration)**.

4   Insert the new stud into the hub flange from the back side and install some flat washers and a lug nut on the stud **(see illustration)**.

5   Tighten the lug nut until the stud is seated in the flange.

6   Reinstall the brake disc. Install the wheel and lug nuts. Lower the vehicle and tighten the lug nuts to the torque listed in the Chapter 1 Specifications.

24   Wheels and tyres - general information

Refer to illustration 24.1

1   All vehicles covered by this manual are equipped with metric-sized steel belted radial

23.3 Use a press tool to push the stud out of the flange

1   *Hub flange*
2   *Lug nut on stud*
3   *Press tool*

23.4 Install a spacer and a lug nut on the stud, then tighten the nut to draw the stud into place

1   *Hub flange*
2   *Spacer*

24.1 Metric tyre size code

25.1 Camber, caster and toe-in angles

tyres **(see illustration)**. Use of other size or type of tyres may affect the ride and handling of the vehicle. Don't mix different types of tyres, such as radials and bias belted on the same vehicle, as handling may be seriously affected. It's recommended that tyres be replaced in pairs on the same axle, but if only one tyre is being replaced, be sure it's the same size, structure and tread design as the other.

2   Because tyre pressure has a substantial effect on handling and wear, the pressure on all tyres should be checked at least once a month or before any extended trips (see Chapter 1).

3   Wheels must be replaced if they are bent, dented, leak air, have elongated bolt holes, are heavily rusted, out of vertical symmetry or if the lug nuts won't stay tight. Wheel repairs that use welding or peening are not recommended.

4   Tyre and wheel balance is important in the overall handling, braking and performance of the vehicle. Unbalanced wheels can adversely affect handling and ride characteristics as well as tyre life. Whenever a tyre is installed on a wheel, the tyre and wheel should be balanced by a shop with the proper equipment.

25 Wheel alignment - general information

Refer to illustration 25.1

A wheel alignment refers to the adjustments made to the wheels so they are in proper angular relationship to the suspension and the ground. Wheels that are out of proper alignment not only affect vehicle control, but also increase tyre wear. The alignment angles normally measured are camber, caster and toe-in **(see illustration)**. Toe-in and camber are the only adjustable angles on the front. Caster should be measured to check for bent or worn suspension parts. Camber and toe-in should be measured on the rear to check for a bent axle.

Getting the proper wheel alignment is a very exacting process, one in which complicated and expensive machines are necessary to perform the job properly. Because of this, you should have a technician with the proper equipment perform these tasks. We will, however, use this space to give you a basic idea of what is involved with a wheel alignment so you can better understand the process and deal intelligently with the shop that does the work.

Toe-in is the turning in of the wheels. The purpose of a toe specification is to ensure parallel rolling of the wheels. In a vehicle with zero toe-in, the distance between the front edges of the wheels will be the same as the distance between the rear edges of the wheels. The actual amount of toe-in is normally only a fraction of an inch. On the front end, toe-in is controlled by the tie-rod end position on the tie-rod. On the rear end, it's not adjustable. Incorrect toe-in will cause the tyres to wear improperly by making them scrub against the road surface.

Camber is the tilting of the wheels from vertical when viewed from one end of the vehicle. When the wheels tilt out at the top, the camber is said to be positive (+). When the wheels tilt in at the top the camber is negative (-). The amount of tilt is measured in degrees from vertical and this measurement is called the camber angle. This angle affects the amount of tyre tread which contacts the road and compensates for changes in the suspension geometry when the vehicle is cornering or traveling over an undulating surface. On the front end, camber is adjusted by altering the position of the steering knuckle in the strut flange. If camber can't be adjusted within the specified range, special adjuster bolts, which replace the standard strut-to-knuckle bolts, are available. On the rear end, camber is not adjustable.

Caster is the tilting of the front steering axis from the vertical. A tilt toward the rear is positive caster and a tilt toward the front is negative caster. Caster is not adjustable on these vehicles

Notes

Chapter 11
Body

Contents

1   General information

The models covered by this manual feature a unibody construction, using a floor pan with front and rear frame side rails which support the body components, front and rear suspension systems and other mechanical components. Certain components are particularly vulnerable to accident damage and can be unbolted and repaired or replaced. Among these parts are the body moldings, bumpers, bonnet and boot lids and all glass.

Only general body maintenance practices and body panel repair procedures within the scope of the do-it-yourselfer are included in this Chapter.

2   Body - maintenance

1   The condition of your vehicle's body is very important, because the resale value depends a great deal on it. It's much more difficult to repair a neglected or damaged body than it is to repair mechanical components. The hidden areas of the body, such as the wheel wells, the frame and the engine compartment, are equally important, although they don't require as frequent attention as the rest of the body.

2   Once a year, or every 20,000 kilometres, it's a good idea to have the underside of the body steam cleaned. All traces of dirt and oil will be removed and the area can then be inspected carefully for rust, damaged brake lines, frayed electrical wires, damaged cables and other problems. The front suspension components should be greased after completion of this job.

3   At the same time, clean the engine and the engine compartment with a steam cleaner or water soluble degreaser.

4   The wheel wells should be given close attention, since undercoating can peel away and stones and dirt thrown up by the tyres can cause the paint to chip and flake, allowing rust to set in. If rust is found, clean down to the bare metal and apply an anti-rust paint.

5   The body should be washed about once a week. Wet the vehicle thoroughly to soften the dirt, then wash it down with a soft sponge and plenty of clean soapy water. If the surplus dirt is not washed off very carefully, it can wear down the paint.

6   Spots of tar or asphalt thrown up from the road should be removed with a cloth soaked in solvent.

7   Once every six months, wax the body and chrome trim. If a chrome cleaner is used to remove rust from any of the vehicle's plated parts, remember that the cleaner also removes part of the chrome, so use it sparingly.

3   Vinyl trim - maintenance

Don't clean vinyl trim with detergents, caustic soap or petroleum-based cleaners. Plain soap and water works just fine, with a soft brush to clean dirt that may be ingrained. Wash the vinyl as frequently as the rest of the vehicle.

After cleaning, application of a high quality rubber and vinyl protectant will help prevent oxidation and cracks. The protectant can also be applied to weather-stripping, vacuum lines and rubber hoses, which often fail as a result of chemical degradation, and to the tyres.

4   Upholstery and carpets - maintenance

1   Every three months remove the carpets or mats and clean the interior of the vehicle (more frequently if necessary). Vacuum the upholstery and carpets to remove loose dirt and dust.
2   Leather upholstery requires special care. Stains should be removed with warm water and a very mild soap solution. Use a clean, damp cloth to remove the soap, then wipe again with a dry cloth. Never use alcohol, petrol, nail polish remover or thinner to clean leather upholstery.
3   After cleaning, regularly treat leather upholstery with a leather wax. Never use car wax on leather upholstery.
4   In areas where the interior of the vehicle is subject to bright sunlight, cover leather seats with a sheet if the vehicle is to be left out for any length of time.

5   Body repair - minor damage

See photo sequence

Repair of minor scratches

1   If the scratch is superficial and does not penetrate to the metal of the body, repair is very simple. Lightly rub the scratched area with a fine rubbing compound to remove loose paint and built-up wax. Rinse the area with clean water.
2   Apply touch-up paint to the scratch, using a small brush. Continue to apply thin layers of paint until the surface of the paint in the scratch is level with the surrounding paint. Allow the new paint at least two weeks to harden, then blend it into the surrounding paint by rubbing with a very fine rubbing compound. Finally, apply a coat of wax to the scratch area.
3   If the scratch has penetrated the paint and exposed the metal of the body, causing the metal to rust, a different repair technique is required. Remove all loose rust from the bottom of the scratch with a pocket knife, then apply rust inhibiting paint to prevent the formation of rust in the future. Using a rubber or nylon applicator, coat the scratched area with glaze-type filler. If required, the filler can be mixed with thinner to provide a very thin paste, which is ideal for filling narrow scratches. Before the glaze filler in the scratch hardens, wrap a piece of smooth cotton cloth around the tip of a finger. Dip the cloth in thinner and then quickly wipe it along the surface of the scratch. This will ensure that the sur-

face of the filler is slightly hollow. The scratch can now be painted over as described earlier in this section.

Repair of dents

4   When repairing dents, the first job is to pull the dent out until the affected area is as close as possible to its original shape. There is no point in trying to restore the original shape completely as the metal in the damaged area will have stretched on impact and cannot be restored to its original contours. It is better to bring the level of the dent up to a point that is about 2 mm below the level of the surrounding metal. In cases where the dent is very shallow, it is not worth trying to pull it out at all.
5   If the back side of the dent is accessible, it can be hammered out gently from behind using a soft-face hammer. While doing this, hold a block of wood firmly against the opposite side of the metal to absorb the hammer blows and prevent the metal from being stretched.
6   If the dent is in a section of the body which has double layers, or some other factor makes it inaccessible from behind, a different technique is required. Drill several small holes through the metal inside the damaged area, particularly in the deeper sections. Screw long, self-tapping screws into the holes just enough for them to get a good grip in the metal. Now the dent can be pulled out by pulling on the protruding heads of the screws with locking pliers.
7   The next stage of repair is the removal of paint from the damaged area and from an inch or so of the surrounding metal. This is done with a wire brush or sanding disk in a drill motor, although it can be done just as effectively by hand with sandpaper. To complete the preparation for filling, score the surface of the bare metal with a screwdriver or the tang of a file, or drill small holes in the affected area. This will provide a good grip for the filler material. To complete the repair, see the subsection on filling and painting later in this Section.

Repair of rust holes or gashes

8   Remove all paint from the affected area and from an inch or so of the surrounding metal using a sanding disk or wire brush mounted in a drill motor. If these are not available, a few sheets of sandpaper will do the job just as effectively.
9   With the paint removed, you will be able to determine the severity of the corrosion and decide whether to replace the whole panel, if possible, or repair the affected area. New body panels are not as expensive as most people think and it is often quicker to install a new panel than to repair large areas of rust.
10   Remove all trim pieces from the affected area except those which will act as a guide to the original shape of the damaged body, such as headlight shells, etc. Using metal snips or a hacksaw blade, remove all loose metal and any other metal that is badly affected by rust. Hammer the edges of the hole in to create a

slight depression for the filler material.
11   Wire brush the affected area to remove the powdery rust from the surface of the metal. If the back of the rusted area is accessible, treat it with rust inhibiting paint.
12   Before filling is done, block the hole in some way. This can be done with sheet metal riveted or screwed into place, or by stuffing the hole with wire mesh.
13   Once the hole is blocked off, the affected area can be filled and painted. See the following subsection on filling and painting.

Filling and painting

14   Many types of body fillers are available, but generally speaking, body repair kits which contain filler paste and a tube of resin hardener are best for this type of repair work. A wide, flexible plastic or nylon applicator will be necessary for imparting a smooth and contoured finish to the surface of the filler material. Mix up a small amount of filler on a clean piece of wood or cardboard (use the hardener sparingly). Follow the manufacturer's instructions on the package, otherwise the filler will set incorrectly.
15   Using the applicator, apply the filler paste to the prepared area. Draw the applicator across the surface of the filler to achieve the desired contour and to level the filler surface. As soon as a contour that approximates the original one is achieved, stop working the paste. If you continue, the paste will begin to stick to the applicator. Continue to add thin layers of paste at 20-minute intervals until the level of the filler is just above the surrounding metal.
16   Once the filler has hardened, the excess can be removed with a body file. From then on, progressively finer grades of sandpaper should be used, starting with a 180-grit paper and finishing with 600-grit wet-or-dry paper. Always wrap the sandpaper around a flat rubber or wooden block, otherwise the surface of the filler will not be completely flat. During the sanding of the filler surface, the wet-or-dry paper should be periodically rinsed in water. This will ensure that a very smooth finish is produced in the final stage.
17   At this point, the repair area should be surrounded by a ring of bare metal, which in turn should be encircled by the finely feathered edge of good paint. Rinse the repair area with clean water until all of the dust produced by the sanding operation is gone.
18   Spray the entire area with a light coat of primer. This will reveal any imperfections in the surface of the filler. Repair the imperfections with fresh filler paste or glaze filler and once more smooth the surface with sandpaper. Repeat this spray-and-repair procedure until you are satisfied that the surface of the filler and the feathered edge of the paint are perfect. Rinse the area with clean water and allow it to dry completely.
19   The repair area is now ready for painting. Spray painting must be carried out in a warm, dry, windless and dust free atmosphere. These conditions can be created if you have

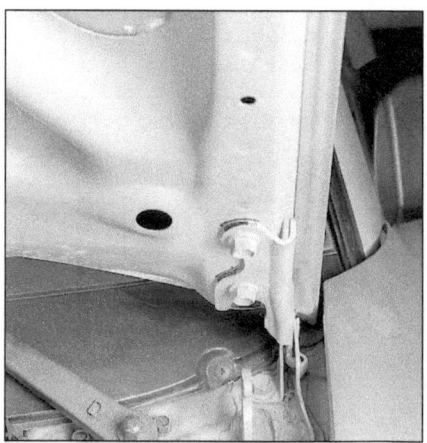

9.1 Before removing the bonnet, make marks around the hinge plate

access to a large indoor work area, but if you are forced to work in the open, you will have to pick the day very carefully. If you are working indoors, dousing the floor in the work area with water will help settle the dust that would otherwise be in the air. If the repair area is confined to one body panel, mask off the surrounding panels. This will help minimize the effects of a slight mismatch in paint colour. Trim pieces such as chrome strips, door handles, etc., will also need to be masked off or removed. Use masking tape and several thickness of newspaper for the masking operations.

20   Before spraying, shake the paint can thoroughly, then spray a test area until the spray painting technique is mastered. Cover the repair area with a thick coat of primer. The thickness should be built up using several thin layers of primer rather than one thick one. Using 600-grit wet-or-dry sandpaper, rub down the surface of the primer until it is very smooth. While doing this, the work area should be thoroughly rinsed with water and the wet-or-dry sandpaper periodically rinsed as well. Allow the primer to dry before spraying additional coats.

21   Spray on the top coat, again building up the thickness by using several thin layers of paint. Begin spraying in the centre of the repair area and then, using a circular motion, work out until the whole repair area and about two inches of the surrounding original paint is covered. Remove all masking material 10 to 15 minutes after spraying on the final coat of paint. Allow the new paint at least two weeks to harden, then use a very fine rubbing compound to blend the edges of the new paint into the existing paint. Finally, apply a coat of wax.

6   Body repair - major damage

1   Major damage must be repaired by an auto body shop specifically equipped to perform unibody repairs. These shops have the specialized equipment required to do the job properly.

2   If the damage is extensive, the body

9.10 Loosen the bonnet latch bolts, move the latch and retighten bolts, then close the bonnet to check the fit - repeat the procedure until the bonnet is flush with the fenders

must be checked for proper alignment or the vehicle's handling characteristics may be adversely affected and other components may wear at an accelerated rate.

3   Due to the fact that all of the major body components (bonnet, fenders, etc.) are separate and replaceable units, any seriously damaged components should be replaced rather than repaired. Sometimes the components can be found in a wrecking yard that specializes in used vehicle components, often at considerable savings over the cost of new parts.

7   Hinges and locks - maintenance

Once every 5000 kilometres, or every three months, the hinges and latch assemblies on the doors, bonnet and boot should be given a few drops of light oil or lock lubricant. The door latch strikers should also be lubricated with a thin coat of grease to reduce wear and ensure free movement. Lubricate the door and boot locks with spray-on graphite lubricant.

9.11 Adjust the bonnet height by screwing the bonnet bumpers in-or-out

8   Windscreen and fixed glass - replacement

Replacement of the windscreen and fixed glass requires the use of special fast-setting adhesive/caulk materials and some specialized tools. It is recommended that these operations be left to a dealer or a shop specializing in glass work.

9   Bonnet - removal, installation and adjustment

Refer to illustrations 9.1, 9.10 and 9.11

Note: *The bonnet is heavy and somewhat awkward to remove and install - at least two people should perform this procedure.*

Removal and installation

1   Make marks around the hinge plate to ensure proper alignment during installation **(see illustration)**.

2   Use blankets or pads to cover the cowl area of the body and fenders. This will protect the body and paint as the bonnet is lifted off.

3   Disconnect any cables or wires that will interfere with removal. On some models, it may be necessary to remove the lower two bonnet insulation retaining pins and peel the insulation back enough to disconnect the windscreen washer hoses.

4   Have an assistant support one side of the bonnet while you support the other. Simultaneously remove the hinge-to-bonnet bolts.

5   Lift off the bonnet.

6   Installation is the reverse of removal.

Adjustment

7   Fore-and-aft and side-to-side adjustment of the bonnet is done by moving the hinge plate slot after loosening the bolts.

8   Scribe a line around the entire hinge plate so you can judge the amount of movement **(see illustration 9.1)**

9   Loosen the bolts or nuts and move the bonnet into correct alignment. Move it only a little at a time. Tighten the hinge bolts and carefully lower the bonnet to check the position.

10   If necessary after installation, the entire bonnet latch assembly can be adjusted up-and-down as well as from side-to-side on the radiator support so the bonnet closes securely, flush with the fenders. To make the adjustment, scribe a line around the bonnet latch mounting bolts to provide a reference point, then loosen them and reposition the latch assembly, as necessary **(see illustration)**. Following adjustment, retighten the mounting bolts.

11   Finally, adjust the bonnet bumpers on the radiator support or bonnet so when closed, it is flush with the fenders **(see illustration)**.

12   The bonnet latch assembly, as well as the hinges, should be periodically lubricated with white, lithium-base grease to prevent binding and wear.

These photos illustrate a method of repairing simple dents. They are intended to supplement *Body repair - minor damage* in this Chapter and should not be used as the sole instructions for body repair on these vehicles.

1 If you can't access the backside of the body panel to hammer out the dent, pull it out with a slide-hammer-type dent puller. In the deepest portion of the dent or along the crease line, drill or punch hole(s) at least one inch apart . . .

2 . . . then screw the slide-hammer into the hole and operate it. Tap with a hammer near the edge of the dent to help 'pop' the metal back to its original shape. When you're finished, the dent area should be close to its original contour and about 1/8-inch below the surface of the surrounding metal

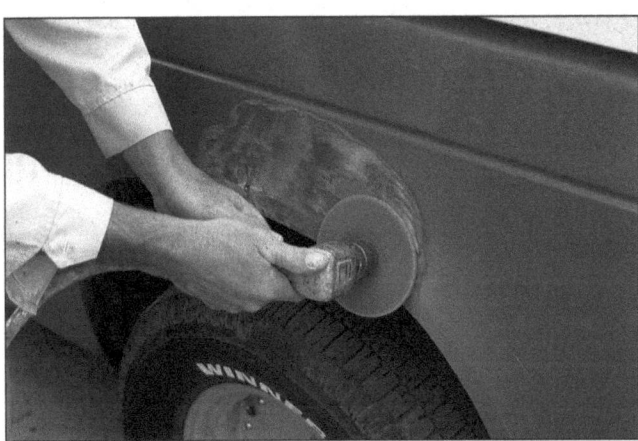

3 Using coarse-grit sandpaper, remove the paint down to the bare metal. Hand sanding works fine, but the disc sander shown here makes the job faster. Use finer (about 320-grit) sandpaper to feather-edge the paint at least one inch around the dent area

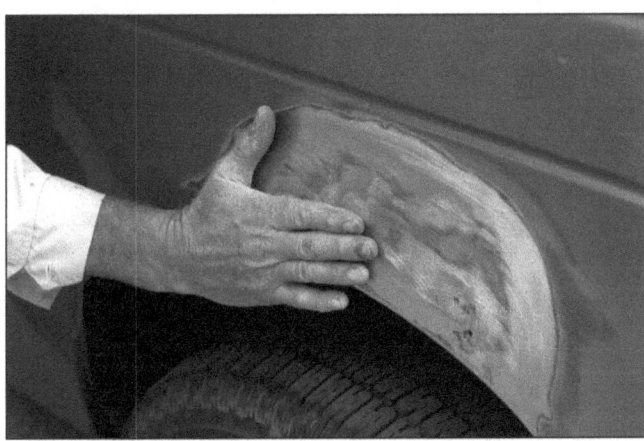

4 When the paint is removed, touch will probably be more helpful than sight for telling if the metal is straight. Hammer down the high spots or raise the low spots as necessary. Clean the repair area with wax/silicone remover

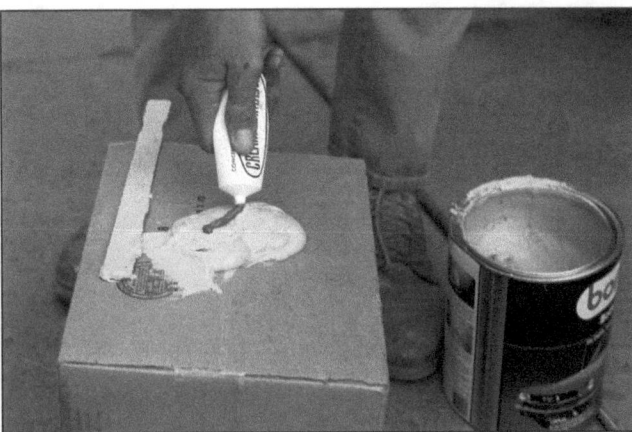

5 Following label instructions, mix up a batch of plastic filler and hardener. The ratio of filler to hardener is critical, and, if you mix it incorrectly, it will either not cure properly or cure too quickly (you won't have time to file and sand it into shape)

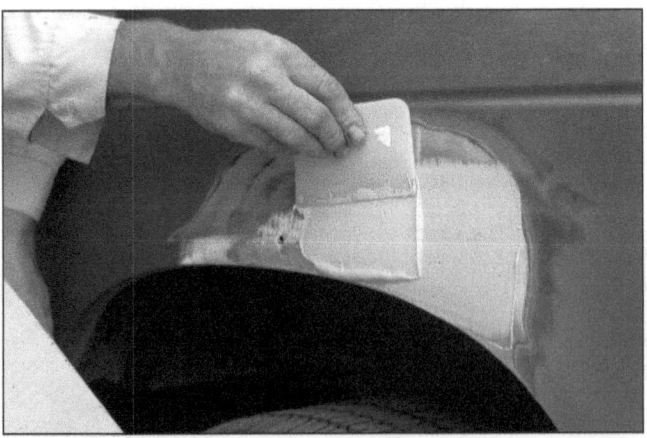

6 Working quickly so the filler doesn't harden, use a plastic applicator to press the body filler firmly into the metal, assuring it bonds completely. Work the filler until it matches the original contour and is slightly above the surrounding metal

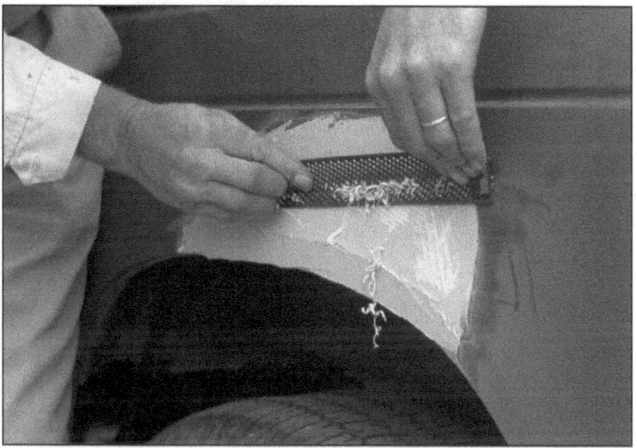

7 Let the filler harden until you can just dent it with your fingernail. Use a body file or Surform tool (shown here) to rough-shape the filler

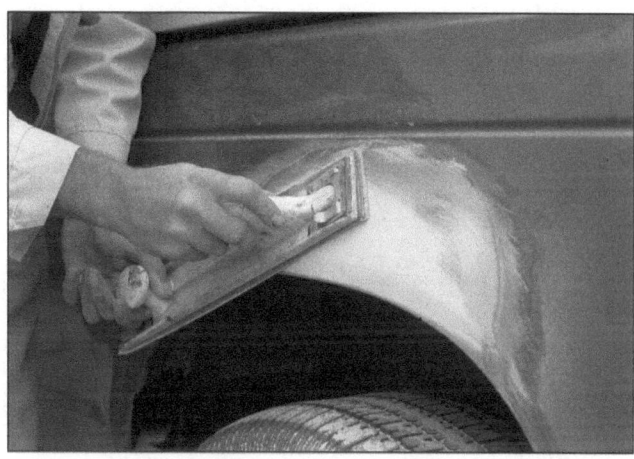

8 Use coarse-grit sandpaper and a sanding board or block to work the filler down until it's smooth and even. Work down to finer grits of sandpaper - always using a board or block - ending up with 360 or 400 grit

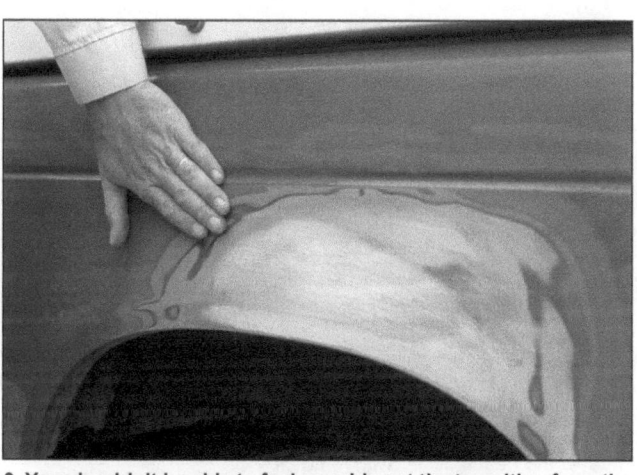

9 You shouldn't be able to feel any ridge at the transition from the filler to the bare metal or from the bare metal to the old paint. As soon as the repair is flat and uniform, remove the dust and mask off the adjacent panels or trim pieces

10 Apply several layers of primer to the area. Don't spray the primer on too heavy, so it sags or runs, and make sure each coat is dry before you spray on the next one. A professional-type spray gun is being used here, but aerosol spray primer is available inexpensively from auto parts stores

11 The primer will help reveal imperfections or scratches. Fill these with glazing compound. Follow the label instructions and sand it with 360 or 400-grit sandpaper until it's smooth. Repeat the glazing, sanding and respraying until the primer reveals a perfectly smooth surface

12 Finish sand the primer with very fine sandpaper (400 or 600-grit) to remove the primer overspray. Clean the area with water and allow it to dry. Use a tack rag to remove any dust, then apply the finish coat. Don't attempt to rub out or wax the repair area until the paint has dried completely (at least two weeks)

10.2 Remove the plastic retainers and the boot lid trim panel

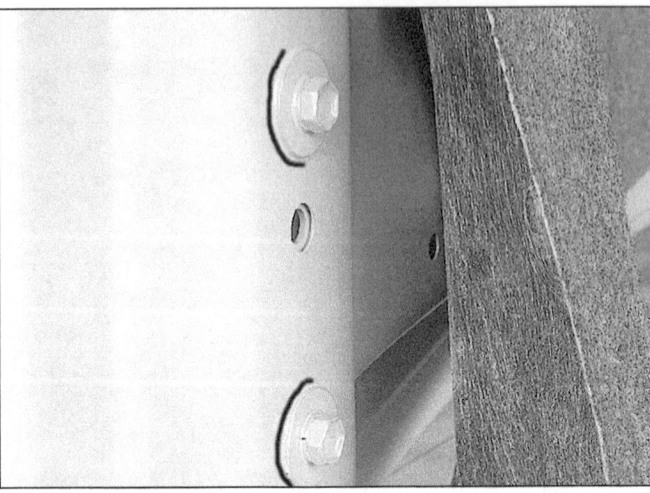

10.3 Draw a mark around the bolt heads to help with lid realignment on installation

10 Boot lid - removal, installation and adjustment

Refer to illustrations 10.2, 10.3 and 10.8

1   Open the boot lid and cover the edges of the boot compartment with pads or cloths to protect the painted surfaces when the lid is removed.

2   Open the boot lid and remove the boot lid trim cover **(see illustrations)**. Follow the wiring harness into the boot lid, mark and disconnect all electrical connectors, then pull the harness out of the lid.

3   Make alignment marks around the hinge mounting bolts **(see illustration)**.

4   While an assistant supports the lid, remove the lid-to-hinge bolts on both sides and lift it off.

5   Installation is the reverse of removal. **Note:** *When reinstalling the boot lid, align the lid-to-hinge bolts with the marks made during removal.*

6   After installation, close the lid and make sure it's in proper alignment with the surrounding panels.

7   Forward-and-backward and side-to-side adjustments are made by loosening the hinge-to-lid bolts and gently moving the lid into correct alignment.

8   To adjust the lid so it is flush with the body when closed, loosen the mounting bolts and move the lock and striker **(see illustration)**.

11 Liftgate (wagon and hatchback) - removal, installation and adjustment

Refer to illustrations 11.2, 11.3 and 11.9

Note: *The liftgate is heavy and somewhat awkward to remove and install - at least two people should perform this procedure.*

1   Open the liftgate and cover the edges of the compartment with pads or cloths to protect the painted surfaces when the lid is removed.

2   Open the liftgate/hatch and remove the boot lid trim cover **(see illustration)**. Disconnect any cables or wire harness connectors attached to the liftgate that would interfere

10.8 Loosen the bolts, then adjust the latch and striker position

with removal.

3   Use a marking pen to make alignment marks around the hinge mounting flanges **(see illustration)**.

4   Have an assistant support the liftgate and detach the support struts (see Section 12).

11.2 Carefully prise the hatch cover back and remove the plastic retainers and the cover - back side of the hatch cover shown with clips (arrows)

11.3 Draw lines at the hinge plate on the liftgate before removing the bolts

11.9 Adjust the lock striker by loosening the mounting screws slightly and tapping the striker with a soft-faced hammer

12.1a Using a small screwdriver remove the upper clip (arrow) . . .

12.1b . . . and then the lower clip (arrow)

5   While an assistant supports the liftgate, remove the lid-to-hinge bolts on both sides and lift it off.

6   Installation is the reverse of removal. **Note:** *When reinstalling the liftgate, align the hinges with the marks made during removal.*

7   After installation, close the liftgate and make sure it's in proper alignment with the surrounding panels.

8   Adjustments to the liftgate position are made by loosening the hinge-to-liftgate bolts or nuts and gently moving the liftgate into correct alignment.

9   The liftgate latch position can be adjusted by loosening the adjusting bolts and moving the latch. The latch striker can be adjusted by loosening the mounting screws and gently tapping it into position with a plastic hammer **(see illustration)**.

12   Liftgate support strut - replacement

Refer to illustrations 12.1a and 12.1b

Warning: *The support strut is filled with pressurized gas - do not disassemble this component. If it is faulty replace it with a new one.*
Note: *The liftgate is heavy and somewhat awkward to hold securely while replacing the struts - at least two people should perform*

this procedure.

1   Open the liftgate and support it in the open position. Remove the clips at the ends and detach the strut from the liftgate **(see illustrations)**.

2   Installation is the reverse of the removal procedure.

13   Door trim panel - removal and installation

Refer to illustrations 13.2a, 13.2b, 13.2c, 13.5a, 13.5b, 13.6 and 13.8

Caution: *If the stereo in your vehicle is equipped with an anti-theft system, make sure you have the correct activation code before disconnecting the battery.*

Removal

1   Disconnect the negative cable from the battery.

2   On manual window regulator equipped models, remove the window crank by working a cloth back-and-forth behind the handle to dislodge the retaining clip **(see illustrations)**. A special tool is available for this purpose but it's not essential. With the retainer removed, pull off the handle. On power window models,

13.2a Work a cloth up behind the regulator handle and move it back-and-forth . . .

pry out the switch assembly, unplug the electrical connector and remove it **(see illustration)**.

3   Remove the outside mirror trim cover (see Section 18).

4   Remove the inside door handle trim piece. One of the screws securing the door panel is in the handle trim.

5   Pry up the armrest panel with a trim tool and remove the two door panel screws under the armrest **(see illustrations)**.

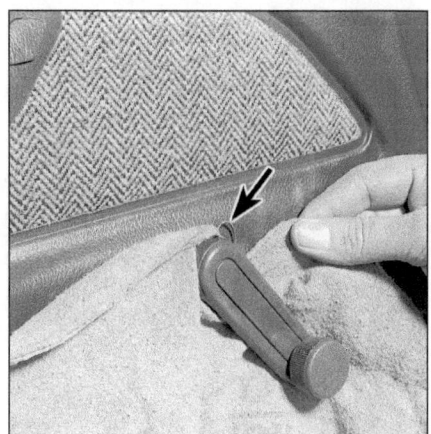

13.2b . . . until the retaining clip is pushed up so you can remove it

13.2c Pry up on the power window switch and disconnect the electrical connector

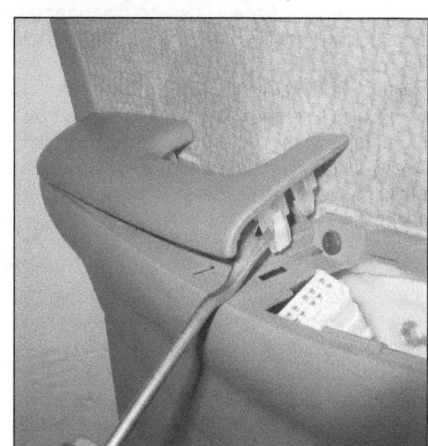

13.5a Pry the armrest up with a screwdriver or trim tool . . .

13.5b . . . and remove the door panel screws

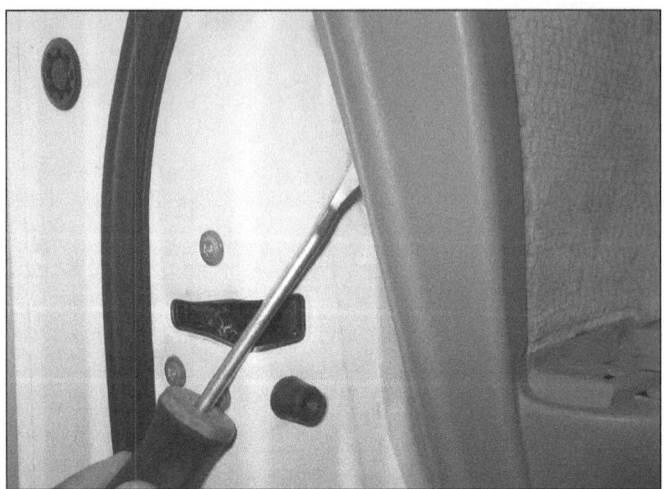

13.6 Use a trim panel removal tool to detach the trim panel retaining clips, then pull the door trim up and out to remove it

13.8 If the plastic watershield is peeled off carefully it can be reused

14.2 Use two jackstands padded with rags (to protect the paint) to support the door during the removal and installation procedures

6   Insert a wide putty knife, a thin screw-driver or a special trim panel removal tool between the trim panel and door to disengage the retaining clips. Work around the outer edge until the panel is free **(see illustration)**.

7   Once all of the clips are disengaged, detach the trim panel, unplug any electrical connectors and remove the trim panel from the vehicle by gently pulling it up and out.

8   For access to the inner door remove the plastic watershield. Peel back the plastic cover, taking care not to tear it **(see illustra-tion)**. Remove the plastic grommets, if neces-sary.

Installation

9   To install the trim panel, first press the watershield back into place. If necessary, add more sealant to hold it in place.

10   Prior to installation of the door panel, be sure to reinstall any clips in the panel which may have come out during the removal proce-dure and stayed in the door.

11   Plug in any electrical connectors and place the panel in position. Press it into place

until the clips are seated and install any retain-ing screws and armrest/door pulls. Install the manual regulator window crank or power switch assembly.

14   Door - removal, installation and adjustment

Removal and installation

Refer to illustrations 14.2, 14.3 and 14.4

1   Remove the door trim panel (see Sec-tion 13). Disconnect any electrical connectors and push them through the door opening so they won't interfere with removal.

2   Position a jack or jackstands under the door or have an assistant on hand to support the door when the hinge bolts are removed **(see illustration)**. **Note:** *If a jack or stand is used, place a rag between it and the door to protect the door's paint.*

3   Remove the door stop strut bolt **(see illustration)**.

4   Draw a mark around the hinges to aid in alignment **(see illustration)**.

5   Remove the hinge-to-door bolts and carefully detach the door. Installation is the reverse of removal.

14.3 Remove the bolt and detach the stop strut

14.4 Mark the position of each hinge to the door, then remove the hinge bolts

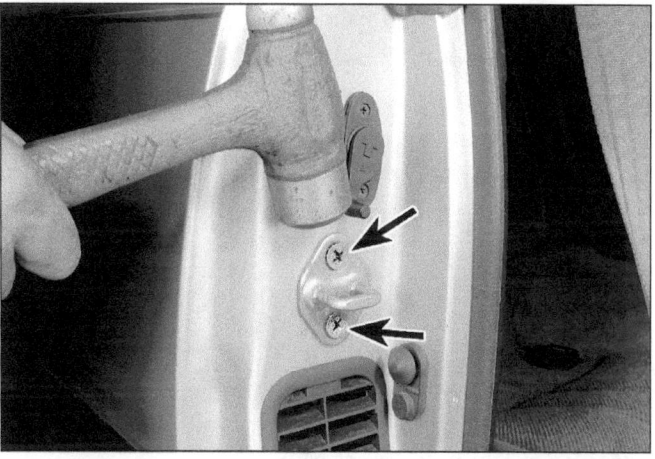

14.6 Adjust the door lock striker by loosening the mounting screws and gently tapping the striker in the desired direction

Adjustment

Refer to illustration 14.6

6   Following installation, make sure the door is aligned properly. Adjust it if necessary as follows:

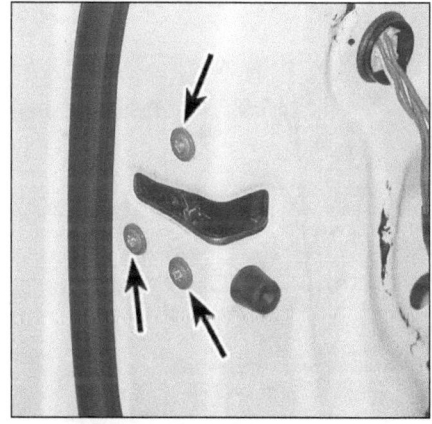

15.3 Remove the latch screws from the end of the door

a) *Up-and-down and forward-and-backward adjustments are made by loosening the hinge-to-body bolts and moving the door, as necessary. A special offset tool may be required to reach some of the bolts.*

b) *In-and-out and up-and-down adjustments are made by loosening the door side hinge bolts and moving the door, as necessary. A special offset tool may be required to reach some of the bolts.*

c) *The door lock striker can also be adjusted both up-and-down and sideways to provide a positive engagement with the locking mechanism. This is done by loosening the screws and moving the striker, as necessary* **(see illustration)**.

---

15 Door latch, lock cylinder and handles - removal and installation

---

1   Remove the door trim panel and the plastic water shield (see Section 13).

Door latch

Refer to illustration 15.3

2   Reach inside the door and disconnect the control links from the latch.
3   Remove the latch retaining screws from the end of the door **(see illustration)**.
4   Detach the door latch and (if equipped) the door lock solenoid.
5   Installation is the reverse of removal.

Lock cylinder and outside handle

Refer to illustrations 15.7 and 15.8

6   Working through the access holes in the door, disconnect the control rods from the lock cylinder and outside handle.
7   Loosen the screw with a Torx bit and pull the lock cover and lock cylinder from the outside of the door **(see illustration)**.
8   To remove the outside handle, disconnect the control rod and remove the two mounting screws inside the door **(see illustration)**.

15.7 Remove the plastic cover, and the outside handle cover/lock cylinder retention screw can be reached through the access in the door frame

15.8 Disconnect the rod and fasteners from the outside handle (shown inside door)

15.13a Rotate the handle clips out of the door and pull the handle assembly away

9   If the outside handle assembly is to be replaced, disconnect the rod and door operating cable from the handle assembly and transfer them to the new handle.
10   Use a screwdriver to pry the retaining clip off or remove the lock cylinder retaining

bolt and remove the lock cylinder from the handle.
11   Installation is the reverse of removal.

Inside handle

Refer to illustrations 15.13a and 15.13b

12   Remove the retaining screw **(see illustration 13.5b)**.
13   Pull the handle free, disconnect the cables from the inside handle control and remove the handle from the door **(see illustrations)**.
14   Installation is the reverse of removal.

---

16   Door window glass - removal and installation

Refer to illustrations 16.2 and 16.4

1   Remove the door trim panel and the plastic watershield (see Section 13).
2   Lower the window glass. Remove the door access plate from the door frame **(see illustration)**.

3   Carefully pry the inner weatherstrip out of the door window opening.
4   Place a rag inside the door panel to help prevent scratching the glass, then remove the two glass mounting bolts **(see illustration)**.
5   Remove the glass by pulling it up.
6   Installation is the reverse of the removal procedure.

---

17   Bumper covers - removal and installation

Warning: *The models covered by this manual are equipped with Supplemental Restraint systems (SRS), more commonly known as airbags. Always disable the airbag system before working in the vicinity of any airbag system component to avoid the possibility of accidental deployment of the airbag, which could cause personal injury (see Chapter 12).*
Caution: *If the stereo in your vehicle is equipped with an anti-theft system, make sure you have the correct activation code before disconnecting the battery.*

15.13b Detach the control cables with a small screwdriver

16.2 Remove the screws and this plate for access to one of the glass mounting bolts

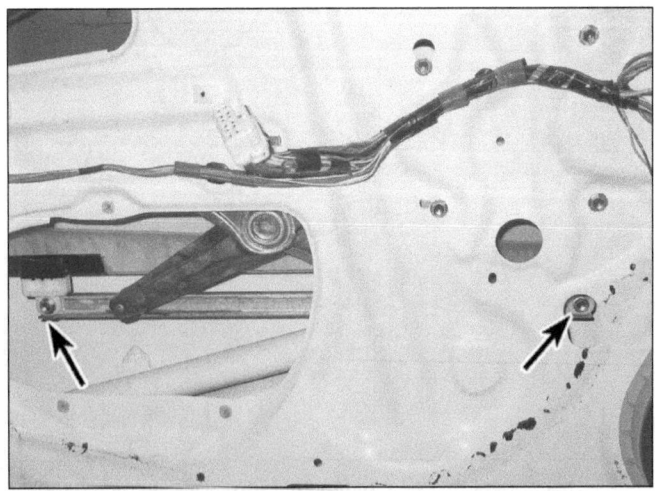

16.4 Location of glass mounting bolts

17.3a Remove the fasteners and the inner fenderwell liner

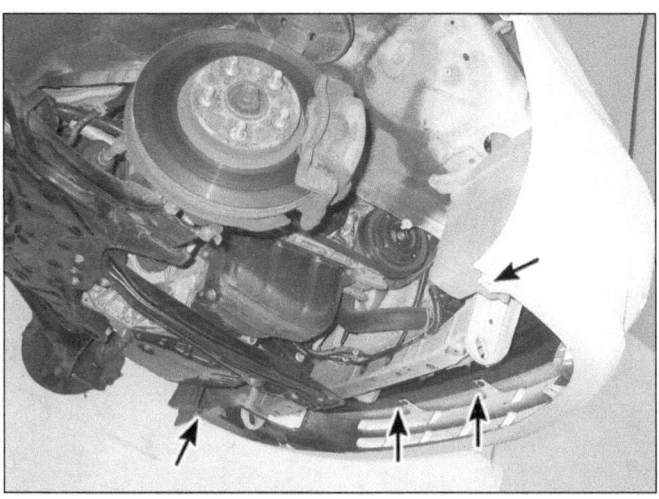

17.3b From below (shown without engine splash panels) remove the screws and plastic pins securing the bumper cover

17.3c Remove the two screws (one shown) at either side of the grille - these screws also secure the bumper cover

Front bumper

Refer to illustrations 17.3a, 17.3b, 17.3c and 17.4

1   Apply the parking brake, raise the vehicle and support it securely on jackstands.

2   Disconnect the negative battery cable, then the positive battery cable and wait two minutes before proceeding any further. On models equipped with fog lights, disconnect the electrical connectors at the fog lights on the back of the bumper fascia.

3   Detach the screws and/or pushpins securing the top, bottom, sides and top of the bumper cover **(see illustrations)**. **Note 1:** *Use a small screwdriver to pop the centre button up on the plastic fasteners, but do not try to remove the centre buttons. They stay in the ferrules.* **Note 2:** *Don't try to remove the cover until all fasteners have been located and removed.*

4   If the bumper beam itself is to be replaced, remove the nuts and pull the beam off its mounts **(see illustration)**.

5   Installation is the reverse of removal. Make sure the tabs on the back of the bumper cover fit into the corresponding clips on the body before attaching the bolts and screws. An assistant would be helpful at this point.

17.3d On models where the grille is part of the bumper cover, the centre plastic pin (arrow) must be removed to allow the cover to be removed

Rear bumper

Refer to illustrations 17.6, 17.7, 17.8a and 17.8b

6   Working under the vehicle, detach the plastic clips and screws securing the lower edge of the bumper cover **(see illustration)**.

17.4 Front bumper beam mounting nuts (access through holes)

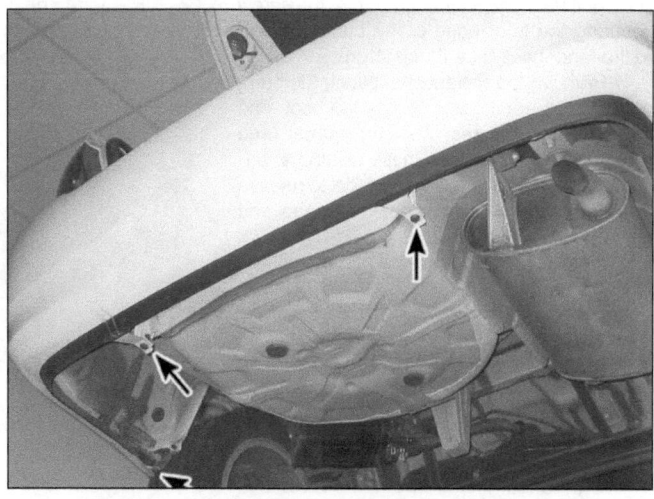

17.6 Remove the fasteners securing the bottom lip of the rear bumper cover

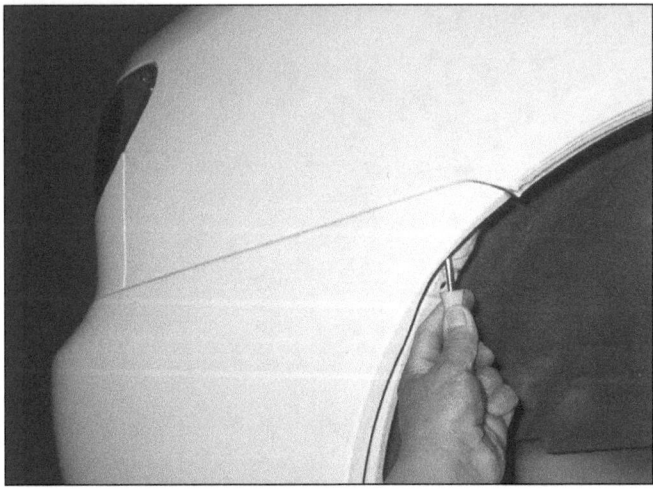

17.7 With the rear of the fenderwell liner pulled back, you can access the one bumper cover screw on each side

17.8a Pry out the plastic fasteners (three shown) and remove the left and right side trim panels in the boot

17.8b With a socket and extension remove the rear bumper cover mounting nuts through the body holes (three of the four are seen here)

18.1a On manually operated side view mirrors, remove the screw and detach the mirror control handle

7   In the rear fenderwells, remove the fasteners securing the rear of the fenderwell liner, pull back the liner and remove the screw securing the front edge of the bumper cover to the fenderwell **(see illustration)**.

8   Remove the fasteners securing the bumper cover in each corner inside the boot, and those behind the rear boot trim panel **(see illustrations)**. To access these fasteners, pull up the boot mat, then use a trim tool to release the clips securing the rear boot trim panel and the left and right rear corner panels.

9   Installation is the reverse of removal.

18   Outside mirror - removal and installation

Refer to illustrations 18.1a, 18.1b, 18.2a and 18.2b

1   On manually operated mirrors, remove the control handle **(see illustration)**. On all models, detach the mirror cover by using

a small screwdriver to pry the retainers free from the door **(see illustration)**.

2   Remove the three retaining nuts and detach the mirror **(see illustration)**. On power

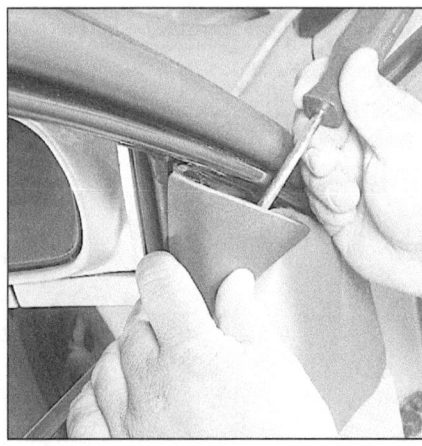

18.1b Detach the cover and lift it out (power mirror shown)

mirrors, unplug the electrical connector **(see illustration)**.

3   Installation is the reverse of removal.

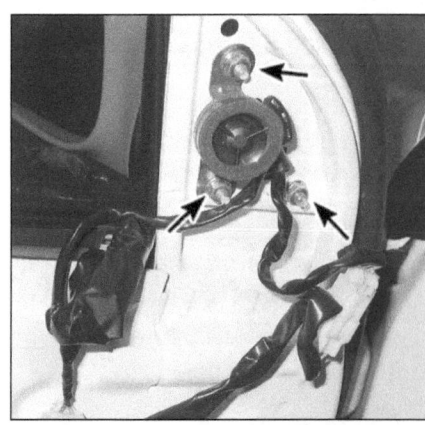

18.2a Remove the three nuts securing the outside mirror to the door - on some models, the nuts also secure a small speaker

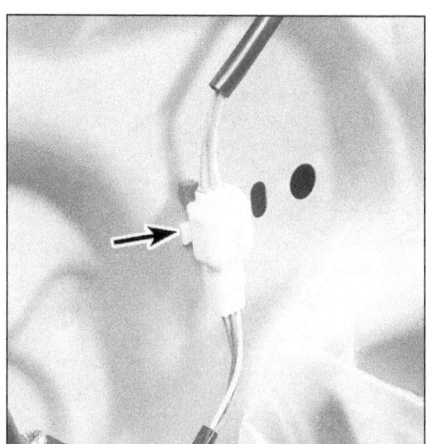

18.2b On vehicles equipped with power side view mirrors, unplug the electrical connector

19.1a Slide the seat rearward and remove the front mounting bolts

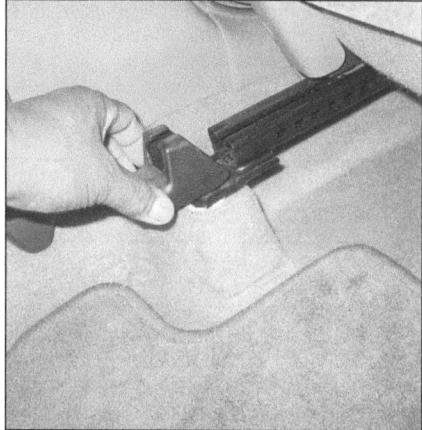

19.1b Slide the seat forward and remove the two covers over the tracks, then remove the two seat mounting bolts

19 Seats - removal and installation

Warning: *These models are equipped with airbags. Always disable the airbag system before working in the vicinity of any airbag system component to avoid the possibility of accidental deployment of the airbag(s), which could cause personal injury (see Chapter 12).*

Front seats

Refer to illustration 19.1a and 19.1b

1   Pry off the seat bolt covers, if equipped, and remove the retaining bolts, unplug any electrical connectors and lift the seats from the vehicle **(see illustrations)**.

2   Installation is the reverse of removal.

Rear seats

Refer to illustrations 19.3, 19.5. 19.6a and 19.6b

3   Lift the front of the cushion up, then pull it out toward the front of the vehicle **(see illustration)**.

4   On models with a one-piece seatback, remove the seat back retaining bolts at the floor, then lift up on the back to release the seat back from the body.

5   On models with a split-back rear seat, open the boot and release the two seatback cables, allowing the seatbacks to fold down **(see illustrations)**.

6   Remove the bolts in the middle securing the seat-back assembly to the floor **(see illustration)**. Lift each section up and out to disengage its pins from the brackets at each side.

7   Installation is the reverse of removal.

20 Instrument cluster bezel - removal and installation

Refer to illustrations 20.2a and 20.2b

Warning: *These models are equipped with airbags. Always disable the airbag system before working in the vicinity of any airbag system component to avoid the possibility of accidental deployment of the airbag(s), which could cause personal injury (see Chapter 12).*

Caution: *If the stereo in your vehicle is equipped with an anti-theft system, make sure*

19.3 Pull up on the seat bottom to release the one clip at each side

you have the correct activation code before disconnecting the battery.

1   Disconnect the cable from the negative battery terminal.

2   Tilt the steering column to its lowest position. Remove the one pushpin at the top of the bezel, then detach the bezel clips at the

19.5 On split-back models, pull the release cables for each half of the seatback

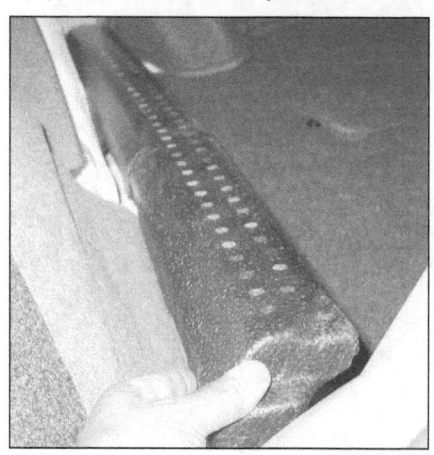

19.6a With the split seat-backs folded down, pull back the carpet and remove this trim piece

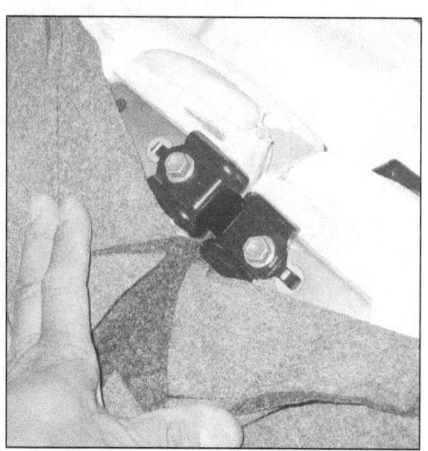

19.6b Remove the mounting bolts securing the seat-backs to the floor - centre bolts shown

lower edges by prying with a screwdriver to release the clips **(see illustrations)**.

3   Grasp the bezel securely and remove it.
4   Installation is the reverse of the removal procedure.

21 Glove box - removal and installation

Refer to illustration 21.1

Warning: *These models are equipped with airbags. Always disable the airbag system before working in the vicinity of any airbag system component to avoid the possibility of accidental deployment of the airbag(s), which could cause personal injury* (see Chapter 12).

1   Open the glove box and remove the screw at the lower right corner **(see illustration)**.
2   Squeeze the sides of the glove box toward the centre enough to clear the stoppers on each side. Remove the glove box.
3   Installation is the reverse of removal.

22 Centre trim panels - removal and installation

Warning: *These models are equipped with airbags. Always disable the airbag system before working in the vicinity of any airbag system component to avoid the possibility of accidental deployment of the airbag(s), which could cause personal injury* (see Chapter 12).

Caution: *If the stereo in your vehicle is equipped with an anti-theft system, make sure you have the correct activation code before disconnecting the battery.*

1   Disconnect the cable from the negative battery terminal.

Lower trim panel

Refer to illustrations 22.3, 22.4a and 22.4b

2   Refer to Section 23 and remove the top trim panel at the front of the floor console.

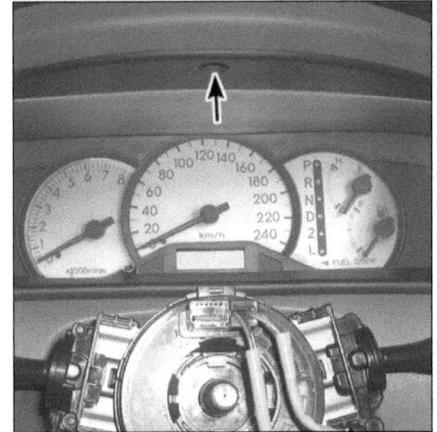

20.2a Remove the one pushpin fastener at the centre-top of the instrument bezel

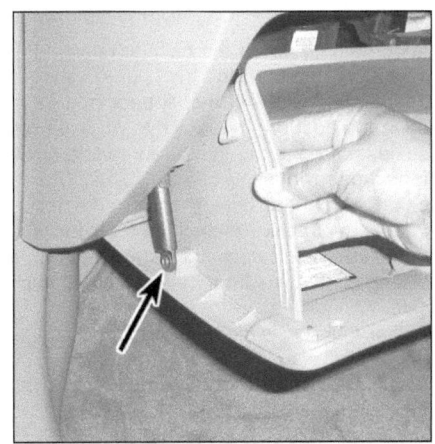

21.1 Remove the stop screw at the right side of the glove box

3   Remove the centre knob from the heating/air-conditioning control panel, then remove the screw behind it **(see illustration)**.
4   Using a small screwdriver, detach the retaining clips at each corner, then remove the panel and unplug the electrical connectors **(see illustrations)**.

20.2b Pop the centre out of the pushpin, then remove it from the bezel

22.3 Pull off this knob for access to the panel screw behind it

Upper trim panel

Refer to illustrations 22.6 and 22.7

5   Follow the Steps above and remove the lower trim panel.
6   Remove the screws at the bottom of the panel, then pry the panel from its clips with a

22.4a Use a trim tool to release the clips holding the lower trim panel and pull it out

22.4b After the lower centre trim panel is detached from the instrument panel, disconnect the electrical connectors at the back

22.6 Remove the four bolts at the bottom of the upper trim panel - the other fasteners are clips

22.7 Pull the upper panel out far enough to disconnect the electrical connectors and the aerial cable

trim tool or taped screwdriver **(see illustration)**.

7   Pull the upper trim panel out and unplug the electrical connectors and aerial cable from the radio **(see illustration)**.

8   Installation is the reverse of the removal procedure.

23.1 Remove the lower column cover screws (steering wheel removed for clarity)

23   Steering column covers - removal and installation

Refer to illustration 23.1

Warning: *These models are equipped with airbags. Always disable the airbag system before working in the vicinity of any airbag system component to avoid the possibility of accidental deployment of the airbag(s), which could cause personal injury* (see Chapter 12).

1   Remove the screws securing the lower steering column cover **(see illustration)**.
Note: *These models have three screws in the lower cover (two mounted horizontally and one mounted vertically). It will be necessary to rotate the steering wheel in order to access the forward facing (horizontally mounted) screws on the lower cover.*

2   Separate the cover halves and detach them from the steering column.

3   Disconnect any electrical connections and the covers.

4   Installation is the reverse of the removal procedure.

24   Console - removal and installation

Refer to illustrations 24.2, 24.3a, 24.3b and 24.4

Warning: *These models are equipped with airbags. Always disable the airbag system before working in the vicinity of any airbag system component to avoid the possibility of accidental deployment of the airbag(s), which could cause personal injury* (see Chapter 12).
Caution: *If the stereo in your vehicle is equipped with an anti-theft system, make sure you have the correct activation code before disconnecting the battery.*

1   Disconnect the cable from the negative battery terminal.

2   Lift up the console armrest and remove the retaining screws from the storage compartment, then remove the mounting screws **(see illustration)**.

3   Detach the shift bezel, using a plastic trim tool, then disconnect the 12-volt power source connector **(see illustrations)**.

24.2 Remove the retaining screws in the console storage box

24.3a Carefully pry up the shift bezel to release the clips . . .

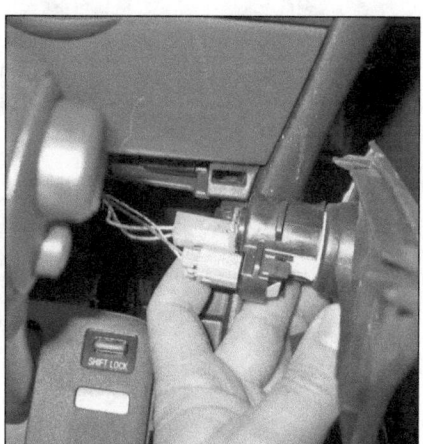

24.3b . . . then pull up the bezel and disconnect the electrical connector

24.4 Remove the four screws securing the front portion of the console to the floor, then disconnect the electrical connector

25.3 Typical passenger side airbag module electrical connector

4   Remove the four screws, disconnect the electrical connector and remove the floor console **(see illustration)**.

5   Installation is the reverse of the removal procedure.

25   Instrument panel - removal and installation

Warning: *These models are equipped with airbags. Always disable the airbag system before working in the vicinity of any airbag system component to avoid the possibility of accidental deployment of the airbag(s), which could cause personal injury (see Chapter 12).*
Note: *This procedure requires the removal of the instrument panel, the cross-cowl support tube and steering column. This involves disconnecting numerous electrical connectors and there is the potential for breakage of delicate plastic tabs on various components. This is a difficult job for the average home mechanic.*

Caution: *If the stereo in your vehicle is equipped with an anti-theft system, make sure you have the correct activation code before disconnecting the battery.*

Instrument panel

Refer to illustrations 25.3, 25.8, 25.10, 25.11, 25.12, 25.13 and 25.14

1   Disconnect the cable from the negative battery terminal.

2   Remove the driver's airbag module and the steering wheel (see Chapter 10).

3   Remove the glove box assembly (see Section 19), disconnect the passenger airbag module electrical connector **(see illustration)**. The electrical connectors used in the airbag system are a twin-lock design; use the proper method for disconnecting these connectors or damage to the connector may occur (see Chapter 12).

4   Remove the instrument cluster bezel (see Section 20) and remove the instrument cluster (see Chapter 12).

5   Remove the centre trim panels (see Sec-

tion 22) and the heater and air conditioning control panel (see Chapter 3).

6   Remove the steering column covers (see Section 23).

7   Remove the centre console (see Section 24).

8   Remove the front door scuff plates and the kick panels from both sides **(see illustration)**.

9   Pry out the left and right air vents in the upper instrument panel.

10   Use a trim tool to remove the left and right trim pieces along the inside of the windscreen pillars **(see illustration)**.

11   Remove the three fasteners and release the clips, then remove the upper instrument panel **(see illustration)**. Be sure to disconnect any electrical connectors attached behind the upper instrument panel.

12   On the right side of the lower instrument panel, disconnect and remove the release handle for the bonnet **(see illustration)**. Also, separate the diagnostic connector under the right edge of the instrument panel.

25.8 Pry up the scuff plate from the sill, then remove the one screw and the kick panel (right-side shown)

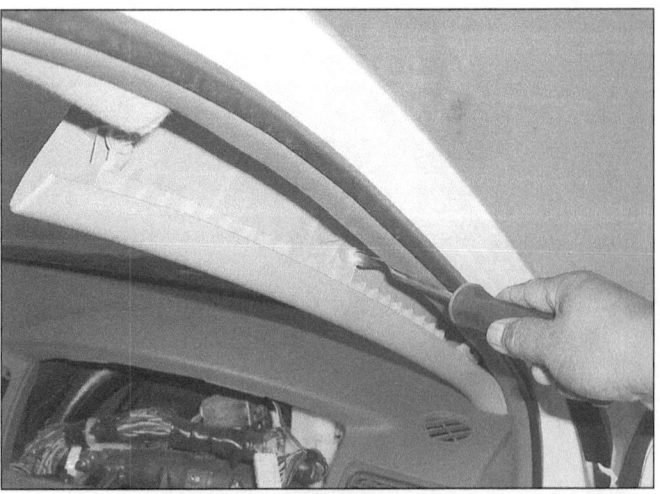

25.10 Carefully pry off the windscreen pillar trim panels

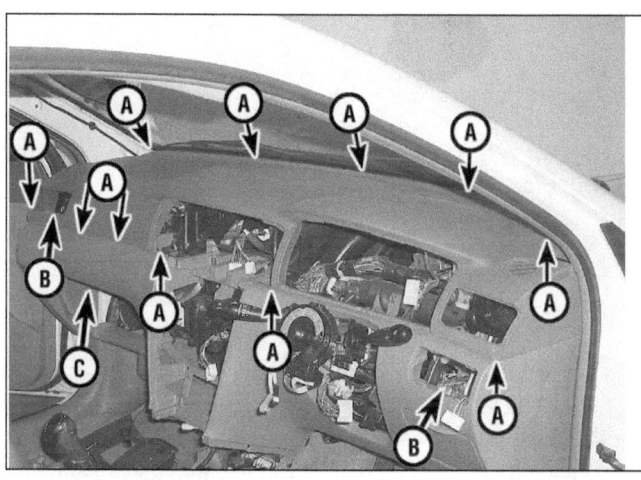

25.11 Indicated here are the clips (A), screws (B) and the one mounting bolt (C) for removal of the upper instrument panel

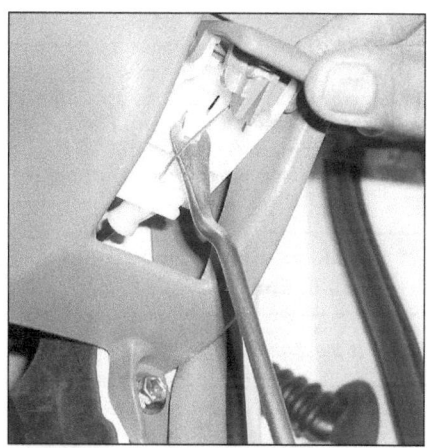

25.12 Pry open the clip and release the cable end from the bonnet release handle, then pry the plastic housing from the lower instrument panel

13   Pry up the plastic pins securing the vent ducts at the centre and each side of the lower instrument panel **(see illustration)**.

14   Remove the fasteners and remove the lower instrument panel **(see illustration)**. Do not force the panel off, make sure you have found all the fasteners first. Make notes and use plastic bags to keep track of which fasteners go where.

15   The remainder of installation is the reverse of removal.

Cowl reinforcement beam

Refer to illustrations 25.16, 25.17a, 25.17b, 25.17c and 25.18

16   If the cowl reinforcement beam must be removed for a service procedure, follow Steps 1 through 15, then proceed to disconnect all components fastened to the reinforcement beam **(see illustration)**.

17   Disconnect the electrical connectors at the steering column and remove the bolts securing the column to the beam **(see illustrations)**.

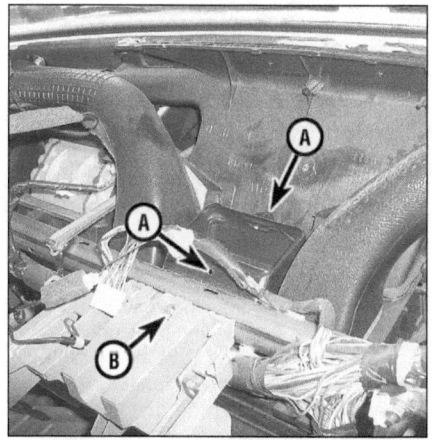

25.13 Remove the pins (A) securing the left, right and centre (shown) ducts - also remove the centre bolt (B) securing the lower instrument panel to the reinforcement tube

25.14 Location of lower instrument panel screws (A) and pins (B)

25.16 Go along the width of the beam, disconnecting electrical components bolted to the beam and harnesses attached with pins

25.17a Remove the bolts and this reinforcement plate below the steering column

18   At the left and right sides of the beam, remove the bolts holding braces from the tube to other components, then remove the two bolts holding the beam into the body saddles at either end **(see illustration)**. Remove the beam from the vehicle.

19   Installation is the reverse of removal.

26   Radiator grille - removal and installation

Refer to illustration 26.1

Note: *On later models the radiator grille is part of the front bumper cover (see Section 19) for removal.*

1   Remove three fasteners along the top of the grille **(see illustration)**.

2   Pull the top of the grille out for access and disengage the lower retaining clips with a screwdriver.

3   Installation is the reverse of removal.

27   Cowl louver panels - removal and installation

1   Mark the position of the windscreen wiper blades on the windscreen with a wax marking pen.

2   Remove the wiper arms (see Chapter 12).

3   With a trim tool, release the clips and peel up the cowl-to-bonnet rubber seal.

4   Remove the cowl louver retaining pins, disconnect the windscreen washer hoses and detach the cowl louver panels from the vehicle. **Note:** *Remove the right-side panel first, then the left.*

5   Installation is the reverse of removal. Make sure to align the wiper blades with the marks made during removal.

25.17b Remove the lower steering column mounting bolt . . .

28   Seat belts - check

1   Check the seat belts, buckles, latch plates and guide loops for any obvious damage or signs of wear.

2   Make sure the seat belt reminder light comes on when the key is turned on.

3   The seat belts are designed to lock up during a sudden stop or impact, yet allow free movement during normal driving. The retractors should hold the belt against your chest while driving and rewind the belt when the buckle is unlatched.

4   If any of the above checks reveal problems with the seat-belt system, replace parts as necessary.

29   Front fender - removal and installation

1   Raise the vehicle, support it securely on jackstands and remove the front wheel.

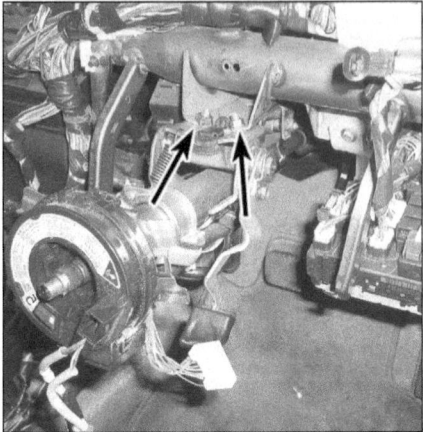

25.17c . . . and the two upper mounting bolts (upper captive nuts indicated, bolt heads are below bracket)

2   Remove the headlight housing (see Chapter 12).

3   Detach the inner fenderwell screws and clips, then remove the inner fenderwell liner **(see illustration 17.3a)**.

4   Open the front door, and remove the upper fender-to-body bolt and the one bolt inside the fenderwell.

5   Under the headlight housing area, remove the two fender fasteners.

6   Remove the cowl louver panel and the rubber bonnet sealing strip along the top of the fender, then remove the remaining fender mounting bolts.

7   Lift off the fender. It's a good idea to have an assistant support the fender while it's being moved away from the vehicle to prevent damage to the surrounding body panels.

8   Installation is the reverse of removal. Check the alignment of the fender to the bonnet and front edge of the door before final tightening of the fender fasteners.

25.18 At the right side of the beam, disconnect the brace to the blower housing (A), the two end mounting bolts (B), and the bottom screw (C). Then move to the left side and detach the braces and mounting bolts

26.1 Along the top of the grille, remove the screws at each side and the pushpin at the centre, then disengage the clips at the bottom and pull the grille forward and out

Chapter 12
Chassis electrical system

Contents

1 General information

The electrical system is a 12-volt, negative earth connection type. Power for the lights and all electrical accessories is supplied by a lead/acid-type battery, which is charged by the alternator.

This Chapter covers repair and service procedures for the various electrical components not associated with the engine. Information on the battery, alternator and starter motor can be found in Chapter 5.

It should be noted that when portions of the electrical system are serviced, the cable should be disconnected from the negative battery terminal to prevent electrical shorts and/or fires. **Caution:** *If the stereo in your vehicle is equipped with an anti-theft system, make sure you have the correct activation code before disconnecting the battery.*

2 Electrical troubleshooting - general information

Refer to illustrations 2.5a, 2.5b, 2.6 and 2.9

A typical electrical circuit consists of an electrical component, any switches, relays, motors, fuses, fusible links or circuit breakers related to that component and the wiring and connectors that link the component to both the battery and the chassis. To help you pinpoint an electrical circuit problem, wiring diagrams are included at the end of this Chapter.

Before tackling any troublesome electrical circuit, first study the appropriate wiring diagrams to get a complete understanding of what makes up that individual circuit. Trouble spots, for instance, can often be narrowed down by noting if other components related to the circuit are operating properly. If several components or circuits fail at one time, chances are the problem is in a fuse or earth connection, because several circuits are often routed through the same fuse and earth connections.

Electrical problems usually stem from simple causes, such as loose or corroded connections, a blown fuse, a melted fusible link or a failed relay. Visually inspect the condition of all fuses, wires and connections in a problem circuit before troubleshooting the circuit.

If test equipment and instruments are going to be utilized, use the diagrams to plan ahead of time where you will make the necessary connections in order to accurately pinpoint the trouble spot.

The basic tools needed for electrical troubleshooting include a circuit tester or voltmeter (a 12-volt bulb with a set of test leads can also be used), a continuity tester, which includes a bulb, battery and set of test

2.5a The most useful tool for electrical troubleshooting is a digital multimeter that can check volts, amps, and test continuity

2.5b A simple test light is a very handy tool for testing voltage

leads, and a jumper wire, preferably with a circuit breaker incorporated, which can be used to bypass electrical components **(see illustrations)**. Before attempting to locate a problem with test instruments, use the wiring diagram(s) to decide where to make the connections.

Voltage checks

Voltage checks should be performed if a circuit is not functioning properly. Connect one lead of a circuit tester to either the negative battery terminal or a known good earth connection. Connect the other lead to a connector in the circuit being tested, preferably nearest to the battery or fuse **(see illustration)**. If the bulb of the tester lights, voltage is present, which means that the part of the circuit between the connector and the battery is problem free. Continue checking the rest of the circuit in the same fashion. When you reach a point at which no voltage is present, the problem lies between that point and the last test point with voltage. Most of the time the problem can be traced to a loose connec-

tion. **Note:** *Keep in mind that some circuits receive voltage only when the ignition key is in the Accessory or Run position.*

Finding a short

One method of finding shorts in a live circuit is to remove the fuse and connect a test light in place of the fuse terminals (fabricate two jumper wires with small spade terminals, plug the jumper wires into the fuse box and connect the test light). There should be voltage present in the circuit. Move the suspected wiring harness from side-to-side while watching the test light. If the bulb goes off, there is a short to earth somewhere in that area, probably where the insulation has rubbed through.

Earth connection check

Perform a earth connection test to check whether a component is properly earthed. Disconnect the battery and connect one lead of a continuity tester or multimeter (set to the ohms scale), to a known good earth connection. Connect the other lead to the wire or

earth connection being tested. If the resistance is low (less than 5 ohms), the earth connection is good. If the bulb on a self-powered test light does not go on, the earth connection is not good.

Continuity check

A continuity check is done to determine if there are any breaks in a circuit - if it is passing electricity properly. With the circuit off (no power in the circuit), a self-powered continuity tester or multimeter can be used to check the circuit. Connect the test leads to both ends of the circuit (or to the "power" end and a good earth connection), and if the test light comes on the circuit is passing current properly **(see illustration)**. If the resistance is low (less than 5 ohms), there is continuity; if the reading is 10,000 ohms or higher, there is a break somewhere in the circuit. The same procedure can be used to test a switch, by connecting the continuity tester to the switch terminals. With the switch turned On, the test light should come on (or low resistance should be indicated on a meter).

2.6 In use, a basic test light's lead is clipped to a known good earth connection, then the pointed probe can test connectors, wires or electrical sockets - if the bulb lights, the circuit being tested has battery voltage

2.9 With a multimeter set to the ohms scale, resistance can be checked across two terminals - when checking for continuity, a low reading indicates continuity, a high reading or infinity indicates lack of continuity

3.1a On early models the interior fuse block is located on the drivers side kick panel

3.1b The interior fuse box is tucked up under the instrument panel, behind the glove box - it's fairly difficult to reach without removing the glovebox

Finding an open circuit

When diagnosing for possible open circuits, it is often difficult to locate them by sight because the connectors hide oxidation or terminal misalignment. Merely wiggling a connector on a sensor or in the wiring harness may correct the open circuit condition. Remember this when an open circuit is indicated when troubleshooting a circuit. Intermittent problems may also be caused by oxidized or loose connections.

Electrical troubleshooting is simple if you keep in mind that all electrical circuits are basically electricity running from the battery, through the wires, switches, relays, fuses and fusible links to each electrical component (light bulb, motor, etc.) and to earth, from which it is passed back to the battery. Any electrical problem is an interruption in the flow of electricity to and from the battery.

Connectors

Most electrical connections on these vehicles are made with multi-wire plastic connectors. The mating halves of many connectors are secured with locking clips molded into the plastic connector shells. The mating halves of large connectors, such as some of those under the instrument panel, are held together by a bolt through the centre of the connector.

To separate a connector with locking clips, use a small screwdriver to prise the clips apart carefully, then separate the connector halves. Pull only on the shell, never pull on the wiring harness as you may damage the individual wires and terminals inside the connectors. Look at the connector closely before trying to separate the halves. Often the locking clips are engaged in a way that is not immediately clear. Additionally, many connectors have more than one set of clips.

Each pair of connector terminals has a male half and a female half. When you look at the end view of a connector in a diagram, be sure to understand whether the view shows the harness side or the component side of the connector. Connector halves are mirror images of each other, and a terminal shown on the right side end-view of one half will be on the left side end view of the other half.

3   Fuses and fusible links - general information

Fuses

Refer to illustrations 3.1a, 3.1b, 3.1c and 3.3

The electrical circuits of the vehicle are protected by a combination of fuses, circuit breakers and fusible links. The fuse blocks are located under the instrument panel and in the engine compartment **(see illustrations)**.

Each of the fuses is designed to protect a specific circuit, and the various circuits are identified on the fuse panel cover.

Miniaturized fuses are employed in the fuse blocks. These compact fuses, with blade terminal design, allow fingertip removal and replacement. If an electrical component fails, always check the fuse first. The best way to check a fuse is with a test light. Check for power at the exposed terminal tips of each fuse. If power is present on one side of the fuse but not the other, the fuse is blown. A blown fuse can also be confirmed by visually inspecting it **(see illustration)**.

3.1c The main engine compartment fuse/relay box is located near the left strut tower

3.3 When a fuse blows, the element between the terminals melts

5.3a These two relays are typical normally open types; the one above completes a single circuit (terminal 5 to terminal 3) when energized - the lower relay type completes two circuits (6 and 7, and 3 and 5) when energized

5.3b These relays are normally closed types, where current flows though one circuit until the relay is energized, which interrupts that circuit and completes the second circuit

Be sure to replace blown fuses with the correct type. Fuses of different ratings are physically interchangeable, but only fuses of the proper rating should be used. Replacing a fuse with one of a higher or lower value than specified is not recommended. Each electrical circuit needs a specific amount of protection. The amperage value of each fuse is molded into the fuse body.

If the replacement fuse immediately fails, don't replace it again until the cause of the problem is isolated and corrected. In most cases, this will be a short circuit in the wiring caused by a broken or deteriorated wire.

Fusible links

Some circuits are protected by fusible links. The links are used in circuits which are not ordinarily fused, such as the ignition circuit, or which carry high current.

Cartridge type fusible links are located in the engine compartment fuse box and are similar to a large fuse. After disconnecting the negative battery cable, simply unplug and replace it with a fusible link of the same amperage.

A wire-type fusible link, installed in the harness between the battery and the fuse/relay blocks, protects the entire chassis electrical system. It's located near the positive battery terminal. If the fusible link melts, the cause of the short must first be repaired, then the fusible link must be replaced with a fusible link of the same gauge. Never substitute a regular wire for a fusible link.

To replace a wire-type fusible link, disconnect the cable from the negative terminal of the battery, cut the damaged link out and solder a new one in its place. Cover the exposed wires with shrink-wrap tubing or plenty of electrical tape.

4   Circuit breakers - general information

Circuit breakers protect certain circuits, such as the power windows or heated seats. Depending on the vehicle's accessories, there may be one or two circuit breakers, located in the fuse/relay box in the engine compartment **(see illustration 3.1b)**.

Because the circuit breakers reset automatically, an electrical overload in a circuit-breaker-protected system will cause the circuit to fail momentarily, then come back on. If the circuit does not come back on, check it immediately.

For a basic check, pull the circuit breaker up out of its socket on the fuse panel, but just far enough to probe with a voltmeter. The breaker should still contact the sockets.

With the voltmeter negative lead on a good chassis earth connection, touch each end prong of the circuit breaker with the positive meter probe. There should be battery voltage at each end. If there is battery voltage only at one end, the circuit breaker must be replaced.

Some circuit breakers must be reset manually.

5   Relays - general information and testing

General information

1   Several electrical accessories in the vehicle, such as the fuel injection system, horns, starter, and fog lamps use relays to transmit the electrical signal to the component. Relays use a low-current circuit (the control circuit) to open and close a high-current circuit (the

power circuit). If the relay is defective, that component will not operate properly. Most relays are mounted in the engine compartment fuse/relay box. If a faulty relay is suspected, it can be removed and tested using the procedure below or by a dealer service department or a repair shop. Defective relays must be replaced as a unit. Identification of the circuit the relay controls is often marked on the top of the relay, but the decal or imprint inside the cover of the relay box should also indicate which circuits they control. **Note:** *Some relays are an integral part of the interior fuse box. These include the starter relay, the IG1 relay, the defroster relay, the power window relay, the circuit opening relay and the integration relay.*

Testing

Refer to illustrations 5.3a, 5.3b and 5.6

2   Refer to the wiring diagrams for the circuit to determine the proper connections for the relay you're testing. If you can't determine the correct connection from the wiring diagrams, however, you may be able to determine the test connections from the information that follows.

3   There are four basic types of relays used on these models **(see illustrations)**. Some are normally open type and some normally closed, while others include a circuit of each type.

4   On most relays, two of the terminals are the relay control circuit (they connect to the relay coil which, when energized, closes the large contacts to complete the circuit). The other terminals are the power circuit (they are connected together within the relay when the control-circuit coil is energized).

5   Some relays may be marked as an aid to help you determine which terminals make

5.6 To test a typical four-terminal normally open relay, connect an ohmmeter to the two terminals of the power circuit - the meter should indicate continuity with the relay energized and no continuity with the relay not energized

6.1 Location of the turn signal and hazard flasher (seen here through the opening for the small utility compartment to the left of the steering wheel)

up the control circuit and which make up the power circuit. If the relay is not marked, refer to the wiring diagrams at the end of this Chapter to determine the proper hook-ups for the relay you're testing.

6   To test a relay, connect an ohmmeter across the two terminals of the power circuit, continuity should not be indicated **(see illustration)**. Now connect a fused jumper wire between one of the two control circuit terminals and the positive battery terminal. Connect another jumper wire between the other control circuit terminal and earth connection. When the connections are made, the relay should click and continuity should be indicated on the meter. On some relays, polarity may be critical, so, if the relay doesn't click, try swapping the jumper wires on the control circuit terminals.

7   If the relay fails the above test, replace it.

---

6   Turn signal and hazard flasher - check and replacement

Refer to illustration 6.1

Warning: *The models covered by this manual are equipped with Supplemental Restraint Systems (SRS), more commonly known as airbags. Always disable the airbag system before working in the vicinity of any airbag system components to avoid the possibility of accidental deployment of the airbags, which could cause personal injury (see Section 26).*

1   The turn signal and hazard flasher is a single combination unit, located on the interior fuse/relay box **(see illustration)**.

2   When the flasher unit is functioning properly, an audible click can be heard during its operation. If the turn signals fail on one side or the other and the flasher unit does not make its characteristic clicking sound, or if a bulb on one side of the vehicle flashes much faster than normal but the bulb at the other end of the vehicle (on the same side) doesn't light at

all, a faulty turn signal bulb may be indicated.

3   If both turn signals fail to blink, the problem may be due to a blown fuse, a faulty flasher unit, a defective switch or a loose or open connection. If a quick check of the fuse box indicates that the turn signal fuse has blown, check the wiring for a short before installing a new fuse.

4   To replace the flasher, disconnect the electrical connector and remove the flasher unit from the electrical centre.

5   Make sure that the replacement unit is identical to the original. Compare the old one to the new one before installing it.

6   Installation is the reverse of removal.

---

7   Steering column switches - replacement

Refer to illustration 7.4

Warning: *The models covered by this manual are equipped with Supplemental Restraint Systems (SRS), more commonly known as airbags. Always disable the airbag system before working in the vicinity of any airbag system components to avoid the possibility of accidental deployment of the airbag(s), which could cause personal injury (see Section 26).*

Caution: *If the stereo in your vehicle is equipped with an anti-theft system, make sure you have the correct activation code before disconnecting the battery.*

1   Disconnect the cable from the negative terminal of the battery.

2   Remove the steering column covers (see Chapter 11).

3   The steering column switches on these models are two separate switch units connected to a central plastic housing. The left-side switch is for the headlight and turn signal control, while the right-side switch is for the washer/wiper control. Either switch can be replaced separately. Unplug the electrical connectors from the combination switch to

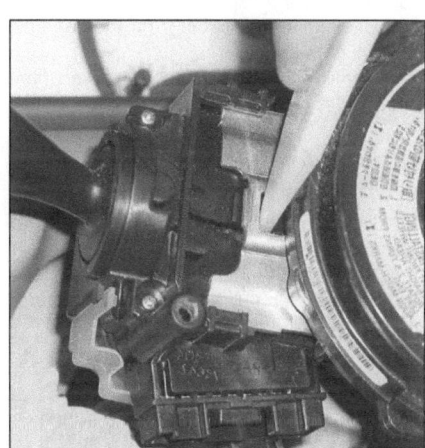

7.4 Release the switch retaining claw with a plastic tool - wiper/washer switch shown, headlight/turn signal switch similar (steering wheel removed for clarity, but it isn't necessary to remove the steering wheel for switch removal)

be replaced.

4   Depress the claw in the switch, then pull the switch from the steering column **(see illustration)**. **Note:** *Excessive force may break the claw.*

5   Installation is the reverse of removal.

---

8   Ignition switch and key lock cylinder - replacement

Warning: *The models covered by this manual are equipped with Supplemental Restraint Systems (SRS), more commonly known as airbags. Always disable the airbag system before working in the vicinity of any airbag system components to avoid the possibility of accidental deployment of the airbag(s), which could cause personal injury (see Section 26).*

Caution: *If the stereo in your vehicle is equipped with an anti-theft system, make sure*

8.3 Disconnect the electrical connectors at the bottom of the ignition switch housing

8.4 Unscrew the retaining screws to remove the electrical portion of the ignition switch

8.8 With the lock cylinder in the ACC position, depress the retaining pin with a small screwdriver, then pull the cylinder straight out

you have the correct activation code before disconnecting the battery.

1   Disconnect the cable from the negative terminal of the battery.

2   Remove the steering column covers (see Chapter 11).

Ignition switch

Refer to illustrations 8.3 and 8.4

3   Unplug the ignition switch wiring harness connectors **(see illustration)**.

4   Remove the switch retaining screws **(see illustration)** then pull the switch from the lock cylinder housing.

5   Installation is reverse of the removal.

Lock cylinder

Refer to illustration 8.8

6   On models equipped with the engine immobilizer system, gently prise off the plastic shroud around the key-lock cylinder and disconnect the electrical connector. Lift the shroud edge from the locating tab only enough to slip the shroud off. The shroud houses the amplifier for the special transponder keys. Prise lightly to remove the illumination ring, then remove the unlock arming switch.

7   Insert the key and turn it to the ACC position.

8   Use a small screwdriver or punch to depress the lock cylinder retaining pin, then withdraw the key cylinder **(see illustration)**.

9   To install the lock cylinder, depress the retaining pin and guide the lock cylinder into the housing until the retaining pin extends itself back into the locating hole in the housing.

10   The remainder of the installation is the reverse of removal.

---

9   Instrument panel switches - replacement

Warning: *The models covered by this manual are equipped with Supplemental Restraint Systems (SRS), more commonly known as airbags. Always disable the airbag system before working in the vicinity of any airbag system components to avoid the possibility of accidental deployment of the airbag(s), which could cause personal injury (see Section 26).*
Caution: *If the stereo in your vehicle is equipped with an anti-theft system, make sure*

you have the correct activation code before disconnecting the battery.

Hazard warning switch

1   Disconnect the negative battery cable (see Chapter 1).

2   Carefully remove the centre cluster finish panel (see Chapter 11) from the instrument panel and pull the assembly out until you can disconnect the electrical connector at the rear of the switch.

3   Use two screwdrivers to depress the switch retaining tangs, then remove the switch cluster from the panel.

4   Installation is the reverse of the removal procedure.

Power mirror control switch and dimmer switch

Refer to illustrations 9.5 and 9.6

5   The switches are located in a small panel to the left of the steering column. Carefully prise the panel from the dash with a trim tool **(see illustration)**.

6   Disconnect the electrical connector and remove the switches **(see illustration)**.

9.5 Use a trim tool to prise the dimmer/mirror switch panel from the left side of the dash

9.6 Disconnect the electrical connector and release the two clips securing the light control switch - mirror switch removal is similar

10.3 Remove this screw at the top of the instrument cluster . . .

7   Installation is the reverse of the removal procedure.

Defogger switch

8   The rear window defogger switch is located in the heating and air conditioning control panel.
9   Refer to Chapter 3 and remove the control panel, then pull the assembly out until you can disconnect the electrical connector at the rear of the switch. Depress the tab and remove the switch from the bezel.
10   Installation is the reverse of the removal procedure.

10   Instrument cluster - removal and installation

Refer to illustrations 10.3, 10.4 and 10.5
Warning: *The models covered by this manual are equipped with Supplemental Restraint Systems (SRS), more commonly known as airbags. Always disable the airbag system before working in the vicinity of any airbag*

system component to avoid the possibility of accidental deployment of the airbag(s), which could cause personal injury (see Section 26).
Caution: *If the stereo in your vehicle is equipped with an anti-theft system, make sure you have the correct activation code before disconnecting the battery.*
1   Disconnect the negative battery cable. Remove the steering wheel (see Chapter 10).
2   Remove the instrument cluster trim panel (see Chapter 11).
3   Remove the cluster mounting screw at the top **(see illustration)**.
4   Prise at the two bottom clips to release them, then pull the cluster out **(see illustration)**.
5   Disconnect the electrical connectors **(see illustration)**.
6   Cover the steering column with a cloth to protect the trim covers, then remove the instrument cluster from the vehicle.
7   Installation is the reverse of removal.

11   Wiper motor - check and replacement

Wiper motor circuit check

Note: *Refer to the wiring diagrams for wire colours and locations in the following checks. When checking for voltage, probe a earthed 12-volt test light to each terminal at a connector until it lights; this verifies voltage (power) at the terminal. If the following checks fail to locate the problem, have the system diagnosed by a dealer service department or other properly equipped repair facility.*
1   If the wipers work slowly, make sure the battery is in good condition and has a strong charge (see Chapter 5). If the battery is in good condition, remove the wiper motor (see below) and operate the wiper arms by hand. Check for binding linkage and pivots. Lubricate or repair the linkage or pivots as necessary. Reinstall the wiper motor. If the wipers still operate slowly, check for loose or cor-

roded connections, especially the earth connection. If all connections look OK, replace the motor.
2   If the wipers fail to operate when activated, check the fuse in the driver's side interior fuse panel. If the fuse is OK, connect a jumper wire between the wiper motor's earth terminal and earth connection, then retest. If the motor works now, repair the earth connection. If the motor still doesn't work, turn the wiper switch to the HI position and check for voltage at the motor. **Note:** *The cowl cover will have to be removed (see Chapter 11) to access the electrical connector.*
3   If there's voltage at the connector, remove the motor and check it off the vehicle with fused jumper wires from the battery. If the motor now works, check for binding linkage (see Step 1). If the motor still doesn't work, replace it. If there's no voltage to the motor, check for voltage at the wiper control relays. If there's voltage at the wiper control relays and no voltage at the wiper motor, have the switch tested. If the switch is OK, the wiper control relay is probably bad. See Section 5 for relay testing.
4   If the interval (delay) function is inoperative, check the continuity of all the wiring between the switch and wiper control module.
5   If the wipers stop at the position they're in when the switch is turned off (fail to park), check for voltage at the park feed wire of the wiper motor connector when the wiper switch is OFF but the ignition is ON. If no voltage is present, check for an open circuit between the wiper motor and the fuse panel.

Replacement

Caution: *If the stereo in your vehicle is equipped with an anti-theft system, make sure you have the correct activation code before disconnecting the battery.*

Windscreen wiper motor

Refer to illustrations 11.7, 11.9 and 11.11
6   Disconnect the negative cable from the battery.

10.4 . . . then release the clips and pull the cluster out at the bottom

10.5 Disconnect the electrical connectors at the back of the cluster

11.7 Lift the end cap to access the wiper arm nut, remove the nut, then make a reference mark before removing the arm

7   Remove the covers over the wiper arm mounting nuts. Remove the nuts, mark the relationship of the arms to the spindles, then prise up the wiper arms **(see illustration)**.
8   Remove the cowl louver panels.
9   Disconnect the wiper motor harness connector and remove the windscreen wiper motor/linkage assembly mounting bolts **(see illustration)**.
10   Slide the assembly toward the passenger side to detach the rubber pin near the motor from the cowl sheetmetal, then lift the windscreen wiper motor assembly from the cowl area.
11   Prise the linkage from the motor arm, remove the wiper motor mounting bolts and separate the motor from the frame **(see illustration)**.
12   Installation is the reverse of removal.

Rear wiper motor

Refer to illustration 11.15

13   Lift the covers over the wiper arm mounting nut. Remove the nut, mark the relationship of the arm to the spindle, then prise up the wiper arm.
14   Remove the liftgate cover (see Chapter 11).
15   Disconnect the wiper motor harness connector and remove the windscreen wiper motor assembly mounting bolts (see illustration).
16   Remove the wiper motor from the liftgate.

17   Installation is the reverse of removal.

12   Radio and speakers - removal and installation

Warning: *The models covered by this manual are equipped with Supplemental Restraint Systems (SRS), more commonly known as airbags. Always disable the airbag system before working in the vicinity of any airbag system components to avoid the possibility of accidental deployment of the airbag(s), which could cause personal injury (see Section 26).*
Caution*: If the stereo in your vehicle is equipped with an anti-theft system, make sure you have the correct activation code before disconnecting the battery.*

1   Disconnect the negative battery cable.

Radio

Early models

Refer to illustrations 12.3a and 12.3b

2   Remove the centre trim panel (see Chapter 11).
3   Remove the mounting screws and pull the radio out of the dash as far as possible **(see illustrations)**.

11.9 Location of the wiper linkage mounting bolts

11.11 Prise the link from the motor arm (A), then remove the wiper motor mounting bolts (B)

11.15 Disconnect the rear wiper motor electrical connection (1), remove the mounting bolts (2) and remove the motor

12.3a Remove the radio mounting screws (two on each side)

12.3b Pull the radio unit out, disconnect the electrical connectors and aerial cable

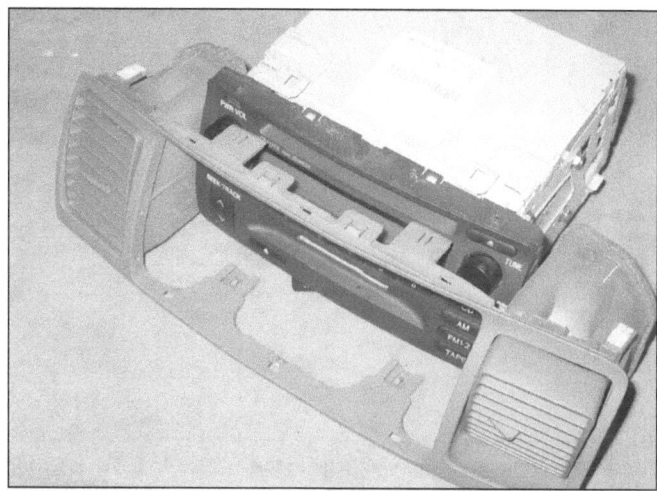

12.7 The radio comes out with this panel and two vents - release the clips top and bottom to remove the radio from the vent panel

4　Disconnect the electrical connector and the aerial lead and remove the radio.
5　Installation is the reverse of removal.

Later models

Refer to illustration 12.7

6　The air conditioning control panel must be removed before the radio mounting screws can be accessed (see Chapter 11).
7　Remove the retaining screws and pull the radio panel outward to access the backside, then disconnect the electrical connectors and the aerial lead. Release the clips and separate the radio from the panel **(see illustration)**.
8　Installation is the reverse of removal.

Door speakers

Refer to illustration 12.10

9　Remove the door trim panel (see Chapter 11). All models have speakers in both front and rear doors. Rear door speakers are mounted similarly to the front door speakers.
10　Remove the speaker mounting rivets **(see illustration)**. Disconnect the electrical connector and remove the speaker from the vehicle
11　Installation is the reverse of removal.

Tweeters

Refer to illustration 12.14

12　In addition to the standard door and rear speakers, some models are equipped with small tweeters for improved high-range sound.
13　The tweeters are mounted in the front of the doors under the mirror cover. Refer to Chapter 11 and remove the outside mirror covers.
14　Remove the tweeter mounting nuts and disconnect the electrical connector **(see illustration)**.
15　Installation is the reverse of removal.

13　Aerial - replacement

1　The vehicles covered by this manual are equipped with a mast-type aerial attached to the rear of the roof.
2　If the aerial mast is damaged, it can be removed by turning it anticlockwise. Wrap the aerial with tape for a good grip and it can be removed by hand.
3　The aerial cable runs from the radio up through the passenger-side windscreen pillar under the headliner at is joined with a connector at the rear of the roof.
4　It's a difficult job for the home mechanic to remove all the panels and the headliner for access to the cables or replacement of the aerial mast base. This procedure is best left to a qualified shop.

12.10 Drill out the rivets securing the door speaker, then pull the speaker out and disconnect the electrical connector

12.14 The tweeters are the small speakers located behind the outside mirror mounting nut covers. They're secured by two of the mirror mounting nuts

14.4 When measuring the voltage at the rear window defogger grid, wrap a piece of aluminum foil around the positive probe of the voltmeter and press the foil against the wire with your finger

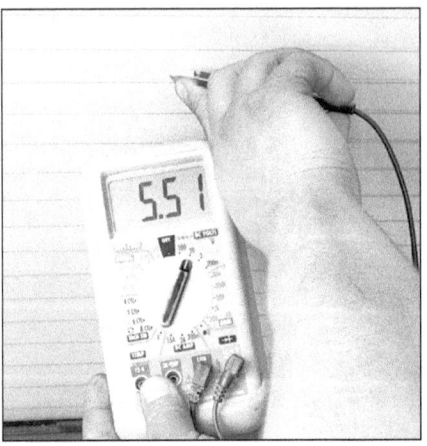

14.5 To determine if a heating element has broken, check the voltage at the centre of each element - if the voltage is 5 or 6-volts, the element is unbroken - if the voltage is 10 or 12-volts, the element is broken between the centre and the earth side - if there is no voltage, the element is broken between the centre and the positive side

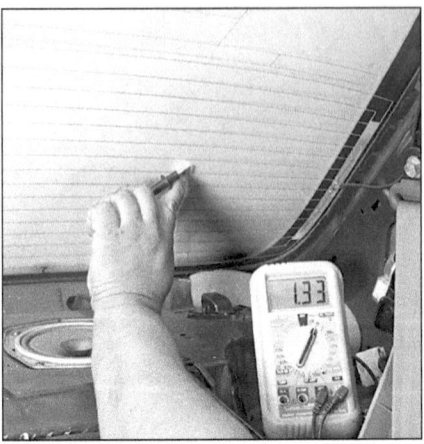

14.7 To find the break, place the voltmeter negative lead against the defogger earth terminal, place the voltmeter positive lead with the foil strip against the heating element at the positive terminal end and slide it toward the negative terminal end - the point at which the voltmeter reading changes abruptly is the point at which the element is broken

14   Rear window defogger - check and repair

1   The rear window defogger consists of a number of horizontal elements baked onto the glass surface. If the defogger isn't working, first check the defogger relay and fuse in the interior fuse/relay box.

2   Small breaks in the element can be repaired without removing the rear window.

Check

Refer to illustrations 14.4, 14.5 and 14.7

3   Turn the ignition switch and defogger system switches to the ON position. Using a voltmeter, place the positive probe against the defogger grid positive terminal and the negative probe against the earth terminal. If battery voltage is not indicated, check the defogger switch and related wiring. If voltage is indicated, but all or part of the defogger doesn't heat, proceed with the following tests.

4   When measuring voltage during the

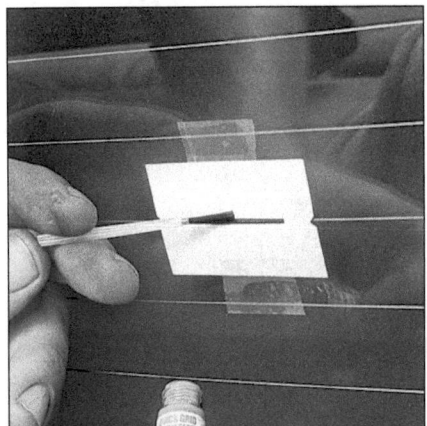

14.13 To use a defogger repair kit, apply masking tape to the inside of the window at the damaged area, then brush on the special conductive coating

next two tests, wrap a piece of aluminum foil around the tip of the voltmeter positive probe and press the foil against the heating element with your finger **(see illustration)**. Place the negative probe on the defogger grid earth terminal.

5   Check the voltage at the centre of each heating element **(see illustration)**. If the voltage is 5 or 6-volts, the element is okay (there is no break). If the voltage is 0-volts, the element is broken between the centre of the element and the positive end. If the voltage is 10 to 12-volts the element is broken between the centre of the element and earth connection. Check each heating element.

6   Connect the negative lead to a good body earth connection. The reading should stay the same. If it doesn't, the earth connection is bad.

7   To find the break, place the voltmeter negative probe against the defogger earth terminal. Place the voltmeter positive probe with the foil strip against the heating element at the positive terminal end and slide it toward the negative terminal end. The point at which the voltmeter deflects from several volts to zero is the point at which the heating element is broken **(see illustration)**.

Repair

Refer to illustration 14.13

8   Repair the break in the element using a repair kit specifically recommended for this purpose, available at most auto parts stores. Included in this kit is plastic conductive epoxy.

9   Prior to repairing a break, turn off the system and allow it to cool off for a few minutes.

10   Lightly buff the element area with fine steel wool, then clean it thoroughly with isopropyl alcohol.

11   Use masking tape to mask off the area

being repaired.

12   Thoroughly mix the epoxy, following the instructions provided with the repair kit.

13   Apply the epoxy material to the slit in the masking tape, overlapping the undamaged area about 3/4-inch on either end **(see illustration)**.

14   Allow the repair to cure for 24 hours before removing the tape and using the system.

15   Headlight bulb - replacement

Refer to illustrations 15.1 and 15.2

Warning: *Halogen gas filled bulbs are under pressure and may shatter if the surface is scratched or the bulb is dropped. Wear eye protection and handle the bulbs carefully, grasping only the base whenever possible. Do not touch the surface of the bulb with your fingers because the oil from your skin could cause it to overheat and fail prematurely. If you do touch the bulb surface, clean it with isopropyl alcohol.*

1   Open the bonnet. Reach behind the headlight assembly and unplug the electrical connector, depressing the clip on the harness connector **(see illustration)**. **Note:** *On later models, remove the access cover from the back side of the assembly.* To access the left-side headlight bulbs, remove the battery (see Chapter 5).

2   Release the spring clip and pull out on the bulb **(see illustration)**.

3   Pull straight out on the bulb to remove from it from the bulb holder. Without touching the glass with your bare fingers, insert the new bulb assembly into the headlight housing.

4   Plug in the electrical connector.

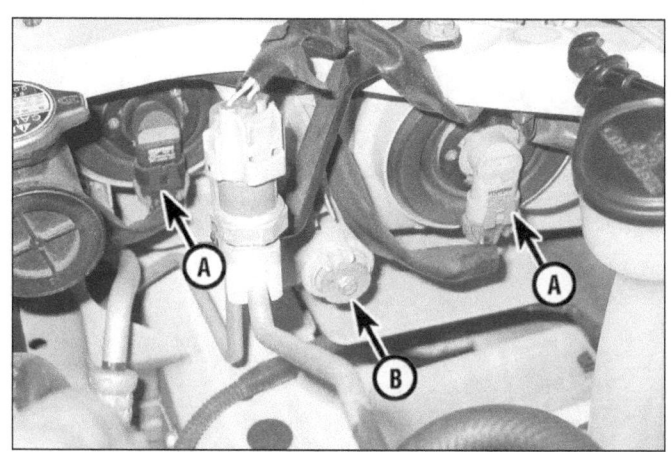

15.1 Location of the two headlight bulbs (A) and the aiming screw (B)

15.2 Release the retaining clip and remove the bulb

16.1a Typical early model adjusting screw locations

16.1b Typical later model adjusting screw locations

16   Headlights - adjustment

Refer to illustrations 16.1a, 16.1b and 16.3

Note: *The headlights must be aimed correctly. If adjusted incorrectly they could blind the driver of an oncoming vehicle and cause a serious accident or seriously reduce your ability to see the road. The headlights should be checked for proper aim every 12 months and any time a new headlight is installed or front-end bodywork is performed. It should be emphasized that the following procedure is only an interim step, which will provide temporary adjustment until the headlights can be adjusted by a properly equipped shop.*

1   The vertical adjustment screws are located behind each headlight housing **(see illustrations)**.

2   There are several methods for adjusting the headlights. The simplest method requires masking tape, a blank wall and a level floor.

3   Position masking tape vertically on the wall in reference to the vehicle centreline and the centrelines of both headlights **(see illustration)**.

4   Position a horizontal tape line in reference to the centreline of all the headlights. **Note:** *It might be easier to position the tape*

16.3 Headlight adjustment details

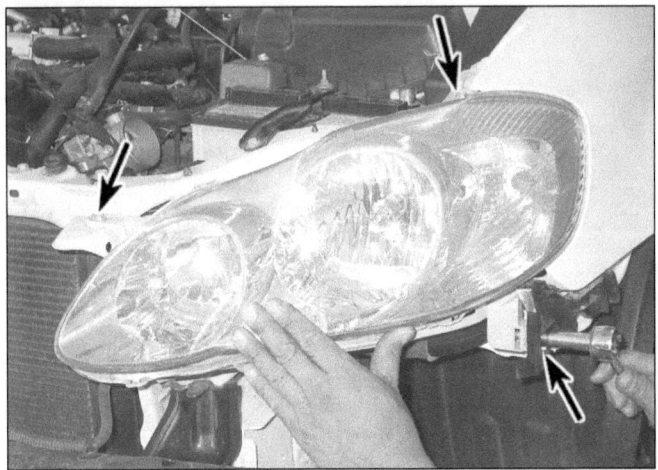

17.2 Headlight housing mounting screws

17.4 Remove the harness lock clips and disconnect the connectors

on the wall with the vehicle parked only a few inches away.

5   Adjustment should be made with the vehicle parked 5 metres from the wall, sitting level, the petrol tank half-full and no heavy load in the vehicle.

6   Starting with the low beam adjustment, position the high intensity zone so it is 50 mm below the horizontal line and 50 mm to the side of the headlight vertical line, away from oncoming traffic. Adjustment is made by turning the adjusting screw clockwise to raise the beam and anticlockwise to lower the beam.

7   With the high beams on, the high intensity zone should be vertically centred with the exact centre just below the horizontal line. **Note:** *It might not be possible to position the headlight aim exactly for both high and low beams. If a compromise must be made, keep in mind that the low beams are the most used and have the greatest effect on safety.*

8   Have the headlights adjusted by a dealer service department or service station at the earliest opportunity.

---

17   Headlight housing - replacement

Refer to illustrations 17.2 and 17.4

Warning: *These vehicles are equipped with halogen gas-filled headlight bulbs that are under pressure and may shatter if the surface is damaged or the bulb is dropped. Wear eye protection and handle the bulbs carefully, grasping only the base whenever possible. Do not touch the surface of the bulb with your fingers because the oil from your skin could cause it to overheat and fail prematurely. If you do touch the bulb surface, clean it with isopropyl alcohol.*

Note: *Headlight housings are expensive to replace, but on most models repair kits are available at Toyota dealerships that can save a headlight housing that has broken mounting tabs.*

1   Remove the headlight bulbs (see Sec-

tion 15) and the parking light bulb (see Section 19).

2   The front bumper cover must be removed to access one of the headlight housing fasteners (see Chapter 11). Remove the retaining bolts, detach the housing and withdraw it from the vehicle **(see illustration).**

3   Pull the housing forward and disconnect the electrical connectors **(see illustration).**

4   Installation is the reverse of removal. Be sure to check headlight adjustment (see Section 16).

---

18   Horn - check and replacement

Warning: *The models covered by this manual are equipped with Supplemental Restraint Systems (SRS), more commonly known as airbags. Always disable the airbag system before working in the vicinity of any airbag system components to avoid the possibility of accidental deployment of the airbag(s), which could cause personal injury (see Section 26).*

Check

Note: *Check the fuses before beginning electrical diagnosis.*

1   Disconnect the electrical connector from

the horn.

2   To test the horn, connect battery voltage to the horn terminal with a jumper wire. If the horn doesn't sound, replace it.

3   If the horn does sound, check for voltage at the terminal when the horn button is depressed. If there's voltage at the terminal, check for a bad earth connection at the horn.

4   If there's no voltage at the horn, check the relay (see Section 5).

5   If the relay is OK, check for voltage to the relay power and control circuits. If either of the circuits is not receiving voltage, inspect the wiring between the relay and the fuse panel.

6   If both relay circuits are receiving voltage, depress the horn button and check the circuit from the relay to the horn button for continuity to earth. If there's no continuity, check the circuit for an open. If there's no open circuit, replace the horn button.

7   If there's continuity to earth through the horn button, check for an open or short in the circuit from the relay to the horn.

Replacement

Refer to illustration 18.9

8   To access the horn, open the bonnet. The horn is located in front of the radiator.

9   To replace the horn, disconnect the elec-

18.9 Location of the horn mounting bolt (A) and electrical connector (B)

19.2 Rotate the bulb holder anticlockwise to remove the park/ turn/marker bulb from the headlight housing

19.4 Open the access panel inside the boot (panel removed in this photo) to access the bulbs

A   *Taillight/stop and rear side marker bulb*
B   *Turn signal bulb*

trical connector and remove the bracket bolt **(see illustration)**.
10   Installation is the reverse of removal.

---

19   Bulb replacement

Front park/turn signal lights

Refer to illustration 19.2

1   The park/turn signal lights and side marker lights are all are part of the headlight housing. These bulbs are accessible from behind the headlight housing (in place), although with some difficulty. If you have trouble, refer to Section 17 and remove the headlight housing for access to these bulbs.
2   Rotate the bulb holder anticlockwise and pull the bulb out **(see illustration)**. Remove the bulb from the holder. On some models, the side marker light is a separate unit mounted in the front fender. On these models, access to the bulb is from underneath the fender.
3   Installation is the reverse of removal.

Rear tail light/brake light/turn signal/side marker/backup

Sedan models

Refer to illustrations 19.4 and 19.6

4   The taillight/brake/turn signal bulbs can be accessed by removing access panels in the boot interior **(see illustration)**.
5   Rotate the bulb holders anti-clockwise and pull the bulbs out to remove them. Remove the bulb from the holder.
6   The backup lights in the boot lid are accessible only after opening a cover on the inside of the boot lid, using a screwdriver to release it **(see illustration)**. Twist the bulb holder anti-clockwise to remove it.
7   Installation is the reverse of removal.

Hatchback and wagon models

Refer to illustrations 19.8, 19.9a and 19.9b

8   The taillight/brake/turn signal bulbs can be accessed by removing access panels in the rear interior **(see illustration)**.
9   Carefully pull or push the locking tabs to

19.6 Swing open this hinged cover on the boot lid to access the backup light bulb

release the assembly **(see illustration)** and remove the bulb assembly from the housing. Twist the bulb from the holder anti-clockwise to remove it **(see illustration)**.
10   Installation is the reverse of removal.

19.8 On hatchback and station wagon models the access is located at the corners

19.9a There are two tabs locking the assembly to the housing. One must be pushed in (as shown) and the other must be pulled outward

19.9b Twist the bulb anti-clockwise to remove them from the assembly

19.11 Rotate the bulb holder and remove it from the high-mounted brake light assembly

19.15 Twist the bulb holders anticlockwise to remove them from the back of the instrument cluster

19.18 Carefully prise off the interior light lens using a flat-bladed screwdriver, then remove the bulb

Centre high-mounted stop light

Refer to illustration 19.11

11   Open the boot and crawl in enough to see the underside of the rear package shelf. Reach the bulb through the opening under the CHMSL housing **(see illustration)**.
12   Twist the bulb holder anticlockwise to remove it, then pull the bulb straight out of the holder.
13   Installation is the reverse of removal.

Instrument cluster lights

Refer to illustration 19.15

14   To gain access to the instrument cluster illumination bulbs, the instrument cluster will have to be removed (see Section 10). The bulbs can then be removed and replaced from the rear of the cluster.
15   Rotate the bulb holder anticlockwise to remove it **(see illustration)**.
16   Installation is the reverse of removal.

Interior light

Refer to illustration 19.18

17   Prise the lens off the interior light housing.
18   Detach the bulb from the terminals **(see illustration)**. It may be necessary to prise the bulb out - if this is the case, prise only on the ends of the bulb (otherwise the glass may shatter).
19   Installation is the reverse of removal.

Number plate light

20   Remove the boot lid lock cylinder by disconnecting the rods and removing the two mounting bolts.
21   Release the four clips inside the boot lid and remove the outside trim panel.
22   On the outside, push the number light bezel to the left to compress the clip, then withdraw the bezel and bulb holder.
23   Installation is the reverse of removal.

Fog light

24   Raise the vehicle and secure it on

jackstands.
25   Remove the splash shield.
26   Twist the bulb holder from the housing and replace the bulb.

Fender marker light

Refer to illustrations 19.27 and 19.28

27   Push forward on the light assembly while prising out the rear **(see illustration)**. Take care to avoid damaging the paint.
28   Rotate the bulb holder anti-clockwise from the housing and separate the holder from the housing **(see illustration)**.
29   Pull the bulb from the holder and replace the bulb.

---

20   Electric side view mirrors - description

1   Most electric rear view mirrors use two motors to move the glass; one for up and down adjustments and one for left-right

19.27 Push forward on the light assembly while prising out the rear - take care to avoid damaging the paint.

19.28 Rotate the bulb holder anti-clockwise from the housing and separate the holder from the housing

adjustments.

2   The control switch has a selector portion that sends voltage to the left or right side mirror. With the ignition ON but the engine OFF, roll down the windows and operate the mirror control switch through all functions (left-right and up-down) for both the left and right side mirrors.

3   Listen carefully for the sound of the electric motors running in the mirrors.

4   If the motors can be heard but the mirror glass doesn't move, there's a problem with the drive mechanism inside the mirror.

5   If the mirrors do not operate and no sound comes from the mirrors, check the fuse (see Chapter 1).

6   If the fuse is OK, remove the mirror control switch from the dashboard. Have the switch continuity checked by a dealership service department or other qualified automobile repair facility.

7   If the mirror still doesn't work, remove the mirror and check the wires at the mirror for voltage.

8   If there's not voltage in each switch position, check the circuit between the mirror and control switch for opens and shorts.

9   If there's voltage, remove the mirror and test it off the vehicle with jumper wires. Replace the mirror if it fails this test.

21   Cruise control system - description

1   On non electronic throttle body models the accelerator pedal is linked to the throttle body with a pair of cables; one running to the cruise control actuator and another running from the actuator to the throttle body. Electronic throttle body models utilize an electric motor to operate the throttle body, and wiring between the accelerator pedal and the throttle body. The ECM communicates between them. Listed below are some general procedures that may be used to locate common problems.

2   With the ignition switch turned to the On position, turn the cruise control main switch On. The CRUISE light on the instrument panel should light up, and turn off when you turn the cruise control main switch back to Off.

3   Check the fuses (see Section 3).

4   If the check in Step 2 is abnormal, further diagnosis requires a scan tool to read diagnostic trouble codes for the cruise control system. For more information on diagnostic code retrieval, see Chapter 6.

5   The cruise control system uses inputs from the Vehicle Speed Sensor (VSS). Refer to Chapter 6 for more information on the VSS.

6   Test-drive the vehicle to determine if the cruise control is now working. If it isn't, take it to a dealer service department or an automotive electrical specialist for further diagnosis.

22   Power window system - description

1   The power window system operates electric motors, mounted in the doors, which lower and raise the windows. The system consists of the control switches, relays, the motors, regulators, glass mechanisms and associated wiring.

2   The power windows can be lowered and raised from the master control switch by the driver or by remote switches located at the individual windows. Each window has a separate motor that is reversible. The position of the control switch determines the polarity and therefore the direction of operation.

3   The circuit is protected by a fuse and a circuit breaker. Each motor is also equipped with an internal circuit breaker; this prevents one stuck window from disabling the whole system.

4   The power window system will only operate when the ignition switch is ON. In addition, many models have a window lockout switch at the master control switch that, when activated, disables the switches at the rear windows and, sometimes, the switch at the passenger's window also. Always check these items before troubleshooting a window problem.

5   These procedures are general in nature, so if you can't find the problem using them, take the vehicle to a dealer service department or other properly equipped repair facility.

6   If the power windows won't operate, always check the fuse and circuit breaker first.

7   If only the rear windows are inoperativo, or if the windows only operate from the master control switch, check the rear window lockout switch for continuity in the unlocked position. Replace it if it doesn't have continuity.

8   Check the wiring between the switches and fuse panel for continuity. Repair the wiring, if necessary.

9   If only one window is inoperative from the master control switch, try the other control switch at the window. **Note:** *This doesn't apply to the driver's door window.*

10   If the same window works from one switch, but not the other, check the switch for continuity. Have the switch checked at a dealer service department or other qualified automobile repair facility.

11   If the switch tests OK, check for a short or open in the circuit between the affected switch and the window motor.

12   If one window is inoperative from both switches, remove the trim panel from the affected door and check for voltage at the switch and at the motor while the switch is operated.

13   If voltage is reaching the motor, disconnect the glass from the regulator (see Chapter 11). Move the window up and down by hand while checking for binding and damage. Also check for binding and damage to the

regulator. If the regulator is not damaged and the window moves up and down smoothly, replace the motor. If there's binding or damage, lubricate, repair or replace parts, as necessary.

14   If voltage isn't reaching the motor, check the wiring in the circuit for continuity between the switches and motors. You'll need to consult the wiring diagram for the vehicle. If the circuit is equipped with a relay, check that the relay is earthed properly and receiving voltage.

15   Test the windows after you are done to confirm proper repairs.

23   Power door lock system - description

1   A power door lock system operates the door lock actuators mounted in each door. The system consists of the switches, actuators, a control unit and associated wiring. Diagnosis can usually be limited to simple checks of the wiring connections and actuators for minor faults that can be easily repaired.

2   Power door lock systems are operated by bi-directional solenoids located in the doors. The lock switches have two operating positions: Lock and Unlock. When activated, the switch sends a earth signal to the door lock control unit to lock or unlock the doors. Depending on which way the switch is activated, the control unit reverses polarity to the solenoids, allowing the two sides of the circuit to be used alternately as the feed (positive) and earth side.

3   Some vehicles may have an anti-theft system incorporated into the power locks. If you are unable to locate the trouble using the following general Steps, consult a dealer service department or other qualified repair shop.

4   Always check the circuit protection first. Some vehicles use a combination of circuit breakers and fuses.

5   Operate the door lock switches in both directions (Lock and Unlock) with the engine off. Listen for the click of the solenoids operating.

6   Test the switches for continuity. Remove the switches and have them checked by a dealer service department or other qualified automobile repair facility.

7   Check the wiring between the switches, control unit and solenoids for continuity. Repair the wiring if there's no continuity.

8   Check for a bad earth connection at the switches or the control unit.

9   If all but one lock solenoids operate, remove the trim panel from the affected door (see Chapter 11) and check for voltage at the solenoid while the lock switch is operated One of the wires should have voltage in the Lock position; the other should have voltage in the Unlock position.

10   If the inoperative solenoid is receiving voltage, replace the solenoid.

11   If the inoperative solenoid isn't receiving voltage, check the relay for an open or short in the wire between the lock solenoid and the control unit. **Note:** *It's common for wires to break in the portion of the harness between the body and door (opening and closing the door fatigues and eventually breaks the wires).*

Keyless entry system

Refer to illustrations 23.14 and 23.15

12   The keyless entry system consists of a remote control transmitter that sends a coded infrared signal to a receiver that then operates the door lock system. On models so equipped, the transmitter may also engage the alarm system and provide a panic button that flashes the lights and blows the horn for emergencies.

13   Replace the transmitter batteries when the red LED light on the case doesn't light when the button is pushed. As the batteries deteriorate with age, the distance at which the remote transmitter operates will diminish.

14   Use a coin or small screwdriver to carefully separate the case halves for battery replacement **(see illustration)**.

15   Replace the two lithium batteries with the same type as originally installed, observing the polarity diagram on the case **(see illustration)**.

16   Snap the case halves together.

24   Power sunroof - description

1   The power sunroof or sliding roof system consists of the control switch, the module, the roof motor and the glass and track mechanism. The sunroof switch is located in a panel in the headliner, above the rear-view mirror. If there is a problem with sunroof operation, first check the 30-amp Power and 10-amp Gauge fuses in the instrument panel fuse/relay box. If the fuse is OK, check the P/W relay, also in the instrument panel fuse/relay box, as

this relay supplies power to the sunroof relay which is located in the module behind the sunroof control switch bezel.

25   Daytime Running Lights (DRL) - general information

The Daytime Running Lights (DRL) system illuminates the headlights whenever the engine is running. The only exception is with the engine running and the parking brake engaged. Once the parking brake is released, the lights will remain on as long as the ignition switch is on, even if the parking brake is later applied.

The DRL system supplies reduced power to the headlights so they won't be too bright for daytime use, while prolonging headlight life.

26   Airbag system - general information

All models are equipped with a Supplemental Restraint System (SRS), more commonly known as an airbag. This system is designed to protect the driver, and the front seat passenger, from serious injury in the event of a head-on or frontal collision. It consists of two impact sensors behind the front bumper, an airbag module in the centre of the steering wheel and the right side of the instrument panel and a sensing/diagnostic module mounted in the centre of the vehicle, ahead of the floor console. Additionally, some models are equipped with side impact airbags and side curtain airbags.

Airbag module
Driver's side

The airbag inflator module contains a housing incorporating the cushion (airbag) and inflator unit, mounted in the centre of the steering wheel The inflator assembly is

23.14 Use a small screwdriver or coin to separate the transmitter halves

mounted on the back of the housing over a hole through which gas is expelled, inflating the bag almost instantaneously when an electrical signal is sent from the system. A spiral cable assembly on the steering column under the steering wheel carries this signal to the module.

This spiral cable assembly can transmit an electrical signal regardless of steering wheel position. The igniter in the airbag converts the electrical signal to heat and ignites the powder, which inflates the bag.

Passenger's side

The airbag is mounted above the glove compartment and designated by the letters SRS (Supplemental Restraint System). It consists of an inflator containing an igniter, a bag assembly, a reaction housing and a trim cover.

The airbag is considerably larger than the steering wheel-mounted unit and is supported by the steel reaction housing. The trim cover is textured and painted to match the instrument panel and has a molded seam that splits when the bag inflates.

23.15 Replace the lithium batteries with the same type as used originally

26.3 Remove the bolt and two nuts to remove the passenger airbag from behind the instrument panel

Side impact airbags

Extra protection is provided on some models with the addition of optional side-impact airbags. These are smaller devices located in the seat backs on the side toward the exterior of the vehicle. The impact sensors for the side-impact airbags are located at the bottom of the door pillars in the body, in the bottom of the driver and passenger seats, or in the driver and passenger doors.

Side curtain airbags

Extra side-impact protection is provided on some models with the addition of optional side-curtain airbags (in addition to the side-impact airbags in the seatbacks). These are long airbags that, in the event of a side impact, come out of the headliner at each side of the car and come down between the side windows and the seats. They are designed to protect the heads of both front seat and rear seat passengers.

Sensing and diagnostic module

The sensing and diagnostic module supplies the current to the airbag system in the event of the collision, even if battery power is cut off. It checks this system every time the vehicle is started, causing the "AIR BAG" light to go on then off, if the system is operating properly. If there is a fault in the system, the light will go on and stay on, flash, or the dash will make a beeping sound. If this happens, the vehicle should be taken to your dealer immediately for service.

Disarming the system and other precautions

Warning: *Failure to follow these precautions could result in accidental deployment of the airbag and personal injury.*

Whenever working in the vicinity of the steering wheel, steering column or any of the other SRS system components, the system must be disarmed. To disarm the system:

a) *Point the wheels straight ahead and turn the key to the Lock position.*

b) *Disconnect the cable from the negative battery terminal. Make sure the cable is positioned so that it cannot come into contact with the battery terminal.*

c) *Wait at least two minutes for the back-up power supply to be depleted.*

Whenever handling an airbag module, always keep the airbag opening (the trim side) pointed away from your body. Never place the airbag module on a bench of other surface with the airbag opening facing the surface. Always place the airbag module in a safe location with the airbag opening facing up.

Never measure the resistance of any SRS component. An ohmmeter has a built-in battery supply that could accidentally deploy the airbag.

Never use electrical welding equipment on a vehicle equipped with an airbag without first disconnecting the yellow airbag connector, located under the steering column near the combination switch connector (driver's airbag) and behind the glove box (passenger's airbag).

Never dispose of a live airbag module. Return it to a dealer service department or other qualified repair shop for safe deployment and disposal.

Component removal and installation

Driver's side airbag module and spiral cable

1   Refer to Chapter 10, *Steering wheel - removal and installation*, for the driver's side airbag module and spiral cable removal and installation procedures.

Passenger's side airbag module

Refer to illustration 26.3

2   Disarm the airbag system as describes previously in this Section. Under the right side of the instrument panel, disconnect the yellow connectors for the passenger airbag.

3   Remove the glove box (see Chapter 11). The airbag is bolted to the underside of the instrument panel. Remove the fasteners and detach the airbag module from the instrument panel **(see illustration)**. Be sure to heed the precautions outlined previously in this Section.

4   Installation is the reverse of the removal procedure. Tighten the airbag module mounting fasteners to 20 Nm.

---

27 Wiring diagrams - general information

Since it isn't possible to include all wiring diagrams for every year covered by this manual, the following diagrams are those that are typical and most commonly needed.

Prior to troubleshooting any circuits, check the fuse and circuit breakers (if equipped) to make sure they're in good condition. Make sure the battery is properly charged and check the cable connections (see Chapter 1).

When checking a circuit, make sure that all connectors are clean, with no broken or loose terminals. When unplugging a connector, do not pull on the wires. Pull only on the connector housings themselves.

Diagram 1 — EFI and powertrain management systems. 4A-FE engine.

Diagram 2 — EFI and powertrain management systems. 4A-FE engine.

Diagram 3 — EFI and powertrain management systems, automatic transmission and cooling fans. 4A-FE engine.

Diagram 4 — Power distribution and integration module. 4A-FE engine.

Toyota Corolla
1.6 litre 4A-FE
wiring diagram 5 of 15

Earth Locations

8. RH rear of console
9. Behind audio system
10. Behind RHS tailgate trim panel (hatchback)
11. Adjacent to tailgate/boot lid striker
12. LHS, adjacent to rear seat back (sedan)

1. RH inner guard
2. LH inner guard
3. Top of engine
4. Behind LH kickpanel
5. Behind RH C pillar trim panel
6. LH side of console
7. RH side of console

Inhibitor switch (A/T models)

Park / Neutral

To PCM terminal STA (Manual only) Diagram 3

To PCM terminal STA (Auto only) Diagram 3

Manual transmission only

Starter relay

Starter motor

To instrument cluster Diagram 12

Cigarette lighter

To interior lighting See diagram 8

Alternator

Clock

To integration module Diagram 4

To tail fuse Diagram 4

To battery Diagram 4 — BR

To main fusible link Diagram 4

To CIG fuse Diagram 4

To integration module Diagram 4

To ST fuse Diagram 4

To alt fusible link Diagram 4

ALT-S fuse

Dome fuse

Horn fuse

To battery Diagram 4

Horn switch

Horn relay

Horn (low tone)

Horn (high tone)

Colour Code

A — Tan	N — Brown	V — Violet	
B — Black	O — Orange	W — White	
G — Green	P — Purple	Y — Yellow	
K — Pink	R — Red	X — Light green	
L — Blue	S — Grey	Z — Light blue	

Diagram 5 — Starting system, charging system, horn, clock and cigarette lighter. 4A-FE engine.

Diagram 6 — Headlamps, park lamps and fog lamps. 4A-FE engine.

Toyota Corolla
1.6 litre 4A-FE
wiring **diagram 6 of 15**

Earth Locations

1. RH inner guard
2. LH inner guard
3. Top of engine
4. Behind LH kickpanel
5. Behind RH C pillar trim panel
6. LH side of console
7. RH side of console
8. RH rear of console
9. Behind audio system
10. Behind RHS tailgate trim panel (hatchback)
11. Adjacent to tailgate/boot lid striker
12. LHS, adjacent to rear seat back (sedan)

Colour Code

A — Tan
B — Black
G — Green
K — Pink
L — Blue

N — Brown
O — Orange
P — Purple
R — Red
S — Grey

V — Violet
W — White
Y — Yellow
Z — Light green
Z — Light blue

Diagram 7 — Turn signal/hazard lamps, stop lamps and reverse lamps. 4A-FE engine.

Toyota Corolla
1.6 litre 4A-FE
wiring diagram 7 of 15

Earth Locations

1. RH inner guard
2. LH inner guard
3. Top of engine
4. Behind LH kickpanel
5. Behind RH C-pillar trim panel
6. LH side of console
7. RH side of console
8. RH rear of console
9. Behind RHS audio system
10. Behind RHS tailgate trim panel
11. Adjacent to tailgate/boot lid striker (hatchback)
12. LHS: adjacent to rear seat back (sedan)

Colour Code

A – Tan		V – Violet	
B – Black		W – White	
G – Green		Y – Yellow	
O – Orange		X – Light green	
P – Purple		Z – Light blue	
R – Red			
N – Brown			
K – Pink			
S – Grey			
L – Blue			

Diagram 8 — Interior lighting and instrument illumination. 4A-FE engine.

Toyota Corolla
1.6 litre 4A-FE
wiring **diagram 9 of 15**

Earth Locations

1. RH inner guard
2. LH inner guard
3. Top of engine
4. Behind LH kickpanel
5. Behind RH C pillar trim panel
6. LH side of console
7. RH side of console
8. RH rear of console
9. Behind audio system
10. Behind RHS tailgate trim panel
11. Adjacent to tailgate/boot lid striker
    (hatchback)
12. LHS, adjacent to rear seat back
    (sedan)

Colour Code

A — Tan	N — Brown	V — Violet
B — Black	O — Orange	W — White
G — Green	P — Purple	Y — Yellow
K — Pink	R — Red	X — Light green
L — Blue	S — Grey	Z — Light blue

Diagram 9 — Power windows, power mirrors and sunroof. 4A-FE engine.

Diagram 10 — Power door locks. 4A-FE engine.

Diagram 11 — Wipers, washers and demister. 4A-FE engine.

Toyota Corolla
1.6 litre 4A-FE
wiring diagram 11 of 15

Earth Locations

1. RH inner guard
2. LH inner guard
3. Top of engine
4. Behind LH kickpanel
5. Behind RH C pillar trim panel
6. LH side of console
7. RH side of console
8. RH rear of console
9. Behind audio system
10. Behind RHS tailgate trim panel (hatchback)
11. Adjacent to tailgate/boot lid striker
12. LHS, adjacent to rear seat back (sedan)

Colour Code

A – Tan	N – Brown	V – Violet
B – Black	O – Orange	W – White
G – Green	P – Purple	Y – Yellow
K – Pink	R – Red	X – Light green
L – Blue	S – Grey	Z – Light blue

Diagram 12 — Instrument cluster. 4A-FE engine.

Toyota Corolla
1.6 litre 4A-FE.
wiring diagram 12 of 15

Earth Locations

1. RH inner guard
2. LH inner guard
3. Top of engine
4. Behind LH kickpanel
5. Behind RH C pillar trim panel
6. LH side of console
7. RH side of console
8. RH rear of console
9. Behind audio system
10. Behind RHS tailgate trim panel (hatchback)
11. Adjacent to tailgate/boot lid striker
12. LHS, adjacent to rear seat back (sedan)

Colour Code

A – Tan
B – Black
G – Green
K – Pink
L – Blue
N – Brown
O – Orange
P – Purple
R – Red
S – Grey
V – Violet
W – White
Y – Yellow
Z – Light green
Z – Light blue

Diagram 13 — Antilock braking system (ABS) and supplemental restraint system (SRS). 4A-FE engine.

Diagram 14 — Audio system and shift lock system. 4A-FE engine.

Toyota Corolla
1.6 litre 4A-FE
wiring diagram 14 of 15

Earth Locations

1. RH inner guard
2. LH inner guard
3. Top of engine
4. Behind LH kickpanel
5. Behind RH C pillar trim panel
6. LH side of console
7. RH side of console
8. RH rear of console
9. Behind audio system
10. Behind RHS tailgate trim panel (hatchback)
11. Adjacent to tailgate/boot lid striker
12. LHS, adjacent to rear seat back (sedan)

Colour Code

A — Tan
B — Black
G — Green
K — Pink
L — Blue
N — Brown
O — Orange
P — Purple
R — Red
S — Grey
V — Violet
W — White
Y — Yellow
X — Light green
Z — Light blue

Shift lock switch

Shift lock module

Shift lock solenoid

Key interlock solenoid

To stop lamp switch Diagram 7

RHF speaker

RHR speaker

LHF speaker

LHR speaker

18 BY   To ECU-IG fuse Diagram 4
24 S   To integration module Diagram 4
35 LY   To dome fuse Diagram 4

Dual pressure switch

LR

BY

On   On   Off   Off

BW

BW   LY

A/C clutch and thermo sensor

LY   BY   YB

Evaporator temperature sensor

BL   BL

XB   XB

2   1
9   8   7   6
5   4   3   2   1
12 11 10 9
B

To distributor
Diagram 2

B   61

To PCM terminal ACT
Diagram 2

RL   RL   59

To PCM terminal AC1
Diagram 2

YR   YR   60

Air conditioning amplifier

LB

Y   YR

GW

WB

To A/C fan No 3 relay
Diagram 3

BW   58

A/C magnetic clutch relay

BW

LR

LB   LR

WB or N

WB or N

WB

GW   2   1   6
6   8   7   6
Y   11 10
10   3
RL   12
7

Heater control switch

LR   LR   LR

LR   LR

15 A A/C fuse

B   B

BW   **Fan motor**

BW   BW   BW

Fan resistor

LB   LB   LB

R   R   R

WB

WB

Ventilation switch

HI
M2
M1
OFF

LO   WB

WB

WB   WB   WB

Heater relay

RL WB LO

RL   WB LO   WB LO

To integration module
Diagram 4

RL   22

To heater fusible link
Diagram 4

56

To gauge fuse
Diagram 4

RL   57

Toyota Corolla
1.6 litre 4A-FE
wiring diagram 15 of 15

Earth Locations

8. RH rear of console
9. Behind audio system
10. Behind RHS tailgate trim panel
    (hatchback)
11. Adjacent to tailgate/hood lid striker
12. LHS, adjacent to rear seat back
    (sedan)

1. RH inner guard
2. LH inner guard
3. Top of engine
4. Behind LH kickpanel
5. Behind RH C pillar trim panel
6. LH side of console
7. RH side of console

Diagram 15 — Air conditioning. 4A-FE engine.

Colour Code

A – Tan
B – Black
G – Green
K – Pink
L – Blue

N – Brown
O – Orange
P – Purple
R – Red
S – Grey

V – Violet
W – White
Y – Yellow
X – Light green
Z – Light blue

Diagram 1 — EFI and powertrain management systems. 7A-FE engine.

Diagram 2 — EFI and powertrain management systems. 7A-FE engine.

Toyota Corolla
1.8 litre 7A-FE
wiring diagram 2 of 15

60 — To A/C amplifier Diagram 15

59 — To A/C amplifier Diagram 15

ISC valve — RSC, +B, RSO

9 — To EFI relay Diagram 1

To engine bay diagnosis connector Diagram 1 — 10

Oxygen sensor

Knock sensor

MAP sensor

Throttle position sensor

Air temperature sensor

Coolant temperature sensor

Injectors

3 — To ignition switch Diagram 1

Distributor — Igniter

To engine bay diagnosis connector Diagram 1 — 6
To instrument cluster Diagrams 3, 12 — 7
To A/C amplifier Diagram 15 — 61

Earth Locations
1. RH inner guard
2. LH inner guard
3. Top of engine
4. Behind LH kickpanel
5. Behind RH LH pillar trim panel
6. LH side of console
7. RH side of console
8. RH rear of console
9. Behind audio system
10. Behind RHS tailgate trim panel (hatchback)
11. Adjacent to tailgate/boot lid striker (hatchback)
12. LHS, adjacent to rear seat back (sedan)

Colour Code
A – Tan
B – Black
O – Orange
G – Green
K – Pink
L – Blue
N – Brown
V – Violet
W – White
Y – Yellow
X – Light green
Z – Light blue
P – Purple
R – Red
S – Grey

Powertrain control module (PCM)

Diagram 3 — EFI and powertrain management systems, automatic transmission and cooling fans. 7A-FE engine.

Diagram 4 — **Power distribution and integration module. 7A-FE engine.**

Toyota Corolla
1.8 litre 7A-FE
wiring diagram 4 of 15

Toyota Corolla
1.8 litre 7A-FE
wiring diagram 5 of 15

Earth Locations

8. RH rear of console
9. Behind audio system
10. Behind RHS tailgate trim panel (hatchback)
11. Adjacent to tailgate/boot lid striker
12. LHS, adjacent to rear seat back (sedan)

1. RH inner guard
2. LH inner guard
3. Top of engine
4. Behind LH kickpanel
5. Behind RH C pillar trim panel
6. LH side of console
7. RH side of console

Colour Code

A — Tan
B — Black
G — Green
K — Pink
L — Blue

N — Brown
O — Orange
P — Purple
R — Red
S — Grey

V — Violet
W — White
Y — Yellow
X — Light green
Z — Light blue

Diagram 5 — Starting system, charging system, horn, clock and cigarette lighter. 7A-FE engine.

Diagram 6 — Headlamps, park lamps and fog lamps. 7A-FE engine.

Diagram 7 — Turn signal/hazard lamps, stop lamps and reverse lamps. 7A-FE engine.

Diagram 8 — Interior lighting and instrument illumination. 7A-FE engine.

Diagram 9 — Power windows, power mirrors and sunroof. 7A-FE engine.

Diagram 10 — Power door locks. 7A-FE engine.

Diagram 11 — Wipers, washers and demister. 7A-FE engine.

Diagram 12 — Instrument cluster. 7A-FE engine.

Diagram 13 — Antilock braking system (ABS) and supplemental restraint system (SRS). 7A-FE engine.

Diagram 14 — Audio system and shift lock system. 7A-FE engine.

Toyota Corolla
1.8 litre 7A-FE
wiring diagram 14 of 15

Earth Locations

1. RH inner guard
2. LH inner guard
3. Top of engine
4. Behind LH kickpanel
5. Behind RH C pillar trim panel
6. LH side of console
7. RH side of console
8. RH rear of console
9. Behind audio system
10. Behind RHS tailgate trim panel (hatchback)
11. Adjacent to tailgate/hood lid striker
12. LHS, adjacent to rear seat back (sedan)

Colour Code

A — Tan	N — Brown	V — Violet	
B — Black	O — Orange	W — White	
G — Green	P — Purple	Y — Yellow	
K — Pink	R — Red	X — Light green	
L — Blue	S — Grey	Z — Light blue	

Dual pressure switch

On

Off   Off

On

LR

BY

LR

YB   2

A/C clutch and thermo sensor

Air conditioning amplifier

BL   8   BL   BL

XB   12   XB

Evaporator temperature sensor

2   1
11   9   8   7   6
3   4
10   9
11   10   9   8   7   6

B   4   B   To distributor
Diagram 2   B   61

LB   11   RL   6   RL   To PCM terminal ACT
Diagram 2   59

Y   7   YR   1   YR   To PCM terminal AC1
Diagram 2   60

GW   9

WB   5

To A/C fan No 3 relay
Diagram 3

BW   58

A/C magnetic clutch relay

LB   LR

WB or N   8

GW   WB or N

Y

RL

LR   LR

Heater control switch

GW   WB or N   12
2   1
7   6
8
6
10
7   11   10
12

15 A   A/C fuse

B   B   Fan motor

BW

Fan resistor

BW   BW   BW   H

LB   LB   M2

R   R   M1

Ventilation switch

OFF

WB   WB   WB

WB

WB   WB   WB

Heater relay

WB LO

RL   WB LO

To integration module   RL   Diagram 4   22

To heater fusible link   56

To gauge fuse   RL   Diagram 4   57

Colour Code

A – Tan	N – Brown	V – Violet
B – Black	O – Orange	W – White
G – Green	P – Purple	Y – Yellow
K – Pink	R – Red	X – Light green
L – Blue	S – Grey	Z – Light blue

Toyota Corolla
1.8 litre 7A-FE
wiring diagram 15 of 15

Earth Locations

1. RH inner guard
2. LH inner guard
3. Top of engine
4. Behind LH kickpanel
5. Behind RH C pillar trim panel
6. LH side of console
7. RH side of console
8. RH rear of console
9. Behind audio system
10. Behind RHS tailgate trim panel
11. Adjacent to tailgate/hood lid striker (hatchback)
12. LHS, adjacent to rear seat back (sedan)

Diagram 15 — Air conditioning. 7A-FE engine.

Diagram 1 — PCM power supply and earth circuits, fuel pump, diagnosis connector, immobiliser. 1ZZ-FE engine.

Diagram 2 — Various input sensors, ISC valve, ignition coils, variable cam timing solenoid, fuel injectors. 1ZZ-FE engine.

Diagram 3 — Cooling fan, automatic transmission, O/D Off switch. 1ZZ-FE engine.

Diagram 4 — Instrument cluster, vehicle speed sensor, security warning lamp, inhibitor switch, start relay, stop lamp switch. 1ZZ-FE engine.

Diagram 5 — PCM power supply and earth circuits, fuel pump, diagnosis connector, immobiliser, engine oil level switch. 2ZZ-GE engine.

Diagram 6 — Various input sensors, ISC valve, ignition coils, variable cam timing solenoids, fuel injectors. 2ZZ-GE engine.

Diagram 7 — Cooling fan, automatic transmission, O/D Off switch. 2ZZ-GE engine.

Diagram 8 — Instrument cluster, vehicle speed sensor, security warning lamp, inhibitor switch, start relay, stop lamp switch. 2ZZ-GE engine.

Diagram 9 — Power distribution.

Toyota Corolla ZZE122R
1.8 litre 1ZZ-FE and 2ZZ-GE
From 2001

Colour Code

A — Tan
B — Black
G — Green
K — Pink
L — Blue

N — Brown
O — Orange
P — Purple
R — Red
S — Grey

V — Violet
W — White
Y — Yellow
X — Light green
Z — Light blue

Earth Locations

1. On LH front of cylinder block, above transmission housing
2. On LH rear of cylinder block, above transmission housing
3. Engine compartment, LH suspension tower
4. LH/H C pillar
5. On coastbar, behind RH of instrument cluster
6. Behind RHF kickpanel
7. On crashbar, behind LH of instrument cluster
8. RH/H C pillar
9. Adjacent to luggage compartment lock
10. Below RHR fixed glass
11. RH of tailgate
12. Engine compartment, RH suspension tower

Diagram 10 — Power distribution. Interior fuse and relay box.

Diagram 11 — Power distribution. Interior fuse and relay box, body control module (BCM).

Diagram 12 — Starting system, charging system, horn, cigarette lighter, clock.

Toyota Corolla ZZE122R
1.8 litre 1ZZ-FE and 2ZZ-GE
From 2001

Earth Locations

1. On LH front of cylinder block, above transmission housing
2. On LH rear of cylinder block, above transmission housing
3. Engine compartment, LH suspension tower
4. LHR C pillar
5. On crashbar, behind RH of instrument cluster
6. Behind RHF kickpanel
7. On crashbar, behind LH of instrument cluster
8. RHR C pillar
9. Adjacent to luggage compartment lock
10. Below RHR fixed glass
11. RH of tailgate
12. Engine compartment, RH suspension tower

Colour Code

A — Tan
B — Black
G — Green
K — Pink
L — Blue

N — Brown
O — Orange
P — Purple
R — Red
S — Grey

V — Violet
W — White
Y — Yellow
X — Light green
Z — Light blue

Diagram 13 — Headlamps, tail lamps, fog lamps.

Diagram 14 — Turn signal/hazard lamps, reverse lamps, stop lamps, shift lock system.

Diagram 15 — Instrument illumination, sunroof.

Earth Locations

1. On LH front of cylinder block, above transmission housing
2. On LH rear of cylinder block, above transmission housing
3. Engine compartment, LH suspension tower
4. LH C pillar
5. On crashbar, behind RH of instrument cluster
6. Behind RHF kickpanel
7. On crashbar, behind LH of instrument cluster
8. RHR C pillar
9. Adjacent to luggage compartment lock
10. Below RHR fixed glass
11. RH of tailgate
12. Engine compartment, RH suspension tower

Toyota Corolla ZZE122R
1.8 litre 1ZZ-FE and 2ZZ-GE
From 2001

Colour Code

A – Tan
B – Black
G – Green
K – Pink
L – Blue

N – Brown
O – Orange
R – Red
S – Grey

V – Violet
W – White
Y – Yellow
Z – Light green
Z – Light blue

Diagram 16 — Interior lighting.

Body control module (BCM)

Interior fuse and relay box
(for connector identification,
refer to diagram 9)

Engine compartment fuse and relay box

To door fuse
See diagram 10

To gauge fuse
See diagram 10

To battery
Diagram 9

Dome fuse

Diode

Tailgate switch

Wagon and hatchback

Luggage compartment lamp

Noise filter (some models)

RHF courtesy lamp switch

To power window master switch terminal 17
Diagram 19

LHF courtesy lamp switch

To security module terminal 4
Diagram 24

To security module terminal 9
(w/o keycylinder illumination)
Diagram 24

To security module terminal 7
Diagram 24

RHR courtesy lamp switch

LHR courtesy lamp switch

Luggage compartment lamp switch
(sedan only)

Interior lamp

Interior lamp (w/ sunroof)

Off / On / Door

W/O remote central locks

Instrument cluster illumination
(for connector identification
refer to diagram 22)

Door

Ignition key cylinder illumination
(some models)

To security module terminal 9
Diagram 24

Some models

Earth Locations

1. On LH front of cylinder block, above transmission housing
2. On LH rear of cylinder block, above transmission housing
3. Engine compartment, LH suspension tower
4. LHR C pillar
5. On crashbar, behind RH of instrument cluster
6. Behind RH kickpanel
7. On crashbar, behind LH of instrument cluster
8. RHR C pillar
9. Adjacent to luggage compartment lock
10. Below RHR fixed glass
11. RH of tailgate
12. Engine compartment, RH suspension tower

Toyota Corolla ZZE122R
1.8 litre 1ZZ-FE and 2ZZ-GE
From 2001

Colour Code

A — Tan
B — Black
G — Green
K — Pink
L — Blue
N — Brown
O — Orange
P — Purple
R — Red
S — Grey
V — Violet
W — White
Y — Yellow
X — Light green
Z — Light blue

Diagram 17 — Power door locks.

Remote door lock receiver

Luggage compartment switch

Luggage compartment lock motor

LHR door lock motor

RHR door lock motor

LHF door lock motor

To key switch
Diagram 1, 5 or 9

Body control module (BCM)

Connector for internal wiring

Connector for external wiring

RHF door lock detection switch and motor

To security module terminal 10
Diagram 24

To security module terminal 11
Diagram 24

RHF door lock switch

To flasher relay terminal 8
Diagram 14

Wagon and hatchback models

Interior fuse and relay box
(for connector identification,
refer to diagram 9)

To door fuse
See diagram 10

To interior lamps
See diagram 16

To interior lamps
See diagram 16

To gauge fuse
See diagram 10

Dome fuse

To battery
Diagram 9

Engine compartment fuse and relay box

Earth Locations
1. On LH front of cylinder block, above transmission housing
2. On LH rear of cylinder block, above transmission housing
3. Engine compartment, LH suspension tower
4. LHR C pillar
5. On crashbar, behind RH of instrument cluster
6. Behind RHF kickpanel
7. On crashbar, behind LH of instrument cluster
8. RHR C pillar
9. Adjacent to luggage compartment lock
10. Below RHR fixed glass
11. RH of tailgate
12. Engine compartment, RH suspension tower

Toyota Corolla ZZE122R
1.8 litre 1ZZ-FE and 2ZZ-GE
From 2001

Colour Code
A	–	Tan		V	–	Violet
B	–	Black		W	–	White
G	–	Green		Y	–	Yellow
P	–	Purple		X	–	Light green
R	–	Red		Z	–	Light blue
S	–	Grey				
L	–	Blue				

Diagram 18 — Power windows. Models to 2004.

RHF power window switch and motor

LHF power window switch

LHF motor

RHR power window switch

RHR motor

LHR power window switch

LHR motor

Power window master switch

P/W relay

30 A P/W fuse

30 A Power fusible link

10 A Gauge fuse

To IG1 relay terminal 3
See diagram 10

Interior fuse and relay box
(for connector identification, refer to diagram 9)

To ALT fusible link
Diagram 9

Earth Locations

1. On LH front of cylinder block, above transmission housing
2. On LH rear of cylinder block, above transmission housing
3. Engine compartment, LH suspension tower
4. LHR C pillar
5. On crashbar, behind RH of instrument cluster
6. Behind RHF kickpanel
7. On crashbar, behind LH of instrument cluster
8. RHR C pillar
9. Adjacent to luggage compartment lock
10. Below RHR fixed glass
11. RH of tailgate
12. Engine compartment, RH suspension tower

Toyota Corolla ZZE122R
1.8 litre 1ZZ-FE and 2ZZ-GE
From 2001

Colour Code

A – Tan	N – Brown	V – Violet
B – Black	O – Orange	W – White
G – Green	P – Purple	Y – Yellow
K – Pink	R – Red	X – Light green
L – Blue	S – Grey	Z – Light blue

Diagram 19 — Power windows. Models from 2004.

Power window master switch

RHF power window motor

LHF power window switch

LHF power window motor

RHR power window switch

RHR power window motor

LHR power window switch

LHR power window motor

Microprocessor

To RHF courtesy lamp switch
Diagram 16

Interior fuse and relay box
(for connector identification,
refer to diagram 9)

P/W fuse
30 A

Power
fusible link
30
A

P/W relay

Gauge fuse
10 A

To IG1 relay terminal 3
See diagram 10

To ALT fusible link
Diagram 9

Earth Locations
1. On LH front of cylinder block, above transmission housing
2. On LH rear of cylinder block, above transmission housing
3. Engine compartment, LH suspension tower
4. LHR C pillar
5. On crashbar, behind RH of instrument cluster
6. Behind RHF kickpanel
7. On crashbar, behind LH of instrument cluster
8. RHR C pillar
9. Adjacent to luggage compartment lock
10. Below RHR flood glass
11. RH of tailgate
12. Engine compartment, RH suspension tower

Toyota Corolla ZZE122R
1.8 litre 1ZZ-FE and 2ZZ-GE
from 2001

Colour Code
A – Tan
B – Black
G – Green
K – Pink
L – Blue
N – Brown
O – Orange
P – Purple
R – Red
S – Grey
V – Violet
W – White
Y – Yellow
X – Light green
Z – Light blue

Diagram 20 — Wipers and washers, power mirrors.

Toyota Corolla ZZE122R
1.8 litre 1ZZ-FE and 2ZZ-GE
From 2001

Colour Code

A — Tan	N — Brown	V — Violet
B — Black	O — Orange	W — White
G — Green	P — Purple	Y — Yellow
R — Pink	R — Red	X — Light green
L — Blue	S — Grey	Z — Light blue

Earth Locations

1. On LH front of cylinder block, above transmission housing
2. On LH rear of cylinder block, above transmission housing
3. Engine compartment, LH suspension tower
4. LHR C pillar
5. On crashbar, behind RH of instrument cluster
6. Behind RHF kickpanel
7. On crashbar, behind LH of instrument cluster
8. RHR C pillar
9. Adjacent to luggage compartment lock
10. Below RHR fixed glass
11. RH of tailgate
12. Engine compartment, RH suspension tower

Diagram 21 — Instrument cluster.

Toyota Corolla ZZE122R
1.8 litre 1ZZ-FE and 2ZZ-GE
from 2001

Earth Locations
1. On LH front of cylinder block, above transmission housing
2. On LH rear of cylinder block, above transmission housing
3. Engine compartment, LH suspension tower
4. LHR C pillar
5. On crashbar, behind RH of instrument cluster
6. Behind RHF kickpanel
7. On crashbar, behind LH of instrument cluster
8. RHR C pillar
9. Adjacent to luggage compartment lock
10. Below RHR fixed glass
11. RH of tailgate
12. Engine compartment, RH suspension tower

Colour Code
A – Tan   N – Brown   V – Violet
B – Black   O – Orange   W – White
G – Green   P – Purple   Y – Yellow
K – Pink   R – Red   Z – Grey
L – Blue   S – Grey   Z – Light green
                               L – Light blue

Diagram 22 — Instrument cluster.

To right turn signal circuit
Diagram 14

To left turn signal circuit
Diagram 14

To SRS module terminal B3
Diagram 23

Right Indicator

Left Indicator

Oil pressure

Air bag

Park brake

Brake fail

ABS warning

O/D off

MIL lamp

Charge

Instrument cluster connector

Oil pressure switch

Brake fluid level sensor

Late models

To ABS module terminal 4
Diagram 24

To ABS module terminal 26
Diagram 24

To PCM terminal A19
See diagram 4 or 8

To PCM terminal B15
See diagram 4 or 8

To alternator terminal L
Diagram 12

To instrument cluster
Diagram 21

To instrument cluster
Diagram 21

Interior fuse and relay box
(for connector identification,
refer to diagram 9)

15 A
IG2 fuse

To ignition switch terminal IG2
Diagram 9

Toyota Corolla ZZE122R
1.8 litre 1ZZ-FE and 2ZZ-GE
From 2001

Colour Code

A — Tan
B — Black
G — Green
K — Pink
L — Blue
N — Brown
O — Orange
P — Purple
R — Red
S — Grey
V — Violet
W — White
Y — Yellow
X — Light green
Z — Light blue

Diagram 23 — Supplemental restraint system (SRS).

Toyota Corolla ZZE122R
1.8 litre 1ZZ-FE and 2ZZ-GE
From 2001

Colour Code

A — Tan   N — Brown   V — Violet
B — Black   O — Orange   W — White
G — Green   P — Purple   Y — Yellow
K — Pink   R — Red   X — Light green
L — Blue   S — Grey   Z — Light blue

Earth Locations

1. On LH front of cylinder block, above transmission housing
2. On LH rear of cylinder block, above transmission housing
3. Engine compartment, LH suspension tower
4. LH C pillar
5. On crashbar, behind RH of instrument cluster
6. Behind RHF kickpanel
7. On crashbar, behind LH of instrument cluster
8. RHR C pillar
9. Adjacent to luggage compartment lock
10. Below RHR fixed glass
11. RH of tailgate
12. Engine compartment, RH suspension tower

Supplemental restraint system (SRS) module
(Italic terminal numbers refer to models without side airbags)

Models without side airbags

Late models only

Diagram 24 — Security system, antilock braking system (ABS).

Toyota Corolla ZZE122R
1.8 litre 1ZZ-FE and 2ZZ-GE
From 2001

Colour Code

A – Tan	N – Brown	V – Violet
B – Black	O – Orange	W – White
G – Green	P – Purple	Y – Yellow
K – Pink	R – Red	X – Light green
L – Blue	Z – Grey	S – Light blue

Earth Locations
1. On LH front of cylinder block, above transmission housing
2. On LH rear of cylinder block, above transmission housing
3. Engine compartment, LH suspension tower
4. LHR C pillar
5. On crashbar, behind RH of instrument cluster
6. Behind RHF kickpanel
7. On crashbar, behind LH of instrument cluster
8. RHR C pillar
9. Adjacent to luggage compartment lock
10. Below RHR fixed glass
11. RH of tailgate
12. Engine compartment, RH suspension tower

Diagram 25 — Audio system, demister.

Diagram 26 — Air conditioning.

To fan No 1 relay terminal 2
See diagram 3

To fan No 2 relay terminal 2
See diagram 3

Fan resistor

Ventilation switch

Powertrain control module
(for connector identification
refer to diagram 3)

Fan motor

A/C switch

Heater relay

A/C dual pressure switch

Models with cooler

Fan booster switch

Evaporator temperature sensor

A/C compressor and lock sensor

A/C module

IG1 relay

Gauge fuse
10 A

HTR fusible link
40 A

A/C fuse
10 A

Interior fuse and relay box
(for connector identification,
refer to diagram 9)

A/C magnetic clutch relay

Engine compartment fuse and relay box

To ignition switch terminal IG1
Diagram 9

To ALT fusible link
Diagram 9

Earth Locations
1. On LH front of cylinder block, above
    transmission housing
2. On LH rear of cylinder block, above
    transmission housing
3. Engine compartment, LH suspension
    tower
4. LHR C pillar
5. On crashbar, behind RH of instrument
    cluster
6. Behind RHF kickpanel
7. On crashbar, behind LH of instrument
    cluster
8. RHR C pillar
9. Adjacent to baggage compartment
    lock
10. Below RHR fixed glass
11. RH of tailgate
12. Engine compartment, RH suspension
    tower

Toyota Corolla ZZE122R
1.8 litre 1ZZ-FE and 2ZZ-GE
From 2001

Colour Code
A — Tan   N — Brown   V — Violet
B — Black   O — Orange   W — White
G — Green   P — Purple   Y — Yellow
L — Pink   R — Red   X — Light green
L — Blue   S — Grey   Z — Light blue

Diagram 27 — Climate control.

Earth Locations

1. On LH front of cylinder block, above transmission housing
2. On LH rear of cylinder block, above transmission housing
3. Engine compartment, LH suspension tower
4. LHR C pillar
5. On crashbar, behind RH of instrument cluster
6. Behind RHR kickpanel
7. On crashbar, behind LH of instrument cluster
8. RHR C pillar
9. Adjacent to luggage compartment lock
10. Below RHR fixed glass
11. RH of tailgate
12. Engine compartment, RH suspension tower

Colour Code

A – Tan	N – Brown	V – Violet
B – Black	O – Orange	W – White
G – Green	P – Purple	Y – Yellow
K – Pink	R – Red	X – Light green
L – Blue	S – Grey	Z – Light blue

Toyota Corolla ZZE122R
1.8 litre 1ZZ-FE and 2ZZ-GE
From 2001

Index

Zeitfracht Medien GmbH
Ferdinand-Jühlke-Straße 7
99095 Erfurt, Deutschland
produktsicherheit@kolibri360.de